Occupation and Disease

Occupation and Disease

How Social Factors Affect the Conception
of Work-Related Disorders

Allard E. Dembe

Yale University Press   **New Haven and London**

Published with assistance from the foundation established in memory of
Philip Hamilton McMillan of the Class of 1894, Yale College.

Designed by Rebecca Gibb.
Set in New Century Schoolbook type by Keystone Typesetting, Inc.
Printed in the United States of America.

Library of Congress Cataloging-in-Publication Data
Dembe, Allard E.
Occupation and disease : how social factors affect the conception
of work-related disorders / Allard E. Dembe.
p.   cm.
Includes bibliographical references and index.
ISBN 0-300-06436-5 (cloth : alk. paper)
1. Occupational diseases—Social aspects.   I. Title.
RC964.D46   1996
616.9'803—dc20   95-39781
                                                      CIP

A catalogue record for this book is available from the British Library.

The paper in this book meets the guidelines for permanence and durability of the
Committee on Production Guidelines for Book Longevity of the Council on Library
Resources.

10 9 8 7 6 5 4 3 2 1

To Hana and Arielle, with love and gratitude

Contents

Preface

This book examines the process by which certain medical disorders come to be regarded by physicians as work-related. My thesis is that this is not merely a matter of gathering and interpreting empirical evidence but rather a complex social phenomenon. The determination that a disorder is caused by a patient's job occurs in a rich social context colored by the unequal power relationships that generally prevail between employees and management in the work environment and between patients and physicians in the health care setting. The intense social dynamics that permeate these two contexts help determine whether a particular disorder eventually becomes known as an occupational disease.

My interest in this question initially grew out of my professional experience as a health and safety specialist in the workers' compensation insurance industry—an industry predicated on the assumption that medical experts can draw a clear distinction between disorders induced by employment and those that are not. Over the past two decades, a great deal of concern has been expressed about the seemingly ever-increasing assortment of maladies that are considered to be work-related. Many authorities have claimed that the expansion in the definition of what constitutes an occupational disorder has been a major factor contributing to the sharp escalation of workers' compensation costs that has occurred during those years.

Concern over the broadened scope of work-related injuries and illnesses intensified during the late 1980s and early 1990s as an influx of new claims were submitted by workers suffering from a host of unfamiliar disorders such as carpal tunnel syndrome and other so-called cumulative trauma disorders. The reasons underlying the proliferation of these apparently "new" occupational diseases were perceived as mysterious and frustrating by many employers, insurers, and workers' compensation officials. Various explanations were suggested for the sudden appearance of these ailments, including the introduction of new chemicals and technologies into the workplace, the increasing pace of production activities, and better medical knowledge about the relationship between disease and occupational exposure. As a representative of America's largest workers' compensation insurance carrier, I was frequently in the center of these controversies, and had the opportunity to serve on a number of industry and government panels that examined the issue.

At about the same time, I was completing my doctoral studies in work environment policy at the University of Massachusetts, Lowell. Stimulated by these studies, I came to investigate this question from a perspective that places emphasis on understanding the broader social and historical context in which judgments about occupational etiology are made. These investigations revealed to me that medical determinations about work-relatedness are often shaped by deep-seated social, political, economic, and cultural forces. This book represents my attempt to describe those forces and to illustrate through historical examples the variety of ways that social factors can influence the medical recognition and conception of occupational disease.

I should like to express my appreciation to the individuals who assisted me in conducting this investigation. Foremost among these are my mentors and colleagues at the University of Massachusetts, Lowell, including Charles Levenstein, Laura Punnett, and David Wegman. I am particularly indebted to Chuck Levenstein, who, through many hours of insightful conversations, helped me to better appreciate and understand the subtleties of work environment policy. My sincere appreciation is also extended to Deborah Berkowitz of the United Food and Commercial Workers Union, Barbara Silverstein of the State of Washington Department of Labor and Industry, and Leslie Boden of the Boston University School of Public Health, who provided me with useful comments and suggestions on specific portions of this book. Valuable guidance was also provided by David Michaels, Gordon Smith, Eve Spangler, Suzanne Rodgers, Michael Silverstein, Richard Fenton, and Stanley Pihl. I should also like to thank all those at the Countway Library of Medicine at Harvard University, the Dewey Library of Massachusetts Institute of Technology, and the library of the U.S. Department of Labor in Washington, D.C., who aided me in acquiring the historical documents and references used in this book.

The production and editing of the manuscript could not have been accomplished without the contributions of many friends and associates. I am grateful to Janine Doherty, who assisted me in editing and proofreading initial drafts, and to Brigitt Inderfurth, who helped me with the translation of German-language materials. Jean Thomson Black and her colleagues at Yale University Press have provided continuing support and constructive suggestions to help guide me through the publishing process.

Finally, I should like to thank the management and employees of the Liberty Mutual Insurance Company, who gave assistance and encouragement to me during the course of this project. I am especially grateful for the insights and suggestions provided by my former colleagues, Dr. George Benjamin and Dr. Kathleen McCann.

The Social Context
of Occupational Disease

It sometimes seems that every week we hear about a new disease or illness that is potentially caused by work. The news is often a surprise to both employees and management. "I didn't realize that my job was dangerous," a worker might say, when it is discovered that a malady was precipitated by conditions in an office or factory. "We've been performing the same operations for years in this facility," says a perplexed supervisor, "and we've never had any medical complaints before. Why now?"

No sooner is a problem recognized than the newspapers and scientific journals are labeling it a new "occupational disease." Concerned employees rush to seek medical advice. Claims begin to flood into workers' compensation insurers. Safety engineers and consultants show up ready to redesign workstations and production tasks. Vendors appear with the latest in protective equipment and devices.

Seemingly overnight, a new threat to workers' health has emerged. Authorities attempt to discover what caused the outbreak, and how it can best be controlled. Investigators try to uncover clues about what changes may have sparked the rash of complaints: the introduction of a new chemical? Changes in production methods? There may be some suspicion that the malady has always existed but is only now being recognized by physicians who have become more attuned to the problem or more aware of its possible occupational origins. Some skeptics may believe that the appearance of the disorder has little if anything to do with new hazards on the job, but rather is a reflection of underlying problems in management-employee relations, increasingly liberal court decisions, or financial considerations related to insurance or health care administration.

In the twentieth century, the scenario described above has been repeated many times. The rise of concern about black lung disease, silicosis, and asbestos-related respiratory ailments are some well-known examples. The emergence of carpal tunnel syndrome and other cumulative trauma disorders has captured the attention of the public, as well as the medical and legal professions. In each case, the perceived danger to workers increased quickly and unexpectedly. What brings about the dramatic growth of a new occupational disorder?

This question has received little scholarly consideration, perhaps due to the inherent interests and perspectives of the key participants in the issue. Scientists and physicians are apt to see the question in the context of a search for causal agents. Employees and their representatives are concerned about the protection of their health and the need for better working conditions. Insurers and many industrialists tend to focus on financial considerations. It is often difficult to achieve a detached and objective examination of the problem as a whole and an appreciation for the diverse social and scientific circumstances in which the occupational disorder arises.

And yet the implications of this question are enormous. The costs to society associated with occupational illness and injuries continue to rise each year. In addition to the direct financial repercussions, there are substantial effects on worker health, job satisfaction, and labor relations. Public health and safety officials strive to anticipate and control significant workplace hazards. But without a clear understanding of how occupational disorders first materialize and develop into a critical menace, their objective cannot be fully achieved.

The question of how disorders come to be regarded as occupationally related has often been framed as strictly (or at least primarily) an issue of establishing scientific causality between exposure factors on the job and the ensuing health outcome. A number of scholars have examined the issue of how causality is potentially established, the use and misuse of epidemiologic evidence in this regard, and special problems involved with demonstrating occupational causality for illnesses having gradual onset and long latency periods.[1] Rather than concentrating on the narrow issue of causality, I shall examine how the issue of causality is embedded in a particular social and political context and show how that context molds and influences the way in which the causality question is formulated.

The Sociology of Disease

During the past several decades, there has been a growing realization that social forces shape the medical community's recognition of disease. Historical studies by Michel Foucault, George Rosen, and Charles Rosenberg, among others, have portrayed the conception of disease as socially determined, framed by cultural norms and shifting conventions in explanatory language.[2] Sociological investigations have provided additional evidence showing that the diagnosis and treatment of ailments by health care professionals is affected by a variety of social factors, including the ethnicity and gender of patients, financial incentives, political considerations, and the influence of the mass media.[3] These studies suggest that doctors' judgments are not merely impersonal deductions based on immutable empirical "facts," rendered independently from social considerations. They imply a more complex view of medical epistemology in which medical concepts and discoveries depend, in part, on social circumstances affecting physicians and the broader community in which they function.

Much of the interest in this subject stems from modern theories about the growth of scientific knowledge, such as those proposed by Ludwik Fleck (1935) and Thomas Kuhn (1962), which emphasize the social behavior of scientists. In *Genesis and Development of a Scientific Fact,* Fleck argued that scientific and medical "facts" are the products of prevailing models or "thought patterns" that gradually come to be widely adopted by a community of researchers.[4] Scientific facts, according to Fleck, have no objective verity independent of the norms, language, and conventions shared by those investigating the issue. The medical conception of a new disease, in his view, is to be understood in terms of the psychological, institutional, and social forces that impel physicians to adopt a particular terminology and conceptual orientation.

Fleck illustrated these views through a historical study of the development of the Wassermann reaction for syphilis. This serological test detects the unique blood changes arising from infection by the *treponema pallidum* spirochete. The introduction of the Wassermann reaction in 1906 provided physicians with a new way of characterizing and delimiting syphilis. As use of the test increased, syphilis became a distinct, narrowly defined disease entity, more easily distinguished from other venereal diseases and less closely bound to a consideration of a patient's moral character. Fleck argued that this transformation in the meaning of syphilis was a culturally conditioned process, dependent on changing social perspectives and the gradual acceptance of new thought patterns within the medical community.

This view about the sociological nature of science was further popularized by the publication of Kuhn's *Structure of Scientific Revolutions* in 1962. Like Fleck, Kuhn stressed the sociological aspects of the development and acceptance of scientific concepts and theories. According to the Kuhnian model of scientific progress, discoveries do not occur through the gradual accretion of theoretical and empirical knowledge, but rather in discrete episodes that involve major paradigm shifts, where a paradigm is understood to be the constellation of language, perspectives, and modes of interpretation shared by a community of researchers. Paradigm shifts, according to Kuhn, involve the conversion of deeply held beliefs and values within a scientific community. They result in a change of the scientists' "world view," which determines how specific empirical and technological advances are perceived and understood.

Another tenet of the Kuhnian perspective is that the vocabulary used to describe scientific phenomena is itself a fluid and dynamic product of the paradigms and cultural conventions of a research community. The meaning of a particular term embedded in a scientific theory can change dramatically with time as a result of shifting paradigms. According to this view, a scientific "concept," "truth," or "fact" has no static reality that endures independently of a particular community's paradigms. Any scientific concept or discovery remains a "social construction," susceptible to continuing reformulation and linguistic description.

In recent years, scholars have begun to adopt a similar sociological approach in examining the historical events surrounding the emergence and growth of various occupational diseases including black lung disease, silicosis, asbestosis, byssinosis, and lead, radium, and beryllium poisoning.[5] In many of these studies, specific political and social factors were shown to have played a critical role in the initial scientific and medical determination that the disorders are work-related.

A number of common themes have emerged from these social analyses of work-related disorders. They involve such issues as industry control over occupational health research, the influence of the popular media, public concern about environmental and community hazards as a stimulus for action on problems in the workplace, the economic self-interest of various individuals and institutions, underlying class struggle and management-labor conflict, the ideologies and assumptions of health professionals, reaction to the introduction of new technologies, social values related to the class, ethnic, and personal characteristics of workers, and legal and economic considerations pertaining to compensation of the victims.

Unfortunately, most of these studies have tended to focus on the social and scientific forces that led to the emergence of a particular disorder, rather than addressing the question of how health problems, in general, come to be recognized as occupationally related. What has been missing is an underlying theory of the determinants of occupational disease and an analysis of how the identified social factors exert their influence within that overall theoretical framework.

Moreover, essentially all of the previous research in this area has involved diseases resulting from exposure to airborne contaminants, which represent only a small proportion of all occupational diseases. There has been little investigation into the social history of occupational disorders caused by physical agents, which are far more numerous and costly. As the focus moves from rare diseases to those that are more common, the economic and political consequences of characterizing the disorder as job-related increase dramatically. A broader analysis of common physical hazards is needed to understand more completely the way social factors affect the initial recognition and emergence of occupational disorders.

My objective is to identify key social factors that affect the initial emergence and recognition of occupational disorders. Social factors can help shape this process in at least three ways: in the selection by employers and employees of particular equipment or work methods that potentially engenders illness, in the decision by workers to seek medical treatment for a disorder, and in the medical determination by physicians that there is a causal link between a disorder and the work environment.

The primary focus in this book will be on the latter process—the initial recognition and conception of occupational disorders by physicians and other health professionals. There are a number of reasons for focusing on the question of medical recognition: This area of investigation has not been addressed sufficiently by previous researchers. Also, the physician plays a central role in our society as the primary judge of occupational etiology. In this sense, the physician's opinion about occupational causation often determines legal responsibility and eligibility for financial compensation. Conflicts over occupational causation are generally resolved in the court of medical opinion, with physicians acting as experts on both sides of the issue.

In most situations, it is clearly in the interests of employers for disorders to be characterized as not due to occupational causes. Similarly, in most cases, it is in the interest of workers for disorders to be deemed occupational. Therefore, the positions and attitudes of workers and employers regarding the determination of the occupational nature of a disorder are relatively predictable. However, physicians are supposed to be objective and neutral. This creates an increased level of uncertainty and need for an informed judgment based on the available evidence. There is a greater potential to be "swayed," one way or the other, by social determinants. The examination of the way physicians first come to view disorders as occupational thus provides an excellent opportunity to understand the way that social factors exert their influence.

Although the primary focus in this book will be on the effect of social factors on physicians' recognition of new occupational disorders, the influence of social factors on the recognition of occupational disorders by workers, employers, and other groups will also be considered. It is important to realize that these processes are not necessarily independent. For example, social factors stimulating the recognition of an occupational disorder by workers might induce more of them to seek medical care from physicians, who, as a result of the greater reporting of the disorder by workers, might become more convinced of its occupational etiology.

The process whereby a disorder comes to be recognized as occupationally related can be lengthy and complex. Key social factors mediating this process might not be discernible while the events are taking place, and only in retrospect may the most relevant social determinants be identified and evaluated adequately.

In this respect, this investigation can be considered a study in the social history of occupational disease. The defining goal of social history, compared to other historical disciplines, is to understand historical developments in the context of the political and social forces that existed at the time of the events in question.[6] By approaching this subject in historical perspective it is possible to gain a more comprehensive assessment of the multiplicity of social factors which affect the initial recognition and conception of an occupational disorder. In addition, the historical approach allows for the acquisition and careful analysis of documents and other evidence upon which to base the analysis of these factors.

Toward an Integrated Theory of Occupational Disease

Before embarking on the historical analysis of specific disorders, it is important to explore the general circumstances in which occupational diseases occur and are presented to doctors for diagnosis and treatment.[7] Understanding the unique context in which these events takes place will help reveal why physicians' judgments about workers' diseases are especially susceptible to social influences. Our analysis of this process has to begin with the fundamental question of what gives rise to an occupational disorder. There are a number of potential approaches to answering this question, which can be represented by explanatory models reflecting the perspectives of economics, Marxism, medicine, epidemiology, the individual worker, sociology, and workers' compensation.

According to the economics perspective, occupational disease arises as a by-product of techniques used to produce goods and services. An explanation of the initial generation of a new occupational disorder thus depends on an analysis of the economic and political decisions that affect the choice and use of technology, work practices, and the characteristics of the labor market.

In the traditional Marxist perspective, occupational disease is a result of capitalist domination over the methods of production and repression of the laboring class. It is but one manifestation of an inevitable class conflict between workers and management. In this view, occupational diseases occur because capitalists impose working conditions and job methods that are aimed more at ensuring control over workers and maximizing profit than at protecting health.

According to the traditional medical perspective, disease is the result of the action of a pathologic agent on a person. In the medical view, toxic or harmful agents found in the workplace cause occupational disease. The effect of the agent on a worker can be modified by inherent characteristics of the individual or environmental conditions. "New" occupational disorders would thus be a product of the introduction of new disease agents into the workplace, increased susceptibility of workers, changes in environmental conditions, or greater awareness by physicians about the relationship between the agent and the occurrence of the disease.

For an epidemiologist, occupational disease is a matter of statistical probability. The role of the epidemiologist is to identify relationships between occupational "risk factors" and the occurrence of disease in populations of workers. According to this view, causality can never be established by statistical methods alone; equally important are qualitative considerations about the plausibility of the purported causal relationship. Moreover, the epidemiologist, unlike the physician, makes no claims about the specific cause of illness in an individual case.

To an individual worker, occupational disease arises when a connection is made between an ailment and conditions at work. The worker can potentially develop a belief in the validity of that connection in a number of ways—by receiving a diagnosis from a physician, by observing similar conditions in coworkers, from advice given by family or friends, from reading accounts in a newspaper or other publication, and so on. From this perspective, the issue of how new occupational disorders arise may, in part, be a question of how a worker initially comes to the awareness that his ailment is due to working conditions.

Sociologists have tried to understand the diagnosis of disease in terms of factors affecting the interaction between physician and patient. The diagnostic decision has been shown to be influenced by social perspectives of the physician, economic incentives, class and ethnic characteristics of the patients, and other external social variables. Equally important, according to this perspective, are the social factors that prompt a person to seek medical treatment—factors potentially related to the person's socioeconomic status, cultural expectations, demographic attributes, and other considerations. Some sociologists believe that all diagnosis of disease is essentially value-laden, in that disease is always to be considered a normative concept, defined relative to socially and culturally determined expectations.

From the viewpoint of many of those involved with workers' compensation insurance, a disorder is considered work-related if it is determined to be eligible for financial compensation according to a government workers' compensation law. This determination can be generated by the pronouncements of physicians, insurance company representatives, judges, or administrative officers. The designation of a disease as potentially compensable can affect the viewpoint of others (for example, workers, physicians, employers) about the occupational relatedness of the disorder. According to this perspective, the emergence of new occupational disorders can be the result of changes in legal interpretations and court decisions.

The above listing of explanatory models is not intended to be comprehensive or empirically precise. It is merely intended to emphasize the variety of orientations for explaining the meaning and origin of occupational disease. Each model contains an element of truth and potentially important insights about the determinants of work-related disorders. They show that any comprehensive model of the emergence of new occupational disease will be complex and subtle, integrating the perspectives of numerous actors, social variables, and relationships between individuals and social institutions.

Multifactoral Causation and Medical Uncertainty

Many of the aforementioned models start with a presumption that there either is or is not a discrete causal connection between specific workplace factors and an individual's ailment. The initial emergence of an occupational disorder is conceived of as a process of revealing this connection through medical examination, research, worker awareness, or other means. Many traditional types of injury and illness support this presumption. For instance, there is little question about the occupational origin of a traumatic injury like a cut finger, especially when it follows from a specific incident, such as contact with a knife while slicing material at work.

Similarly, a simple model of causality serves well enough in the case of

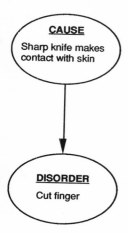

Figure 1 Cut: Causal Model

occupational diseases with a specific etiology that can be traced definitively to the working environment. For example, the medical determination of occupational causality is relatively straightforward in a case where a plastics industry worker presents with liver angiosarcoma following prolonged workplace exposure to large doses of vinyl chloride monomer.

However, for many disorders the analysis of causation is much more difficult and complex, particularly for disorders that potentially stem from a multiplicity of factors both on and off the job. Examples include hearing loss, back pain, and cumulative trauma disorders of the hands and wrists. Causal models for such disorders are further complicated by considerations of personal susceptibility and genetic disposition, repeated exposure to low levels of the suspected causal agent(s), and long latency periods.

The complexity of the causal model determines the extent to which the recognition of disease is affected by external social factors. Consider the example of a cut from the use of a knife at work. A causal model for this type of injury starts with a direct link between the causal agent and the outcome (figure 1).

In the case of such an injury, the treating physician, employer, and worker would have little trouble agreeing about the occupational origin of the malady, after they have ascertained the specific details of the incident and have ruled out overt deception or any alternative explanations for how the injury could have occurred. Because the link between the job activity and the ensuing disorder is so concrete and easily determined, economic, political, and other social factors would probably have little effect on the physician's medical judgment about the work-relatedness of the disorder.

The situation is quite different in the case of a disorder that has multiple possible causes and an indistinct relationship to work—for instance, when a

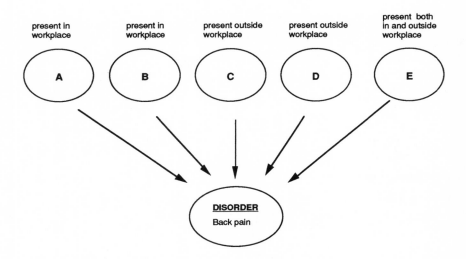

Figure 2 Back Pain: Causal Model

worker reports back pain. It is well known that numerous conditions can produce back pain. Some of these conditions cause back pain directly, yet in
other cases, back pain is a secondary effect of an underlying disease process.
Some of the potential causal conditions may be present in the workplace and
some may not. Several of the conditions may exert their influence in the life
and activities of a particular individual. Consider the model depicted in figure 2, in which a number of possible causes of back pain (A . . . E) are all
assumed to be present in the life of a particular person suffering from this
condition.

Assuming that any of the conditions A . . . E is potentially sufficient to
cause back pain, how is a physician to determine whether or not the disorder
is work-related? To as great an extent as possible, most medical professionals
consider such factors as the strength and magnitude of the conditions which
are present, the temporal sequence in which they occurred relative to the
time of the disorder's onset, and independent research and epidemiological
findings indicating the general patterns under which A . . . E can lead to back
pain.

But, generally speaking, even the best medical inquiry will be unable to
produce an unequivocal judgment about the precise cause of the condition
and the relative contribution of the occupational conditions vis-à-vis those
that are nonoccupational.

Further complicating the medical determination of work-relatedness is
the realization that each of the sufficient causes of a disorder (for example,
A . . . E in figure 2) might potentially be the product of a number of component

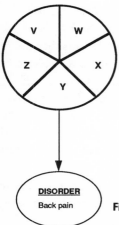

Figure 3 Back Pain: Multifactoral Causation

conditions which must interact conjunctively in order for the causal complex to generate the disorder. Consider, for instance, the causal complex portrayed in figure 3, composed of five conditions, all of which must exist together for back pain to arise.

It is plausible to think that the specific components (V . . . Z) of the causal complex might include both workplace and nonworkplace factors as well as personal characteristics, individual susceptibility, environmental or lifestyle attributes, genetic makeup, and so on. If all components are necessary for the causal complex to produce the disorder, then the removal of any one would eliminate the complex as a possible cause of the condition. Various controlled experiments and research models could be used to measure the relative contribution of this causal complex in a study population.

But for an individual suffering from back pain, epidemiologic studies will never untangle and resolve the true effect of the various possible sufficient causes and causal complexes. At best, such studies can provide a physician with a probabilistic indication of the potential relative strength of the various "risk factors" that may be present.

Thus, for a wide range of disorders that have multiple sufficient causes and multifactoral causal complexes, a range of medical uncertainty will exist about whether the disorder was truly "caused" by work and about the precise contribution of the occupational and nonoccupational factors that were present.

Nevertheless, the physician is frequently compelled to make a judgment about occupational causation because of insurance considerations, workers' compensation, Occupational Safety and Health Administration (OSHA) enforcement and legal proceedings, as well as the need for patients to know the origin of their maladies and for employers to determine whether their work-places are safe. In our society the physician is regularly put in the position of a "gatekeeper," whose pronouncements about occupational causality affect subsequent actions by workers, employers, insurers, and public health officials. During the twentieth century there has been an increasing tendency for physicians to be placed in the position of having to make judgments about occupational causality for disorders with indistinct etiology owing to the existence of multiple sufficient causes and multifactoral causes as described above. Some would say that the concept of an "occupational disorder" has thus become much broader, including disorders in which workplace conditions are only one of many possible explanations. Adopting the probabilistic language of epidemiology, physicians have increasingly rendered their judgments about occupational causation in a discourse emphasizing the risk factors that may be present in a particular situation. The characterization of occupational causality in terms of risk factors is, in a way, an acknowledgment by the medical profession of the inability to make definitive judgments about occupational etiology for many kinds of disorders. Because of this inherent medical uncertainty, there is frequently a wide range of competing plausible and scientifically justifiable opinions about the occupational origins of a disorder. It is in this context of uncertainty that extramedical considerations and social factors can be expected to exert their greatest influence.

Social Context and the Patient-Physician Relationship

Occupational disorders by definition occur among workers, or former workers, who come into contact with various causes or components of causal complexes while on the job. This takes place in a particular setting—a working environment—that establishes the context in which the disorder may have originated. A comprehensive understanding of the disorder thus necessitates a consideration of the features of that environment.

Central to the employment environment is the management's relationship to workers, which ultimately creates the set of conditions and work methods that determines if the disorder is likely to arise. This is true for any kind of occupational disorder, even a minor cut on the finger as described earlier. A simple portrayal of the work environment in which a finger cut occurs is shown in figure 4.[8]

As emphasized by the economic and Marxist models, the fundamental cause of occupational disorders resides ultimately in the decisions made by employers and employees in the workplace concerning the choice of technology, the level of production, acceptable work methods, and the utilization of labor. Numerous social and economic factors influence these choices. For example, a decision to increase profit by minimizing costs may result in the

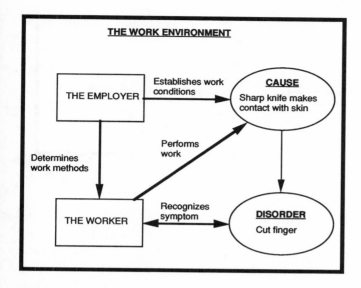

Figure 4 Cut Finger: Employment Context

use of defective equipment or inadequate maintenance. Autocratic management styles may produce worker frustration or noncompliance with safety
procedures.

The characteristics of the working environment may also be determined
by social and economic factors that are external to the immediate employment context. For example, community sentiment, legal and political developments, and government regulation can all exert pressure on management to select equipment and processes that limit the creation of dangerous
conditions. Management's concern about health and safety hazards can be
heightened by escalating workers' compensation costs or in response to
union actions. Vendors of safety equipment can help sway management's
outlook on the seriousness of particular disorders. Class, gender or ethnic
biases that have deep cultural roots can also have an impact on conditions in
the work environment.

External influences can also determine the likelihood that workers will
bring their disorders and fears of occupational injury to the attention of
management. Strong union involvement can encourage workers to come forward with these concerns. Media attention can heighten their awareness of
the dangers.

However, management and workers are rarely the final arbiters of
whether occupational conditions caused a particular worker's disorder.
Workers with maladies are generally sent to a physician for diagnosis and

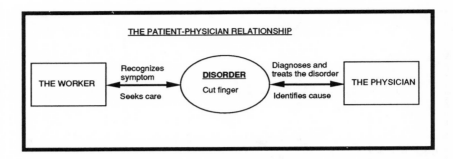

Figure 5 The Patient-Physician Relationship

treatment.[9] In our society, the physician frequently is asked to render a definitive judgment about whether the disorder was due to conditions at work. With the notable exception of "company doctors," physicians normally stand outside of the direct work environment and management-labor relationship.

The restricted focus on social and economic dynamics of the work environment found in the traditional Marxist and economic models of occupational disease fails to give sufficient consideration to the social factors that prompt physicians to render their medical judgments. Too often, theorists have taken the naive view that such judgments are objective and dispassionate, immune from the same type of social determination that affects decisions made in the workplace.

By reporting to a physician or other health care provider for medical attention, a worker is transformed into a patient (figure 5). The relationship between patient and physician is subject to the influence of various social, political, and economic factors.

As in the employer-employee relationship, social factors affecting the patient-physician context can be internal to the relationship, and some can be external. Internal factors might involve the physician's perspectives about the relevance of worker's ethnic or demographic characteristics, place of residence, socioeconomic background, lifestyle, or cultural habits. Inherent class differentiation between physicians and workers may make doctors insensitive to many potential occupational problems. A physician's decisions may be influenced in part by a need to enhance social or professional status or by economic interests. Different forms of compensating the physician may affect the type and quality of medical services rendered to the worker in establishing the diagnosis for a disorder and in selecting the treatment to be provided.

External social factors may also affect the physician's perspective on the question of occupational causality. Physicians selected by the employer's insurance carrier may be reluctant to diagnose occupational diseases for fear of losing future business. On the other hand, the relatively guaranteed reimbursement available through workers' compensation for compensable disorders may induce physicians to view symptoms as work-related. Government payment schemes that require diagnoses to be restricted to pre-defined classifications may obfuscate emerging occupational problems. Media attention, political pressure, and community concern can affect doctors in much the same way that it can workers and employers. Suppliers of drugs and medical instrumentation and others can exert pressure and financial incentives to sway physicians' practices.

A Pluralistic Model of Occupational Disease

A comprehensive model of occupational disease must reflect the fundamental importance of multifactoral causation, medical uncertainty, and the primacy of the employer-employee and patient-physician relationships. The social dynamics within the work environment establish the basic context for the employer-employee relationship and determine the conditions that can generate occupational disorders. Upon reporting to a physician, the worker is transformed into a patient. Subsequent judgments about the occupational etiology of the disorder are governed by the dynamics of the physician-patient relationship and the broader context in which those medical judgments occur. An understanding and analysis of both the employer-employee context and physician-patient context are necessary to appreciate fully the way in which occupational disorders originate. Those contexts are separate but related to one another, with the key point of intersection being the worker who suffers an ailment (figure 6).

The portrayal of unions, government, insurers, researchers, and the community is intended to highlight the importance of those forces exerted on the dynamics of the two principal contexts. But undoubtedly there are additional external forces that affect the decisions made about occupational disorders by the employer, employee, and physician. Examples of other sources of social influence include the mass media, health care institutions, safety professionals, vendors of safety and health products, the legal profession, workers' families, and professional epidemiologists and public health officials. Broad societal determinants—prevailing cultural norms and the overall economic health of a nation or industry, to name a few—create additional pressures.

The influence exerted by a particular external source may affect the various primary groups in different ways. For example, insurers may simultaneously encourage employers to recognize and control occupational disease hazards while at the same time fighting claims made by workers and physicians concerning the occupational causality of the ensuing health disorders. Organized labor may educate workers about serious health dangers while

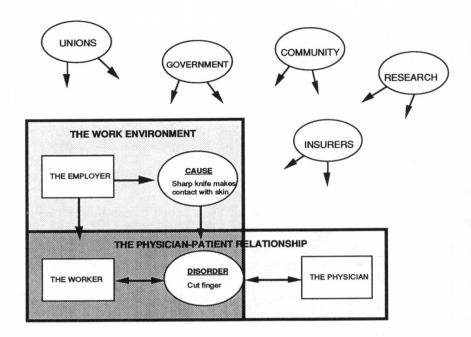

Figure 6 The Social Context of Occupational Disease

sanctioning agreements with employers that provide disincentives to addressing workplace safety deficiencies.

In addition, various groups do not always exert a unified and coherent influence. The history of occupational disease is replete with examples of fragmentation within organized labor, when some factions urged forceful action on issues of occupational disease while others feared the potential economic harm or repercussions of such efforts. The medical profession also speaks with many voices. Alice Hamilton, Irving Selikoff, Harriet Hardy, and Lorin Kerr, among others, are famous for their unrelenting campaigns to bring attention to the ravages of occupational disease. Other physicians are leading protectors of capitalist interests and the domination of the privileged class. Research findings can point to significantly different conclusions, often paralleling the financial backing and social politics of the researchers.

Even for a disorder with an easily discernible cause (a cut finger), the representation of possible social determinants can become quite complex (figure 7).

The model of occupational disease becomes much more complex in the case of a disorder (like back pain) that has a wide array of possible causes and a potentially indefinite etiology. The additional complexity arises because the causes and conditions that can lead to the disorder are no longer

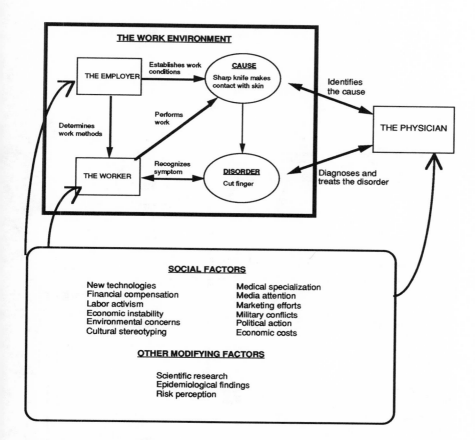

Figure 7 Cut: Social Determinants

necessarily confined to the work environment. The "production" of causal conditions is thus subject to numerous social influences and agents of control. Because of medical uncertainty, there is much wider latitude of reasonable medical judgment open to the physician and thus expanded potential for the patient-physician relationship to be influenced by internal and external social factors. Intricate relationships between social variables and competing interpretations of disease causality come into play (figure 8).

Toward a Comprehensive Model

The preceding analysis has identified several fundamental principles that must be incorporated into any adequate theory of occupational disease:

- The work environment establishes the basic context in which occupational disorders arise and are to be understood. The relationship between employer and employee determines the existence of work condi-

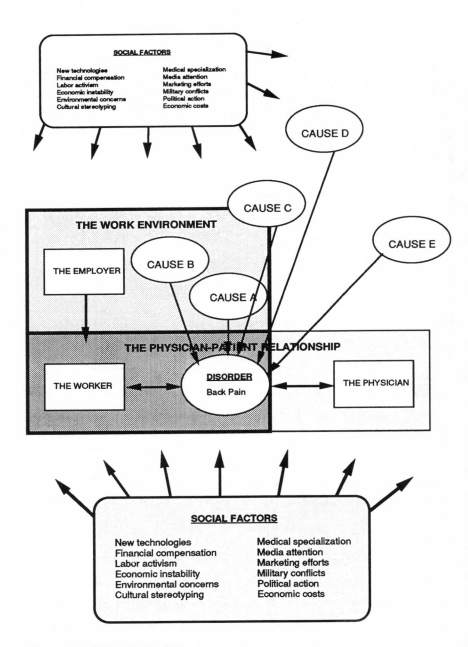

Figure 8 Back Pain: Social Context

tions and work methods necessary for the production of disease. The decisions of employers and employees are shaped within this context by fundamental economic and political realities, some of which are internal to the work environment and some of which are imposed by external forces.

- When a worker reports to a physician for medical attention, the worker is thereby transformed into a patient. The physician is invested by our society with making a definitive judgment as to the occupational etiology of the disorder. In doing so, the judgment is fundamentally affected by social determinants mediating the patient-physician relationship, including economic incentives, class and cultural characteristics, and other factors that are both internal and external to the immediate patient-physician context.

- Attributions of occupational causality are easiest in situations where there is a direct link between one or a few precipitating conditions and the ensuing disorder. In cases where the disorder has a multiplicity of possible causes and the potential contribution of work conditions is indefinite, there is a greater range of reasonable medical opinion and a corresponding increased potential for social determinants to affect the physician's judgment about the occupational nature of the disorder.

- Most previous scholarly work in the social analysis of occupational disease has failed to address the complexity of this process. Marxist and economic theories of occupational disease have generally ignored the dynamics of the patient-physician relationship and the social determinants underlying a physician's judgment about the occupational etiology of a disorder. Traditional sociological approaches have not fully appreciated the social production of disease deriving from the economic terms of the employer-employee relationship. Medical and epidemiologic perspectives share a naive view of objective science, neglecting the social determinants that mold scientists' judgments in the context of uncertainty and multifactoral causation.

Based on previous research and the available empirical evidence, the following social factors appear to be especially relevant for understanding how occupational disorders are initially recognized and conceived.

1. New technologies and the reaction to those technologies by various societal groups can lead to the increased reporting and diagnosis of occupational disorders.
2. Laws and legal decisions establishing financial compensation can bring increased attention to the question of whether or not a disorder is work-related.

3. Union campaigns and labor activism can foster initial concern about the problem of occupational diseases occurring in particular trades.
4. Occupational disorders are apt to be initially recognized during periods of economic instability and potential job loss.
5. Medical interest in disorders caused by hazards in the workplace can be aroused by public reaction to similar environmental hazards present in the wider community.
6. Cultural stereotyping based on class, gender, and ethnicity can distort medical opinion about the relationship between occupation and disease.
7. The growth of medical specialization and the ensuing competition for professional authority, status, and financial rewards can help shape physicians' perceptions about the connection between disorders and job activities.
8. Attention by the national mass media to a particular workplace disorder can heighten medical awareness of the problem.
9. Marketing efforts by vendors of diagnostic, protective, and therapeutic equipment can stimulate initial concern about health disorders in workers.
10. Technology, diagnostic procedures, and medical attitudes arising in the course of military conflicts can influence the way that occupational disorders are subsequently studied and understood.
11. The actions of particular political parties and candidates can generate public and medical consideration of occupational health problems.
12. Resistance to the medical recognition of occupational disease is greatest when there are substantial costs associated with controlling the associated workplace hazards.

Social determinants such as these are always embedded in a complicated and interconnected social dynamic and are not necessarily mutually exclusive. For example, labor action related to an occupational disorder may engender national media attention. The effect of cultural stereotyping on the formulation of the conception of an occupational disorder may be most pronounced when economic instability in an industry has brought about competition between ethnic groups for scarce jobs.

How these social factors shape the initial recognition and conception of occupational disorders is as important as their identification. Some of the factors listed above promote the recognition of a disorder, while others impede it. Their effects may depend on which social group is involved and on the particular disorder. For example, the effect of gender stereotyping might sway some physicians into viewing a disorder as occupationally related if it occurs primarily among men but discourage that same association if the patients are women. The development of a new diagnostic technology, such as X rays, can be seen as a way of validating or refuting the legitimacy of an occupational disorder, depending on whether it is used to confirm underlying injury or to "prove" that a worker's complaint has no objective basis.

One of the primary objectives of this book is to characterize these factors and describe their complex and multifaceted influence on particular disorders. For example, military conflicts might affect the recognition and conception of occupational disorders:

- Disorders occurring through exposure to military weaponry or environments may increase the attention given to disorders arising from similar hazards in the workplace.
- Diagnostic or medical screening procedures first developed or adopted by the military may be extended to civilian workers.
- Physicians who received initial training in the military may tend to apply distinctive techniques and perspectives to the diagnosis and conception of workers' disorders upon their return to civilian life. For example, they may be especially aware of the traumatic origin of various disorders or concerned about detecting feigned illnesses.
- The return of a large number of disabled veterans into the civilian workforce may engender public sympathy and medical interest in health problems affecting them at work.
- Potentially hazardous technologies first developed for military applications may be introduced into civilian work settings (for example, various biological and chemical agents).

Historical Case Studies

In the following chapters, I shall explore the historical development of three specific occupational disorders: cumulative trauma disorders (CTDs) of the hands and wrists (particularly carpal tunnel syndrome), back pain, and noise-induced hearing loss. Despite their extremely high incidence, these physical disorders have not previously received the same level of scholarly historical analysis as have occupational illnesses related to chemical exposures. Back pain and CTDs involve disorders of the musculoskeletal system, which is currently by far the most common source of work-induced disability. Because they are so widespread and costly, these disorders have been the focus of considerable public debate about the need for tighter regulatory control. Gaining a better understanding of the social forces responsible for the contemporary rise of these disorders can thus potentially contribute to the development of cogent occupational health policy. Unlike many traditional occupational diseases, their occurrence is not related specifically to any particular etiologic agent or any single pathological mechanism. For low back pain and CTDs, comparatively little attention has been given to the systematic quantification and testing of exposure levels in the workplace. In both of these respects, the disorders selected differ from many of the other occupational diseases involving exposure to specific chemical or dust contaminants (such as lead, asbestos, and silica) where the controversies about work-relatedness have tended to revolve more explicitly around toxicologic and epidemiologic considerations, such as the existence of a dose-response relationship. It should be easier to isolate and examine the social (rather than medical and epidemiologic) factors that affected the recognition and conception of the selected disorders as occupationally related.

Despite their extremely high incidence, these three physical disorders have not previously received the same level of scholarly historical analysis as have occupational illnesses related to chemical exposures. Back pain and CTDs involve disorders of the musculoskeletal system, which is currently by far the most common source of work-induced disability. Because they are so widespread and costly, disorders caused by physical hazards have been the subject of considerable public debate about the need for tighter regulatory control. Gaining a better understanding of the social forces responsible for the contemporary rise of these disorders thus potentially contribute to the development of cogent occupational health policy.

Chapter 2 recounts the history of the development of the modern conception of work-related CTDs. This case study was chosen as the first to be examined both because of the contemporary popular and scientific interest in the subject as well as the availability of extensive source material showing how these disorders were repeatedly rediscovered and redefined by the medical profession over the course of many years. The seemingly sudden emergence of carpal tunnel syndrome as a significant occupational health problem after the late 1970s will be traced to a number of factors, including labor activism and national media attention. Prior to that time, gender-based stereotyping by one influential physician delayed its characterization as an occupationally related disorder.

Chapter 3 will show how back pain became the single most frequently reported occupational malady and the leading contemporary source of workers' compensation payments. As in the case of CTDs, back pain has plagued individuals for centuries. But unlike CTDs, there were very few medical reports of *occupational* back pain prior to the establishment of workers' compensation laws in the late nineteenth and early twentieth centuries. The growth of reported occupational back pain during the twentieth century exemplifies how professional specialization and technological developments can increase the likelihood that a disorder becomes characterized as work-related.

In chapter 4, I shall explore the history of noise-induced hearing loss. Directly preceding and following World War II, labor actions, economic conditions, and capitalist interests, in different ways, created an atmosphere of heightened concern about the effects of noise in the workplace. This chapter portrays how the definition of an occupational disorder is subject to continual reinterpretation based on technological advances, political and environmental developments, and debates about the relative importance of functional impairment versus occupational or social disability.

Finally, in chapter 5, the relative contribution of each of the key social factors in each case study is assessed. Common trends and patterns are highlighted. I shall compare the action of these social factors in the three case studies to the findings of previous studies regarding various diseases caused by chemical hazards and dust contaminants. The book concludes with a consideration of the importance of the findings for occupational health policy and implications for the question of who is responsible for analyzing and fixing the problem. In most Western nations, separate institutions are responsible for compensating, regulating, and preventing various disorders, depending on whether or not the disorders are classified as work-related. If specific social factors substantially determine this decision, then policy-makers will need to take those into account when establishing strategies for prevention and treatment.

Cumulative Trauma Disorders of the Hands and Wrists

2

In the United States and many other countries, workers are reporting hand and wrist disorders in record numbers. Most of us have heard of such incidents: a newspaper reporter's hand aches after many hours at a computer keyboard; a butcher experiences intense wrist pain while cutting meat; a housekeeper awakens in the middle of the night with numb fingers following a hard day of scrubbing floors. Thousands of workers are reporting to doctors for evaluation and treatment of these kinds of problems. Are they suffering from a cumulative trauma disorder? Is it caused by their work?

Government agencies now view cumulative trauma disorders (CTDs) as one of the nation's most severe occupational health problems. According to the U.S. Bureau of Labor Statistics, the number of these disorders grew more than tenfold between 1983 and 1993. CTDs currently account for more than 60 percent of all occupational illnesses reported in the United States. Costs have skyrocketed, with the average compensable CTD case totaling $8,070 in medical bills, lost wages, and rehabilitation expenses, almost twice the average workers' compensation claim ($4,075). If surgery is required, the cost for a CTD case is approximately $30,000. The total annual cost of workers' compensation payments for upper extremity CTDs in the United States has been estimated to exceed $500 million.[1]

Although there is not unanimous agreement as to what constitutes a CTD, typical examples occurring in the hand and wrist include carpal tunnel syndrome, tendonitis, tenosynovitis, trigger finger, de Quervain's disease, and vibration syndrome (Raynaud's phenomenon).[2] Of these, carpal tunnel syndrome has become the most widely publicized and well-known. Various CTDs have also been identified by the jobs or activities performed by those suffering from the condition. Thus, the medical literature includes descriptions of washerwoman's sprain (now identified as de Quervain's disease), shearer's wrist, seamstress's finger, pipetter's thumb, and tennis elbow.[3]

Despite the variety of names and diagnoses, CTDs are commonly understood to be disorders that can result from chronic and repeated stress of a joint or tendon. They are sometimes poorly localized and nonspecific. CTDs may result from both occupational as well as nonoccupational causes. Epidemiologic studies and biomechanical evidence have implicated frequent repetition, high force, mechanical pressure, awkward posture, vibration, and low temperature as important occupational risk factors.[4] Nonoccupational factors that can lead to similar symptoms include diabetes, rheumatoid arthritis, pregnancy, hypothyroidism, acute trauma, and congenital defects.

Although comprising a relatively small proportion of overall workers' compensation claims for American business, CTDs can be the predominant cause of lost time for specific occupations and tasks.[5] Among meat packers, the prevalence of carpal tunnel syndrome is estimated to be as high as 15 percent of the workforce.[6] Other occupations with reported high rates of CTDs include supermarket checkout clerks, garment workers, operators of video display terminals, keyboard operators, assembly-line workers, and poultry processors. Several studies have reported prevalences of CTDs for the general industrial workforce of 5–10 percent.[7] This has led some investigators to conclude that the true prevalence of CTDs is even higher than that indicated by medical visits and compensation claims.

Whatever the true prevalence of CTDs is, the perception among the American business, academic, and medical communities is that there is an unprecedented epidemic of new CTD cases. Newspaper accounts have portrayed this as a national crisis. Congressional leaders and federal safety officials have called CTDs the "number one occupational hazard of the 1990s." Recent magazine headlines have declared CTDs "The Illness of the Decade," and a "Repetitive Motion Monster."[8] For some industries, such as automobile manufacturing and newspaper publishing, CTDs have become a major collective bargaining issue because of their perceived impact on the health and welfare of a substantial proportion of the workforce.

The tremendous increase in workers' compensation claims, coupled with the intense media attention that CTDs receive, has prompted considerable questioning about the origins of the "epidemic." Business people and physicians alike are naturally perplexed about why so many new cases of CTD have been seen. Numerous questions are being asked about why the increase in CTDs is occurring and if they are actually new diseases.

Many explanations have been offered for the observed rise in CTDs. Authorities have pointed to such factors as higher production rates, the shift toward service and high-technology jobs, and the greater use of computers. Some commentators question whether the disorders are real, or whether they are being purposely or unconsciously feigned by workers.[9] One noted physician has called CTDs an "iatrogenic concept," arguing that doctors are partially responsible for creating a false impression of the disease in many patients.[10] Others are wondering whether these disorders have always occurred but are being detected more frequently because of increased medical surveillance and knowledge, greater worker awareness, or expansion of workers' compensation laws.

These questions can only be answered by examining the history of occupational hand and wrist disorders. The term *cumulative trauma disorder* was first used in the 1970s. But the concept itself has been around for well over a century. There have been a number of distinct historical episodes in which physicians have attempted to understand these disorders using different theoretical models and terminology. To some extent, changes in the medical conception of occupational hand disorders have occurred in response to the introduction of new technologies, shifts in work organization and workforce composition, and advances in medical and epidemiologic research. But underlying these transformations in medical thought were profound social influences involving organized labor, political action, and deep-seated cultural perspectives on the class, gender, and ethnicity of affected workers.

Early History of Hand and Wrist Disorders

"The hand is the most important tool of the human brain," wrote Sir Charles Bell in the early nineteenth century.[11] Because of its central role in executing human actions, the hand has, since prehistoric times, been a locus of severe injuries, burns, infections, and amputations. In addition to these instances of acute trauma, chronic pain to the hands and arms has been known and described since the time of Hippocrates and Galen. Rheumatism and degenerative joint disease of the hands and wrists was fully described by Guillaume de Baillou (commonly known by his Latinized name, Ballonius) in 1591.[12]

Harm to the hands and arms from long-term manual exertion has also been observed since antiquity. The ancient Egyptian writer of the Sellier Papyrus noticed that the arms of masons are often "worn out with work."[13] Hippocrates provided one of the earliest known accounts of chronic disorders caused by repetitive occupational hand movements. In the *Epidemics,* he described a workman who developed paralysis in the hand after prolonged twisting of twigs.[14]

The potential relationship of occupational activities to the development of chronic hand and wrist disorders was articulated by Bernardino Ramazzini in 1713. In *De Morbis Artificum* Ramazzini describes the deleterious effects of hand exertion among bakers: "Now and again I have noticed bakers with swelled hands, and painful, too; in fact the hands of all such workers become much thickened by the constant pressure of kneading the dough; a great quantity of nutritive juice is squeezed out of the orifices of the arteries and is kept in the hands; since the return flow is checked by the constriction of the fibers." Ramazzini also provided one of the first detailed accounts of hand pain and numbness caused by continual writing among professional scribes and notaries:

> The maladies that afflict the clerks arise from . . . incessant movement of the hand and always in the same direction. . . .
> Incessant driving of the pen over paper causes intense fatigue of the hand and the whole arm because of the continuous and almost constant strain on the muscles and tendons, which in the course of time results in failure of power in the right hand. An acquaintance of mine, a notary by profession, still living, used to spend his whole life continually engaged in writing . . . and he made a good deal of money by it; first he began to complain of intense fatigue in the whole arm, but no remedy could relieve this, and finally the whole right arm became completely paralyzed. In order to offset this infirmity he began to train himself to write with the left hand, but it was not very long before it too was attacked by the same malady.[15]

Physicians observed a number of specific work-related disorders of the hand for the first time during the early nineteenth century. The increased reporting of these disorders was associated by physicians of that period with the introduction of factory production methods and mechanized tasks that required the systematic repetition of precise and rapid hand movements. Hand disorders were particularly evident in weavers and other textile workers, tailors, seamstresses, carpenters, and metalworkers. These jobs were often performed under congested conditions, frequently requiring awkward and constrained body postures. Payment for the work was ordinarily based on how much was produced, resulting in high-frequency repetition. During this period, large numbers of workers began performing tasks that demanded a prolonged recurrent work cycle, often without rest or variation in working position.

Accompanying the growth of factory jobs and the emergence of industrial work organization, several cases in the medical literature reported disorders that developed gradually in workers, frequently in the absence of any precipitating traumatic event or identifiable pathologic lesion. For example, several types of musculoskeletal ailments among British factory workers were described by Charles Thackrah in 1832:

> Certain classes of muscles are for twelve or fourteen hours a day scarcely moved, and postures maintained injurious to the proper actions of the internal organs. Tailors are very unfortunately situated in this respect. Sitting all day in a confined atmosphere, and often in a room too crowded, with the legs crossed and the spine bowed, they cannot have respiration, circulation, or digestion well performed. . . . The sensibility of the right fore-finger is sometimes greatly reduced, and sometimes the right brachial nerves have their function impaired. . . .
> Card-makers have two principal departments. The doubling [of] the wire is performed by men, and in a posture the same as that of shoemakers. The disorders produced are also similar. . . . No men live to follow this employ from youth to great age. Card-setting is performed by children from eight to twelve years old. It requires them to sit, to lean much forward, and to use their fingers and eyes with rapidity and accuracy. The rooms are often much too crowded. Beginners suffer from head-ache and pain in the back; but the children in general make no complaint.[16]

Although it was not possible for the physicians of the time to identify a specific disease mechanism or precise diagnosis, each of these disorders had the common feature that the symptoms occurred in parts of the body (particularly the hands and back) that were engaged in repetitive or continuous exertions in the workplace.

Along with these new cases of often vague but localized occupational discomfort, other medical reports began to describe specific musculoskeletal disorders with more readily identifiable causes and lesions. One of these was the "beat" condition among miners, which was noted in 1842 by Edwin Gurney. The beat disorders involve subcutaneous cellulitis or acute bursitis resulting from repeated trauma to the knee ("beat knee"), elbow ("beat elbow"), or hand ("beat hand").[17]

Other disorders that were thought to have a specific, identifiable anatomical locus included traumatic tenosynovitis, first observed by Velpeau (1825), who attributed it to a lesion of the tendon sheath; snapping (trigger) finger, first reported by Notta (1850); and occupational skin diseases of the hands such as palmaris psoriasis among shoemakers (Willan 1798), silk-winder's dermatosis (Potton 1851), and excessive callosities on the hands of various manual workers (Rayer 1827).

Growth of the Clerical Professions and Writers' Cramp

One important and frequently unrecognized aspect of the Industrial Revolution was a dramatic increase in the employment of clerks, particularly copyists, scribes, bookkeepers, legal clerks, and others who earned their living by use of the pen. The increasing complexity of business activity during this period required employment of these clerks, generally educated but lower grade officials responsible for simple tasks of organization, administration, and accounting.

By the mid-nineteenth century, according to British physician Samuel Solly, "the greatest part of the middle classes of London earn their bread by the use of the pen, either as the exponent of their own thoughts or the thoughts of others, or in recording the sums gained, lost, or spent in this great emporium of commerce—this vast Babylon." Census figures indicated that clerical and office employment grew from about 3 percent of the workforce in 1831 to approximately 7 percent in 1900.[18]

The work performed by this new class of industrial clerical workers was often as monotonous, repetitive, and time-pressured as that of manual factory laborers. Thackrah (1832) provided the following description: "Clerks, book-keepers, accountants, &c. suffer from confined atmosphere, a fixed position, and often from long days. At many large manufactories, the book-keepers are kept at the desk, with the intervals of two hours and a half for meals, from half-past six in the morning till nine at night. . . . Their muscles are distressed by the maintenance of one posture; and they complain frequently of pains in one side of the chest."[19]

Beginning in 1830, reports began to document clerical workers who suffered disabling pain, paralysis, and muscular spasm of their hands and wrists after prolonged repetitive writing.[20] The symptoms would often appear gradually and then intensify with continued performance of the repetitive activities. Most commonly the writing was performed with a pen, and the disorder affecting those workers came to be known as *writers' cramp* or *scriveners' palsy*. It is significant that the overwhelming proportion of those suffering from writers' cramp were not authors or occasional writers of letters or manuscripts. The malady almost exclusively affected those who performed their repetitive penmanship writing for businesses or industrial concerns. Charles Dana (1894) observed: "Clerks and professional writers are naturally much more subject to the disease. . . . Copying is much more harmful than composing. Authors seldom have writers' cramp."[21]

A typical case of writers' cramp, as described in nineteenth-century medical literature, involved the gradual development of an aching fatigue in the fingers and hand used for writing, accompanied by dull pain and/or stiffness. The first symptoms could last for months or even years. With continued writing the symptoms progressively intensified, resulting in increased pain and difficulty in pen-prehension and movement. Prickling sensations and numbness in the finger tips were often reported. Eventually writing became nearly impossible. At an advanced stage, anesthesia, paralysis, intense pain, and spasmodic contractions of the fingers or hand were sometimes experienced.

The following descriptions provided by Solly (1864) in one of the first English-language case reports illustrate the typical presentation and course of writers' cramp:

> Case 1: I am a clerk of four years' service in the —— Bank. My duties consist entirely in writing. I first felt pain in my right arm about May, 1862; had then been in the employ of the above-mentioned bank three years, and during that time had worked extremely hard, writing without cessation from morning till evening. . . . The first symptoms were those of a sprain in the wrist, but I could not recollect hurting it in any way. . . . I soon resumed work, though still experiencing slight inconvenience, which gradually increased. At this date the pain was most violent between the knuckles of the first and second, and second and third fingers of my right hand. When I moved my second finger I could feel an uneasy sensation striking up my arm, apparently in the sinews connected with that finger. . . . I still continued to work as before. The pain became a burning, uncomfortable feeling between the knuckles (more especially between the second and third fingers) and in the back of the hand, extending occasionally to the shoulder after writing about an hour, and gradually getting worse whilst writing. I worked on in this state for eight months. . . . [Eventually] on the skin a nasty nervous sensation, accompanied by the old symptoms of burning and bursting became apparent; it troubled me in the night, frequently keeping me awake for hours.
>
> Case 2: Mr. S——, aged twenty-five, clerk in the —— Bank, applied to me for advice on the 20th of October, 1863. He states that he has lost the use of his forefinger and the finger next to it, or middle finger; that he felt a weakness in them about ten days ago, but that he did not like to give up, and therefore worked through it; but it increased so much

that at last he could not hold the pen. . . . There is a certain amount of numbness in the fingers affected, which is increased when holding a pen, or by any pressure upon the fingers. The numbness is not quite constant, but varies from time to time. Sometimes those fingers are fixed, and he has difficulty in extending them. His hand soon gets very cold; but by wrapping it up he can keep the temperature at its natural standard.

Case 3: The first time I ever felt any inconvenient sensation in my right hand was, as well as I can remember, about 1858–59. At that time, I had an unusual quantity of writing on my hands, a great deal that was strictly official, and much that was semi-official. The inconvenience I then felt was a cramp through the entire hand, which made me often lay down my pen and straighten out my right hand with my left. In 1860 a great deal of my writing ceased. I still had much official writing but semi-officially and privately I had much less to do; the cramped state of my hand entirely disappeared. In 1862–3 my duties required more writing than usual, and I imposed upon myself also a great deal of writing which did not, strictly speaking, belong to my office, and my hand began to suffer. Meantime I felt the old sensation of cramp, but towards the end of 1862 it assumed a new form. I then began to feel a pain in my right thumb. . . . By degrees the pain in the thumb ceased, and was succeeded by a sensation difficult to describe in the last two fingers of the right hand. It sometimes was a tingling—a burning sort of feeling—commencing in the tip of the fingers, or more properly most perceptible in the tip of the fingers, and extending up the hand; sometimes it was a numbness in the fingers, occasionally accompanied by sharp but slight shooting pains, which sometimes extended up the arm. . . . It gradually increased, never assuming an acute feeling but practically rendering my hand much less useful to me than formerly. After writing for a while, I was compelled to pause from sheer inability to continue writing. . . . I used to feel the tingling sensation in the two last fingers of my right hand when I went to bed, and it would continue all night, being just as perceptible in the morning.[22]

During the mid-to-late nineteenth century, the reported incidence of writers' cramp steadily increased. According to British neurologist W. R. Gowers (1896), almost all cases (83 percent) occurred to persons of prime working age, between twenty and fifty. The overwhelming majority of cases involved males. This conformed to employment patterns of that time, in which men held a much greater proportion of the newly created professional clerical positions.[23]

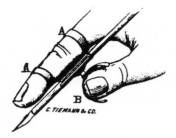

Figure 9 Mathieu's Penholder (from Dana 1894)

Researchers of the time attempted to identify various reasons that the disorder had started to appear in significant numbers throughout the newly industrialized nations of Europe. Four possible explanations were offered.

All authorities agreed that the primary cause of the emergence of writers' cramp was the enormous growth in the class of professional scribes, clerks, and copyists that had followed the introduction of factories, services (banks, insurance, and so on), transportation, and distribution businesses during the late eighteenth and early nineteenth centuries. The same working conditions and pressures imposed on factory labor were extended to early office workers, resulting in a transformation of the writing task into one that was prolonged, regimented, and monotonous. G. Vivian Poore suggested that, in addition to job exertion, there was a broader socioeconomic component of etiology. In 1897, he wrote: "The frequency of writer's cramp is due, in the first place, to the unwholesome life of a clerk who spends his days in a stuffy office in a crowded city."[24]

There was speculation that specific manual actions, which were especially characteristic among professional scribes, were responsible. Several experts believed that the act of pen-prehension was more hazardous in this respect than pen movement because professional clerks and bookkeepers needed to maintain a constant contraction of the affected muscles in grasping the pen for long periods of time.[25] This incessant exertion of the nerves and muscles, without the ability to pause or recover, eventually led to a condition that was termed "localized chronic fatigue" or "irritable weakness."[26]

Another commonly cited factor was the speed and time pressure of writing required by the new class of professional scriveners. Poore (1899) noted that most cases of writers' cramp occurred in those who "write against time," and summed it up in remarking, "'tis the pace that kills." Charles Dana (1894) observed that "the chief exciting cause is excessive writing. But this is not all. The writing that is done under strain or a desire to finish a set task is the harmful thing." James Lloyd believed that the emergence of writers' cramp was due primarily "to the increased speed and recklessness with which [the pen] is driven in our modern struggle for existence."[27]

Figure 10 Nussbaum's Penholder (from Dana 1894)

Many researchers traced the emergence of writers' cramp to the introduction of steel pens, which first occurred around 1820. Steel pens, because of their hard points and rough friction over the paper, were thought to require much greater effort than quill pens to produce steady writing and offered fewer occasions to rest the hand. To address this hazard, a number of prophylactic writing devices were introduced and recommended between the years 1840 and 1900. These included rubber and cork sleeves, as well as mechanical penholders (figures 9 and 10). Lloyd believed that use of a stub-pen was less dangerous than a sharp-pointed pen for persons who do constant writing because "a stub-pen does not require such fine muscular adjustment to keep it in proper contact with the paper as that which a pointed pen requires." After the introduction of mechanical typewriters, in the 1880s, it was also commonly recommended that use of a typewriter should be substituted for manual writing, so as to relieve the need for constant grasping.[28]

From the beginning of these disorders' widespread appearance in the early 1800s, medical authorities struggled with developing an appropriate nomenclature to signify the condition. Their difficulty stemmed from the lack of identifiable underlying anatomical changes and the proliferation of varying and diffuse symptoms that could affect sufferers. There was a belief that neither the use of the term "cramp" in *writers' cramp* or "palsy" in *scriveners' palsy* was entirely satisfactory. One of the leading authorities in the field, G. Vivian Poore, commenting on his experience in treating more than forty cases of writers' cramp, wrote in 1873: "All who have knowledge of this disease are aware that although the word *cramp* has been applied to it, yet actual cramps or spasms of any of the muscles concerned are often not evident even on the most careful examination; and that although the word *palsy* has been used, yet actual paralysis of any nerve, muscle, or group of muscles, is only present as an occasional complication, and when present generally warrants us placing the case in a category other than that of functional spasms."[29]

Physicians were perplexed by the multiplicity of symptoms that could affect workers in unpredictable ways. In this respect, these new occupational disorders were unlike many traditional infectious diseases or acute injuries that progress more rapidly and unambiguously from an identifiable cause to a specific effect. As we shall see, this inability to define a precise clinical pattern remains an important element in controversies about the identification of cumulative trauma disorders as a form of specific occupational disease.

Eventually, medical authorities began to differentiate "varieties" of writers' cramp, depending on the types of secondary symptoms observed during advanced stages of the disease. Moritz Benedikt (1868) suggested a categorization of writers' cramp into the paralytic, the spasmodic, and the tremulous, according to which symptom predominated. This classification became widely accepted during the latter part of the nineteenth century, although there was not universal agreement as to whether the distinction signified distinct disorders or merely different symptoms of a single malady. There was also disagreement about which variety was most prevalent, with some authorities (for example, Wood 1893) claiming the paralytic was by far the most common, and others (for example, Lloyd 1895) claiming the spasmodic predominated.

Although professional writers were the most frequently affected occupational group, other workers were also plagued by the same symptoms seen in writers' cramp. An increasing number of reports began to appear during the mid-nineteenth century of similar ailments among workers in other trades who also used their hands in a prolonged and repetitive fashion, including seamstresses, shoemakers, musicians, and milkers. These case descriptions exemplify this trend:

> Some time ago a smith, aged 37, came under my notice, who applied for relief at the hospital, for a rigid contraction of the muscles of the forearm, occurring whenever he took hold of the handle of his hammer, and wanted to fetch a blow; it was accompanied with violent pain, and the tense muscles were said to project like cords under the skin. This cramp prevented him from attending to his business for the previous six months.[30]
>
> I have been informed of two instances among musicians where prolonged strain . . . has resulted in loss of power. One case was that of a violin player who has lost the power of grasping, and consequently of fingering, the instrument with the left hand. The other case is that of a performer on the violoncello who has lost the power of "making the nut," that is; of shortening the strings of the instrument by means of extreme pressure exerted by the phalangeal joint of the thumb.[31]
>
> Mary Anne C., semptress, 27, was kindly sent to me by Mr. Morrant Baker. In June, 1874, she was working inordinately hard, "often nearly all night," and one day, after using a very big pair of scissors for

"cutting out," thought she had strained her wrist. She then lost the power of plying her needle, and the arm became comparatively useless for all acts, whether coarse or fine.[32]

The normal custom of physicians first examining these cases was to name them according to the type of professional activity performed. This practice derived from the tradition of Ramazzini and Thackrah, in which occupational diseases were conceived as specific to a particular trade, with the trade itself viewed as a fundamental etiologic agent. Thus, from the 1830s until the 1890s, medical journals published case reports of more than forty related maladies with such names as hammerman's palsy, milker's cramp, compositor's cramp, auctioneer's cramp, pianist's cramp, violinist's cramp, sewing spasm, and tailor's cramp.

However, even from the beginning, there was a realization that the symptoms exhibited by all these kinds of manual workers (writers and others) were quite similar, characterized by pain, stiffness, and nerve tenderness in the fingers and hands, accompanied by occasional anesthesia, paralysis and/or spasm. The principal common defining mark of the disorder was a progressive inability to perform normal manual functions of the job. And the primary distinguishing characteristic was the particular vocation in which the work was performed.

It was thus unclear to physicians and patients of the time whether they were dealing with one disease or many. The great variety of vocations along with the multiplicity of symptoms suggested a host of different disorders. But the similarity in symptoms, their progressive nature, and the common origin in prolonged, repetitive manual activity implied a single malady.

Because the symptoms were observed and studied most frequently among professional writers, many physicians of this period began to use the terms *writers' cramp* or *scriveners' palsy* as a generic phrase to describe the related hand and wrist disabilities observed among a wide range of other workers. Some medical studies appeared that specifically designated cases among seamstresses and tailors as varieties of writers' cramp.[33]

The Emergence of Telegraphists' Cramp

Toward the latter part of the nineteenth century, a new important variety of "writers' cramp" began to appear among telegraph workers. The development of the telegraph, with its consequent impact on the growth of communications, was a powerful force driving industrial and business expansion during the late 1800s. The rapid spread of this technology led to the emergence of a large new class of white-collar workers performing intense manual activity: the telegraph operators.

William Fothergill Cooke and Charles Wheatstone patented the first electromagnetic telegraph in 1837. By the early 1840s, demonstration telegraph lines had been laid alongside several railways in Britain. In 1844, Samuel F. B. Morse sent a telegraph message from Baltimore to Washington, D.C. By 1846, London was linked with Dover, and in that same year the Electric Telegraph Company was founded in Great Britain. Western Union came into existence in the United States in 1856, and the first transatlantic cable was laid in 1866. By the mid-1870s, electric telegraphy was in commercial use throughout Europe and the United States. As of 1907, there were nearly 16,000 telegraphic systems in use in Great Britain, with a similar number employed in France and Germany. The number of telegraphists grew steadily until World War I, after which employment declined owing to the development of wireless telegraphy, automatic sending devices, and the telephone.

With the introduction of commercial telegraphy came the first medical reports of chronic hand and wrist disorders among telegraphists. The observed symptoms and the absence of an identifiable underlying pathology exactly paralleled the characteristics of writers' cramp. The "new" disorder, termed *telegraphists' cramp,* was first reported at a meeting of the Paris Société de Biologie by M. Onimus, on March 20, 1875. At that meeting, Onimus described two cases of the affliction, which he said was not uncommon in telegraph clerks, especially those who used the Morse instrument.[34]

A brief English-language report of Onimus' Parisian lecture was carried in the April 17, 1875, edition of the *British Medical Journal.* The announcement provoked a strongly worded editorial in the following week's *Lancet* (April 24, p. 585)—prophetic of the type of response that would characterize the debates on this issue up to the present time. The editorial begins sarcastically by suggesting that, "something like a panic must have been caused amongst the telegraphists of this country by the announcement— for which a French physician is answerable—that their occupation exposed them to a disease which is said to be 'very common amongst telegraph clerks.'" While acknowledging that "this story is likely enough," the editorial's author challenges the authenticity of the disorder by asking why more cases have not been reported. After all, "the number of telegraph clerks is enormous." The writer goes on to predict that telegraphists' cramp will ultimately take its stand among such other reported disorders as milker's cramp and bricklayers' cramp as little more than medical "curiosities."

This anonymous author, undoubtedly a physician, was probably reflecting a growing sense of frustration and dismay, in both the medical community and society at large, with the increasing proliferation of obscure hand and wrist disorders among workers whose jobs did not seem overtly hazardous, at least according to traditional standards. In addition, these maladies were cropping up among the growing class of workers who were neither traditional laborers nor factory owners, whose occupational existence was directly attributable to the rapid changes in work organization and business technology that were occurring during the late nineteenth century. To many in British society, the vague problems that were plaguing these new office workers must have seemed symbolic of their own sense of disbelief and apprehension about the repercussions of industrial progress.

Contrary to the predictions of the *Lancet* editorial, it was not long before a growing number of medical cases of telegraphists' cramp were reported in Britain and elsewhere. In 1882, Edward Robinson, surgeon to the post office at Leeds, described four cases of telegraphists' cramp to the British Medical Association. In the same year, the medical officer of the British General Post Office reported on the complaint. Two years later, in 1884, Thomas W. Fulton, who had been a telegraphist in the Edinburgh post office, published a medical report in which he concluded that the disorder was more common than generally supposed. Charles Dana, in 1894, estimated that approximately 0.5 percent of all telegraphists in New York City were affected. In 1903, an extensive monograph on the subject was published by E. Cronbach describing seventeen cases that had been treated in Berlin.[35]

The following case descriptions, appearing in Robinson's 1882 article, are representative:

Case 1—Miss C, aged 26, has been a telegraph clerk for eight years, and is considered a most efficient one. She was suddenly seized with numbness and weakness in the right forearm and wrist (on the ulnar side), compelling her to relinquish work. On examination I could not find anything wrong with her arm, but she seemed weak. . . . Under this treatment [rest and diet] she gradually improved, the numbness disappeared, and she resumed duty after a month's absence, as I thought, well. On commencing duty, she found she could not do her work nearly as well as formerly; the hand and wrist soon tired, and her messages were sent in an irregular, jerky manner, rendering them frequently unintelligible.

Case 2—Miss D, aged 22, complained of numbness and weakness in the right elbow, forearm, and hand, after only one year's duty as telegraph clerk. This, after troubling her more or less for six months, compelled her to relinquish work.

Case 3—Mr. B, aged 31, has been employed as telegraph clerk sixteen or seventeen years. Four years ago, he felt pain over the front of the right elbow; after some months, pain commenced over the front of the left elbow, followed by cramp in the forearm and hands. . . . After a hard day's work, this cramp in the forearms and hands sometimes lasted for hours, and the pain ran down the ulnar side of the forearm from the elbow to the little and ring fingers.[36]

Most authorities who studied telegraphists' cramp mentioned the unmistakable similarity of this malady to writers' cramp. J. H. Lloyd, in 1895, remarked that telegraphists' cramp "is practically the same disease as writers' cramp." Theodore Thompson and John Sinclair (1912) asserted that "the two conditions are strictly comparable."[37]

In his original case report of 1875, Onimus speculated that the risk of developing telegraphists' cramp was closely associated with the use of the Morse telegraph key. This same reasoning was adopted by other early researchers. Gowers, in 1896, observed that the affliction "affects exclusively those who use the Morse machine." Lloyd, in 1895, also claimed that Onimus' original speculation about the Morse key as the "cause" of telegraphists' cramp "has been confirmed by subsequent observers." However, it should be noted that during the last thirty years of the nineteenth century, the Morse key gradually came to be the predominant instrument used in telegraphy in Great Britain, accounting for 30 percent of telegraphic systems in 1870 and progressively increasing to 64 percent by 1907. Thus, the higher prevalence of telegraphists' cramp among operators of the Morse key may have been merely a reflection of its greater overall use. This seems to have been the conclusion of Cronbach, who, in his 1903 description of seventeen cases of telegraphists' cramp in Germany, noted that only three of the affected workers used the Morse key, while fourteen worked on a Hughes instrument of different design that was at that time more commonly employed in Germany. Cronbach surmised that the substitution of the Hughes instrument for the Morse would not be effective as a preventive measure.[38]

The Morse key worked on the basis of a lever surmounted at one end with a knob (figure 11). Depressing the knob completes a circuit, thereby transmitting an electric signal. The telegraph operator usually held the key loosely with the thumb and index and middle fingers. By using the elbow as a rest, the operator's forearm was held relatively stationary, and most movement was consequently confined to rapid extension and flexion of the wrist. This was accompanied by a constant but variable contraction of the thumb and first two fingers. It was not uncommon for operators to be continually engaged in this activity for periods of eight to fourteen hours, with long documents requiring particularly sustained effort. Fulton (1884) estimated that a typical operator made between thirty and forty thousand contractions per hour (more than twice as many movements per minute as made by the average typist). In this regard, it is also interesting to note the striking

Figure 11 Normal Position of the Hand for Telegraphing (from Lloyd 1895)

similarity between the hand grip and contractions employed in operating a telegraph key and those required in the use of the modern computer mouse, which some contemporary researchers have suggested is a potential risk factor in the development of cumulative trauma disorders.[39]

As was the case with writers' cramp, typewriters were suggested as a means for preventing telegraphists' cramp.[40] Manufacturers of typewriters encouraged this view, as can be seen in a 1906 advertisement on the inside front cover of *The Railroad Telegrapher* (the journal of the railroad telegraphers' trade union), which claimed that a telegrapher using a typewriter "never gets 'nervous prostration,' no matter how swift the pace" (figure 12). Whether or not the claim was justified, this kind of advertising campaign would have served to alert telegraphers to the potential dangers of their work, and the risk for nervous disorders to arise as the result of fast-paced manual activities.

By 1911, telegraphists' cramp reached nearly epidemic proportions among British telegraph operators. A study of 8,153 telegraphists conducted that year by a special committee of the General Post Office showed that 64 percent of telegraph workers were experiencing some physical difficulty from keying. Approximately 9 percent of the workers were diagnosed as suffering telegraphists' cramp, based upon a doctor's clinical examination. Seventy-six percent of those clinically diagnosed with cramp were male, compared to 61 percent of males in the overall workforce of telegraph operators. The average length of employment as a telegraphist amongst those with telegraphists' cramp was sixteen years. A member of the Departmental Committee (T. F. Purves), charged with investigating conditions in the United States, found that in 1911 the percentage of operators showing symptoms of telegraphists' cramp was about 4 percent in the Western Union Company and approximately 10 percent in the Postal Telegraph Company.[41]

In addition to the hand postures and motions involved in operating the Morse key, researchers identified a number of other factors as contributing to cause the disorder. These included aspects of work organization (for exam-

Figure 12 Advertisement from *The Railroad Telegrapher*, 1906

ple, the failure to rotate workers between sending and receiving to reduce periods of continuous key operation), excessive congestion in the operator's workspace, poor training and supervision, improper adjustment and spring resistance of the keys, and the anxiety and nervous "strain" imposed on young workers assigned to high-volume circuits.

In the early twentieth century, telegraphists' cramp became perhaps the first chronic disorder caused by physical hazards to be specifically deemed compensable under workers' compensation laws. Prior to 1897 in Great Britain, there was no prescribed method for employees to seek redress and compensation from employers for injuries that occurred in the workplace. Their only recourse was to sue employers at common law or, if malice was involved, to seek criminal penalties.[42] The Workmen's Compensation Act of 1897, however, prescribed a procedure for compensating injured workers automatically for any injury "arising out of and in the course of employment." To demonstrate that an injury arose out of and in the course of employment, it was necessary to show that an "accident" had occurred, where an accident was understood to be an unforeseen event that took place at a specific place and time.

It soon became clear to workers and insurance administrators that there were several recognized occupational diseases for which it was difficult to isolate a specific accident and injury as defined in the act. For that reason, the Workmen's Compensation Act of 1906 extended the 1897 act to a large number of previously excluded occupations and established a schedule of specific diseases. Each of these occupational diseases was to be treated as if it were an injury resulting from an "accident" as prescribed by the 1897 Act. Six diseases merited this status initially: lead, phosphorous, arsenic, and mercury poisoning, ankylostomiasis, and anthrax. Moreover, the 1906 act established a process for investigating whether other occupational diseases should be added to the schedule. For a disease to be scheduled, evidence needed to be presented to the Departmental Committee on Compensation for Industrial Diseases (the so-called Industrial Diseases Committee) demonstrating that the disease was clinically specific, clearly linked to a specific work process, and resulted in work incapacity lasting more than one week. The committee was comprised of well-known governmental occupational disease authorities, including Dr. Thomas Legge and Dr. Clifford Allbutt.[43]

Shortly after passage of the 1906 act, the British postmaster general asked the Industrial Diseases Committee to consider whether telegraphists' cramp should be added to the schedule. As part of this process, that committee met in 1908 to investigate the prevalence of the disease among British telegraph workers, identify its causes, and make recommendations for prevention. Based upon expert testimony provided by the Post Office's medical officer, independent physicians, and workers' representatives, the Industrial Diseases Committee added telegraphists' cramp to the act's compensation schedule on December 2, 1908. In so doing, they found that telegraphists' cramp met the criteria of being identified with a particular work process, namely the use of the Morse key (cramp resulting from use of the Hughes instrument was excluded). Furthermore, the committee found the disorder clinically differentiable by virtue of the localized hand dysfunction that resulted in coding errors made by afflicted telegraphists when transmitting messages.[44]

A few years later the same Industrial Diseases Committee rejected the scheduling of "twisters' cramp" (which was actually Dupuytren's contracture) in lace makers because, while there was sufficient proof that lace makers suffered from this disorder, there was evidence that other individuals in the same geographical area who were not lace makers also contracted the same malady. The occurrence of Dupuytren's contracture among "twist-hands" or "minders of lace machines" had first been brought to the attention of the Chief Inspector of Factories in 1910 by a representative of the Amalgamated Society of Operative Lace Makers in Nottingham. As a result, an investigation was conducted in 1912 by Edgar Collis and Robert Eatlock of the British Factory Inspectorate. They found 139 cases of the disease among

1,360 workers examined (10.2 percent) and concluded that "(1) Dupuytren's contracture is more than usually prevalent among lace-machine minders; (2) This prevalence has a direct relation to i) the frequency with which the levers and wheels of the machine are manipulated; and ii) the power required to actuate these levers and wheels, and their size, shape, and position."[45]

Unpersuaded by the findings of the factory inspectors' report, the Industrial Diseases Committee relied instead upon evidence supplied by Dr. Kenneth Black, a medical consultant for the employers, indicating that, of 131 cases of Dupuytren's contracture reported to local doctors in the Nottingham area, 63 occurred in manual workers and 68 in "other persons," 32 of whom were persons of "independent means" (not workers). In addition, Black personally examined 270 inmates at the Nottingham prison and found a prevalence rate for the disorder of 21 percent among all inmates compared to 15 percent (three inmates) among the twenty inmates who had been previously employed as "twist-hands."[46] Moreover, independent inquiries made by the Industrial Diseases Committee to Nottingham doctors and the local hospital were not able to confirm any unusual prevalence of the disorder among lace makers. For these reasons, the committee recommended that twisters' cramp should not be scheduled as a compensable occupational disease.

As indicated earlier, telegraphists' cramp itself closely resembled cramps that were common among professional scribes, musicians, and others. So why was the committee willing to accept telegraphists' cramp as a bona fide occupational disease, but not twisters' cramp among lace makers? One explanation involves the criteria used by the committee for defining the two disorders. Twisters' cramp was distinguished by a specific pathology (contracture of the palmar fascia—see section below on Dupuytren's contracture). The presence of this same pathology in persons not engaged in lace making was interpreted by the committee as evidence that the disease was not uniquely associated with that employment. For telegraphists' cramp, by contrast, the lack of a distinguishing pathology led the committee to rely on the presence of clinical symptoms and overt functional behavior (errors in telegraphic coding) to characterize the condition. Defining the disease in that way meant that cases of telegraphists' cramp could always be uniquely related to a particular occupation, as required for compensable occupational diseases by the 1906 act.

In addition, there may have been deeper considerations of a social nature. For example, one significant difference in the two cases was that by 1913 British telegraphers were a strong and well-organized political force. Their occupation was central to the nation's economic growth, and telegraph clerks were comparatively well compensated. A national trade union, the Postal Telegraph Clerks Association, had been established in 1881. Representatives from that union had testified at the committee hearings. Intense canvassing by postal workers' unions was instrumental in achieving a landslide victory for Liberals, supported by Labour, in the general election of 1906. More than half the members of Parliament elected in that year had pledged to support postal workers' demands for better wages and working conditions. The new Liberal postmaster general, Sydney Buxton, declared his support for the postal unions and appointed a select committee to investigate workers' needs for increased benefits and improved working conditions. Following Buxton's lead, other Liberal ministers indicated a willingness to deal with representatives of government workers. As a result, seventy-three new civil service workers' associations were established by 1914.[47]

In contrast, lace makers were poorly organized and politically weak, with no effective national trade association. The workers' representative in the case of the Nottingham "twist-hands" was the Amalgamated Society of Operative Lace Makers, a society representing 2,000 local laborers, approximately half of all the lace makers in that district. These workers were generally poorly paid (on a piecework basis), and most were elderly. According to testimony provided to the committee, the lace trade in Nottingham in 1912 was in a state of "decay," with a rapidly decreasing base of employment.[48] The differing political clout possessed by the workers who brought these two diseases before the Industrial Diseases Committee could help explain why the committee was ready to adopt the seemingly circular and imprecise reasoning that telegraphists' cramp be defined as a disease distinguishable by errors made sending telegraph messages, while refusing to grant compensation for a malady (twisters' cramp) that had been determined by government factory inspectors to affect more than 10 percent of the lace makers in Nottingham.

Occupational Neuroses

By the late 1800s, it was generally agreed that the multiplicity of chronic hand and wrist disorders arising among writers, telegraphists, and other workers were all varieties of a common disease syndrome, related to chronic overuse of the hands and wrists in manually intensive jobs. A number of researchers struggled with the question of developing an appropriate generic descriptive name that would encompass this family of maladies. By the end of the nineteenth century, more than twenty different generic terms had been suggested in the medical literature including professional impotence, craft palsy, overfatigue, exhaustion neurosis, overuse, professional spasms, anapeiratic diseases, fatigue disease, functional dyskinesia, professional ataxia, copodyskinesia, and local chorea. Two terms in particular came into vogue as generic descriptors: occupational neuroses and professional cramps. Of these, occupational neuroses eventually came to be the single most widely used diagnostic appellation used by physicians for the growing number of work-induced hand and wrist disorders.

The name *occupational neuroses* apparently was first suggested by Gowers (1888) in his textbook on diseases of the nervous system. He adapted the term from the German physician H. Berger (1885), who called these disorders *Beschäftigungs-neurosen*. The term *neurosis,* as initially used by Gowers and other physicians between 1830 and 1895, was used not to indicate any mental or psychological condition, but rather to signify that the malady was a neurological disorder of unknown etiology. Gray's textbook of neurology (1895) defined *neurosis* as "Nervous disease without specified lesions. From *neuron,* a nerve, and *osis,* suffix denoting morbid condition."

The classification of these disorders as neurological was a direct outcome of the great nineteenth-century discoveries in neurology made by Sir Charles Bell in Great Britain and G. V. Duchenne in France, which elucidated the anatomy and function of the nervous system and demonstrated the role of electrical stimulation in neuromuscular function. Prior to these advances, physicians since Galen's time had conceived of muscular action as the result of animal spirits or fluids that flowed down hollow nerves to inflate the muscles. Duchenne and others discovered that application of local electric current could excite the muscles, and, with prolonged electrical stimulation, the muscles eventually became fatigued, losing their ability to contract. A prominent role of the nerves, as conceived by Bell and Duchenne, was to supply the electrical stimulation needed for muscular contraction. The function of the brain and higher nerve centers was to control and distribute the electrical stimulation in appropriate amounts as needed by the muscles in use.

In this context, it was natural for Bell and Duchenne to conceive of local functional problems such as writers' cramp as essentially nervous system dysfunctions. It was clear to them and to subsequent researchers that the disorders were not primarily muscular in origin, since the patient with writers' cramp could generally use his or her muscles for many purposes other than one specific vocational activity (like writing). The major unresolved question, according to this model, was whether the neurological dysfunction had its pathological origin (its "morbid anatomy") located in the peripheral nerves or in the higher centers of the central nervous system.[49]

The neurological model of localized functional disorders of the hand first provided by Bell in 1830 helped define many of the concepts and identify issues that were to dominate thinking about these disorders for the next hundred years: "The affections of particular muscles, or classes of muscles, imply a very partial disorder of the nerves. A disease of the brain, or a disease in the course of the nerve, must influence the whole limb, or that portion of it to which the nerve or nerves are distributed. But in these cases, particular subdivisions of the nerves, included in the same sheaths, or running the same course are affected. I am inclined to attribute such partial defects to the influence of visceral irritation."[50]

Duchenne, in 1855, called these disorders *functional spasms* or *functional impotence* and described cases occurring in writers, musicians, tailors, and cobblers. With respect to their neurological basis, he wrote in 1867: "Is the trouble peripheral, i.e., limited to the muscles? Do the nerve centers send their normal stimulus to the muscles? Is the excitability of the muscles sometimes increased and sometimes lost or lessened during voluntary or instinctive movements? Or rather is there a point in the nerve centers which, excited or exhausted by constantly repeated movements, sometimes over discharges causing spasm, sometimes sends the nervous stimulus to the muscles irregularly so as to cause tremor and clonic spasm, and sometimes ceases to distribute its nervous force, and this only during the performance of certain functions? . . . I lean towards the second hypothesis (that which makes the trouble depend upon some derangement of the nerve centers)."[51]

Later writers and investigators reiterated this emphasis on "exhaustion" or "fatigue" of the nerves. Poore, for instance, in 1873, claimed that these disorders are the result of "chronic local fatigue." James Lloyd (1895), another neurologist, termed them "fatigue neuroses." Gowers (1896) believed that they were due to a "morbid lowering of nervous resistance" and said the condition could accurately be described as one of "irritable weakness" of the nerve centers. The emphasis on nervous exhaustion and fatigue to describe occupational hand and wrist ailments paralleled the growth of the concept of "neurasthenia" during the late nineteenth century.

The Relationship of Occupational Neuroses to Neurasthenia

Neurasthenia as a distinct medical entity was introduced by the American physician George M. Beard in a series of books and articles beginning in 1869. By the end of the century it had become one of the most commonly diagnosed of all disorders, both in America and in Europe, allegedly affecting as much as 20 percent of the population. Headlines proclaimed neurasthenia "The National Disease of America." It grew throughout the late 1880s and 1890s and into the early twentieth century, but dramatically decreased in incidence after World War I. By 1930, the concept of neurasthenia had effectively disappeared from the lexicon of the medical community.[52]

A tremendous amount of scholarly analysis has been directed toward the history of neurasthenia during the period 1870–1930. Neurasthenia was conceived to be a generalized state of nervous exhaustion and fatigue, fostered by the frenetic pace of contemporary life, especially in the United States. Its symptoms included lethargy, headaches, sleeplessness, nausea, excitability, bowel problems, sexual dysfunction, and a wide range of nebulous complaints.[53]

The theoretical basis for neurasthenia stemmed from nineteenth-century advances in neurology and physics that demonstrated a relationship between energy and electrical stimulation, on the one hand, and human physiology, particularly muscle function, on the other. The intermediary for relating energy (most notably, electricity) to physiology (most notably, muscles) was the nervous system. The prevailing view in the mid-nineteenth century was that every person had a finite store of "nervous force" or energy that mediated this transfer and that when the available force was depleted, either through overwork or by the general rigors of everyday life, a neurasthenic state of "nervous exhaustion," "nervous fatigue," and "irritable weakness" could result.

Beard and others considered neurasthenia to have a definite psychological aspect, and those with an inherently "nervous" temperament were believed to be especially predisposed to contracting the disease. Men and women, though both susceptible to neurasthenia, were thought to be affected differently. For example, women suffering from neurasthenia were typically prescribed bed rest for a month or longer. Men, in contrast, were advised to engage in vigorous outdoor exercise.[54]

Beard attributed the growing incidence of neurasthenia during the late 1800s to be a direct result of the new pressures of modern civilization. Lutz (1991) analyzes the disease as a social metaphor that provided individuals with a specific way to represent and explain the diverse cultural, social, and economic changes occurring during that period. According to Lutz, "Neurasthenia became then both a medical specialty and a central new cultural articulation of psychological, moral, physical, social, and economic understandings, especially understandings of psychological, social, and economic change. 'Nervousness' in literary, academic, and journalistic discourses was most often used in explaining change in gender roles, change from one stage in life to another, change in financial circumstances, change in cultural values, change in marital status, change in an individual's relation to institutions, or changes in the institutions to which an individual is related."[55]

Another important development that influenced the growth and conception of neurasthenia at the close of the century was the growing acceptance and popularization of the modern theories of psychology, as represented by the work of Jean-Martin Charcot and Sigmund Freud. Charcot's work with patients diagnosed as hysterics in the mid-1880s first introduced Freud to the possibility that mental disorders might be caused by purely psychological factors rather than by organic brain disease. Freud's writings, beginning in 1893–1895 with the publication of *Studien über Hysterie* (*Studies in Hysteria,* co-authored with Josef Breuer), emphasized the role of the individual personality in various diseases that had previously been thought of as essentially neurological. In *Studien über Hysterie,* Freud first introduced the distinction between "psycho-neuroses" and "actual neuroses," with the former being of emotional origin and the latter caused by organic conditions. As Lutz points out, Freud initially classified neurasthenia as a physiological disease but gradually came to interpret it as predominately psychological: "Freud in 1895 made a distinction between 'psycho-neuroses' (which were psychogenic) and 'actual neuroses' (which were organic), and he placed neurasthenia in the second category and thereby outside the ken of psychoanalysis. But before he appropriated them as distinct syndromes, the majority of symptoms of what he termed psychoneuroses had been considered symptoms of neurasthenia, not specific disease entities. Nevertheless Freud continued to maintain the importance of neurasthenia as a general term and argued for the value, for instance, of Mitchell's rest cure. And in his middle writings neurasthenia, anxiety neurosis, and other 'actual neuroses' were analyzed as psychogenic as well."[56]

The terminology used to describe occupational neuroses closely resembled that used in the neurasthenia model, with both disorders being rooted in "nervous exhaustion and fatigue" and "irritable weakness." It is thus not surprising that investigators began to see these types of hand and wrist disorders as intimately related to neurasthenia. After a period of time, many physicians began to interpret the occupational neuroses as localized forms of neurasthenia. The American neurologist Horatio Wood (1893) stated that "occupational neuroses may indeed be looked upon as local neurasthenia, having the same relations to general neurasthenia that every local neurasthenia has." Southard and Solomon (1916) cite eighteen studies linking neurasthenia with occupational neuroses and conclude that occupational neuroses can be considered to be "in some way dependent upon a general neurasthenic condition which might be focalized in a particular muscular activity."[57]

Despite the fact that the original descriptions of chronic hand and wrist disorders as *occupational neuroses* did not imply any psychoneurosis in the Freudian sense, they were nevertheless typically conceived as possessing an underlying psychological component. Even such early researchers as Poore and Gowers referred to emotional and temperamental manifestations of writers' and telegraphists' cramp. Poore (1872, 1873) observed that those suffering from writers' cramp commonly exhibited "mental irritation and distress and sleeplessness" and are often "nervous people, such as are easily startled by sudden noises and the like." Several authors (for example, Rosenthal 1879) commented on the "nervous excitability" of patients with writers' cramp. Dana (1894) described those suffering from occupational neuroses as often nervous, emotional, mentally depressed, and plagued by insomnia and vertigo. Lloyd (1895) referred to the "mental and moral symptoms" of writers' cramp such as anxiety, depression, hypochondria, and hysterical phenomena.

Other physicians (for example, Osler 1892) implicitly or explicitly suggested that nervous temperament itself was a predisposing causal factor for the development of occupational neuroses of the hands and wrists. Wood (1893) cited anxiety and "depressing emotion" as etiologic factors. Dana (1894) listed "excessive worry and intemperance" as predisposing causes.

As the neurasthenia model grew in popularity, physicians began to expand their conception of the importance of the psychological component of occupational neuroses. By the late 1890s and early 1900s, the medical discourse about hand and wrist disorders placed equal emphasis on the psychological basis of the malady. For example, the British *Departmental Report on Telegraphists' Cramp* (1911) concluded that the condition was a result of two factors; one being fatigue caused by repeated hand movements when operating the Morse key and the other "a nervous instability on the part of the operator."[58]

By 1896, Gowers was beginning to question the verity of writers' cramp because of its supposed psychological underpinnings: "Writers' cramp is a disease that is readily imagined. Most persons who have to write much, experience at times some discomfort in the hand after writing, and, since such discomfort is one of the early symptoms of writers' cramp, they are apt to fancy that they are the subjects of the disease, and a slight tendency to spasm is readily imagined in such a case."[59]

With the emergence of workers' compensation as a matter of legal and medical debate, especially during the first two decades of the twentieth century, even more speculation arose about the psychological origin of occupational neuroses. The popular and medical literature began to shift focus toward the question of how to detect the deliberate feigning of these symptoms by patients. A number of books and articles were published between 1912 and 1930 on this subject, several by physicians giving detailed advice on clinical methods to detect such "fakers." In the same vein, the British *Departmental Report on Telegraphists' Cramp* (1911) speculated that "a neurasthenic telegraphist might believe difficulties to be real which exist only in his imagination, and occasionally a telegraphist who wished to give up operative work might feign the symptoms of cramp." When a follow-up study of telegraphists' cramp was conducted in 1927 by the British Industrial Fatigue Board, an even stronger conclusion was reached: namely, that telegraphists' cramp was a condition primarily attributable to the "psychoneurotic predisposition" of certain telegraphists.[60]

Physicians and others studying occupational hand and wrist disorders thus gradually shifted their attention from neurology to psychology. Most authorities came to believe that certain specific psychological tendencies caused workers to suffer from ill-defined hand and wrist ailments, spasms, and paralysis. Further evidence for this conclusion was found in the well-documented post-traumatic responses of many soldiers who, upon returning from the horrors of the first World War, experienced chronic pain, paralysis, and other symptoms in the upper and lower extremities that lacked organic causes and were undeniably psychological in origin.

A temperamental predisposition to nervous excitability came to be recognized by physicians as a major factor in the development of occupational neuroses. In the medical and popular literature of this period, two types of people were singled out as possessing these traits in a disproportionately high degree: females and Jews.

The Alleged Susceptibility of Women and Jews

Building upon Freud's original studies of hysterical females in the 1890s, a number of medical authorities commented on the nervous temperament of women and their predisposition to neurasthenia. Physicians of the nineteenth century put forward a number of rationalizations for women's special predisposition to nervous exhaustion, including frail constitution, smaller brain size, greater indoor confinement, rigors of childbearing, and the weight of their clothes. Physician Abraham Myerson, in his 1920 book *The Nervous Housewife,* attributed this susceptibility to such "female" characteristics as liability to worry, wounded pride, desire for sympathy, monotony of life, over-aesthetic tastes, secret jealousy, and passions and longings. Fulton (1884), in discussing Onimus' observations of telegraphists' cramp, remarked, "those of a nervous temperament—and, *ergo* women—are especially prone to be affected; the condition is accompanied by insomnia, palpitations, vertigo, and that melancholia, loss of memory, moral and physical atony, and even insanity may supervene."[61]

As several modern historians have observed, one of the primary reasons that physicians at the turn of the century considered women especially vulnerable to nervous disorders was their apprehension about the increased role that women were beginning to assume in the workplace, particularly in white-collar positions. Most medical authorities believed that these social roles were unnatural and unhealthy for females. They maintained that a woman's nervous system, being naturally inferior to a man's, was incapable of handling the additional stresses imposed by these new roles. G. M. Hammond, a professor of mental and nervous diseases at the New York Post-Graduate School, wrote that women, through no fault of their own, inherited a "weak nervous system" which, while "ample in all probability to meet the requirements of an even placid, and uneventful existence, [was] absolutely inadequate to stand against a strong current of misfortune, care, or overwork." British physician Sir Thomas Oliver expressed warnings about the potentially destructive effect that can result from overtaxing a woman's nerves in a working environment: "On the part of girls there is a growing tendency for them to enter shops, offices and factories than to stay at home or enter domestic service. . . . The telephone has given a new occupation to women, but by highly-strung girls of an excitable nature and whose nervous system is likely to break down under strain it ought to be avoided." This warning was echoed by Canadian physician Robert Dwyer (1907), who believed that after four or five years on the job, women telephone operators were prone to "break down nervously and have nervous children." Dr. S. Weir Mitchell, originator of the widely prescribed Weir Mitchell Rest Cure for women, saw female neurasthenia as the most characteristic form of the disease. He advised physicians to be particularly sensitive when treating their women patients, asserting, "the man who does not know sick women, does not know women." The solution to the health problems of the New Woman, according to the prevailing medical view, was for her to return to the protective surroundings of the home, which offered a healthy environment, more "proper" and "natural" to a woman's innate character.[62]

During the first forty years of the twentieth century, medical and popular literature also contained frequent references to the "special susceptibility" of Jews and other immigrant groups to nervous disorders. This passage, written in 1919 by Dr. Harry Mock, a noted surgeon and chief medical adviser to the Sears, Roebuck Company, is typical: "It has been the common observation of all authorities on this subject that the Jewish race, especially the very poor or the very rich, are the most susceptible to neuroses. This is undoubtedly due to the emotional temperament, characteristic of the Hebrew. The condition, however, is not more common among the intelligent Jews than among other nationalities. I have found the Irish and Italians, especially among the very poor and less educated classes, also quite susceptible to these conditions."[63]

This alleged nervous temperament was also thought to predispose Jews to neurasthenia. Dr. James Huddleson, a neurologist at Columbia University, concluded that the high prevalence of neurasthenia among garment workers (25–30 percent) could be attributed to the presence of Russian

Jews as operatives in that industry. In making that judgment he draws on evidence from a number of studies including those by DaCosta and Jones (1923), Hughes (1928), Wechsler (1929), Schwab (1926), Fishberg (1911), and Baker (1915). He cited, for instance, DaCosta and Jones' finding that "Russian Jews often become frantic with terror after an accident and develop many secondary nervous phenomena." Even the venerable *Jewish Encyclopedia* expounded this belief in its 1905 edition. The entry on "Nervous Diseases" states:

> The Jews are more subject to diseases of the nervous system than the other races and peoples among which they dwell. Hysteria and neurasthenia appear to be most frequent. Some physicians of large experience among Jews have even gone so far as to state that most of them are neurasthenic and hysterical. . . . Binswanger, Erb, Jolly, Möbius, Löwenfeld, Oppenheim, Féré, Charcot, Bauveret, and most of the other specialists in nervous diseases, speak of this in their monographs on neurasthenia and hysteria, and point out that hysteria in the male, which is so rare in other races, is quite frequent among the Jews. In New York City it has been shown by Collins that, among 333 cases of neurasthenia which came under his observation, more than 40 per cent were of Jewish extraction, although his clientele was not conspicuously foreign.[64]

The traits that made Jews supposedly prone to neurasthenia and other disorders of mental origin were also noticed by the medical community in other ethnic groups, particularly those of Slavic and Eastern European origin. Church and Peterson (1899) asserted that "Hebrews and Slavs" were especially subject to neurasthenia. An article by G. H. Benton in the *Journal of the American Medical Association* (1921) stated that the neurotic symptoms displayed by Italian, Greek, Austrian, and Polish immigrants stemmed from their general belief that "the United States . . . is due . . . to provide for them the rest of their lives. These people are often unable to demonstrate any somatic maladies."[65]

The medical community's "scientific" linkage of women and Jews to nervous traits had a long and well-established history. In the early twentieth century, this doctrine provided physicians and others with an additional model for understanding why these obscure hand and wrist disorders had appeared in the workplace when they had. Both groups began to dramatically increase their presence in the workplace, especially in the United States, from 1890 to 1920. During this period of intense immigration, more than ten million Jews and Slavs arrived. Many Americans naturally feared the economic consequences and competition for scarce jobs that resulted from this huge influx of low-skilled Eastern European workers.

Women had also made tremendous strides in entering the modern workplace. Prompted in part by labor shortages during World War I, women had flooded into factories and offices, often taking over positions that traditionally had been occupied by men. This was particularly true for the expanding force of white-collar office workers, which became predominately female by 1930. Between 1900 and 1930 white-collar employment in the United States rose by almost 800 percent (nearly three million workers), more than two-thirds of whom were women.[66]

After 1900, occupational neuroses of the hands and wrists increasingly came to be interpreted by physicians as forms of neurasthenia, psychoneuroses, and other psychological abnormalities. At the same time, physicians continued to allege that women, Jews, and immigrants were especially susceptible to those types of psychological disorders. Physicians' linkage of such groups with psychological abnormality was part of a broader social reaction to the unprecedented entry of large numbers of these individuals into the modern workplace. As observed by a number of contemporary social commentators, including feminist writers Barbara Ehrenreich and Deirdre English (1973), the medical allegation that sickness is due to supposedly inherent psychological traits can be a way for the prevailing privileged classes to maintain social control over the less advantaged. The historical evidence suggests that the redefinition of occupational neuroses of the hand into varieties of psychological illness may have stemmed in part from an attempt to exert such social control.

The Decline of Occupational Neuroses after World War I

From the end of World War I onward, the incidence of reported occupational neuroses of the hand and wrist began to decline significantly. By the end of the 1920s, very few cases were reported. This decline can be understood in terms of many of the aforementioned changes.

The decline of reported occupational neuroses paralleled the demise of the neurasthenia model as an accepted clinical entity by the medical community. By 1920, neurasthenia had shifted from the domain of neurology to that of psychiatry. Since occupational neuroses had also been transformed into varieties of neurasthenia and psychoneuroses, many occupational physicians and safety experts came to dismiss or ignore these cases and relegated them to the domain of mental illness, akin to hypochondria, depression, and anxiety. Workers would understandably have been reluctant to report disorders that could stigmatize them as neurotic or psychologically abnormal.

In many cases, the ailments were considered to be nothing more than a manifestation of the personal nervous characteristics of women, Jews, and recent immigrants. The association of these symptoms with Jews, the poorly educated, and lower-class immigrant groups further discouraged recognition of the problem. British psychiatrist and historian Simon Wessely (1990) traces the decline of neurasthenia to the changes in social demography that occurred in the early twentieth century. Beard, Charcot, and other early theorists had conceived of neurasthenia as principally a disease of modern civilization that thus affected primarily the civilized and privileged social classes. Wessely contends that as neurasthenia began to be identified in the immigrant and lower classes during the early 1900s, prominent physicians and intellectuals became less concerned with the problem. As a result, according to Wessely, neurasthenia gradually fell into disrepute with both psychiatrists and neurologists.[67]

These developments also need to be seen against the backdrop of the more general social reaction against labor that occurred in the years following World War I. In the United States, events during the period from 1917 to 1922 included bans on immigration, the institution of espionage and sedition acts, prosecution of socialists, and a wave of major strikes. Unemployment rose from 9 percent in 1916 to 19.5 percent in 1921. Workers were in a weak position politically. There was widespread reaction against protective legislation that had been passed during the Progressive Era and numerous attacks on organized labor. There was no guarantee of employment security for injured or disabled workers. Immigrants, women, blacks, and others at the low end of the labor market were most vulnerable. The redefinition of occupational neuroses as psychological abnormalities of immigrants, Jews, and women was one indication of the pervasive antilabor and antiforeign sentiment in the United States during the decade following World War I.

The new class of office workers was paid comparatively less and was more female than in the past and, thus, had relatively less power to bring minor physical problems to the attention of their employers. The vast majority of these workers were young and single, most between seventeen and twenty-four years of age. For many, employment constituted a temporary interval preceding marriage. Among female telephone operators, for instance, the average duration of employment was approximately fifteen to twenty months. A report by the U.S. Women's Bureau confirmed that many women during the 1920s either decided to leave their employment or were forced to leave because of sickness, exhaustion, or injury. To some extent, the low reporting of occupational hand disorders after World War I may have been indicative of a healthy worker effect (diseased workers having left the workforce) and/or workers' reluctance to report cases due to fear of reprisal.[68]

Moreover, any hand disorder that an office worker may have acquired was probably less disabling than in previous years: a clerk of 1875 who could not write could not work, but a secretary of 1925 who experienced hand pain or numbness could likely still handle the occasional writing, typing, and other tasks required in the modern office. According to medical authorities of the period, the use of the typewriter was less hazardous in that it avoided the prolonged prehension and static muscular contraction that was needed by the nineteenth-century scrivener or telegraphist.

Many traditional sources of occupational exposure to repetitive motions of the hands were reduced or eliminated as the result of technological changes. The replacement of manual telegraph operation with radio, telephone, and automated telegraphy proved particularly significant. Also, manual writing was no longer the defining characteristic of a discrete occupational class. The dedicated scribes, clerks, and scriveners were eventually replaced by a new generation of white-collar workers who primarily used typewriters for business correspondence, and whose jobs included a variety of other tasks including answering telephones, taking dictation, and performing assorted activities that eliminated the need for prolonged and prescribed manual exertion.

The decision by the designers and administrators of the workers' compensation system to specifically exclude chronic hand disorders with nonspecific pathology, both in the United States and Britain, also affected reporting and recognition. In Britain, compensation was predicated upon inclusion in a specific schedule, in which telegraphists' cramp and writers' cramp were the only chronic hand disorders listed. In the United States, compensation could be sought only for disorders that occurred at a specific time and place and had an identifiable organic pathology. Although most chronic hand and wrist ailments lacked a specific pathology, there were two noteworthy exceptions that attracted medical attention during the nineteenth and early twentieth centuries: Dupuytren's contracture and Raynaud's phenomenon.

Dupuytren's Contracture and Raynaud's Phenomenon

The emphasis on the identification of a specific pathological abnormality, an organic "lesion," as a necessary component of medical disease has been traced by some historians to French and German advances in anatomy and physiology during the early 1800s.[69] With the development of modern psychological theory during the years 1895–1920, the ability to isolate an underlying anatomical lesion became an important method for distinguishing "real" disease from psychoneuroses and other mental or emotional conditions. This criterion found its way into medico-legal discourse and the decision-making process used in the workers' compensation system. The inability to isolate such an abnormality for most chronic occupational hand and wrist disorders became an important reason behind their decline in the years following World War I. Because Dupuytren's contracture and Raynaud's phenomenon are each characterized by distinctive and observable physical signs, questions never arose about their being genuine medical conditions. However, in both cases, controversies eventually developed about whether the anatomical abnormality stems from occupational causes. The history of both these diseases was highlighted by dramatic shifts of opinion regarding this issue.

Dupuytren's disease is characterized by the chronic contracture of the fourth and fifth fingers of the hand toward the palm, usually accompanied by ridging of the palmar skin. This abnormality has been reported in the medical literature since the early 1600s. A noteworthy aspect of the history of this disease is that almost all of the early references related the disorder to occupational activities. For instance, Felix Plater, in 1614, wrote: "Contraction of the fingers of the left hand into the palm. A certain well-known master stone mason, on rolling a large stone, caused the tendons of the ring and little fingers in the palm of the left hand to cease to function. They contracted and in so doing were loosed from the bonds by which they are held and became raised up, as two cords forming a ridge under the skin. These two fingers will remain contracted and drawn in forever."[70]

Henry Cline, Sr., a prominent London physician, recognized the disease in 1787 as one of "laborious people."[71] Astley Cooper (1822) attributed the contracture to "excessive action of the hand, in the use of the hammer, the oar, ploughing, etc." Baron Guillaume Dupuytren, in his presentation of December 5, 1831, at the Hôtel-Dieu in Paris, clearly identified the disorder's lesion as contracture of the palmar fascia, which he asserted could be surgically treated by excision of the palmar aponeurosis. In that lecture, Dupuytren associated the disease with chronic local trauma caused by occupation:

> Most people with this disease have been obliged to do hard work with the palm of the hand or to handle hard objects. Thus the wine merchant and the coachman whose case histories we will report were accustomed, one to broaching casks with a puncheon or to binding up staves, the other to plying his whip unceasingly on the backs of his jaded horses. We could also cite the example of a clerk in an office who took particular care in applying the seal to his dispatches. It is also found in masons who grasp stones with the ends of their fingers, with ploughmen, etc. From this it is clear that the disease affects particularly those who are obliged in their work to use the palm of their hand as a pressure point.[72]

The historical irony is that Dupuytren's contracture, which was clearly recognized by its early investigators as work-related, is now generally considered not to be produced by occupational activities. The contemporary medical perspective is that the etiology of Dupuytren's contracture is unknown, with chronic or acute trauma playing no role in its development.[73]

In many ways, this transformation is itself a result of Dupuytren's success in identifying a specific lesion responsible for the disorder. Unlike the other nineteenth-century hand disorders discussed earlier, Dupuytren's contracture could be diagnosed objectively in terms of anatomical characteristics. This led to an increased diagnosis of Dupuytren's contracture in patients whose hand disorders would previously have been attributed to rheumatism, gout, or infection. As the diagnosis of Dupuytren's contracture expanded in the late nineteenth century, epidemiologic evidence began to accumulate demonstrating that the disorder was prevalent in nonworking as well as working populations. For example, the findings of the 1913 Industrial Diseases Committee Report found no increased prevalence of Dupuytren's contracture among lace makers in Nottingham, England, compared to the prevalence in the general population of that community. By the early twentieth century, investigators had verified that Dupuytren's contracture occurs more often in workers who do *not* use their hands for manual work than in those who do (55 percent versus 45 percent).[74] Patients range from eleven years to old age, with the elderly being more prone to the disease. The disorder generally occurs bilaterally, even in those who predominately use one hand in their work. In addition, there is a strong hereditary tendency. All of these data were considered to be indicative of a localized structural dysfunction unrelated to occupational activity.

Another consequence of the identification of a specific anatomical lesion by Dupuytren was the removal of this disorder from the province of neurologists. Because the pathology was clearly not localized in the nervous system, Dupuytren's contracture never came to be identified with the cramps and spasms that were epidemic in workers during the late nineteenth century and which were eventually subsumed by the generic descriptor *occupational neuroses*. This disease thus escaped both the original explosion of scientific and public concern about work-induced nervous disorders (including neurasthenia) that occurred in the late 1800s, as well as the subsequent "psychologization" of these disorders that took place in the early twentieth century.

A somewhat similar history characterized investigations of Raynaud's phenomenon. The first medical report on this condition was made in 1862 by Maurice Raynaud, who called it "local asphyxia and symmetrical gangrene of the extremities."[75] The disorder is characterized by recurrent episodes of finger numbness and blanching, generally thought to result from arterial vasospasm. As in the case of Dupuytren's contracture, the signs of Raynaud's phenomenon are "objective" and readily discernible through clinical examination. It is now customary for physicians to distinguish between *primary* Raynaud's phenomenon (also called Raynaud's disease), which is considered to be an idiopathic congenital condition occurring most frequently in young women, and *secondary* Raynaud's phenomenon, attributable to an underlying systemic disease, such as scleroderma, or exposure to physical agents, including cold and segmental vibration.

When Raynaud and other early researchers first described the syndrome, they were convinced that it was not caused by occupational activities, despite the fact that the symptoms typically occurred among manual workers. For Raynaud, the primary consideration in deciding that this was not an occupational disorder was its occurrence in the general, nonexposed, population: "A certain number of patients had manual occupations, such as washerwomen, chambermaid, burnisher, sculptor, etc. But as this circumstance was wanting in many other cases it appears to me we cannot attach any importance to it."[76]

Jonathan Hutchinson (1893, 1901) and other researchers realized that the symptoms described by Raynaud can arise from a number of sources, and thus do not necessarily indicate a single disease or etiologic process. For this reason, Hutchinson advocated use of the term *Raynaud's phenomenon* to connote a complex of associated syndromes rather than one specific disease.

In the early twentieth century, a number of studies were undertaken to investigate outbreaks of similar symptoms among users of vibratory tools in the mining, stone-cutting, iron-casting, and heavy manufacturing industries. Many of these studies were prompted by labor unrest and concern by workers and public health officials that dust produced by new mechanized equipment (especially pneumatic power tools) could increase the risk of contracting tuberculosis. Particularly influential were the studies conducted by Alice Hamilton (1918) on stone cutters in Indiana, in which she discovered episodic finger blanching and discomfort among thirty-four of thirty-eight limestone workers, forty-five of fifty granite workers, and forty-four of seventy-eight marble workers. Subsequent European studies confirmed the occurrence of these symptoms in other manual workers.[77] By the mid-1930s, a considerable amount of epidemiological evidence had been accumulated, demonstrating a clear association between digital vasospasm and occupational exposure to cold and vibration, especially vibration caused by the use of pneumatic tools. At first, there was considerable debate about what to call these cases of occupationally induced vasospasm. The workers themselves termed the condition "dead hand" and "white fingers." Hamilton preferred to label the ailment "spastic anæmia of the hands," in part to differentiate it from constitutional Raynaud's and to highlight its distinctively occupational nature.

Eventually, the similarity of the symptoms of this condition and Raynaud's led several authorities, including Sir Thomas Lewis and G. W. Pickering (1934) and John Hunt (1936a, 1936b) to suggest that the occupational cases be categorized as a variety of Raynaud's phenomenon. This suggestion soon took hold in the medical community. By the end of World War II, job-induced Raynaud's phenomenon (also called "vibration white finger" and "hand-arm vibration syndrome") was discussed extensively in the medical literature and had been recognized as a potentially compensable disorder within the workers' compensation systems in both Great Britain and the United States.[78]

Interestingly, the epidemiologic evidence has continued to show a sizable occurrence of Raynaud's phenomenon in the general non-exposed population. Recent estimates for the prevalence of Raynaud's symptoms in the general population are in the range of 3–11 percent for men and 4–19 percent for women.[79] The study of Lewis and Pickering found that the prevalence of this disorder was approximately 28 percent among a sample of medical students and nurses.

One might wonder why the medical and scientific establishment has come to acknowledge Raynaud's phenomenon as a potential work-related disorder despite its frequent occurrence in the general population, while dismissing the occupational etiology of Dupuytren's contracture for essentially the same reason. In this regard, one factor may be the composition and characteristics of the affected workforce. For example, occupational Raynaud's phenomenon is most frequently diagnosed among operators of pneumatic tools in "heavy" industries such as quarrying, construction, and mining. Almost all of these workers are males. This profile may fit the preconceived expectations of many physicians (and others) who conceive of a "legitimate" occupational disorder in the traditional sense of traumatic injuries related to heavy industrial work. By contrast, there is no similar pattern of occurrence for Dupuytren's contracture in workers performing traditional "heavy" and male-dominated jobs.[80]

Occupational Hand Disorders between the Wars

Medical and public attention directed at chronic occupational hand disorders declined after World War I and continued relatively dormant until the 1980s. During that sixty-year interval, the reported incidence of these cases remained low and was confined generally to problems that arose subsequent to acute injuries or to those disorders that were considered to have a specific detectable pathology, such as Raynaud's phenomenon or tenosynovitis crepitans.

The history of occupational tenosynovitis during this period provides a fascinating illustration of the way the social perspective of physicians can affect the recognition of a disease's work-relatedness. Tenosynovitis, the inflammation of a tendon sheath, was first observed by French surgeon Alfred Velpeau in 1818 and was later described by him in his *Anatomie Chirurgicale,* published in 1825. Several varieties of tenosynovitis affect the hands and wrist, including tenosynovitis crepitans, stenosing tenosynovitis, and infectious tenosynovitis. During the 1920s and 1930s, both tenosynovitis crepitans and stenosing tenosynovitis began to be associated by physicians with the repetitive and forceful use of the hands.[81]

Claims for compensation of these disorders started to appear in the workers' compensation system in limited numbers, confined to a few specific geographical areas. Most notable were the cases of tenosynovitis filed in the state of Ohio. Apparently, the recognition of tenosynovitis in Ohio stemmed from the pioneering work of Dr. Emery R. Hayhurst, one of the founders of American industrial hygiene, and director of the Division of Occupational Diseases of the Ohio State Board of Health from its inception in 1913 until 1930.

The establishment of state bureaus of industrial welfare and health was an outgrowth of Progressive Era interest in extending the public health perspective to problems of the workplace. This movement led to the establishment of Industrial Hygiene sections by the U.S. Public Health Service and the American Public Health Association, as well as to the creation of a number of state bureaus of occupational health and hygiene.[82] In 1911, a state-sponsored survey of occupational diseases in Illinois was undertaken by Dr. Alice Hamilton. Prompted by the findings in Illinois, which included a significant incidence of lead poisoning, the Ohio legislature, in 1913, authorized a similar comprehensive survey of industrial health hazards and occupational diseases to be conducted by Hayhurst, who had assisted Hamilton in Illinois.

The survey, conducted by fourteen field inspectors over a two-year period, covered 1,067 establishments and 235,984 workers in more than thirty Ohio industries.[83] As part of the survey, medical records were examined, trade unions were contacted, and hundreds of employees were interviewed. A comprehensive assessment was made of all workers' health complaints. Questionnaires on occupational disease occurrence were sent to 7,500 Ohio physicians. Through this process, Hayhurst documented the occurrence of numerous occupational diseases as well as an assortment of chronic musculoskeletal problems including lumbago, neuritis, sciatica, rheumatism, and inflammation and tenderness of tendons in the hands and wrist. In his final report to the state, Hayhurst recommended that a number of these disorders, including tenosynovitis, be scheduled as compensable occupational diseases.

When Ohio's first occupational disease act was enacted in 1921, fifteen specific occupational afflictions were listed as compensable, but tenosynovitis of the hands and wrist was not one of them. Hayhurst continued to argue for its inclusion. He was familiar with synovitis disorders because of early work on the "beat" conditions among miners that had been investigated since the nineteenth century in Great Britain and elsewhere in Europe. However, based on the results of the Ohio survey, Hayhurst recognized that tenosynovitis often took a different form among industrial workers. He advocated amending Ohio's schedule to conform more closely to that of New York, which included "miner's diseases including cellulitis, bursitis, ankylostomiasis, tenosynovitis, and nystagmus." But Hayhurst offered an alternative wording for the hand and wrist disorders to be scheduled, along with this explanation for the different terminology:

> Cellulitis, bursitis, or tenosynovitis of the hand, wrist, elbow or shoulder from any work involving continuous local pressure, twisting or straining of parts named. These features are now included in the New York Law in the case of miners only, but as such they are rarely reported in Ohio. On the other hand, they are fairly common in many other industries, especially among new workers or those just returning from a period of idleness who attempt to turn out the old "day's output" before they are again accustomed to the work. Some cases become suppurative, but most end within a few days, and after simple treatment. The conditions are fairly easily diagnosed—soreness, swelling, crepitus and even grating sounds on moving the parts may be evinced.[84]

As Progressive Era reforms dissipated after World War I, Hayhurst's recommendation languished until August 1929, when the Ohio Legislature passed an amendment to its workers' compensation act that specifically included as compensable "primary tenosynovitis characterized by a passive effusion or crepitus into the tendon sheath of the flexor or extensor muscles of the hand due to frequently repetitive motions or vibrations." In a 1931 study of tenosynovitis in Ohio, Dr. Harold Conn of Akron stated that the reporting of compensable tenosynovitis increased substantially after passage of the amendment, accounting for 0.15 percent of total lost days from all causes in 1929 and 0.99 percent in 1930. In 1933, 191 cases of compensable tenosynovitis were reported in Ohio, representing 15.2 percent of all reported occupational disease cases.[85]

One factor that helped establish tenosynovitis as a legitimate occupational ailment was the presence of a detectable pathology. This was particularly true in cases of tenosynovitis crepitans, in which adhesions on the tendon sheaths produce the sound of crunching snow upon sliding of the tendon, and stenosing tenosynovitis of the digital flexors ("trigger finger"), in which a thickening of the tendon sheath physically restricts finger movement. Unlike occupational neuroses of the late nineteenth century, it was hard to argue that the crepitans sound or the overt snapping of the tendon observed in trigger finger were psychological illusions.

The situation was less clear in other forms of tenosynovitis, or in other related musculoskeletal inflammatory conditions such as tendonitis and bursitis. Many physicians of the period noted the difficulty in making a precise diagnosis as well as differentiating these conditions from other musculoskeletal ailments such as rheumatism, arthritis, and neuritis.[86]

In addition to the issue of identifying a distinct pathology, the other important aspect of establishing tenosynovitis as a occupational disorder was tracing its etiology to motions, activities, and trauma occurring in the workplace. In the late 1920s and early 1930s a number of medical studies attempted to draw this connection. One disorder that attracted considerable attention in this regard was stenosing tenosynovitis (or tendovaginitis) at the radial styloid process, also called de Quervain's disease.[87]

This condition had first been noted in five female patients by Fritz de Quervain in 1895. In 1912, de Quervain reported eight additional cases that were claimed to be cured by surgery. He stated that the most frequent exciting cause of the condition was overexertion from household duties. E. Eichhoff in Germany (1927) reported on five cases and concluded that the disorder is "an injury to the gliding mechanism of the tendon sheath resulting from work requiring a constantly repeating movement of the wrist."

Apparently, there was no American knowledge of this disorder or comment on it in English medical literature until the pioneering work of Dr. Harry Finkelstein and his colleagues at the Hospital for Joint Diseases in New York in the late 1920s. The first American report on this condition was published by Dr. H. C. Stein, a colleague of Finkelstein's, in July 1927. An independent study of the same condition was made by Dr. Chester Schneider of Milwaukee in 1928 describing fifteen cases of his own and summarizing 119 cases previously reported in German and French medical journals. In his landmark study published in 1930, Finkelstein reported on twenty-four cases that he had treated surgically between 1926 and 1928. Finkelstein wrote: "The fact that so few reports on stenosing tendovaginitis appear in the American literature does not mean that the condition is uncommon in our country, for during the period between 1926–1928 twenty-four cases were operated on for this lesion at our institution. This condition is apt to be erroneously diagnosed as rheumatism, neuritis, periostitis, tenosynovitis and even tuberculous osteitis."[88]

The profile and work history of Finkelstein's patients precisely matched those of Schneider and the previous European investigators. Of Finkelstein's twenty-four surgical patients, twenty were female. Of the twenty women, fourteen were housewives, and the other six worked as a maid, a governess, a dancer, a piano player, a bookkeeper, and a factory worker. Among the men, two were tailors, one a cutter, and one a grocery clerk. Of Schneider's fifteen patients, six were housewives, three were nurses, two were students, one was a dressmaker, one an architect, one a milliner, and one a laborer. (Schneider did not indicate the gender of his patients.) In his summary of 133 cases combining his own and those reported from previous European literature, 119 were female (89.5 percent). Significantly, of eighty-nine cases where the side was noted, forty-seven were right, forty-four were left, and four were bilateral.

Thus, by 1930, it was known that patients suffering from de Quervain's disease were overwhelmingly female, generally housewives and others who worked outside of industrial factories, and that the cases were about equally divided between the right and left hands. Based upon the available information, Finkelstein concluded that the disorder was of an occupational and traumatic origin: "Stenosing tendovaginitis is encountered most frequently in the laboring classes, which leads to the assumption that it is of traumatic origin. An acute traumatic onset is rather infrequent, having occurred in but six of the author's series. The general impression prevails that the inciting factor must be attributed to a chronic trauma. Cases are reported to have developed after prolonged piano-playing, following the use of a typewriter or adding machine, as the result of excessive writing, washing and wringing out clothes, chopping wood, carrying heavy objects, farm labor, cutting cloth with heavy scissors, etc. . . . The laboring classes are most frequently affected. Chronic trauma and overexertion are the most common causes."[89]

Finkelstein clearly believed that his patients represented workers from the laboring classes. Some of the terminology he adopts underscores this perspective. For example, of the twenty-four patients, six are described as a "housewife" and eight others as a "houseworker." In the article's summary statistics on occupation, Finkelstein uses the term *houseworker* to refer to all fourteen. He does not clarify the distinction between a housewife and a houseworker, but those terms are evidently meant to denote someone other than a domestic servant, since the word *maid* is used to describe the work done by another patient. Presumably both housewives and houseworkers worked in their own homes—the terminological distinction may have been intended to differentiate married from single women.[90]

Finkelstein notes twice that the patients were from the laboring classes, not just that they performed work. He also notes that two were "colored." The terminology used to describe their work activities is highly evocative: *prolonged* piano playing, *excessive* writing, carrying *heavy* objects, cutting with *heavy* scissors. Finkelstein viewed the activities of housewives as *work,* part of the life of the laboring class. In his mind they were house*workers.* Their hand disorders originated from their toil.

Some indication of how Finkelstein, a successful orthopedic surgeon, adopted what seems by contemporary standards to be an extremely progressive, feminist, and labor-oriented perspective toward these conditions can be gleaned from the circumstances of his own personal history.

Harry Finkelstein was born in 1883 in New York City, the eldest of seven surviving children (six other brothers and sisters had died either at birth or in infancy).[91] His mother and father, who were Jewish immigrants, had arrived in the United States from southern Russia during the 1870s. Harry's father initially supported his family by buying and selling cloth in New York's garment district. As a child, Harry sold newspapers to help his family survive. Despite working part-time, he managed to graduate from De Witt Clinton High School and then complete medical college in 1904, at the age of twenty—the only member of his immediate family to receive a formal education.

Along with several other young Jewish physicians, he helped found the Hospital for Joint Diseases in two old brownstone buildings in New York in 1905. In 1911, he married Rae Blum, herself the daughter of Jewish Russian immigrants. Over the next several years he and his wife had three children, including a son, Dr. Richard Fenton, who followed in his father's footsteps as an accomplished orthopedic surgeon.

For Harry Finkelstein, the world of the "laboring classes" was not an abstraction, but rather the world of the people he knew and served in New York between 1905 and 1930. The first ten years of his practice saw the height of Progressive Era labor activism in his own neighborhood. Radical Jewish women in the textile district of New York were leading the fight for improved working conditions. In 1909, four years after the founding of the Hospital for Joint Diseases, the great labor uprising occurred in New York's garment district led by "socialist feminists" from the International Ladies Garment Workers Union. In 1911, 146 young Jewish women were killed in the infamous fire at the Triangle Shirtwaist Company on the Lower East Side.

When Finkelstein began to see tendovaginitis in the radial styloid of women at the Hospital for Joint Diseases it was natural for him to look beyond his patients' status as housewives to perceive more deeply their working-class roots and the hardness of their daily labor. It was also perhaps no coincidence that his wife, Rae, was an accomplished pianist, and that the first patient he diagnosed with de Quervain's disease was a young female piano player. It is also significant that, after having achieved professional success, Finkelstein became a personal friend of President Franklin D. Roosevelt and embraced the Democratic party's New Deal politics during the 1930s.

Finkelstein's judgment about the traumatic and occupational etiology of de Quervain's disease corresponded with that of Schneider in Milwaukee and the previous European investigators, including de Quervain himself. In reaching that judgment Finkelstein and the others were undoubtedly also influenced by biomechanical considerations concerning the lesion's appearance and its presentation generally at the precise position where the abductor longus and extensor brevis pollicis tendons slide over the radial styloid process. In addition, Finkelstein was able to reproduce experimentally a similar lesion in animals by external and internal traumatization of the tendons at that spot.

Due to the medical pronouncements of Finkelstein and other authorities, de Quervain's disease was generally accepted as a compensable work-related disorder under state workers' compensation plans. Seeking compensation for any form of tenosynovitis in New York became easier after 1935, when a new occupational disease law was enacted (in response to the silicosis crisis —see chapter 3) that liberalized criteria for occupational disease compensation. Statistics from New York state show that claims for "synovitis and bursitis" increased 87 percent between 1936 and 1939. In 1952, Finkelstein's son, Dr. Richard Fenton, reported on 423 cases of de Quervain's disease in 369 patients. In an interview, Fenton observed that most of these cases were submitted as compensable work disorders in New York and that "not one" was denied.[92]

Low Reporting of Occupational Hand Disorders, 1920–1980

Despite the widespread medical acceptance of the occupational character of de Quervain's disease and other forms of tenosynovitis, the number of compensated cases remained small and geographically isolated until the 1980s. In New York state, although cases of synovitis and bursitis increased 87 percent during the four years after passage of the 1935 occupational disease act, the total number of claims for these disorders reached only 127 in 1939. In Ohio the total was similarly low, with 191 cases of tenosynovitis reported in 1933. A report issued in 1941 by the Women's Bureau of the U.S. Department of Labor indicated that claims for tenosynovitis among women had been reported in Connecticut, Illinois, Wisconsin, and Michigan, as well as Ohio and New York. However, the number of cases involving women was low, with only nine such cases reported in 1938 from Connecticut, seven from Illinois, four from Michigan, and eleven from Wisconsin. A summary of tendonitis and other "soft-tissue" disorders from Wisconsin in 1961 revealed twenty-two such reports.[93]

There was a similar absence of reporting for occupational Raynaud's phenomenon, despite the wide body of evidence documenting its potential occupational etiology. Few cases were reported between 1920 and 1980 to the state departments of industrial health or to workers' compensation boards. A survey conducted in 1960 by the U.S. Public Health Service could find no reported prevalence of Raynaud's phenomenon in the United States; the report's authors concluded that it "may have become an uncommon occupational disease approaching extinction in this country." In 1979, the U.S. Bureau of Labor Statistics Supplementary Data System contained fewer than thirty-nine cases that may have been job-related Raynaud's phenomenon.[94]

Several explanations have been offered to account for the low reporting of occupational hand disorders during this sixty-year period. As indicated above, physicians and the workers' compensation system were reluctant to acknowledge nonspecific syndromes lacking a distinct pathology as occupational diseases. But the history of vibration-induced Raynaud's phenomenon and de Quervain's disease shows that even disorders with both a specific pathology and evidence for occupational etiology were seldom reported.

Some of this may be due to the absence of professional education and knowledge concerning occupational hand disorders. In their 1952 study of stenosing tenosynovitis of the wrists and fingers, Lapidus and Fenton note that "the general practitioner and even the general surgeon, as will be shown in our series, are still often baffled by these cases and not infrequently fail to diagnose and treat them properly."[95] These authors found that many cases of stenosing tenosynovitis were still being misdiagnosed as arthritis, neuritis, or rheumatism.

Other authorities attributed the low reporting of occupational hand disorders to the minor extent of the disability that resulted in most cases. Dr. W. C. Arthur, commenting on Conn's paper in 1931, believed that "tenosynovitis would have been included in the [Ohio occupational disease] law long ago save for the fact that disability rarely extended beyond the waiting period of seven days." The Public Health Service drew the same conclusion about Raynaud's phenomenon in 1960, commenting that the disorder constituted more of a "nuisance" than a real disability. In their 1962 article on occupational Raynaud's, Ashe, Cook, and Old suggested that the Public Health Service study was unable to find cases of the disorder in the United States due to shorter work weeks, increased automation, and the generally warmer climate in the United States compared to Canada and Scandinavia (where colder conditions presumably create a greater risk for contracting the disorder).[96]

With respect to Raynaud's phenomenon, it is also important to note that most occupational cases, such as those originally studied in the early investigations of Hamilton and Loriga, occurred among stone cutters. Between 1920 and 1960 the stone cutting industry was preoccupied with a much more serious health issue—silicosis—which became the focus of an intense national debate involving public health officials, occupational physicians, industrial hygienists, state legislators, and affected workers. In the context of the enormous national concern about the health hazards of silica dust among stone cutters, attention to a relatively minor disorder like Raynaud's phenomenon languished.

Although a limited number of chronic occupational hand disorders continued to be reported in the years between World War I and 1980, a major increase of cases did not take place until the mid-1980s. At that point, in the course of a few years, a new surge of public, legal, and medical attention was directed at occupationally induced hand and wrist disorders. The reported incidence of these disorders began to rise and has increased substantially each year since. During this period, new medical terms—*cumulative trauma disorders* and *repetitive stress injuries*—became part of the common lexicon of occupational safety and health. In the remainder of this chapter I will explore this contemporary phenomenon, attempt to explain why the expansion of cases occurred and how the growth in cumulative trauma disorders relates to previous historical episodes involving writers' cramp, occupational neuroses, and other related maladies.

The History of Carpal Tunnel Syndrome

Renewed interest in work-related hand and wrist disorders has been dominated by a concern with one particular disorder, *carpal tunnel syndrome*. Carpal tunnel syndrome has now become one of the most frequently diagnosed cumulative trauma disorders, and one of the most serious and disabling. Sectioning of the transverse ligament in the wrist to relieve the symptoms of carpal tunnel syndrome is one of the most frequently performed surgical procedures in the United States. It is estimated that more than 26,000 persons have this procedure performed every year, which averages out to 65 surgical cases per year for every hand surgeon in the United States. The popular press has latched onto this phenomenon, calling carpal tunnel syndrome "the 'in' injury" and "the malady of the information age." The former head of the U.S. National Institute for Occupational Safety and Health, Dr. J. Donald Millar, considers carpal tunnel syndrome to be a "mega-epidemic." In many popular and scientific publications, the term *car-*

pal tunnel syndrome is (imprecisely) employed as a generic descriptor for all CTDs, in a manner reminiscent of the way the term *writers' cramp* was once used to classify similar disorders affecting various vocational groups.[97]

The history of how the medical community first recognized and characterized carpal tunnel syndrome during the twentieth century provides an interesting insight to the more general question of how disorders come to be associated with working conditions. In the case of carpal tunnel syndrome, the opinion of one prominent medical authority was extremely influential in retarding this recognition and in obscuring the relationship of carpal tunnel syndrome to the various chronic hand and wrist disorders that had been reported previously.

Clinical symptoms of carpal tunnel syndrome include pain, numbness, and tingling in the hand, usually, but not always, confined to the distribution of the median nerve in the thumb, index finger, third finger, and half of the fourth finger. A hallmark for clinical diagnosis is night pain or tingling that is generally relieved by hanging, shaking, massaging, or exercising the hand. Physical findings can include reduced sensitivity to pinpricks or vibration, reproduction of symptoms upon provocative testing (for example, Phalen's test, Tinel's sign), and nerve conduction deficit as measured by electromyographic testing. Carpal tunnel syndrome is typically progressive with increasing intensity of pain and numbness, and the eventual development of motor weakness and inability to perform normal manual functions. In advanced cases, wasting of the thenar muscle can occur.

The medical literature contains a long history of descriptions of patients suffering exactly these kinds of symptoms. For instance, in 1833, Ormerond provided an excellent clinical description in a patient suffering night pain, digital dyesthesias, and onset with manual work.[98] E. Onimus (1876) described three cases in workers of what he called "professional muscular atrophy," one involving an enameler who had to hold an object between his thumb and forefinger all day. This patient, after a progressive development of cramps, palsy, and tremor, eventually developed a wasting of the thenar eminence. James Putnam, in 1880, reported on a series of thirty-one patients, twenty-eight of whom were women, suffering from local numbness in the hands and fingers. Several presented signs of discomfort at night, as evidenced by the following case description: "A married woman, 50 years of age, always strong and well. As a young girl, used to have neuralgia in the face; never since. For the past four weeks she has suffered from intense sense of numbness of one or both hands, from wrists down. It is present to a greater or less degree nearly all the time, but is worse at night, especially from about 3 A.M. till daylight, and also when, after doing housework, she sits down to sew. At such times she finds, after a few minutes, that she can scarcely hold a needle; the numbness, subjective and objective, is so intense, especially on the palmar surface of the thumb and fingers."[99]

Similar reports were provided by Ludwig Hirt (1893) who describes an "angio-neurosis" of night palsy which, he says, is particularly prevalent in women, especially those in the menopausal years. J. Ramsey Hunt (1911), in describing professional palsies related to occupational movements and frequent repetition, described cases of thenar atrophy and paralysis in jewelers, brass polishers, machinists, and oyster openers. Hunt speculated that the symptoms were due to a compression of the ulnar or median nerves. Brouwer (1920) provided detailed case descriptions of what he called "neuritis of the medianus" in patients including tailors, cigar makers, women who perform hand washing, and other manual workers.

The case descriptions provided in studies of writers' cramp, telegraphists' cramp, and other occupational neuroses also provide evidence suggesting that carpal tunnel syndrome existed during the nineteenth century. For example, in the first description of writers' cramp provided by Sir Charles Bell (1830), reference was made to the "wasting of the ball of the thumb" that may occur. Solly's early case descriptions of writers' cramp (1864) contained several references to "night pain and tingling." Poore (1897) also included several cases of writers' cramp that are suggestive of carpal tunnel syndrome, including one involving a man who had been "disturbed at night by a pricking sensation in the hand, and the next morning he wrote with great difficulty," and other cases of "tailor's cramp" and "goldbeater's cramp" characterized by tenderness over the course of the median nerve, wasting of the thenar eminence, and lack of sensation in the area served by that nerve.

The contemporary understanding of carpal tunnel syndrome depends heavily on the concept of *pathological lesion*, which became a dominant concern of neurologists and physiologists in the nineteenth century. The defining anatomical sign of carpal tunnel syndrome is a compression of the median nerve within the small opening inside the wrist known as the carpal tunnel. This compression is presumed to interfere with normal nerve conductance. The conclusive criterion for diagnosing carpal tunnel syndrome is observable median nerve compression upon surgical exploration of the carpal tunnel in symptomatic patients. This kind of surgical approach first revealed the lesion to physicians and led to the development of the modern concept of carpal tunnel syndrome as a distinct disease entity.

The first surgical characterization of the lesion is commonly attributed to Sir James Paget (1854), who described chronic compression of the median nerve in a patient who had previously suffered a fracture of the carpal tunnel. In 1913, French surgeons Pierre Marie and Charles Foix observed median nerve swelling during the postmortem examination of a patient with bilateral atrophy of the thenar muscles and suggested sectioning of the transverse ligament as a means of surgical treatment. This operation was first performed by J. R. Learmouth in 1930. F. P. Moersch discussed the use of this approach at the Mayo Clinic and, in 1938, coined the term *carpal tunnel syndrome*. In 1946, B. W. Cannon and J. G. Love published the results of median nerve decompression surgery performed in nine cases out of thirty-eight patients suffering from what they termed "tardy median nerve palsy." Thus began the popularization of surgical intervention as an accepted treatment for this disorder.

However, the major turning point in twentieth-century awareness and understanding of carpal tunnel syndrome came from Dr. George S. Phalen's work at the Cleveland Clinic. Beginning in 1950, Phalen published a series of articles that drew considerable attention to carpal tunnel syndrome and proved highly influential in both the American and European medical communities.[100] At the Cleveland Clinic, Phalen treated 823 patients with carpal tunnel syndrome, representing 1,254 affected hands. He saw 439 of those patients between 1947 and 1964, and an additional 384 patients between August 1964 and January 1969. About 40 percent of Phalen's patients were treated surgically by sectioning of the transverse carpal ligament.

Phalen's work documented conclusively the presence of the median nerve lesion in many patients presenting the clinical symptoms of the disorder, and demonstrated the potential effectiveness of surgical decompression in alleviating their symptoms. Phalen thus confirmed the "medical reality" of carpal tunnel syndrome as an actual organic disorder of the nervous system. Phalen's success in identifying the lesion and refining an effective surgical treatment established him one of America's premier hand surgeons and a leading medical authority on the subject of chronic hand and wrist disorders.

The scientific search for an underlying "lesion" responsible for chronic occupational hand disorders dominated medical investigation of this problem for more than one hundred years. The inability to identify a specific lesion was a major factor in the transformation of occupational neuroses to the realm of psychology and contributed to the lack of recognition afforded these disorders by workers' compensation and medical authorities during the early twentieth century. The eventual discovery of a specific lesion by Phalen, combined with the similarity of CTS symptoms to those of previously reported occupational hand disorders, thus held tremendous importance and the potential to explain why workers had been experiencing these problems in many different occupations for so many years. Investigators in this field had been seeking the answer since 1830, and this discovery provided concrete evidence to address the original problem that had been debated by Bell, Duchenne, Poore, Gowers, and others about the location of the neurological lesion. Phalen's work provided strong evidence that the lesion in most cases is peripheral rather than central.

But rather than validating or explaining the nature of chronic occupational hand disorders, Phalen's discovery had exactly the opposite effect. Phalen's work produced a deepening suspicion and rejection by physicians of claims that these disorders are potentially work-related. This result stemmed from Phalen's ardent pronouncements about the etiology of the lesion he had discovered. Phalen was absolutely convinced that the cause of carpal tunnel syndrome was not occupational, a conclusion he strongly and repeatedly voiced in medical publications and to the public at large. Phalen maintained that he did not know what caused the disorder. The compression of the median nerve in most cases, he asserted, was idiopathic, and he insisted on calling the disorder "spontaneous compression of the median nerve at the wrist" to emphasize the nonoccupational and unknown origins of the lesion.

Physicians knew of or at least strongly suspected several causes of median nerve neuropathy, including diabetes, rheumatoid disease, lupus erythematosus, neoplasms, exposure to neurotoxins, acute traumatic injury, and congenital abnormalities. But the majority of patients in Phalen's series did not suffer from any of these systemic or acute conditions. In addition, Phalen acknowledged that his patients' symptoms were often aggravated by active use of the affected hand. Yet Phalen was sure that the lesion could not be caused occupationally:

> (1951—11 cases) The cause of this spontaneous compression of the median nerve at the wrist is not readily apparent. Occupational trauma may play some part in the production of the syndrome, but only one patient in this series was doing a type of work requiring a little more than normal use of the hands. . . . If this syndrome of median neuropathy were due to occupational trauma alone, the condition certainly should be encountered much more commonly than it evidently has been.
>
> (1957—37 cases) We believe that spontaneous compression neuropathy of the median nerve in the carpal tunnel is not an occupational disease. Often repeated, forceful grasping movements might cause some tenosynovitis of the flexor tendons in the carpal tunnel, but this is certainly not a common finding. . . . It is true that almost every patient in our series described an aggravation of symptoms after strenuous use of the hands, and the symptoms were almost always worse in the dominant hand. None of these patients, however, consistently did an excessive amount of work with the hands.

(1966—439 cases) The common, typical, carpal-tunnel syndrome—spontaneous compression neuropathy of the median nerve in the carpal tunnel—is not an occupational disease. A chronic tenosynovitis of the flexor tendons in the carpal tunnel might result from prolonged excessive forceful grasping movements, but such a tenosynovitis is not a common finding in industrial workers. Most patients with a carpal-tunnel syndrome have an aggravation of symptoms after strenuous use of the hands, and the symptoms are usually worse in the dominant hand. . . . Men certainly subject their hands to more trauma than do women, but men contributed only 33 per cent of all cases in this series. Excluding the seventy cases directly associated with trauma, men comprised only 29 per cent of the remaining cases. An occupation may aggravate but seldom produces a carpal-tunnel syndrome.

(1972—384 cases) Thickening of the flexor synovialis may be caused by prolonged forceful grasping movements, and carpal-tunnel syndrome may result. Under these conditions, carpal-tunnel syndrome could be classified as an occupational disease, but this is an exceedingly rare cause of median nerve compression. Patients with carpal-tunnel syndrome usually will aggravate their symptoms by strenuous use of the hands, but occupational trauma is seldom the initiating factor in the production of the syndrome.[101]

Despite the overt evidence of aggravation by strenuous use of the hands, consistently worse symptoms in the dominant hand, and the acknowledgment that prolonged forceful grasping causes tenosynovitis in the carpal tunnel, Phalen invariably maintained that the disorder is not caused occupationally. He apparently based this judgment on the small percentage of his patients who performed "excessive" or "little more than normal" use of their hands vocationally. He pointed to the large proportion of women in his sample as providing additional evidence against work-relatedness, because "men certainly subject their hands to more trauma than do women." To further support his position he noted that in the first group of eleven cases (1951), there was only "one case, however, which is the only case of a man in our series, [where] we felt the patient was doing a type of work which might possibly produce some tenosynovitis of his flexor tendons."[102]

So Phalen's position, which proved highly influential for three decades, was based on his judgment about the "type of work" that could potentially involve strenuous use of the hands, combined with his perception that essentially only the men in his series (but not the women) performed this type of work. Phalen observed that most of the patients who came to his clinic were women, many of whom were in their middle years (aged thirty to sixty), and

Table I   Patients' Occupations

	Total	Men	Women
Housekeeper or cook	210	3	207
Laborer	26	25	1
Assembly worker	18	10	8
Salesman, saleswoman	18	10	8
Clerk, accountant	16	5	11
Mechanic, machinist	15	15	0
Executive	11	11	0
Teacher	9	0	9
Secretary	8	0	8
Nurse	8	0	8
Physician	6	6	0
Dentist	1	1	0
Other professions	8	8	0
Carpenter, painter, electrician	7	7	0
Waitress	5	0	5
Barber, beautician	4	1	3
Farmer	4	4	0
Draftsman	2	2	0
Telephone operator	2	0	2
Dressmaker, tailor	2	1	1
Florist	2	1	1
Dry cleaner	2	1	1
Professional golfer	1	1	0
Retired	14	12	2
No excessive use of hands	29	20	9
Not recorded	11	6	5
Total	439	150	289

Source: Phalen (1966)

most of whom did not work in traditional industrial settings. He concluded that manual work could not be a cause of the disorder because, to him, these women did no "manual" work. But the cases tell another story. In the 1951 series of eleven patients, the lone man who, in Phalen's opinion, performed the "type of work that could involve strenuous use of the hands," worked as a drop-forge hammer operator. Phalen mentions that one woman was employed as a stenographer and that another performed sewing, but no indication was given as to the employment of the others. In his 1966 article, Phalen provides a better breakdown of the patients' occupations (table 1).

Phalen stated that "recent excessive use of the hands was thought to be an etiological factor in only twenty-one of the cases in this series."[103] He did not indicate which of the 439 cases represent the twenty-one having "excessive" use of the hands, but it presumably includes some proportion of the twenty-six laborers, all but one of whom were men. Although he does not explain how the specific twenty-one exceptions were ascertained, it is clear he considered most all of the occupations listed above to require no "excessive" use of the hands. At best, he regarded only a minority of those who perform assembly work or laborers as engaging in "excessive" manual work (because there were forty-four of those), and he apparently saw little manual work involved in such occupations as machinist, carpenter, draftsman, farmer, and barber. The predominantly female occupations like cook, housekeeper, clerk, secretary, waitress, dressmaker, and nurse were not included among those he thought required strenuous use of their hands.

Thus a seemingly medical and scientific judgment about disease causation was based on a social perspective that regarded males performing work in heavy industry to be the type of patients who could be judged legitimately to engage in strenuous use of the hands. Other work, whether cooking, typing, sewing, or working in an office, was relegated to the domain of "women's work," perceived as being inherently less demanding upon the hands and wrists.

By contemporary standards, this orientation seems naive, sexist, and demeaning. It stemmed in part from a tradition whose preoccupation with the technical and procedural aspects of surgery often trivialized a patient's personal activities and work history. The profile of Phalen's patients is remarkably similar to that of Finkelstein's and Schneider's. And yet the contrast in Phalen's interpretation of his patients' occupational background is striking. As with Finkelstein, Phalen's medical judgment may have been reflective of his own personal background and experiences.

George Smith Phalen, who was born in 1911 in Peoria, Illinois, received his medical degree at Northwestern University Medical School in 1938 and completed his residency in orthopedics at the Mayo Clinic in 1942. After serving as a lieutenant colonel in the Medical Corps during World War II, he practiced hand surgery in Springfield, Missouri. During his army duty Phalen had met and worked with the famous hand surgeon Dr. Sterling Bunnell, thereby developing a professional interest in surgical treatment of the hand. His experience in hand surgery during the war involved mostly reconstructive repair of severe combat wounds. Phalen never received training in oc-cupational medicine, nor did he ever work in an industrial setting.[104]

From July 1946 until his retirement in 1970, Phalen became a wealthy and highly distinguished orthopedic hand surgeon practicing at the Cleve-land Clinic, one of the nation's finest medical institutions. During that period, the Cleveland Clinic was principally a specialty referral center. Seventy-five percent of its patients came from out-of-town. The patients re-ferred to Phalen for carpal tunnel surgery at the Cleveland Clinic may have seemed to him very much like his own wife: middle-aged women, many of whom spent their days in or around the home. In his view, this did not constitute demanding work, and he could not understand how their com-plaints could be considered in any way "occupationally" based.

Phalen, retired and living in Dallas, still believes that "a woman doing housework doesn't affect her wrist by what she does." He stands by his origi-nal assessment of the Cleveland Clinic cases as not work-related, noting that the majority of his patients were women, and "they weren't digging ditches or using hammers." Phalen maintains that the majority of CTS cases in the workplace are spurious, that "it's in their minds, not their wrists."[105]

This attitude may help explain why Phalen did not obtain a more detailed work history on his patients or investigate the kind of hand activities they performed. But this inattention to occupational history was not unique to Phalen. In general, twentieth-century medicine had seen a shift away from the careful clinical observation and case descriptions that characterized much nineteenth-century investigation. The approaches used in modern oc-cupational epidemiology, emphasizing the identification of discrete job risk factors and the precise analysis of exposure variables such as hand motions and forces, had not yet been refined or widely used. If they had been, a careful analysis of Phalen's data may have yielded a different conclusion.

For example, Radford C. Tanzer, a plastic surgeon at the Hitchcock Clinic in Hanover, New Hampshire, conducted surgical studies on carpal tunnel syndrome at about the same time as Phalen. From 1956 to 1959 he operated on thirty-four cases in twenty-two patients exhibiting symptoms of carpal tunnel syndrome. The profile of his patients was very similar to Phalen's, comprised of sixteen middle-aged women and six men. But unlike Phalen, Tanzer collected a much more complete occupational history on each and details about the specific manual activities required in their daily work:

> Two patients recently had started to milk cows on a dairy farm. Three
> were engaged in shop work involving handling of objects on a conveyor
> belt, with the wrists repeatedly flexed. Two had undertaken gardening
> which involved considerable hand weeding and another had been en-

gaged for the preceding year in automobile-body spraying in which he repeatedly pressed the trigger of a spray gun with the index and long fingers, alternately flexing and extending the wrist. One was a woman who, for a year prior to the onset of symptoms, had been ladling soup twice daily for about 600 students, holding the ladle between index and long fingers and flexing the wrist. Another patient had for three years prior to the onset of symptoms been doing kitchen work involving much stirring and ladling. A careful review of the mechanics of exercise established that almost half of our patients had been engaged for varying periods of time prior to the onset of symptoms in prolonged activity involving forceful flexion of the fingers with the wrist either held in flexion or moving through some range of flexor motion.[106]

Because of this closer consideration of the specific manual functions performed on the job, Tanzer reached a different conclusion than did Phalen about the disorder's etiology. For Tanzer, the detailed occupational histories provided support for the notion that occupational hand exertions potentially caused the lesion. Based on this, Tanzer asserted: "A study of the occupations in twenty-two cases of carpal-tunnel syndrome involving thirty-four hands suggests that repeated, forceful flexion of the wrist and fingers is frequently a precipitating factor."[107]

Similar conclusions were reached by other investigators, including J. G. Love, who in his 1955 study of median neuritis noted three occupations which he thought might have contributed to the development of the lesion, namely, "very busy secretarial work, milking of cows by hand, and tailoring." In their early (1947) report on median nerve compression, W. R. Brain, A. D. Wright, and M. Wilkinson came to the same conclusion based upon surgery performed in England on six patients, all of whom were middle-aged or elderly women. Five of the six were housewives (the other was a tailor), but in each case the surgeons were able to document the recent occurrence of increased and unaccustomed manual activities, mainly due to the absence of their husbands during World War II. These investigators summarized their findings as follows: "There can be little doubt that occupation is a causal factor. One of our patients, like four of Brouwer's, was employed in tailoring; four of the others said they had done much unaccustomed housework during the war; and in the last the onset occurred at a time when she had to carry buckets of water."[108]

Different conclusions were reached based upon a consideration of the occupational activities performed by patients who had similar profiles— predominantly females of middle age, many of whom worked in domestic settings. But Phalen's assessment stopped there, with the assumption that women who worked outside of heavy industrial settings rarely stressed their hands and wrists. Other investigators probed deeper, looking at the specific manual activities performed by their patients.

In the end, Phalen's view proved to be more influential, based as it was on his experience with almost a thousand patients and his standing as a renowned surgeon at a prestigious institution. His acknowledged leadership in the orthopedic community made it difficult for other hand surgeons to question his authority or judgment. In addition, the renowned hand surgeon Sterling Bunnell, Phalen's mentor in the army and close personal friend, supported Phalen's view on the disorder's etiology. At a meeting of the Orthopedic Section of the American Medical Association, Bunnell stated that his views on CTS were "entirely in accord" with Phalen's, based on his own experience with a dozen surgical cases, all but one of which were in women.[109]

The result was that between 1950 and 1980 carpal tunnel syndrome was most often viewed as a disease of middle-aged women which was probably associated with hormonal changes.[110] Although some investigators voiced their suspicion that occupational factors could be relevant, there was no general agreement or wide acceptance of that view by the medical community. Consequently, industrial safety officials, workers' compensation administrators, and others who looked to the medical authorities for guidance and evidence about occupational disease paid little attention to the malady.

George Phalen's social views and his stereotyping of what constitutes "women's work" shaped the history of occupational hand disorders for thirty years. The similarity between the symptoms of carpal tunnel syndrome and those of writers' cramp, telegraphists' cramp, and other disorders that had plagued workers for almost one hundred years were never discussed in the writings of the many surgeons who worked on this problem during the years following World War II. There was a general absence of recognition that the lesion of carpal tunnel nerve compression may indicate a bigger problem concerning chronic disorders of the hands and fingers affecting workers in many occupations.

To some degree, this medical orientation may have reflected widely held societal perspectives concerning the nature of work itself. Traditional male-dominated jobs were performed increasingly by women throughout the twentieth century, beginning with the changeover from (male) clerks to the modern (female) secretary that expanded further into other industries during World War II. Immigrant groups like Jews, Poles, and Slavs had made considerable progress in entering many occupations. These changes may have been threatening to many Americans, especially those like Phalen and other surgeons, who represented the traditional elite class of well-educated wealthy white males. Their response was often an inability to see "real" occupational health problems potentially affecting anyone other than traditional male laborers in heavy industrial settings. It was easier perhaps for them to relegate health problems affecting women, Jews, and others to the patient's personal characteristics, such as their hormones, nervous disposition, and other innate traits, rather than to the nature of the work performed.

Interest in Occupational Hand Disorders during the 1970s

This situation began to change during the mid-1970s as greater medical interest in occupational hand and wrist disorders emerged, particularly in such traditional heavy industries as automaking and jet engine manufacturing. Medical interest grew during this period due to a combination of increasing epidemiological evidence, government intervention, and labor activism. The developments of the 1970s paved the way for the dramatic rise in reported cumulative trauma disorders that occurred during the mid-1980s.

Following Phalen's studies of carpal tunnel syndrome during the 1950s and 1960s, a small group of medical researchers continued to explore the possible linkage between CTS and hand movements on the job. A few isolated studies in the medical literature during the mid-1970s provided expanded evidence for the possible connection of CTS to workplace activities. During this period, the first claims were submitted for carpal tunnel syndrome as a compensable disorder under state workers' compensation insurance. In one 1972 case from Missouri, an appellate court ruled that CTS in a woman engaged in luggage manufacturing was job-related because her work required "repetitive flexions under pressure." However, a 1975 Delaware appellate court reached the opposite conclusion in a CTS case involving a worker who continually used a vibrating air gun at a General Motors plant.[111]

The claim against General Motors may have been stimulated by safety and health initiatives newly introduced throughout the auto industry. In 1973 an agreement between the Big Three automakers (General Motors, Chrysler, and Ford) and the United Auto Workers (UAW) called for the hiring of a full-time union health and safety representative and the establishment of a joint management-labor safety and health committee in every auto plant with more than six hundred workers. Dan MacLeod, who worked for the UAW health and safety department during the mid-1970s, recalls how the meetings of these joint committees provided a forum for bringing instances of occupational hand and wrist disorders to light: "In the late 1970s, while employed by the UAW in Detroit, I routinely attended meetings of auto workers. As we began to learn more about CTDs, I began to ask, 'Have any of you ever had surgery on your wrists?' Those who had surgery would raise their hands. Then there would be stunned glances around the room as everyone realized that a good portion of the group had their hands in the air. 'I thought it was just me,' several people would say simultaneously. What everyone had thought was a rare affliction based on personal factors turned out to be common among those who did repetitive handwork in auto plants. There was an epidemic under our noses, but no one knew it until then."[112]

In 1976, a case of carpal tunnel syndrome at an Eastman Kodak plant in Windsor, Colorado, prompted the first government study of occupational hand disorders caused by repetitive motions. In that case, a young woman employee became disabled after contracting perplexing neurological symptoms in her hands and wrists. Several physicians failed to produce a specific diagnosis, although at least one physician suspected that the condition may have been due to chemicals used at the Kodak plant. Realizing that the condition could potentially be caused by her work, she notified the Colorado OSHA office and contacted an attorney to help file a claim for workers' compensation benefits.[113] The lawyer placed an advertisement in a local newspaper, attempting to locate other workers in the area who had experienced similar problems.

On August 5, 1976, the Colorado Occupational Safety and Health Program, lacking the expertise to analyze and evaluate the complaint adequately, requested technical assistance from the National Institute for Occupational Safety and Health (NIOSH) in Cincinnati. NIOSH medical and ergonomics personnel visited the plant from September 28 to October 1, 1976. The NIOSH researchers were astounded to discover a very large number of hand and wrist disorders recorded on the facility's industrial health log, OSHA Form 100 (see table 2).[114]

Fifteen additional cases of hand or wrist discomfort were discovered through a survey questionnaire NIOSH administered to current employees. In their final report, issued in December 1976, the NIOSH investigators concluded that the disorders were clearly due to "repetitive trauma" caused by arm and hand motions required in packaging and paper-trimming operations at the plant. The NIOSH investigators also noted that Eastman Kodak had, since 1973, begun to institute a number of significant improvements that had been effective in eliminating most of the repetitive motion hazards. As a follow-up to the NIOSH investigation, officials from federal OSHA revisited the plant in February 1978, issuing a citation under OSHA's general duty clause (Section 5.a.1) for "excessive ergonomic stress caused by repetitive motion," accompanied by a small penalty of $4,300.[115] This was the first citation issued by OSHA for cumulative trauma disorders of the hands and wrists.

It is interesting to speculate on why this episode arose at this particular plant when it did. The plant safety director during those years, Tom Majors, attributes it to the unusually detailed and comprehensive injury and illness

Table 2   Industrial Health Log Entries at Kodak Plant, Windsor, Colorado, 1972–1976

Tendonitis	84
Ganglion cyst of hand	10
Epicondylitis of elbow	2
Bursitis	4
Myositis	1
Carpal tunnel syndrome	2
Thoracic outlet syndrome	1
Total	104

records that were maintained by Eastman Kodak at the Windsor facility. Plant officials responsible for maintaining the log, including Majors and the plant's medical staff, had been personally trained in recognition of these disorders by Kodak's corporate medical director, Dr. Christian Amoroso (a rheumatologist), and its ergonomist, Suzanne Rodgers. Wanting to be particularly thorough, plant safety and health personnel recorded every complaint on the logs, even those that were minor and involved no work disability. Most of the "tendonitis" cases, according to Majors, were nothing other than minor complaints for sore hands.[116]

Kodak's employment of a corporate ergonomist and its insistence on thorough medical recordkeeping was an outgrowth of the company's longstanding interest in the recognition and prevention of musculoskeletal disorders.[117] In 1957, Kodak had established one of the nation's first human factors and ergonomics programs, patterned on a similar program instituted at Du Pont Chemical in the 1950s by a physiologist, Dr. Lucien Brouha. Kodak's original motivation for establishing its human factors organization was to evaluate ways of improving manufacturing productivity through better understanding the limits of workers' physical tolerances. After its ergonomics research laboratory was established in 1960, the orientation of Kodak's human factors efforts gradually evolved to include studies of work disability. For example, from 1960 to 1979, studies of the causes of low back pain were undertaken at Eastman Kodak's main Kodak Park manufacturing complex in Rochester, New York, under the direction of Dr. M. Laurens Rowe, a noted orthopedic surgeon and professor of orthopedic surgery at the University of Rochester.[118] During that twenty-year period, some 1,500 workers with recurrent or chronic back pain were evaluated. As a result of those studies, Kodak management became particularly attuned to the ergonomic risk factors that were associated with back pain and other musculoskeletal ailments.

The Windsor, Colorado, facility opened in 1972, the same year that Kodak's ergonomics and human factors staff took on company-wide responsibilities (previously, their work had been confined to the Rochester manufacturing facility). The new plant employed a relatively young, inexperienced, and nonunionized workforce of 3,300 persons, which included a high proportion of females and Hispanics. The opening of this new plant was viewed by Rodgers and Kodak's medical department as an opportunity to establish methods for monitoring musculoskeletal injury risk factors and assessing the effectiveness of ergonomic controls. The irony for Kodak is that its attention to recording all possible musculoskeletal ailments eventually helped bring about the United States' first punitive enforcement action for cumulative trauma disorders.

A similar corporate concern for the identification of musculoskeletal injury risk factors led to the nation's first large-scale epidemiological study of occupational carpal tunnel syndrome. In that retrospective study of workers at four United Technologies Corporation facilities in central Connecticut, Lawrence Cannon, Edward Bernacki, and Stephen Walter found thirty cases of CTS occurring between 1977 and 1979 in a population of 20,000 workers performing aircraft engine assembly.[119] In addition to corroborating Phalen's claim about the likely precipitating influence of female hormones, these researchers observed a highly elevated risk among workers who used vibratory hand tools.

The study drew widespread attention, in part because it was sponsored by United Technologies and in part because one of its authors, Dr. Bernacki, served as medical director of the company. Thus, the publication of this study in 1981 represented one of the first public acknowledgments by representatives of corporate management that an industrial CTS problem might exist.

According to Bernacki, the principal aim of the study was to determine if carpal tunnel syndrome was work-related and, if so, to assess whether employees at high risk could be "selected out" through medical screening examinations.[120] United Technologies' interest in this question had been prompted by the filing of several workers' compensation cases for carpal tunnel syndrome, which was compensable under Connecticut law so long as it resulted from a discrete "injury." Bernacki's recollection is that the study was initiated by management concern at United Technologies and its aircraft engine subsidiary, Pratt & Whitney, without involvement of the workers' union, the International Association of Machinists and Aerospace Workers (IAM).

However, according to workers who were at Pratt & Whitney during the late 1970s, IAM activities had a major influence in bringing awareness of occupational hand disorders both to workers and to the corporate doctors. Beginning in 1978, the IAM local ran a series of educational articles in the union newspaper, *IAM Shoptalk,* aimed at occupational health problems at Pratt & Whitney. The series, entitled "Bad Medicine," documented a number of workers' health ailments and concerns, including repetitive motion complaints from work at the "burr bench" (where parts were held manually against a rotating abrasive wheel to remove burrs) and ganglionic cysts of the hands from loosening screws on gages.[121]

Moreover, the IAM provided free representation for union members wishing to pursue workers' compensation claims for these disorders before the Connecticut Workers' Compensation Board. This was to entice members to join and remain in the IAM, since Pratt & Whitney was an open shop, and workers could withdraw from the union after their initial one-year membership. In addition, the IAM sponsored various educational activities that heightened worker awareness of occupational hand disorders and other health problems occurring at the facility. These educational sessions included talks to workers by activists from New Directions, a labor-oriented health advocacy program based at the University of Connecticut, and health professionals of the Yale Occupational Health Clinic. Both the program and the clinic were founded in 1978, at the same time as the IAM media campaign and the filing of the initial claims for work-related CTS at Pratt & Whitney.

Cannon, Bernacki, and Walter's study recommended the reduction or elimination of low-frequency vibration in hand tools as a preventive approach. This strategy of redesigning manual tasks and hand tools to accommodate the biomechanical tolerances of the working population had recently received an increasing amount of attention from a group of researchers in an entirely different discipline, industrial engineering. Popularized by the pioneering work in the 1960s and 1970s of E. R. Tichauer of Texas Tech University (later, of New York University) and Don Chaffin at the University of Michigan, engineers had begun to examine the biomechanical function of the hands and wrists with the intention of improving hand tool design.

Their objective was to redesign industrial tools to utilize the mechanical properties of the tendons and muscles in the hand better and thereby increase the efficiency and safety of the job. This approach employed principles of ergonomics, the science of designing jobs to closely match the physical and mental capabilities of the affected workers. It was clear to Tichauer and Chaffin that the ergonomic approach to hand tool design could effectively decrease the likelihood of workers sustaining strains, sprains, and other disorders in the hands and wrists. Articles extolling the ergonomic approach for the control of CTS and other occupational hand disorders began to appear during the late 1970s.[122] This approach was to become quite prominent as the reporting of hand and wrist cumulative trauma disorders began to escalate during the mid-1980s.

The Impact of Labor Activism during the 1980s

According to the U.S. Bureau of Labor Statistics, reported cases of repetitive motion injuries of the upper extremities increased throughout the 1980s, with a notable surge occurring after 1985 (figure 13).[123]

In the decades preceding the 1980s, concern about occupational hand disorders had been confined to a relatively small group of physicians, researchers, ergonomists, and public health advocates. This situation changed dramatically in the 1980s with the emergence of hand and wrist disorders as a major concern for trade unions, politicians, government safety officials, and the media. In 1980, for instance, the Occupational Safety and Health Administration (OSHA) had responded to complaints by garment workers in Galax, Virginia, by fining their employer, Hanes Corporation, for allegedly subjecting workers to "excessive muscular stress" that led to repetitive motion trauma. In a 1983 *Wall Street Journal* interview, Dr. Charles Gunn, the Hanes medical director, attributed the outbreak of hand and wrist injuries to be a by-product of the successful organizing drive of the Amalgamated Clothing and Textile Workers Union (ACTWU) that had taken place during the same period as the reported injuries.[124]

Awareness about this problem expanded during the mid-1980s with the emergence of hand and wrist disorders as a focus of union activism in one of the most traditional heavy and hazardous of industries, meat packing. Safety concerns, particularly regarding hand disorders, became an important issue for management-labor relations owing to the tremendous economic changes in the meatpacking industry during the late 1970s and early 1980s. The meatpacking industry had always been recognized as one of the most hazardous in America. The industry's dangerous working conditions had first come to national attention with the publication of *The Jungle,* Upton Sinclair's 1906 classic portrayal of Chicago's slaughterhouses. Although many improvements had been made in meatpacking facilities during the sixty years since Sinclair's account, that industry still possessed the nation's worst accident record. In 1985, for instance, the rate of OSHA-recordable injuries and illnesses for meat packing was 30.4 per 100 full-time workers, almost four times worse than the national average of 7.7 for all private sector industries. This accident rate placed meat packing at the top of OSHA's list of most hazardous industries for five years in a row.[125]

Contributing to this deplorable safety record were several changes in the nature of corporate control and production that were sweeping that industry during the 1970s and 1980s. Prior to that time, the industry had been dominated by family owned and operated businesses, such as Swift & Company, Armour & Company, Patrick Cudahy Incorporated, and Wilson Foods Corporation. Wages were relatively high, averaging $10.69 per hour in 1983.[126]

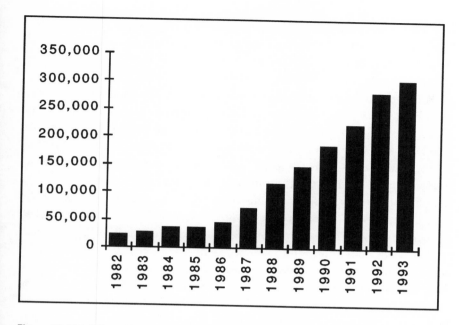

Figure 13 Total Cases Reported of Repetitive Trauma Disorders 1982–1992

Many workers possessed a considerable loyalty and identification with their employer. The plants served as a valued focus of business and social life in many small meatpacking towns scattered around Iowa, Wisconsin, Minnesota, South Dakota, and Nebraska.

This situation began to change during the 1970s. Due to expanded global competitiveness and changing American dietary habits, there was less demand for red meat at the same time that more firms were entering the meatpacking business. To stay competitive, there was tremendous pressure to modernize facilities and increase productivity. Because capital and resources were needed to survive, many traditional meatpacking companies were sold to corporate conglomerates including ConAgra, Occidental Petroleum, Cargill, Sara Lee, and United Brands. Several new production facilities were built, such as the sprawling (more than one million square feet) and highly automated George A. Hormel & Company facility in Austin, Minnesota, which was completed in 1982.

Along with the transition from family to corporate control, the nature of the traditional relationship that had been established with workers began to change. New non-union facilities were set up, fueled in part by the availability of cheap labor, particularly East Asian immigrants who had resettled in the Midwest after the Vietnam War. Starting in 1978 and continuing into the 1980s, corporate management throughout the meatpacking industry demanded sizable wage concessions from union workers. An ultimatum was essentially issued to workers that without wage concessions, facilities would be closed. The industry conglomerates made good on this threat in a number of instances.[127]

An associated result of the emphasis on modernizing facilities and boosting productivity was a significant increase in machine speeds and production rates. According to one account, the number of hogs slaughtered and boned per hour rose from 365 in 1960 to 640 in 1970, and to more than 1,000 by 1985. In most cases, this speed-up was not accompanied by a corresponding increase in personnel. On the contrary, there was often a decrease in the number of workers performing those production operations. The result was that the majority of laborers were being asked to work much harder (up to 40 percent faster) while receiving considerably less compensation (up to 23 percent less) for their efforts.[128]

By 1985, many workers had reached the end of their rope. What followed was a series of bitter strikes and the greatest amount of labor unrest the industry had seen since the 1930s. Workers walked out at more than a dozen plants during the early and mid-1980s, including Wilson Foods (seven plants in 1983), John Morrell (1985), Swift (1986), FDL (1986), IBP (1986–1987), and Cudahy (1987–1988). The most prominent and notorious strike occurred at the flagship Hormel plant in Austin, Minnesota. This walkout, which occurred from August 1985 to September 1986, was national news. It became the focus of a social upheaval that was to influence national politics and the safety movement for years to come.

That strike, by workers represented by local P–9 of the United Food and Commercial Workers Union (UFCW), was characterized by National Guard intervention, violence, arrests, and mass demonstrations. In a highly publicized manner, it pitted the local union against the international UFCW in a battle about control of strike tactics and the degree to which workers should sacrifice wages and working conditions for job security. The strike resulted in a national boycott of Hormel products and the formation of a coalition representing a diverse mixture of America's liberal activists including Native Americans, farm workers, and politicians such as Jesse Jackson and Bruce Babbitt.[129]

The most controversial aspect of the strike was the decision by the P–9 local to retain the services of Ray Rogers, an independent consultant with Corporate Campaign, Inc., to develop and lead the local's strike efforts. The hallmark of Rogers's approach was the revolutionary idea of a national "corporate campaign," that is, an attack directed against the financially sensitive elements of the targeted corporation's entire commercial operations, including its banking and investment partners and the associated enterprises run by members of the company's board of directors. The essence of such a campaign is high visibility, the extensive use of media attention to garner public sympathy, and national political pressure.

This approach had been developed initially by Rogers during the late 1970s through his work as principal strategist for the ACTWU's organizing drive of southern textile workers. Rogers utilized a corporate campaign in the successful effort to unionize the J. P. Stevens Company by applying pressure on its corporate sponsors at Seaman's Bank and the Metropolitan Life Insurance Company. Employer representatives suggested that this organizing drive was at least partially responsible for the reporting of occupational hand disorders at the Hanes Corporation plant in Galax, Virginia, during the late 1970s. (The parent company of Hanes Corporation was Consolidated Foods, many of whose employees were represented by the UFCW.)

From the very beginning of labor unrest at Hormel, safety had been a primary issue, and it became a central feature of Rogers's corporate campaign. Concern about accidents among Hormel workers had increased steadily throughout the late 1970s. Most workers attributed the company's deplorable accident record to the enormous increases that had been made in production speed in the slaughtering and boning operations. Workers claimed that this resulted in more numerous serious injuries including knife cuts, amputations, and machine-related incidents. Particularly distressing to workers was an increasing number of problems involving chronic pain and numbness in the hands and wrists. Many workers had become disabled due to this problem, and several received medical diagnoses of carpal tunnel syndrome.

The local workers made the issue of carpal tunnel syndrome a key aspect of their complaints against the company, bringing the problem to public attention. For instance, in the spring of 1985, P–9 workers drafted a brochure entitled, "Legacy of Pain: Hormel's Injured Workers in Austin." In this publication, the incidence of carpal tunnel syndrome was documented, along with the pain and suffering that had befallen its victims. One Hormel worker, Elizabeth Anderson, described how, in 1982, she had first begun to experience pain and numbness in her wrists and arms. After two carpal tunnel surgeries and transfer to a dozen "rehabilitation" jobs, she finally lost all use of her hands and became permanently disabled. As part of the local's publicity campaign, the "Legacy of Pain" brochure was published by the thousands and distributed door-to-door throughout Minnesota.[130]

Before long, the issue of carpal tunnel syndrome spread to other labor actions in the meatpacking industry. Much of the credit for the dissemination of this information can be traced to the efforts of Deborah Berkowitz, health and safety director of the UFCW.[131] From the time of her appointment in 1979, Berkowitz had been aware of the growing incidence of CTS in the meatpacking industry. Berkowitz and the UFCW adopted a conscious and deliberate strategy of bringing this issue to the forefront in the union's organizing and negotiating efforts. It was Berkowitz who, in 1980, had first suggested that a NIOSH health hazard evaluation be performed at the Swift turkey boning facility in Harrisonburg, Virginia. The ensuing NIOSH study by Dr. Thomas Armstrong and his associates from the University of Michigan Center for Ergonomics was one of the earliest and most influential ergonomic studies conducted on the problem of occupational CTS.

Berkowitz and the UFCW used the CTS issue to amass public support and sympathy for the labor strikes occurring in the meatpacking industry in the 1980s. At the height of the strikes against Hormel and John Morrell in 1986 and 1987, major news stories on the CTS "epidemic" in the meatpacking industry appeared in the *Los Angeles Times,* the *New York Times,* the *Washington Post,* and the ABC News program *20 / 20.*[132]

Based upon the publicity and news stories in 1986 and 1987 related to the strikes at Hormel and other meatpackers, OSHA began a concentrated inspection and enforcement effort of that industry. The OSHA investigation was closely monitored and assisted by Berkowitz and the UFCW. In addition to Hormel, targeted facilities included the large IBP facility in Dakota City, Nebraska, and the John Morrell plant in Sioux Falls, South Dakota. Workers at both plants had reported soaring rates of CTS and other hand disorders. The IBP plant had previously been granted immunity from unannounced OSHA inspections under a government program that exempted facilities if their accident record was much better than the industry's average. When the OSHA and UFCW officials examined the "official" OSHA accident logs at the plant, they found a low number of injuries or hand disorders reported. However, local workers were aware that when they reported hand pain to company officials, a record was kept of the incident in a different set of accident records. The UFCW complained to OSHA about the allegedly deliberate maintenance of two sets of accident logs by IBP. OSHA's investigation verified the union's claim and uncovered significant health and safety problems at the IBP and Morrell plants. Management at both companies was found to have purposely ignored the identified safety problems, preferring instead to view them as merely "bargaining ploys" used by the union in contract negotiations.[133]

To make matters worse for management, highly publicized congressional hearings on the subject of safety problems in the meatpacking industry were held by Democratic Representative Tom Lantos of California during 1987. The extensive publicity stemming from the P–9 strike against Hormel and other labor actions during 1986 and early 1987 had prompted Lantos to initiate the hearings. The OSHA investigation showed that IBP management officials had lied in their testimony during the congressional hearings, which infuriated Lantos and further diminished political and public sympathy for the meatpacking companies and their parent corporate entities.[134]

As a result, OSHA lowered the boom throughout the industry, imposing record fines of $2.59 million against IBP in July 1987 and $4.3 million against Morrell the following year. Remaining strikes were quickly settled and conciliatory labor agreements were forged. Under the supervision of OSHA, a progressive joint management-union ergonomics program was established at IBP.[135] This effort culminated with the official codification of such programs in the 1990 publication of OSHA's *Ergonomics Program Management Guidelines for Meatpacking Plants*.

By 1990, a decade of bitter labor conflict had subsided in the meatpacking industry. The P–9 strikers had been defeated at Hormel, but safety conditions in the industry as a whole ultimately improved. The original goal of the meatpackers' labor action was aimed primarily at winning better wages and job security, not specifically at addressing the problem of hand disorders. But a by-product of the violent strikes was increased national attention directed at the issue of occupational carpal tunnel syndrome, thereby helping to stimulate medical and public recognition of the problem.

Through the influence of the union and the media, occupational hand disorders had been pushed to the forefront of the national health agenda. This, combined with the accumulation of additional epidemiologic and medical evidence, convinced most physicians and government authorities about the potential work-relatedness of these afflictions. Awareness about these disorders became widespread among the medical community, workers, and the general public, reporting increased, and CTD cases gained acceptance within state workers' compensation systems. The era of cumulative trauma disorders as the "occupational disease of the 1990s" had arrived.

In retrospect, according to Deborah Berkowitz, two key developments were largely responsible for winning widespread recognition of the CTD problem in industry during the 1980s: the deliberate illegal double recordkeeping at IBP and Rep. Lantos' congressional hearings in response to the strikes at Hormel and other meatpackers. These unexpected "miracles," says Berkowitz, helped bring about the political climate and public support that ultimately established CTS and other cumulative trauma disorders as important occupational health concerns.[136]

It was also probably no coincidence that the flurry of government activity and OSHA enforcement efforts peaked in the year directly preceding the 1988 presidential elections. Publicity surrounding the meatpacking strikes of 1986 and 1987 afforded liberal-minded politicians an opportunity to use that struggle to gain support among labor, farmers, and the political left. Lantos clearly wished to embarrass the Republican administration over its allegedly lax enforcement of health and safety laws. Both Jesse Jackson and Bruce Babbitt made highly publicized visits supporting strikers at Hormel and Morrell to foster their own presidential aspirations.[137] The record $4.3 million OSHA fine against Morrell was imposed on October 28, 1988, just two weeks before the presidential election, presumably in part to ensure that the incumbent administration was seen as sufficiently forceful in its protection of workers.

With the Republican victory came a marked reduction of tensions in the meatpacking industry and the rapid growth of ergonomics control programs directed at CTDs. On November 23, 1988, two weeks after George Bush's election, OSHA, IBP, and the UFCW announced their landmark cooperative agreement to adopt an industry ergonomics program directed at CTDs, thereby freeing IBP of more than $5 million in accumulated OSHA fines.[138] Union activism prior to the 1988 presidential election, along with the adoption of safety and health as a major campaign issue by labor and liberal Democrats, were major factors in stimulating the federal government enforcement agencies to recognize and take action on the CTD problem. If OSHA had not acted forcibly when it did, the Republican administration would have played into the arguments raised by the liberals. Acknowledging and addressing the CTD problem in the meatpacking industry effectively deflected this potential political liability.

Popularization of the Term *Cumulative Trauma Disorders*
By 1990, the problem of occupational hand and wrist disorders had migrated to a host of other industries, particularly auto assembly, textiles, apparel manufacturing, electronics, offices, and newspaper publishing. The growth of CTD cases in the newspaper industry was especially pronounced and occurred concurrently with highly publicized periods of labor unrest at the *Los Angeles Times, Newsday*, and other major publications.

During the growth of concern about occupational hand disorders during the 1980s, a transformation took place from an initially narrow focus on carpal tunnel syndrome into a more broadly based effort to address many types of chronic upper extremity pain. The use of the phrase *cumulative trauma disorders* came into increasingly popular use during this period as a generic descriptor to encompass not only carpal tunnel syndrome, but also tendonitis, tenosynovitis, occupational Raynaud's phenomenon, and other disorders stemming from repetitive use of the hands and wrists.

The medico-legal term *cumulative trauma* first appeared during the 1970s in the context of debates about the compensability of nontraumatic back pain under state workers' compensation laws. Prior to that time, workers' compensation statutes typically recognized only those injuries that occurred at a specific place and time. The doctrine of "cumulative trauma" was introduced as a means of distinguishing chronic musculoskeletal disorders from acute injuries (the compensability of which required a specific precipitating event), and to promote the idea that they be treated analogously to occupational diseases, which were acknowledged to develop gradually over time as a result of prolonged exposure.

This attempt to create a new category of cumulative trauma back pain cases first achieved success in Michigan and California in 1977–1978 and then gradually was adopted in several other states.[139] When claims were first made for carpal tunnel syndrome as a compensable disorder, it was unclear whether they ought to be submitted as injuries (requiring a specific causal event) or occupational diseases. Initial claims met with resistance and were often difficult to pursue because of the need for claimants to satisfy stringent state criteria for treatment of their claim as either an injury or an occupational disease. For example, the 1975 claim against General Motors in Delaware (see above) was denied on the basis that a legitimate occupational disease under that state's workers' compensation law cannot arise outside of employment or as a consequence of "everyday life."

The submission of cases under the doctrine of cumulative trauma in California and Michigan was intended to avoid this problem, because the cumulative trauma disorders in those states, like cumulative back pain, needed to be neither recognized occupational diseases nor acute injuries in order to qualify for compensation. Thus, as the scientific and political concern with CTS and other hand disorders accelerated during the 1980s, the use of the term *cumulative trauma disorders* may have reflected a deliberate attempt by claimants, attorneys, and physicians to couch the discussion in terms appropriate for expediting adjudication within the prevailing legal system.

The term *cumulative trauma disorders* gained additional stature in the 1980s through its adoption by ergonomics researchers from the University of Michigan, the site of pioneering work in ergonomics and the biomechanics of musculoskeletal injuries conducted by Don Chaffin during the 1960s and 1970s. This subject also captured the interest of Thomas Armstrong, a student and later a colleague of Chaffin's at Michigan. It was Armstrong who first focused on applying ergonomics techniques specifically to the prevention of carpal tunnel syndrome. With the number of reported CTS cases beginning to increase rapidly during the late 1970s and early 1980s, a team of researchers began to assemble at the University of Michigan that focused on this problem, including Chaffin, Armstrong, an epidemiologist, Barbara Silverstein, Brad Joseph, and others. With the growing attention to this issue in the meatpacking, textile, and automaking industries, prompted by worker complaints and union activism, the Michigan ergonomics team soon became the preeminent scientific authorities in the field in the United States, often working in conjunction with unions and OSHA to study and confirm the existence of the problem at various facilities.

The contributions of the University of Michigan researchers culminated in the publication in 1985 of Barbara Silverstein's influential Ph.D. dissertation, "The Prevalence of Upper Extremity Cumulative Trauma Disorders in Industry." In this publication and the subsequent journal articles based on the same data set, Silverstein documented the relevance of two specific industrial risk factors, repetition and forcefulness, in the development of chronic hand disorders.[140]

Deborah Berkowitz first looked to Armstrong and his associates for help in examining the carpal tunnel syndrome outbreak at the Swift turkey boning facility in Harrisonburg, Virginia, in 1979. From that original interaction, a long and continuing relationship developed between the UFCW and the University of Michigan researchers that helped add scientific credence to the UFCW's publicity campaign about hand disorders in the meatpacking industry during the mid-1980s.

The Michigan researchers developed other ties to organized labor—ties that proved important in bringing awareness about CTDs to American workers and articulating the scientific basis for the compensability of those disorders. For instance, during the late 1970s and early 1980s Silverstein's husband, Dr. Michael Silverstein, was a colleague of Dan MacLeod's in the safety and health department of the United Auto Workers. When complaints of occupational hand disorders began to be reported among autoworkers in the late 1970s, MacLeod and Michael Silverstein turned to Chaffin and Armstrong at the University of Michigan for technical assistance and guidance. This culminated in the 1982 publication by the UAW of an educational pamphlet on the subject, *Strains and Sprains,* which was disseminated widely by labor organizations to workers in a variety of industries. In that pamphlet, the UAW advised workers that disorders such as carpal tunnel syndrome, tendonitis, and Raynaud's phenomenon, referred to collectively as cumulative trauma disorders, could result from a variety of job activities including repetitive movements, vibrating tools, and excessive pressure against the hand.[141]

In these ways, the concept of cumulative trauma disorders became more widely known and discussed. Gradually, the use of that phrase came to supplant other generic terms that had also been in common use, such as *repetitive motion disorders* and *overuse injuries*. OSHA, NIOSH, and other government agencies began to adopt this terminology in their reports and enforcement actions.[142] During the 1990s, OSHA involvement in the problem of cumulative trauma disorders accelerated with the heightening of enforcement activity under the general duty clause and its attempt to enact a national standard for the control of CTDs, an effort led by Barbara Silverstein, who became OSHA special assistant in charge of developing the standard, and Michael Silverstein, OSHA's director of policy.

Repetition Strain Injuries: The Australian Experience

Although I am interested principally in examining how this issue emerged in the United States, the rapid growth of reported cases in Australia during the mid-1980s, followed by their equally dramatic decline, has prompted a number of scholarly analyses that shed light on the way that social determinants shape the initial recognition and conception of occupational disease.

In Australia a different phrase, *repetition strain injury* (RSI), came into widespread use to describe carpal tunnel syndrome and other related problems that became epidemic among office and manufacturing workers during the period 1983–1985.[143] The reporting of RSIs began to rise in late 1983, peaked in 1984 and 1985, and then declined in 1986 and 1987. This trend can be seen in two sets of workers' compensation statistical data that have been published, one from the Australian national telephone company, Telecom Australia (figure 14), and the other from compensation reports collected by the Australian Bureau of Statistics for South Australia (figure 15).

A number of commentators have pointed to specific social developments that could have contributed to the growth of Australian RSI claims in the mid-1980s. One explanation that has been offered is that administrative and court decisions liberalizing the criteria for compensability under Australian law helped promote the reporting of RSI claims. For example, the Australian government Office of the Commissioner for Employee Compensation, which administers compensation for Australian public service workers, issued a directive in 1985 specifying that claims for RSI should be granted in all cases "where the employee has been engaged in work of a manual, repetitive nature and the doctor certifies the condition to be consistent with the stated cause." It has been suggested that this relatively liberal interpretation, combined with the provision to provide compensation equaling 100 percent of the employee's normal salary, were significant factors in the large outbreak that occurred among Australian public sector workers.[144]

The election of a new Labor party government in 1983, supportive of workers' concerns, is often cited as another possible contributing factor. Other scholars have suggested that the increased reporting of RSIs was fueled by intense media attention and trade union educational campaigns, such as that which resulted in the publication in 1984 of *Sufferers' Handbook: Repetition Strain Injury* by the Australian Public Service Association.

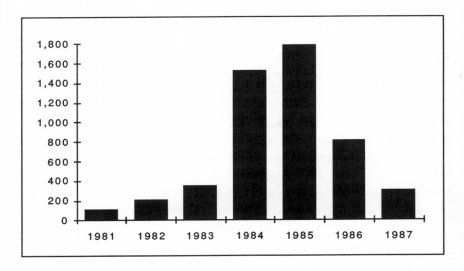

Figure 14 Cases of RSI Reported at Telecom Australia 1982–1987 (from Hocking 1987)

Media stories frequently painted the RSI epidemic as a by-product of larger social issues concerning workers' response to the introduction of new technologies and the ensuing changes that had occurred in industrial work organization. As in the United States, the initial surge in Australian RSI claims arose first among workers in industries facing job losses due to automation and recession.[145]

But there were at least two important differences in the Australian experience with RSIs compared to the growth of CTDs in the United States. The incidence of RSI in Australia fell dramatically in the years following 1985, in contrast to the United States, where the occurrence of CTDs has continued to rise each year since the early 1980s. A number of explanations have been offered for the observed reduction in RSIs. Some authorities attribute it to substantial improvements in ergonomic job design and work methods that were enacted by many Australian employers in response to the outbreak.

David Michaels, an American epidemiologist who studied the Australian phenomenon for the World Health Organization, has suggested that the decline may, in part, be a statistical artifact related to "instant prevalence bias." According to this suggestion, the liberalization of compensation benefits and media attention to RSI in 1983–1985 gave workers license to report ailments that might actually have been prevalent, but unreported, before this time. Once the "backlog" of previously unreported cases had been filed, the incidence of new cases appeared to drop.[146]

Hall and Morrow (1988) have credited the decline to "growing medical skepticism about the existence of 'RSI.'" Some commentators maintain that

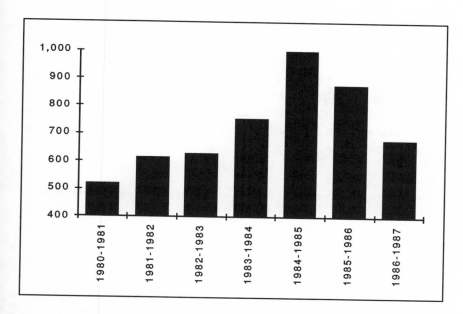

Figure 15 Cases of RSI Reported in South Australia 1980–1981 to 1986–1987 (from Gun 1990)

there was a social backlash against the epidemic that culminated in a well-publicized decision by the Australian Supreme Court in *Cooper vs. Commonwealth of Australia*. In that case, the court found no evidence of employer negligence and ruled that the plaintiff (who professed to have RSI) had not suffered any injury as defined by Australian compensation law. Ireland (1992) claims that subsequent to this court decision, "many suits pending by RSI sufferers against their employers [were] withdrawn on the advice of their trade union leaders and sections of the legal industry."[147]

The other difference between the two countries is that from the beginning of the RSI epidemic in Australia, there has been much more public discussion and scholarly attention given to the social and psychological factors influencing the diagnosis and reporting of RSI. A large number of articles have appeared in Australian medical and popular journals examining the relationship of the RSI outbreak to legal, insurance, economic, and psychological factors.[148] Many of these studies have challenged the reality of RSI as a legitimate medical condition, preferring instead to view it as a "nonphysical and psychosomatic condition" (Ireland 1992), an "iatrogenic process" (Hall and Morrow 1988, Bell 1989, Lucire 1988), a form of "epidemic hysteria" (Ferguson 1987), a type of "compensation neurosis" (Bloch 1984), or a "psychological conversion disorder" (Lucire 1986).

The attempt to portray RSI in Australia as primarily a social or psychological problem, rather than a medical or safety issue, is reminiscent of the transformation of occupational neuroses to psychoneuroses that occurred in the United States and Europe during the early twentieth century. A question raised by the Australian experience is whether history will repeat itself in the United States, with CTDs eventually being subsumed as varieties of "occupational stress," "nervous fatigue," or some other comparable concept that implies a fundamentally psychological origin.

Summary

Where did upper extremity cumulative trauma disorders come from? Why have they begun to increase in number? As the incidence of reported occupational CTD cases grew in the United States during the 1980s and 1990s, these questions were asked repeatedly by physicians, the media, workers, and employers. The history of occupational hand and wrist disorders presented here can begin to provide some answers.

1. Cumulative trauma disorders of the hands and wrists are not new. The detailed case descriptions provided by physicians in the nineteenth and early twentieth centuries make it clear that precisely the same types of hand and wrist problems plaguing contemporary workers have been reported in significant numbers since the Industrial Revolution. The consistency in clinical presentation of nocturnal paresthesia, gradual onset, tenderness over the course of the median nerve, along with the pattern of usage and progressive development, provides strong evidence that even occupationally induced median nerve compression in the carpal tunnel, now called carpal tunnel syndrome, was prevalent more than one hundred years ago.

2. The history of occupational CTDs suggests that outbreaks typically occur in response to the introduction of new technologies and/or systems of work organization. For example, writers' cramp began to appear with the growth of professional clerical positions and the introduction of steel pens. Telegraphists' cramp followed closely upon the development of telegraphic technology, and its accompanying job structuring. Carpal tunnel syndrome arose in concert with production changes in the meatpacking industry. And we see the same phenomenon as office workers attempt to accommodate to the new demands created by the widespread introduction of computer equipment.

These episodes suggest that the emergence of "new" occupational disorders is, in part, related to a process of adaptation and accommodation to unfamiliar production processes and technologies. Additional evidence for this is provided by studies showing that, in general, workers face a greater risk of injury when they begin work on a new piece of machinery or in a new process.[149] Robert Arndt of the University of Wisconsin (1990) has argued that the performance of unaccustomed activity increases the risk of developing cumulative trauma disorders. It may be that people can adapt only at a limited rate to new and unfamiliar job demands. If so, then we would expect to continue to see the expansion of cumulative trauma disorders and other diffuse ailments during periods of rapid "technology shifts."

3. A corollary to the previous observation is that the decline of particular forms of CTDs often accompanies the removal or demise of specific technologies. Thus, the incidence of writers' cramp declined with the advent of typewriters, and telegraphists' cramp decreased as communications methodology shifted to telephones and wireless transmission. One can speculate that hand and wrist CTDs among office workers may similarly subside as hand-intensive methods of computer input utilizing a keyboard and/or mouse are eventually replaced with voice recognition or other nonmanual input devices.

4. The history of occupational CTDs illustrates that occupational disorders are especially likely to emerge as major problems during periods of economic instability and potential job loss. This seems to have been a factor in both the Australian RSI experience and in the outbreak of carpal tunnel syndrome in the American meatpacking industry. However, this association between an increasing incidence of CTDs and poor economic conditions does not imply that the disorders are therefore fabricated or unreal. There are a number of possible explanations for this association. Workers may be more apt to report these ailments when economic conditions are poor, for example, as a way of accounting for substandard job performance or to seek a medical "cure" so they can stay employed. In addition, management may ask workers to labor faster, longer, or harder when the economic conditions are bad in a particular industry, thereby contributing to the onset of these health problems.

5. The activities of trade unions and labor conflict can play an important role in bringing occupational disorders to the attention of physicians, employers, and the general public. This was seen clearly both in the contemporary rise of CTS among meatpackers and textile workers as well as in the emergence of telegraphists' cramp as a major issue in that industry during the early 1900s. Particularly during the 1980s, CTDs would not likely have had the major impact they did without the deliberate and concerted attempt of organized labor to make them the focus of organizing and negotiating actions.

However, the role of organized labor should not be overemphasized. Though potentially important and effective, labor activism ought not to be interpreted as a necessary condition for the emergence and recognition of an occupational disorder. This is clear from the history of writers' cramp, which became a significant occupational health problem despite the absence of organized labor representation for most lower-middle-class clerks, notaries, and scribes in the mid- and late nineteenth century.[150] This episode demonstrates that if workers start to become incapacitated to the extent that they cannot perform the normal requirements of their job, then their health problems will probably eventually get recognized, even without the assistance of an effective labor movement.

6. Several authors have argued that the creation and existence of many occupational disorders, including CTDs, are primarily a result of the prevailing compensation system. According to this view, these disorders would not be reported or recognized as a distinct disease entity if the compensation system did not give a financial incentive to workers to report them as such.

The history presented here shows that changes in the compensation system and court-imposed expansion of the criteria for compensability have played a role in the growth of CTDs. But the issue of workers' compensation for CTDs has typically emerged as a late-stage effect of the appearance and diagnosis of these disorders rather than their initial cause. For example, writers' cramp and telegraphists' cramp arose before the establishment of the British workers' compensation system. Moreover, neither of those disorders stimulated a large amount of common-law employer-negligence suits prior to that time. It was only after the establishment of the Workmen's Compensation Act of 1906 that the issue of compensability for telegraphists' cramp as a scheduled occupational disease arose as a major topic for inquiry by government and insurance regulators and the telegraphists' union. By that time, however, the incidence of reported cases had already begun to rise substantially. In the same vein, later debates about the compensability of Dupuytren's contracture and Raynaud's phenomenon generally followed their emergence and medical recognition among lace makers (Dupuytren's) and quarry workers (Raynaud's).

The introduction and acceptance of CTS and other CTDs into state workers' compensation systems in the United States during the 1980s also occurred subsequent to their emergence as issues in the meatpacking strikes and the resulting attention they drew from the national media. That attention and public concern generally stimulated their rapid acceptance as compensable disorders within the state workers' compensation systems, not vice versa.

However, the historical evidence suggests that one way insurance compensation *does* exert an influence is with respect to the terminology used to describe hand disorders and the selection of methods by which they are defined and clinically diagnosed. For example, the choice of the phrase *cumulative trauma disorders* by contemporary researchers and labor activists to describe generically hand and wrist disorders stemming from occupational usage seems to have been related to the earlier development of the "cumulative trauma" doctrine within the state courts of California and Michigan.

Similarly, the movement to distinguish hand-arm vibration syndrome from other forms of Raynaud's phenomenon might reflect the need to couch the description of that disorder in a manner that helps establish its compensability. Contemporary attempts to "define" legitimate cases of carpal tunnel syndrome in terms of nerve conduction velocity decrements could be a reaction to the need for "hard" physical evidence in insurance and legal proceedings.

7. The historical analysis presented here has shown that there was a consistent pattern of bias against the recognition of occupational hand disorders afflicting women, Jews, and other immigrant groups. Many authorities have displayed a preference to view legitimate work-related disorders within a traditional model of occupational injury potentially affecting male workers engaged in manual labor such as found in mining, quarrying, metalworking, and other supposedly heavy industrial jobs. As suggested earlier, this perspective reflects an attitude about the nature of work itself, in which "real" excessive or strenuous labor is confined to those activities traditionally performed by men in manufacturing industries. According to this view, other work, such as clerical activities, cannot be truly "excessive" or potentially hazardous. After all, the argument goes, men have been performing much "harder" work for years without suffering from these kinds of medical problems.

To some extent, this reasoning reflects naiveté about the real demands of the "other" nontraditional occupations and an unfamiliarity with the biomechanical stresses actually imposed upon the hands and wrists during those activities. But the common adoption of this perspective by many authorities may also have a deeper root, embedded in a particular class consciousness and its orientation to many of the social changes that have occurred in modern industrial society, including gender roles and the influx of immigrants and other nontraditional groups into the working force.

It is not a coincidence, I suspect, that those who have been influenced by this orientation are generally, like George Phalen, members of the privileged, wealthy, Caucasian establishment. The inability to see occupational disorders affecting Jews, women, and others may literally be that—an *inability* predicated on a world-view based on fear about the potential loss of one's own status and position, and a reaction to the dizzying pace of change that has occurred in societal and occupational roles. By contrast, Harry Finkelstein's view of houseworkers as representatives of the laboring class was likely predicated on his own experiences growing up among the Jewish immigrant garment workers in New York during the Progressive Era.

8. Beginning at the turn of the century, writers' cramp and other occupational neuroses were transformed from disorders regarded as fundamentally organic to ones that were deemed to be essentially psychological in nature.

Those disorders, originally conceived as neurological and later as forms of neurasthenia, were finally cast as psychoneuroses whose verity and legitimacy came to be questioned by medical and government authorities. To some degree, this transformation can be viewed as a consequence of the ascendancy of Freudian psychoanalytic theory during the early twentieth century and its pervasive influence in creating an awareness about the psychological underpinnings of human behavior and health.

In another sense, this transformation grew out of the inability of medical researchers, over many decades of investigation, to uncover a specific pathological lesion to explain these disorders. The medical profession, especially neurologists, had come to require the isolation of an organic lesion to constitute the "biological basis" of a disease process. It became difficult for physicians to conceive of the presentation of clinical symptoms without a distinct pathology as constituting "real" medical entities. Especially for disorders thought to be work-related, physical harm needed to have a physically detectable consequence (a lesion).

The alternative, for many authorities, was to label such conditions as pseudo-ailments, relegated to the world of psychology and quackery. It was against this backdrop that Phalen's discovery of a frequently occurring lesion in the median nerve held such great potential importance, and why his relentless insistence on dissociating this condition from occupational activities was ultimately so disappointing.

But the transformation of chronic occupational hand disorders from the domain of neurology to that of psychology has deeper roots. The suggestion that these disorders are psychogenic, which was supported by much of the medical establishment, was readily accepted by corporate management, the insurance industry, lawyers, and others with something to gain from this diagnosis. For underlying much of this history is the tension that comes from the ongoing struggle between workers and those who control and benefit from their labor. There are those in society who inherently mistrust the motives of workers and who see in the emergence of chronic hand and wrist disorders a veiled but deliberate attempt to subvert the system. And undoubtedly some workers are eager to exploit this opportunity.

In such a context of mistrust and class conflict it is inevitable that the focus of discussion reverts to that of intentions, motivation, and tactics. It ought not be surprising, therefore, that the assessment of chronic hand disorders has tended to gravitate to the psychological. This phenomenon can be observed in the Australian response to RSIs, with sides taken in the debate along traditional political lines; workers and their advocates arguing for the scientific reality of these diseases, and management and their allies tracing the roots of the ailments to psychosocial influences. Physicians have generally been caught in the middle, torn between a medical tradition that imparts validity to pathological states with discrete causal agents, and new research models that find evidence for occupational causation in multivariate analyses of data that often seem vague and inconclusive.

9. The emergence of modern occupational epidemiology in the twentieth century has had a significant impact on promoting the recognition of a relationship between working conditions and the development of chronic hand disorders. The application of epidemiological reasoning was instrumental in convincing scientists that Raynaud's phenomenon can be caused by the use of vibratory tools. As employed by Barbara Silverstein and her colleagues at the University of Michigan, epidemiological techniques were important in drawing causative inferences about occupational CTDs in the absence of definitive pathological or physiological evidence. Likewise, without the epidemiologic approach, it would have been far more difficult for researchers to establish a connection between carpal tunnel syndrome and occupational activities.

Many who still dispute the occupational origin of CTDs, like Dr. Nortin Hadler of the University of North Carolina, question whether epidemiological research of the type conducted by Silverstein provides a sound basis for drawing judgments about the work-relatedness of disease. In arguing against the credibility of studies relating patterns of usage with the onset of musculoskeletal disease, Hadler has stated, "Only prospective studies in which there are few and defined variables can be interpreted as cogent evidence of causality."[151] This claim reflects an older medical tradition that affords primacy to controlled laboratory experimentation as the hallmark of a legitimate scientific inquiry.

Modern epidemiology, by contrast, often relies on a wide array of research approaches (including retrospective cohort, case-control, and cross-sectional studies) to identify the potential causes of occupational disease. Although there are limitations with many of these approaches (such as imprecise case definitions), they are sometimes the only practical research methods available, because usually such studies can be conducted much more quickly and inexpensively than can a prospective study. In matters of public health and worker protection, those considerations are often paramount. The broad acceptance of contemporary epidemiologic methodology by the scientific community has provided researchers with new and compelling evidence for the occupational origin of many CTDs.

10. In discussing the forces that have coalesced to produce a widespread recognition for occupational CTDs, we should not fail to mention the effect of the popular media. Unquestionably, the major stories that appeared in the national print and broadcast media had a profound influence on the recogni-

tion of the carpal tunnel syndrome problem in the meatpacking industry by physicians, workers, and the general public. The same can be said in respect to earlier episodes of chronic hand and wrist disorders, such as the outbreak of telegraphists' cramp at the turn of the century, which also attracted considerable media attention. It can be debated whether the news media creates the recognition of the work-relatedness of an ailment, or whether they merely report on it. At least for carpal tunnel syndrome in the meatpacking industry, the original press stories were based on a few anecdotal reports, provided by unions and affected workers, that generally preceded widespread medical familiarity with occupational CTS and recognition of the disorder by workers in other industries. In that respect, the media coverage of CTS produced and actively promoted the contemporary concept of CTS as an occupational disease.

11. Along with the media coverage, there were associated political influences that help shaped the way in which CTDs are now conceived. The political goals of Tom Lantos, Jesse Jackson, and Bruce Babbitt, for instance, originally helped frame the discussion of these disorders around matters of workplace safety and unfair labor practices. This helped set a precedent for later investigations of CTD outbreaks in the newspaper publishing and communications industries. As was the case with the environmental movement, the issue of what constitutes a hazard has become intertwined with a national political agenda and, in both cases, became part of a popularist, liberal, and generally Democratic attempt to disparage the accomplishments of a conservative, business-oriented, Republican government in the area of health and safety. A similar division of political loyalties, along generally the same political lines, has emerged as an important component of the RSI debate in Australia.

12. The history of occupational CTDs also demonstrates some of the effects of increasing specialization and fragmentation of the medical profession. For example, after World War II, orthopedic surgeons became the acknowledged medical experts in the area of musculoskeletal disorders. Not surprisingly, their orientation was focused on surgical treatment, rather than epidemiologic analysis or prevention. The initial characterization of carpal tunnel syndrome as a surgically treated disorder—and the large number of wrist surgeries that have been performed in the decades following World War II—is a testimonial to this perspective. The relatively narrow focus of orthopedists may have helped obscure the potential relationship of contemporary cases of CTDs to the "occupational neuroses" that occurred during the nineteenth century. In that era, such cases were exclusively the province of neurologists, who developed their own terminology and theoretical models for understanding and treating the malady. A fuller consideration by Phalen

and others of the relationship between modern investigations of CTS cases and earlier research on writers' and telegraphists' cramp may have expanded the alternatives for diagnosis and treatment and led to earlier recognition and control of the occupational risk factors. Similarly, the study of psychological factors has been led primarily by psychologists, especially during the early twentieth century. In general, their perspectives have been rejected or ignored by many in mainstream medical practice.

Ultimately, those who have been most confused and distressed by the changing perspectives on cumulative trauma disorders have been its victims. The affected workers have frequently ended up caught in a cross fire between competing medical judgments, political agendas, or labor conflicts. Generally, the workers want only to avoid becoming disabled and to be treated sympathetically and effectively when an injury does occur. As with many nonspecific ailments, CTDs probably arise from the multiple effects of many different factors, both occupational and nonoccupational. A political and medical obsession on establishing a specific unique etiology and "placing blame" often diverts attention from recognizing the multiplicity of physical, psychosocial, and technological approaches that could effectively address the problem.

Given the history of these disorders since the Industrial Revolution, chances are good that cumulative trauma disorders related to prolonged and repeated movement of the hands and wrists will continue to occur. As controls are established over risk factors from the use of one technology, such as keyboards, pens, or knives, it is probable that similar disorders will arise through the use of other new manually intensive technologies. My hope is that those investigating the chronic hand disorders of the future will examine the history of how similar disorders have been recognized and treated in the past, and that all those involved in occupational health—whether physicians, ergonomists, managers, or workers—adopt a common objective and coordinated strategy for preventing and treating these maladies.

Back Pain 3

The extent of the occupational back pain problem is staggering. Back pain is far and away the most frequently compensated disorder under state workers' compensation insurance plans, accounting for more than 30 percent of all workers' compensation claims filed each year.[1] The majority of the American workforce suffers from disabling back pain at some time during their career, with approximately 2 percent of workers affected annually. This makes it the leading source of work disability in the United States, accounting for 40–45 percent of all lost workdays.[2] The annual direct insurance cost nationwide for job-related back pain is estimated to exceed $11 billion, with an average cost per case of more than $8,000.[3]

Back pain is known to have many potential causes, including acute trauma, strains and sprains, musculoskeletal degenerative processes, congenital conditions, and certain systemic diseases. It is often difficult for physicians to ascribe any specific etiology, pathology, or set of multiple causes to a particular worker's back pain. A large proportion of cases cannot be diagnosed by any objective pathological criteria.

In most cases, it is not possible to trace an occurrence of occupational back pain to any specific activity or job task. One study found that workers could clearly relate the onset of back pain to a definite trauma only 15 percent of the time.[4] Examples of traumatically induced back pain include cases in which a worker is struck in the back by an object or falls on the back from a height or slippery surface. In cases where back pain results from a specific traumatic incident involving an external impact or blow, its occupational origin is generally easily recognized and acknowledged. More controversial and ambiguous are the majority of cases in which back pain develops in the absence of any discernible precipitating blow or underlying disease process.

Despite the inability in most instances to trace a worker's case of back pain to a particular job activity or accident, the reported incidence of occupationally induced back pain has increased dramatically during the twentieth century, especially in the years directly preceding and following World War II. Back pain is now recognized as a potential occupational disorder by the workers' compensation statutes in all fifty states of the United States. A similar recognition of back pain as a compensable occupational disorder exists in most other developed countries. Medical authorities and safety experts are generally in agreement that back pain can result from such job activities as manual materials handling, awkward postures, and vibration.[5]

In light of the considerable medical uncertainty about the specific cause of back pain in most cases, how has it become the most frequently diagnosed work-related disorder? A number of commentators have traced the growth of occupationally induced back pain during the twentieth century to changes that took place in the workers' compensation system, often as the result of court decisions that liberalized the criteria for compensability.[6] Other commentators have attributed the rise in reports of occupational back pain to the accumulation of epidemiologic evidence demonstrating a statistically significant association between nonspecific back pain and such job-related risk factors as lifting and twisting.[7] Still others have emphasized the role that advancing medical knowledge has played in stimulating a broader recognition of occupational back pain. For example, Nortin Hadler has attributed this phenomenon to the development of the theory of the "ruptured" intervertebral disc in 1934 by W. J. Mixter and J. S. Barr, two surgeons at Massachusetts General Hospital, and the subsequent popularization of the *ruptured disc* model by physicians, surgeons, and officials involved in the adjudication of workers' compensation cases.[8]

Although the emergence and recognition of occupational back pain during the twentieth century involved developments in workers' compensation, epidemiology, and medicine, it is equally important to consider the social, political, and economic backdrop against which these developments took place. Particularly important were the social dynamics surrounding the introduction of rail travel in the nineteenth century and the Great Depression of the 1930s. But the history of back pain extends much further back than that, so let us begin by looking at how back pain was understood by physicians prior to the Industrial Revolution.

Early History

There is considerable evidence that back pain has been a common affliction throughout recorded history.[9] Early references appear in the medical writings of Hippocrates (550 B.C.E.).[10] Fractures and deformities of the spine were described in the works of Galen and other classical writers.[11] There is also abundant paleontological evidence that prehistoric humans suffered from degenerative changes in the spine.[12]

The modern conception of back pain and lumbago began with the emergence of the concept of rheumatism during the seventeenth century. This concept stemmed from the classic humoral theory of disease as caused by disturbances in the flow of bodily fluids, called humors, which issued from the brain. Rheumatism, as conceived by such early theorists as Guillaume de Baillou (1538–1616) and Thomas Sydenham (1624–1689), referred to the build-up of noxious fluids in the joints and muscles. This process was thought to be aggravated by cold and damp conditions. The pain experienced in those tissues was attributed to inflammation caused by the collection of the irritating rheumatic fluid and phlegm. The use of the term *rheumatism* was originally very broad, encompassing not only lumbago but also a wide range of diverse pathologies including gout, acute rheumatic fever, sciatica, as well as many forms of arthritis.

For most of the eighteenth and nineteenth centuries, lumbago was regarded as a form of rheumatism. The condition was treated by techniques commonly used to counteract the effect of rheumatic humors, including bloodletting, changing diet, blistering, cupping, and prescribing drugs such as opium, calomel, antimonials, alkalis, and cinchona bark.[13]

In the early nineteenth century, Thomas Brown, a physician at the Glasgow Royal Infirmary, introduced a new theory to explain a wide variety of idiopathic body pains that were occurring mainly in young women.[14] His patients exhibited a variety of symptoms, including pains in the chest, legs, arms, abdomen, neck, and back, as well as fatigue, constipation, and digestive problems. Most patients had been previously diagnosed as suffering from rheumatism and had been treated, unsuccessfully, by the common therapies for rheumatism mentioned above.

Upon examination, Brown discovered that pressure applied to the spinal column of these patients elicited reports of extreme pain and tenderness, most commonly in the area between the fourth and fifth dorsal vertebrae, and sometimes in the area between the seventh and eighth dorsal vertebrae. Moreover, he found that leeching, cupping, and other external applications to these vertebral regions relieved the symptoms. Brown conjectured that the symptoms were really the manifestation of spinal disease that he termed *spinal irritation*.

Brown's theory of spinal irritation, introduced in 1828, was the first to suggest a connection between disorders of the spinal column with pains occurring in remote regions of the body. He speculated that lesions in the spine, particularly the vertebrae and their surrounding nerves, caused these pain syndromes. A great number of physicians were influenced by Brown's arguments. In the years immediately following the introduction of the concept, dozens of additional papers on spinal irritation appeared in the medical journals of Britain, France, Germany, and the United States.[15] The diagnosis of spinal irritation as a specific disease entity grew rapidly during that period.

However, by the mid-nineteenth century, medical authorities were beginning to question the validity of the diagnosis because of the inability to detect any specific physical lesion in the spinal column. A number of physicians began to suggest that the symptoms reported among these patients were really psychosomatic and hysterical in origin.[16] During the 1860s, the popularity of spinal irritation as a medical diagnosis declined significantly, and by 1876 Wilhelm Erb, in the *Cyclopaedia of the Practice of Medicine*, stated that spinal irritation "has almost passed from the memory of the present generation of physicians."[17]

Brown's basic idea that disorders of the spinal structures could account for many cases of remote pain continued to be highly influential, however. Although spinal irritation disappeared as a discrete disease syndrome, physicians continued to speculate that back pain could emanate from irritation to the spine and its surrounding nerves. This idea proved to be critical in establishing the theoretical groundwork for the eventual development of the concept of "railway spine" during the late nineteenth century.

Earliest Reports of Occupational Etiology

From ancient times until the late nineteenth century, physicians paid comparatively little attention to the possibility that work causes back pain. Virtually no mention is made of occupational etiology in the extensive medical writings from that period on the subject of lumbago, sciatica, and rheumatism. Other than the obvious cases in which back pain resulted from fractures or blows to the body during work, there are few specific instances in which physicians acknowledged possible occupational causes for the condition. Perhaps the earliest reported case of work-induced back pain can be found in the Edwin Smith papyrus, which may be dated to approximately 3,000–2,500 B.C.E. The author of this papyrus, thought to be the Egyptian physician Imhotep, provided medical care to workers involved in moving and lifting great stone blocks during the building of the pyramids. In this papyrus, Imhotep furnished instructions for the diagnosis and treatment of traumatic injuries occurring to these workers, including back pain originating from what is termed a "sprain of a vertebra in the spinal column."[18]

Other historical documents describe the practice of children walking on their parents' backs used as both a preventive and therapeutic treatment for manual workers in ancient Greece, Egypt, and Bohemia.[19] Hippocrates draws an association between horseback riding among the Scythians and the frequency of their "chronic defluxions of the joints," particularly in the lower back and hips.[20] Another physician of the classical period, Caelius Aurelianus, writing during the fourth century C.E., described sciatica as a syndrome involving intense low back pain and spasms, radiating into the buttocks, perineum, and lower extremities. He provided several possible causes for this syndrome including "a sudden jerk or movement during exercise, unaccustomed digging in the ground, lifting a heavy object from a low place, lying upon the ground, a sudden shock, a fall, or continuous and immoderate sexual intercourse."[21]

Bernardino Ramazzini's 1713 classic *De Morbis Artificum* briefly mentions backache and "pains in the loins" stemming from a variety of occupational activities. In one passage, Ramazzini states that "all sedentary workers suffer from lumbago," presumably related to their prolonged maintenance of a static posture.[22] Ramazzini also comments briefly on related problems among other workers, such as hernia among millers from carrying sacks of grain and flour on their shoulders, and sciatica among tailors from prolonged sitting in an awkward posture.[23]

Charles Thackrah, in his 1832 study of the health effects of various occupations in Great Britain, drew an explicit association between lumbago and manual exertion. For example, with respect to stonecutters Thackrah commented, "Quarry-men, or stone-getters, have the strongest muscular labour. They are subject to pain in the back, but to no other disorder." Thackrah's writings were also important in that they began to challenge the prevailing medical opinion that interpreted almost all idiopathic cases of back pain as forms of rheumatism: "With the exception of pains which they term rheumatic, but which are more probably the result of stress on particular muscles, carpenters have no marked disease." He challenges the prevailing notion in other cases: "Old men in all occupations, and especially those which are laborious, complain of pains in the back and limbs. Though these affections are always called rheumatic, I doubt the truth of the opinion. Are they dependent on injury of the muscular fibres, the result of excessive labour; or are they dependent on the senile change in the structure of blood-vessels?" Thackrah here expressed the view that back pain may develop over time due to the stresses and strains imposed by heavy labor. This idea eventually became the foundation of many contemporary models of occupational back pain.[24]

Thackrah also believed that, in addition to the effects of heavy labor, the prolonged maintenance of static working postures by sedentary workers could evoke lumbago. Among such workers, he observed, "certain classes of muscles are for twelve or fourteen hours a day scarcely moved, and postures maintained injurious to the proper actions of the internal organs." As examples of these ill effects, he cites the experience of card-setters, "It [card setting] requires them to sit, to lean much forward, and to use their fingers and eyes with rapidity and accuracy. The rooms are often far too much crowded. Beginners suffer from head ache and pain in the back." Needlework, because it requires "sitting for hours," also "leaves a numerous class of muscles wasting for want of exercise. The muscles of the back are especially enfeebled."[25]

Railway Spine

Despite the writings of Ramazzini and Thackrah, most physicians of the nineteenth century were either not concerned about or not aware of the possibility that occupational activities could precipitate back pain. In the vast majority of medical textbooks and major journal articles on the causes and treatment of lumbago written before 1890, no mention was made of suspected occupational etiology for the condition, nor of the possibility that back pain could result from work-induced trauma, lifting, or other forms of manual exertion.[26]

During the latter part of the nineteenth century, medical interest in traumatic back pain increased due to heightened public and scientific concern about the growing number of railway accidents. The first commercial railway was opened in Great Britain in 1825.[27] Between 1830 and 1870, about 30,000 miles of track were laid, totaling 15,500 miles.[28] This new mode of transportation gained immediate popularity as a means of intercity travel. By 1842, the British railways were carrying 24.5 million passengers per year. That number grew, to 43.6 million by 1846, 72.9 million by 1850, 251.9 million by 1865, and 507 million by 1875. By 1914, this number had increased fourfold.[29]

The growth of rail transportation had an immediate and profound effect on many aspects of society. For example, it was a major factor in the development of the British middle class, insofar as it allowed large numbers of clerical and administrative workers in London and other large cities to move away from the deplorable living conditions in urban centers to more decent housing available within commuting distance by train.

Never before in human experience had such large numbers of people been subjected to the significant forces, acceleration, and continual vibration that characterized rail travel. Trains went much faster than any previous mode of transportation. The average speed of a train on express mail routes was 44 miles per hour, stoppages included.[30] The velocity on passenger routes was estimated to average between 20–40 miles per hour in 1845.[31] This was about three times faster than that previously experienced when traveling by stages and horse-drawn carriages.[32]

The rapid expansion of rail traffic during the period 1825–1860 led to the emergence of a new and alarming public health concern—the danger of train collisions and other railway accidents. High speeds, combined with congested rail lines, poor traffic controls, and extremely long working hours for train operators, produced a potentially deadly and frightening situation. The resulting carnage was unparalleled in modern society. The extent and type of traumatic injuries that occurred were matched only by those previously seen in war. Between 1830 and 1865 there were approximately 1,200 deaths and 13,000 serious railroad injuries recorded in Great Britain alone. The number of passenger fatalities in train accidents steadily increased from an average of fifteen per year in the 1850s to forty-three per year by 1874.[33] Severe traumatic injuries were common, with 23 percent of the cases involving amputated limbs. One statistical analysis performed in 1864 showed that 34 percent of the injuries to the traveling public occurred as the result of train collisions. The remainder resulted mainly from sudden stops, falls from carriages, and derailments. The hard wooden interior surfaces of the train, especially in the third-class carriages, contributed to the severity of the injuries.[34]

As a result of the increase in serious railway accidents and injuries, there was a tremendous surge of public concern over railway safety. The dangers of rail transportation became a major political and media issue in Britain between 1860 and 1900. Most of the public debate was concerned with the railway companies' practice of requiring their employees to work long hours. Both a Board of Trade study in 1860 and the Lancet Commission Report of 1862 concluded that most train accidents were caused by human error resulting from the exceptionally long working hours imposed upon railroad employees.[35] It was not uncommon for engine-drivers and other railway crew members to work sixteen- to eighteen-hour days, with occasional shifts of twenty-four to forty-eight hours continuously on duty.[36]

The struggle to guarantee shorter working hours for rail crews led to the formation of the first trade unions of railwaymen, the Railway Clerks Association in 1865, the Railway Guards, Signalmen, and Switchmen's Society and the Engine Drivers and Firemen's United Society in 1866, and, finally, a consolidated union representing all rail workers, the Amalgamated Society of Railway Servants (ASRS), in 1871. The campaign to ensure shorter working hours was pressed by the unions, and the debate was taken up by their supporters in Parliament. Editorials in *The Times,* the *Lancet,* the *Daily News* and the *Daily Telegraph* decried the growing spate of rail disasters and supported the workers' demands for shorter hours.[37] A number of strikes and public demonstrations occurred during this period. The unions used the public's fear of rail accidents to argue for their efforts to achieve improved working conditions.

The national concern about the dangers of rail travel and the growing number of injuries sustained by the general public resulted in enactment of the Campbell Act by Parliament in 1864.[38] This act made railroad companies legally liable for the compensation of passengers injured by collisions, sudden stops, and other rail accidents. Under this law, damages were to be awarded only if it could be medically established that the victim's injury resulted from the rail accident and that it had a demonstrable pathological cause.[39] Maladies stemming from a purely psychological reaction to an accident were not considered compensable. During the first year after enactment of the Campbell Act, the total amount of compensation awarded for personal injuries due to railroad accidents in Great Britain was £304,816 (about $2.6 million in 1865 U.S. dollars).[40]

The epidemic of rail injuries also stimulated increased medical and scientific research. To better understand the public health dangers of rail traffic, a special medical commission was established in 1861 under the auspices of the medical journal *Lancet.* In the Lancet Commission report, issued in January 1862, a number of potential concerns about rail travel were addressed, including ventilation, vibration, and the injurious effect of collisions.[41] A new area of concern raised in the commission's report was the possibility that the continual jarring and shock of rail travel could lead to cerebral or spinal concussions. The authors of the report speculated that passengers who stand during their journey and persons who are tall and thin may be especially susceptible to musculoskeletal injuries and pains in the knees, legs, and low back.[42]

In 1867, Dr. J. E. Erichsen echoed the Lancet Commission's concerns about injuries to the spine that can result from the jars and jolts of rail travel and collisions. Drawing upon a review of cases he had treated, Erichsen defined a new syndrome called "concussion of the spine," which he described as follows: "A certain state of the spinal cord occasioned by external violence; a state that is independent of, and usually, but not necessarily, uncomplicated with any obvious lesion of the vertebral column, such as its fracture or dislocation—a condition that is supposed to depend on a shake or jar received by the cord, in consequence of which its intimate organic structure may be more or less deranged, and by which its functions are greatly disturbed, various symptoms indicative of loss or modification of innervation being immediately or remotely induced."[43]

There were a number of unique and original aspects of Erichsen's theory of spinal concussion. One was his assertion that the symptoms of this disorder could occur at a different time or location than that of the trauma. So, for example, many of his patients did not start exhibiting ill effects until days or even weeks after their spines had allegedly first been injured. Also, the site and type of symptoms could be quite varied, ranging from pain or numbness in the lower back and legs to more serious conditions such as paralysis and death. The symptoms were rarely localized at the site of the primary concussion.

Another provocative idea of Erichsen's was that spinal concussion could occur in the absence of any identifiable lesion or sign of a specific blow upon the spine. In addition, Erichsen proposed that the spinal concussion could develop as a cumulative effect of slight shocks or injuries to the spine, rather than a specific, severe impact.

Although spinal concussion was not considered unique to rail travel, Erichsen believed it to be particularly common in rail accidents because of the high speed and intense shock that can occur under those conditions. Many commentators soon adopted the phrase "railway spine" to denote essentially the same syndrome as that first described by Erichsen, although he personally disliked the term.[44]

Two other studies on this subject were published at about the same time as Erichsen's: William Camps' "Railway Accidents or Collisions: Their Effects Immediate and Remote, Upon the Brain and Spinal Cord and Other Portions of the Nervous System" (1866) and a three-part article by Dr. Thomas Buzzard in the *Lancet* called "On Cases of Injury from Railway Accidents" (1867). All three studies documented the existence of a syndrome among victims of railroad accidents characterized by delayed onset of symptoms, concussion to the spine, and diverse effects to the nervous system. Wolfgang Schivelbusch points out that it is remarkable that none of these authors (all of whom were British) refer to one another or to any previous publications.[45] It is interesting that these studies, all of which provide evidence for a special organic syndrome attributable to railroad accidents, appeared within three years after the enactment of the Campbell Act, which required a pathological basis for compensation.

In the years immediately following its introduction, the theory of railway spine became extremely controversial. The medical literature was soon filled with articles about this supposed condition. The articles tended to be approximately equally divided between those that supported the theory and those that did not. According to the U.S. Army's Surgeon General's *Index Catalogue* of medical literature, more than one hundred scholarly articles on railway spine were published between 1866 and 1890.

It was not long until the issue of railway spine was introduced into court proceedings dealing with liability claims under the Campbell Act. The question of the legitimacy of railway spine quickly became a prominent aspect of legal actions submitted by passengers claiming damages from injuries sustained in train collisions, rapid starts and stops of passenger cars, and other rail accidents. According to one authority, 58 percent of all cases submitted for compensation involved alleged injuries to the back or spine. Similar statistics were provided from Germany, where, during the eight years following passage of their railway compensation law (1871–1879), 78 percent of legal cases of railway injuries involved back injuries.[46]

The courts soon became a highly visible stage for the discussion of the question of back injuries. For what may have been the first time in modern history, the medical profession found its members challenging one another's opinions and credibility in public legal proceedings. Many in the medical establishment were dismayed and embarrassed by this disagreement between prominent medical authorities in public testimony on both sides of the issue. Not surprisingly, the physicians who believed that railway spine was a legitimate disorder often testified on the behalf of claimants and other concerned citizens. Opponents of this theory were often surgeons employed by or otherwise affiliated with the railway companies.

The theory's supporters relied heavily on clinical experience gathered from actual case studies, as well as physiological arguments and some post mortem findings. The opponents typically based their arguments on the absence of a detectable lesion, along with the lack of a plausible biological mechanism to account for the connection between spinal concussion and the remote symptoms that were observed. They also commonly cited the implausibility of a significant gap of time existing between the precipitating incident and the onset of symptoms. A good example of this viewpoint can be seen in the following passage from James Syme, a surgeon from the University of Edinburgh who, in 1867, challenged the theory of railway spine in the *Lancet*:

On the 27th of April last a commercial traveler drove out in the evening to my residence in the neighborhood of Edinburgh, and informed
me that he had been shaken the night before in a railway collision
near Berwick-on-Tweed. He had walked immediately afterwards a
mile and a half to see Dr. Maclagan, of Berwick, and having been as-
sured by him that there was no local complaint, I desired him to call
the next morning at my house. . . . He accordingly did so, and then exhibiting the most perfect freedom in all his movements, without any
sign of local injury, I concluded that if he felt any uneasiness, it must
be more mental than bodily. . . . On the same day, the 28th of April, it
appears that this person applied to a surgeon of experience in cases
like his own, who discovered that he had sustained a 'severe wrench of
the spine and sacro-iliac synchondrosis,' put him to bed, called in a
trustworthy coadjutor, and visited his interesting patient at least once
a day for months. . . . I deem it unnecessary to offer any observations
on this case, but would suggest the following questions: Could anyone
who had sustained a severe wrench of the back and sacro-iliac synchondrosis immediately afterwards walk a mile and a half, or on the
two following days travel sixty miles by railway, drive about in cabs,
and make visits without local complaint?[47]

By the late nineteenth century, the critics of the railway spine concept
increasingly challenged the validity of this disorder on the grounds that the
symptoms observed were primarily psychological in origin. An increasing
number of medical studies interpreted these complaints as psychosomatic or
manifestations of underlying hysteria.[48] Representative of this trend are the
perspectives of American surgeon R. M. Hodges. In his 1881 article entitled
"So-Called Concussion of the Spinal Cord," Hodges summarized the results
of investigation into forty-nine cases of that alleged disorder, finding that,
"thirty-six or three fourths of the whole number were really or probably de-
ceptions." Based on his investigations, he concluded, "The subjective symptoms following alleged concussion of the spine are ill defined, vary in degree
and character, are such as permit of ready simulation. . . . Recovery, or improvement of a fixed and permanent character, never takes place until after
the adjustment of any existing claim for compensation; and, so long as this is
final it makes little difference whether the settlement is a favorable or unfavorable one for the claimant."[49]

Herbert Page, who practiced for nine years as surgeon for the London and
North Western Railway, expressed similar views in *Injuries of the Spine and
Spinal Cord and Nervous Shock in Their Surgical and Medico-Legal Aspects*
(1883). Page describes the alleged effects of railway spine as "litigation

symptoms" and considers them to be what he calls "neuromimetic disorders," that is, disorders with symptoms that mimic those of a true pathological state.[50]

By 1900, more articles appeared which argued that many if not most cases of railway spine were feigned.[51] A large number of medical and legal inquiries were made into "malingering" in railway injuries and how best to identify the malingerer.[52] At least one prominent authority, in 1889, classified railway spine as a variety of "traumatic neurosis."[53]

Courts continued to award compensation for injuries attributable to railway spine in judgments for negligence against rail companies through the late nineteenth century. After about 1900, however, as medical opinion tended increasingly to identify this syndrome as a form of hysteria or neurosis, the problem of railway spine, as a matter for compensation in the courts, began to subside.

Inattention to Railway Spine among Workers

Throughout the course of the medical and legal debate about railway spine that occurred between 1866 and 1900, the focus was placed on injuries to the traveling public. There was little direct attention given to the incidence of this disorder among rail workers. Those victims who sued for compensation under the Campbell Act were generally not employees (or "servants," as they were called) of the railway companies. Railway spine among railway servants never emerged as a major topic in the medical literature, government inquiries, the courts, or the popular press during most of the nineteenth century.

This is startling in light of the apparent magnitude of the occupational injury problem in the railroad industry. For example, in Great Britain between 1874 and 1876 there was an annual average of 742 accidental deaths and 3,500 nonfatal injuries suffered by railroad employees *per year*. Although safety conditions gradually improved, there was still an annual average of 505 employee fatalities and 3,040 injuries per year during the period 1890–1892. This compares to an average annual casualty rate for the general traveling public of 28 deaths and 534 injuries per year in Great Britain during the period 1857–1860 and 43 fatalities per year by 1874.[54]

The experience was much the same in other countries. A report summarizing railroad accidents occurring between 1879–1889 on one rail line in the United States indicated that there were 1,332 incidents of non-employee injuries compared to 8,016 cases of employee injuries.[55] Statistics provided by the chief physician of the Lyons and Paris Railway which were cited (but not further commented upon) in the 1862 Lancet Commission Report showed that approximately one-fourth of all railway drivers and fireman

disabilities were subject to termination on the basis of unfitness for duty. The generally servile position of British rail labor is evident in this (unsuccessful) plea made to the directors of the Stockton and Darlington line of the North Eastern Railway by drivers and firemen let go as a result of their participation in a brief strike against that company in 1867:

> We pray you to entertain the humble petition of your humble servants the engine drivers and firemen lately on your section. We have surrendered ourselves to William Bouch, esquire, and are now at his disposal. We had no quarrel with our employers; the course we took was to support the North Eastern men. We were betrayed into a false position and have acknowledged our error already. There were circumstances in the case we were not made acquainted with. We repent of what we have done and promise the act shall never be repeated. "To err is human, to forgive is divine." We cast ourselves entirely on thy mercy. Hoping you will manifest towards us a true chivalrous spirit and have compassion on a fallen foe. And in proportion to your magnanimity, benevolence and humanity on the present occasion, will be our devotion, fidelity and obedience in the future. We petition you, gentlemen, to be so kind, so forgiving and condescending as to pay the money standing to our account. You will be aware, gentlemen, that most of the money was earned in the storm and tempest, whilst exposed to the howling wind and pelting snow.
>
> P.S. Some of the families are now on the point of starvation. We hope, gentlemen, you will favor us with the money standing to our account. It is now sixteen weeks since we received any from you. And your humble servants will ever pray, etc.[64]

A related impediment to the recognition of railway spine was the absence of any effective mechanism for obtaining financial compensation for employees' work injuries. Unlike the legal protection afforded to passengers by the Campbell Act, rail servants had no special statutory remedy for seeking redress for injuries incurred in occupational accidents. Their only recourse was to file a civil liability action for damages against the employer, a tactic that was easily thwarted by the rail companies' reliance on the prevailing common-law defenses of fellow-servant, contributory negligence, and assumption of risk. It was not until 1897, with the enactment of Britain's first workers' compensation law, that rail employees gained a practical means of pursuing claims for work-related injuries.[65]

Thus, for a combination of reasons, few cases of railway spine were reported among British rail servants during the nineteenth century, despite an overall high incidence of employee injuries and death. Perhaps railway spine

was merely too "subtle" or inconsequential an ailment to provoke much concern from rail workers, who regularly faced the more immediate threat of
death and dismemberment from severe rail accidents. Quite likely, their
preoccupation with job security, better wages, and working conditions took
precedence over chronic health concerns, including back pain. As we have
seen, reports of railway spine as an occupational malady were further hin-
dered by lack of an effective method for compensation and the absence of
accurate recording of work injuries by the railway companies and government agencies.

Although railway spine never emerged as a significant *occupational*
health issue during the 1800s, the highly publicized medical and legal debates that took place in connection with public liability cases posed many of
the same theoretical and political questions about back pain that surfaced in
the workers' compensation arena during the twentieth century. A number of
important ideas that first became prominent in connection with railway
spine foreshadowed later thinking about the nature of job-induced back
pain. These included: the notion that trauma to spinal structures can induce
a host of obscure symptoms at remote locations in the body, including pain in
the lower back, hip, and thigh; the belief that symptoms may appear well
after the time of the original trauma; and the idea that injurious insult to the
spine can consist of repeated minor stresses and shocks, rather than a single
severe blow. In addition, considerable emphasis began to be placed on determining whether back disorders were feigned or real and on detecting fakers
and malingerers. Physicians were assumed to have a prominent role in making this determination.

The medical distinction between signs and symptoms took on expanded
importance, with *signs* being understood as physically objective and measurable manifestations of disease, and *symptoms* as those manifestations of a
purely subjective nature. Pain, for example, was considered to be a symptom,
not a sign. Many medical authorities believed that a disorder should not be
considered legitimate if a patient presented exclusively symptoms with no
overt signs. Representative of this trend is this passage from Erichsen's
(1877) work on spinal concussion:

> In effecting a diagnosis in these as in all other surgical cases, you will
> find that the patient will present two distinct classes of phenomena,
> and it is very important to bear in mind the distinction and the differ-
> ence that exist both in kind and in importance of those two classes. He
> will, in the first place, present a series of phenomena which are recog-
> nizable by the surgeon himself, however unable the patients may be,
> from his injury or disease, to explain them. These are commonly called

objective, and are described, or ought to be described, in surgical language as *signs.* But there is another series of phenomena presented by the patient which are of less importance than those that I have just mentioned, and that series of phenomena goes by the name of *symptoms.* They are *subjective*—that is to say, they are not recognizable by the surgeon, but are taken upon the statement made by the patient. . . . Pain is a symptom. All symptoms are taken upon the assertion of the patient, and they are all incapable of proof by the surgeon, except so far as his reliance on the patient's statement is concerned, whatever be the value of that as a matter of proof. You will therefore see that there is an immense difference in point of value as well as in kind between a sign and a symptom.[66]

Discussions about the legitimacy of railway spine came to be couched in the context of a debate about the appropriateness of financial compensation for its victims. The issue of back or spinal injuries thus became the focus of a larger question concerning corporate responsibility for negligence and harm resulting from industrial operations. As the debate raged, it became increasingly impossible to separate the medical issues regarding diagnosis and treatment from legal questions about compensation and blame. Medical authorities were thrust into the forefront of these disputes, with contradictory expert medical testimony provided on both sides.

Some contemporary scholars have viewed the nineteenth century controversy about railway spine as symbolic of a more generalized public reaction to the effects of the Industrial Revolution.[67] According to these commentators, the notion of railway spine grew out of a widespread apprehension about the lack of personal control and the ensuing sense of imminent threat posed by new industrial organizations and technologies. The large corporations were seen as the primary agents of these threatening changes. The rapidly expanding railway system was the most visible public manifestation of the new industrial age, and railway corporations were the epitome of growing capitalist power. In this context, catastrophic railway accidents became a dominant metaphor for the faults of the new industrial system and technology's failure to live up to its initial promise for improving the general social welfare.

Railway spine, according to this interpretation, is one representation of the potential malevolence of the new industrial environment, the danger of physical abuse and diminution of the human spirit, and the sense of personal impotence that can result from one's inability to escape from the ubiquitous and surreptitious threats imposed by emerging production technologies. These themes of corporate control, social welfare, and personal security became central issues in the twentieth century as cases of nonspecific back pain began to appear more frequently in the context of workers' compensation claims.

The Inception of Workers' Compensation

I have suggested that at least three developments fostered the emergence of the concept of railway spine during the nineteenth century. One was the public's concern about rail safety. A related development was the rail union's efforts to drum up public support for shorter hours and improved working conditions. A third was the passing of the Campbell Act and other similar laws that made it easier for citizens to receive compensation for rail injuries through liability suits.

Throughout most of the nineteenth century, workers hurt on the job had a difficult time obtaining financial compensation for their injuries, especially those that were not acute and severe. This may explain why there was comparatively little medical attention given to occupational back pain prior to 1880. The advent of government-sponsored social insurance and the initial establishment of workers' compensation acts throughout Europe and the United States made it easier for workers to collect financial compensation for work-related disorders and payment for medical treatment of their conditions.

Many critical studies have discussed the factors that influenced the emergence of workers' compensation insurance between 1880 and 1910.[68] I do not plan to explore fully these studies here. Suffice it to say that the emergence of workers' compensation insurance was due, at least in part, to dissatisfaction by workers and employers with previous civil liability laws, including the early employers' liability statutes that had been enacted in Germany (1871) and Great Britain (1880). This dissatisfaction was related to the costs, delays, and inequities that had resulted, along with the tremendous growth in the number of tort cases brought under these laws.

On a deeper level, social analysts have traced the growth of European workers' compensation laws during the late nineteenth century to an attempt by conservative governments of the time (for example, Bismarck in Germany) to preemptively stifle growing Socialist and democratic political movements. According to this view, government advocacy of modest state-sponsored accident insurance was intended to quell worker demands for more extensive and potentially revolutionary social reform.[69]

Another significant stimulus for the inception of workers' compensation laws was the specific accident conditions affecting the railroad industry. Public alarm in Great Britain about the dangers of railroad travel had led to the passage in 1864 of the Railroad Liability Act. Most claims made under this law were for members of the traveling public—few rail employees received compensation. However, the number of occupational deaths and injuries to railroad workers was staggering. In Great Britain in 1908, for example, 461 railroad employees were killed and 20,688 disabled by injuries, accounting for approximately 13 percent and 7 percent, respectively, of work-related accidental deaths and injuries for all industries.[70] Railroad workers, and their supporters, used this public concern to press hard for enactment of liberalized compensation remedies.

For all of these reasons, workers' compensation laws were eventually established and accepted in most industrialized countries. Germany's 1884 law is considered to have been the first. Great Britain, modeling its initiative on Germany's, enacted its first workers' compensation act in 1897. The British Workmen's Compensation Act of 1897 applied at first only to employees of railroads, docks, factories, storehouses, stone quarries, and building trades, but not to domestic servants, clerks, agricultural laborers, or sailors. The act was amended in 1900 to include common and agricultural laborers, and a new act passed in 1906 extended coverage to virtually all occupations. The 1906 act also adopted a schedule of occupational diseases, which were to be treated as "injuries" compensable under the act. Similar workers' compensation laws were adopted in Austria (1887), Hungary (1891), Norway (1894), Finland (1895), Denmark (1898), Italy (1898), France (1898), Spain (1900), Netherlands (1901), Sweden (1901), Greece (1901), Russia (1903), Belgium (1903), and Switzerland (1911).

In the United States, an early attempt at social insurance for injured workers was made in 1908 with the passage of the Federal Employers Liability Act (FELA), applicable to railroad employees engaged in interstate commerce. Here again, the deplorable accident record in the railroad industry was a major stimulus to the passage of this act. Accidents involving the traveling public directed attention to the plight of injured railway workers. As in Britain, occupational injuries to railroad workers were at epidemic proportions. For instance, in 1910 3,602 railroad employees were killed and 126,039 were injured in the United States.[71] A report issued by the New York state legislature showed that in that state alone between 1907 and 1910 there were 22,694 work-related accidents reported among railway employees, resulting in approximately 1,800 deaths.[72]

Because of the severe accident toll affecting their industry, railroad workers were among the most vocal proponents for passage of FELA in that it eliminated the three notorious employer "defenses" then available under common law (fellow-servant, contributory negligence, and assumption of risk), and addressed certain specific concerns affecting railroad safety. For example, according to FELA, any employer violation of the Federal Safety

Appliance Act presumptively creates absolute liability under FELA, thus ensuring a compensation award for the injured railroad employee.

However, getting compensation under FELA still required filing civil actions in state and Federal courts, resulting in an inevitable administrative burden on the judicial system. Unpredictable jury decisions led to delayed settlements and inconsistencies in compensation judgments. Dissatisfaction with employers' liability legislation by both workers and employers culminated in state actions to abolish common-law practices and adopt state-administered systems of workers' compensation. The first state workers' compensation act was passed in 1910 in New York. Support for the movement spread quickly, and by 1921 forty-two states had enacted similar laws.

Medical Reporting of Occupational Back Pain, 1880–1915

As mentioned earlier, there were very few medical reports of occupational back pain in the nineteenth century prior to 1880. The only exceptions appear to be Thackrah's observations in 1832 and a brief mention in the 1862 Lancet Commission report of back problems among railway officials in France.

Beginning in the late 1800s, a few preliminary medical reports reflected a nascent recognition of the relationship of back pain to the performance of certain specific industrial activities, most notably the lifting and handling of heavy materials. Although I do not have any evidence directly linking the emergence of this medical literature to the inception of employers' liability and workers' compensation laws, the timing of the medical reports suggests this possibility. The following report, by L. S. Oppenheimer, appeared in the *Louisville Medical Journal* in 1884: "Lumbago is readily diagnosed by exclusion. Most of the cases are probably due to catching cold (rheumatism). Others are due to straining in lifting heavy weights or to traumatism. . . . Strained back from lifting, or from labor requiring continuous bending of the body, is likely to be underestimated, and may give rise to permanent weakness of the lumbar muscles." Adolf Strümpell made a similar observation in 1893: "Lumbago is not always of a rheumatic character, but of traumatic origin, as from lifting a heavy weight, or from sudden stooping." American physician Pearce Bailey, in 1898, described "traumatic lumbago" as potentially resulting from "sudden twists or wrenches of the spine, such as are so frequently received in railway and similar accidents, or as may occur through blows or falls on the back, or through lifting heavy weights."[73]

Medical reports suggesting occupational etiology accelerated rapidly after the turn of the century. One of the most influential medical treatises on the subject was written by William Gowers in 1904. Gowers, in examining the pathological nature of muscular rheumatism in general and lumbago in

Table 3   Number of Accidents per Thousand Workers, 1888–1907

	Total	Fatal	Permanent Injury (Complete)	Permanent Injury (Partial)	Temporary Injury
1888	4.35	0.68	0.43	2.38	0.86
1890	5.29	0.72	0.37	3.23	0.97
1895	6.24	0.67	0.15	3.57	1.85
1900	7.46	0.74	0.08	3.58	3.06
1905	8.34	0.63	0.07	3.59	4.05
1906	8.26	0.63	0.07	3.49	4.07
1907	8.36	0.68	0.06	3.36	4.26

Data from Frankel and Dawson 1910, p. 105.

to be a medical condition. During most of the nineteenth century, prior to the enactment of workers' compensation laws, an individual case of back pain would arise as a medical matter only if a patient voluntarily sought treatment for this disorder from a physician. Because it was often expensive and inconvenient for a working person to receive medical care, this presumably resulted in a self-selection of only serious cases that involved an especially high degree of pain or incapacity. As new laws required compulsory reporting of all industrial injuries, the reported cases of back pain likely included a much larger proportion of *minor* ailments than in the past. Evidence for this conclusion can be seen in table 3, using data drawn from the German workers' compensation system for the years 1888–1907.

These statistics show that in the twenty-three years after enactment of the German workers' compensation law (1884), the rate of fatal and permanent partial injuries stayed essentially the same, and the rate of complete permanent injuries decreased. But the rate of reported temporary minor injuries rose dramatically, increasing fivefold between 1888 and 1907. Similar trends were observed in Great Britain and the United States following the enactment of their workers' compensation laws.[93]

These statistics are consistent with contemporary American studies showing that the rate of claims filed generally rises following an increase in the benefits available under workers' compensation insurance.[94] In Finland, T. Tunturi and H. Pätiälä (1980) reported that the number of persons receiving disability payments for spinal disorders increased twelvefold between 1965 and 1978, after the liberalization of criteria used in awarding government financial assistance for work disabilities.[95]

Appliance Act presumptively creates absolute liability under FELA, thus ensuring a compensation award for the injured railroad employee.

However, getting compensation under FELA still required filing civil actions in state and Federal courts, resulting in an inevitable administrative burden on the judicial system. Unpredictable jury decisions led to delayed settlements and inconsistencies in compensation judgments. Dissatisfaction with employers' liability legislation by both workers and employers culminated in state actions to abolish common-law practices and adopt state-administered systems of workers' compensation. The first state workers' compensation act was passed in 1910 in New York. Support for the movement spread quickly, and by 1921 forty-two states had enacted similar laws.

Medical Reporting of Occupational Back Pain, 1880–1915

As mentioned earlier, there were very few medical reports of occupational back pain in the nineteenth century prior to 1880. The only exceptions appear to be Thackrah's observations in 1832 and a brief mention in the 1862 Lancet Commission report of back problems among railway officials in France.

Beginning in the late 1800s, a few preliminary medical reports reflected a nascent recognition of the relationship of back pain to the performance of certain specific industrial activities, most notably the lifting and handling of heavy materials. Although I do not have any evidence directly linking the emergence of this medical literature to the inception of employers' liability and workers' compensation laws, the timing of the medical reports suggests this possibility. The following report, by L. S. Oppenheimer, appeared in the *Louisville Medical Journal* in 1884: "Lumbago is readily diagnosed by exclusion. Most of the cases are probably due to catching cold (rheumatism). Others are due to straining in lifting heavy weights or to traumatism. . . . Strained back from lifting, or from labor requiring continuous bending of the body, is likely to be underestimated, and may give rise to permanent weakness of the lumbar muscles." Adolf Strümpell made a similar observation in 1893: "Lumbago is not always of a rheumatic character, but of traumatic origin, as from lifting a heavy weight, or from sudden stooping." American physician Pearce Bailey, in 1898, described "traumatic lumbago" as potentially resulting from "sudden twists or wrenches of the spine, such as are so frequently received in railway and similar accidents, or as may occur through blows or falls on the back, or through lifting heavy weights."[73]

Medical reports suggesting occupational etiology accelerated rapidly after the turn of the century. One of the most influential medical treatises on the subject was written by William Gowers in 1904. Gowers, in examining the pathological nature of muscular rheumatism in general and lumbago in particular, postulated that the underlying root of the ailment was an inflammation of the fibrous tissues of the muscles. Gowers coined the term *fibrositis* to denote this sort of inflammation and concluded that fibrositis could be induced by habitual or sudden muscular strain, of the sort involved in lifting and handling heavy objects.[74]

The growth of medical awareness about the onset of back pain and its relationship to industrial activities can be vividly traced by examining the medical textbooks of the period. Sir William Osler's *Principles and Practices of Medicine*, which appeared in thirteen editions spanning the years 1892–1939, was considered at the time to be one of the most authoritative compendiums of medical knowledge. A portion of Osler's article on lumbago appeared unchanged in the third (1898) through seventh (1910) editions of the textbook: "It [muscular rheumatism] is most commonly met with in men, particularly those exposed to cold and whose occupations are laborious. It is apt to follow exposure to a draught of air, as from an open window in a railway carriage. A sudden chilling after heavy exertion may also bring on an attack of lumbago. . . . Lumbago, one of the most common and painful forms, affects the muscles of the loins and their tendinous attachments. It occurs chiefly in workingmen. It comes on suddenly, and in very severe cases completely incapacitates the patient, who may be unable to turn in bed or to rise from the sitting posture."[75] The text in the eighth edition (1914) is slightly different: "Lumbago, one of the most common and painful forms, affects the muscles of the loins and their tendinous attachments. *Some patients are subject to attacks at short intervals.* It occurs chiefly in workingmen *and often after a strain in lifting.* It comes on suddenly, and in very severe cases completely incapacitates the patient, who may be unable to turn in bed or to rise from the sitting posture" (changes from previous editions in italics).[76] These passages, along with the timing of Osler's textbook revisions, suggest that medical attention to the dangers of occupational activities (especially heavy muscular exertion of the back muscles) increased at about the same time that the first workers' compensation laws were being enacted in Europe and the United States.

One immediate consequence of the enactment of workers' compensation legislation was a dramatic improvement in the reporting of industrial accidents and the ability to compile occupational injury statistics. Before the advent of workers' compensation laws, occupational injury statistics were almost totally unavailable in the United States. In Great Britain, there had been some systematic reporting of industrial accidents by means of the factory inspectorate system that had been established in 1833 to enforce Britain's Factory Acts. But with the introduction of compulsory reporting by employers of all work-related accidents came a vastly improved and reliable

There are a number of additional reasons to believe that the development of the workers' compensation system influenced the emergence of the recognition of back pain as an occupational disorder during the early twentieth century. One piece of evidence can be seen in the increasing appearance of the term *back strain* in the medical literature to describe occupational back injuries. Prior to 1910, there had been almost no use at all of this term—the traditional vocabulary used to describe pain occurring in the back included *lumbago, muscular rheumatism,* and *myalgia,* as well as the specialized terms we examined earlier such as *railway spine, fibrositis,* and *spinal irritation.*

The term *strain* relates directly to the injury and accident provisions of all the new workers' compensation laws. According to the statutes enacted in the United States, Britain, and continental Europe, compensation was to be awarded only for "personal injury by accident arising out of and in the course of employment," where an *injury* was understood to be an acute condition with specific anatomic locus and an *accident* was interpreted as a sudden unforeseen event occurring at a specific place and point in time.[96] The medical notion of "strains" fit both these requirements insofar as they were conceived to be tears of particular muscles arising from "stresses" placed on those muscles during the performance of specific actions.

By 1915, the incidence of work-related back strains was increasing dramatically. In that year Dr. Howard King of New Orleans wrote, "Pain in the back as a result of injury, is the most frequent affection for which compensation is demanded from the casualty company."[97] Dr. Harry Mock (1919) declared industrial lumbago to be at "epidemic proportions," adding that it was not uncommon "to see ten men in the examining room at the same time all complaining of pain in the back."[98] Also in 1919, Dr. Robert Osgood in Boston wrote that back strain is "the commonest industrial lesion."[99] E. W. Hope, in 1923, called industrial back pain "one of the most common grounds of claims."[100] Popular and medical literature began to focus on the problem of the "industrial back" as one of the most significant occupational injury problems.[101] One medical report written in 1920 indicated that 50 percent of all injuries among railroad workers were related to low back pain.[102]

Along with the development of the workers' compensation system during the early 1900s came the initial growth of industrial safety associations, such as the National Safety Council, founded in 1913 and based upon the Association of Iron and Steel Electrical Engineers that had been in existence since 1907.[103] These early safety groups essentially had an engineering orientation and stressed the control of industrial accident hazards through machine guarding and other physical modifications of production processes.

The same approach to industrial safety characterized the initial safety efforts of the large insurance companies, some of which created safety engineering departments to help their insureds prevent accidents and thereby control workers' compensation costs.[104]

The engineering orientation to industrial accident prevention employed by these groups may have also contributed to the recognition of the hazards of heavy materials handling and its potential relationship to the inducement of back strains. The model of a mechanical stress-producing strain is an engineering concept that was widely applied in industry during this period. This orientation can be seen in the remarks made by Beyer and other early safety engineers about the capabilities and limitations of what was called the "human mechanism" compared to other available electromechanical materials-handling devices.[105]

The emphasis on handling heavy material with respect to its potential to produce muscular strains (particularly in the lower back) became common during the 1920s—a perspective that had been almost entirely missing from medical writings about back pain during most of the nineteenth century. Concern about the injurious effects of heavy muscular exertion and its potential for causing back injuries was also notably absent from the nineteenth-century literature concerning the nature of muscular fatigue and the detrimental effects of overwork.[106]

However, between 1890 and 1930 the emergence of scholarly writings describing a relationship between occupational materials handling and back pain should not be construed as indicative of the introduction of new production technologies or new industrial methods requiring more frequent handling of heavy materials or heavier loads. There is ample evidence that strenuous material handling had been a part of many occupations for centuries and was particularly common in the industrial factories of the early nineteenth century. Public concern during the 1800s about the employment of women and children in the workplace became a major factor stimulating passage of the British Factory Acts in the mid-nineteenth century. Several government reports documented the handling of very heavy weights by women and children. For example, a government investigation into working conditions among female nail-makers described a case of a woman who "carried a quarter of a mile, on her neck, chain weighing, it would seem, on an average half a hundredweight [50 pounds]. Another woman carried a hundredweight of chain 20 or 30 yards, and Mr. Hoarse said that women carried a 60 lb. bundle of nails a mile."[107] The *Annual Report of the Chief Inspector of Factories and Workshops* for 1909 concluded that "women have been used as beasts of burden for over 40 years," citing evidence for the "constant lifting" of fifty- to sixty-pound weights by both women and children, particularly in the textile mills.[108] In contrast to the early twentieth century, in which attention to heavy material handling focused on the danger of injuries (particularly back strains), the major concern expressed during the 1800s about heavy materials handling by women and children revolved around its supposed potential for stunting their growth, inducing curvature of the spinal column (rounded shoulders), and/or causing "uterine displacement."[109]

Although the common practice when filing workers' compensation claims for back pain was to label the affliction a case of back "strain" or "sprain," it was evident to physicians and to others involved in administering the workers' compensation system that most cases of work-related back pain were devoid of any identifiable lesion or specific proximate trauma. Rufus Crain and Benjamin Slater (1921), two physicians from the Eastman Kodak Company, estimated that 90 percent of all reported cases of workers' compensation back strains were really idiopathic, unable to be attributed to any specific event or precipitating cause. Dr. James Sever (1923) reflected a commonly held perspective about the difficulties of using the term "back strain" to describe these workers' compensation cases: "The diagnosis of the so-called 'industrial back' is a subject which the writer undertakes with a great many reservations. . . . The term 'back strain' is used advisedly, for any definite classification of these cases from these causes is difficult."[110]

Because physicians could find no specific lesion in most cases, and because medical examinations for back ailments arose increasingly in the context of claims for financial compensation related to work disability, many medical authorities began to question the legitimacy of these alleged back injuries. By 1916, Archibald McKendrick, in *Back Injuries and Their Significance Under the Workmen's Compensation and Other Acts,* concluded: "Back injuries have a bad reputation. The workman looks upon them with apprehension, the insurance company with doubt, the medical examiner with suspicion, the lawyer with uncertainty, and the Court with as open a mind as is possible under the circumstances. . . . The medical examiner is faced with the difficulty of estimating the true value of the subjective symptoms in the comparative absence of physical signs. His suspicion is born of the frequent disparity between the two."[111]

During the 1920s, an increasing amount of attention began to be directed at the question of whether claims for cases of nonspecific back strains should qualify for treatment under workers' compensation. Crain and Slater (1921) argued that because it was not possible to relate most back strain cases to a specific precipitating event, they should not be deemed to have resulted from an "accident" as defined in the prevailing workers' compensation codes, and thus were not compensable under those laws. Similar arguments were raised in a host of other articles appearing in the 1920s.[112]

Social Class and the Problem of Malingering

During the 1920s, articles attempted to portray many cases of idiopathic back pain as varieties of neurotic and hysterical behavior.[113] Several authorities related the observed rise in workers' compensation back strain cases to the concept of "traumatic neuroses," a diagnosis that had grown in prominence as a result of soldiers' post-combat medical complaints during and immediately after World War I.[114] Medical and legal discussions concerning industrial back pain began to focus on the issue of malingering, its detection, and the psychological causes of the malingerer's actions. Many commentators of the period were inclined to interpret malingering and, therefore, the industrial back pain problem, as symptomatic of a broader social and class conflict.

Malingering first became a significant social issue in connection with the railroad liability laws. As noted above, physicians and other observers believed that many injuries reported by persons involved in railroad accidents were exaggerated or feigned, either deliberately or subconsciously. It was suggested that this was due to their desire to receive increased recompense in legal proceedings pursuant to the accident. The term *malingering* was used to describe this behavior. Other related terms, such as *compensation neurosis* and *litigation injury*, also arose in the mid-1800s in connection to the debates about compensation for railway spine and other supposed effects of rail mishaps.

After passage of the workers' compensation laws in the late 1800s and early 1900s, similar cases of nonspecific back pain began to be reported by workers. In a manner reminiscent of the earlier reports of railway spine, many of the new cases of occupational back pain came about gradually or considerably after the time of the alleged precipitating event. As in railway spine, the pathology of the pain was often obscure, with no specific lesion. The symptoms often mimicked those of such known systemic conditions as arthritis and rheumatism.

It is thus not surprising that the earlier controversies about malingering and railway spine were resurrected, re-emerging in the context of the new "industrial back" problem of the 1920s. The arguments of those who believed that many of these cases were psychologically related were bolstered by the experiences of soldiers in World War I, many of whom reported lingering physical complaints as a result of traumatic war experiences. The complaints commonly involved symptoms without signs or evidence of organic disease. Such complaints were generally ascribed to be "hysterical" in origin—the term "traumatic neurosis" was frequently used to denote this type of war-related syndrome. The British physician H. N. Barnett (1909) summarizes the popular thinking of the time about traumatic neuroses of the back: "It was first thought that the condition was one of injury to the meninges of the cord with resulting inflammation; then came the theory of pure hysteria, and now the generally accepted theory is that a trauma causes symptoms which are hysterical in character and sometimes simulate organic lesions."[115]

Barnett was among those who quickly perceived the applicability of these considerations to similar cases that were beginning to appear within the workers' compensation system. In *Accidental Injuries To Workmen With Reference to Workmen's Compensation Act of 1906,* he discusses the difficulties involved in making a proper medical diagnosis: "If the case were difficult before the passing of the Workmen's Compensation Act, it is doubly so now, for the injured workman has an Act of Parliament at his back which makes it worth his while to magnify his troubles. Without casting any unjust aspersion on the honest workman, we must be alive to the possibility of simulation especially with regard to injuries of the nervous system. It is wonderful how the malingerer learns the symptoms he has to simulate, and the only pity from his point of view is that he usually overdoes them, and thus betrays himself."[116] H. R. Conn (1922), an Ohio physician, remarked, "traumatic back still enjoys an unenviable notoriety as a sort of rock-bound refuge for malingerers."[117] King (1915), a physician for the Texas and Pacific Railway, traces the transformation of the nineteenth-century concept of railway spine (as a supposed organic ailment) into the twentieth-century concept of hysterical spine (a purely psychic state), a condition that he, with great derision, ascribes to the deviant personality of the malingerer:

> Railway spine, while not the dreadful bogey of former days, is still a
> source of worriment to the physician. In the days of Erichsen, what
> was regarded as "railway spine," or "concussion of the spine," and sup-
> posed to be based on definite organic changes in the spinal cord, is now
> correctly diagnosed as "hysterical spine." In "hysterical spine" there is
> alleged hypersensitiveness over certain parts of the back—as a rule,
> the sacro-lumbar area. This condition, a purely psychic one, often
> proves intractable to treatment; some of my confreres claim it is abso-
> lutely incurable. This view is wrong, as an adverse court decision has
> cured several of my most obstinate cases. Other cases require copious
> applications of "greenback salve," after which rapid recovery ensues.
> A condition curable with money is not a disease—it is a swindle. In for-
> mer days railway corporations were defrauded out of large amounts of
> money by victims of "railway spine." Through introspection and gross
> exaggeration many fakers have been gloriously rewarded with large
> damages. The present-day methods of psycho-therapeusis would have
> changed the picture.[118]

A number of medical authorities believed that many, if not most cases of compensable, nonspecific back pain were really manifestations of arthritis and other systemic conditions. Dr. J. C. Landenberger (1926) attributed the confusion to a deliberate and "flagrant" attempt on the part of claimants to mislead the workers' compensation industrial boards: "The sense of corporation liability for injury, with its monetary remuneration, together with compensation laws which pay indemnity for injury, present a lure to the industrial worker which it is difficult for him to resist. And this is undoubtedly the reason why cases of chronic infectious arthritis in industrial workers are always connected with a history of an injury, whereas the same pathological conditions occurring in individuals in other positions in life seldom or never are accompanied by a history of injury."[119] A similar view was expressed in 1926 by Dr. James Donohue, who was a member of the Connecticut Board of Compensation Commissioners:

> Many of us, I feel sure, when we see a man coming in for about the tenth time and claiming a back strain, wish that our prehistoric ancestors in their progress of evolution had handed down to us an anatomical structure devoid of any vertebrae whatever; in other words, when the spineless vertebrate presents himself, we often wish that heredity had dealt differently with the human race anatomically, and so might have eliminated many of the claims for back strain. We have heard of railway spine, which, in the past, was the bugbear of the railroad companies. Today we have the sacroiliac strain and the lumbar muscle strain, both of which are among the most fertile sources of contention when it comes to disability disputes. . . . Oftentimes the man with a back strain, though he may not be a malingerer, still lacks that stamina and self-confidence which are necessary to send him forward and shake off the imaginary pain magnified by his self-consciousness and self-sympathy.[120]

Donohue goes on to classify such individuals as "neurotic," and then, in a manner reminiscent of the similar accusations made several years earlier about those suffering from writers' and telegraphers' cramp, presents his view that certain ethnic classes are more prone to such behavior: "My observation leads me to feel that people coming from southern European climates —that is, the warm countries—are the ones who are most spineless and who have the biggest idea of the size of their injuries, magnifying a trifling ailment out of all proportion to the injury actually received, shouting with pain if you look at them, and going into hysterics if you attempt to bend or exercise an injured member in an attempt justly to estimate the amount of specific injury."[121]

Donohue was not alone in viewing the question of malingering and injury simulation within the workers' compensation system as ultimately a matter of ethnic and class distinctions. Sir John Collie, a prominent British physician and chief Home Office referee for the Workmen's Compensation Act, attributed malingering to inherent class conflict between poor and generally uneducated workers and those representing industry and government. In 1917 he wrote:

> Pain in the back is the most common element in claims for compensation which are litigated in the Courts. The number of complaints to which pain in the back is added as a species of make-weight is surprising. A friend of mine was told by a workman that, prior to his visit for the purpose of being examined, he received the following sage advice from a "pal": *When yer git 'urt, 'e says, say it's yer back; the doctors can't never get round yer back.* . . . Experience shows that the idea that doctors cannot "get around" the back still prevails with a large number of those who are prone to malinger. . . .
>
> It is abundantly apparent to those who have much to do with working-men that there are certain persons who deliberately set class against class, who day by day breed discontent, who prolong the period of incapacity caused by illness, and debase honest working-men. . . . As long as medical men who attend the working-classes are dependent on the working-men for their position, so long will gross exaggeration and malingering be rampant. . . .
>
> It must be remembered that most sick and injured workmen belong to a class whose education is incomplete, and that they are peculiarly unfit to take a detached view of themselves, especially when ill. . . . The stricken soldier in the industrial warfare is, because of distrust, too often over-anxious, at all hazards, to guard himself against the possibility of future incapacity arising out of his disability. He assumes that the State, or the insurance company by which his master is protected, will minimize his illness, and therefore he must exaggerate; he considers that, in any case, the fullest demand he makes must be as nothing compared with the vast sums at the command of the Government or insurance company.[122]

The portrayal of malingering as a manifestation of inherent class prejudice and bigotry has a long history in British medical literature. Dr. Michael Dewar, the secretary of the Edinburgh Branch of the British Medical Association, wrote in "Medical Training for the Detection of Malingering" (1912): "Malingering is fairly common and widespread among the wage-earning classes who are members of friendly societies. It is rare, though not unknown, among salaried officials. A highly developed and conscientious principle of right and wrong is not a characteristic feature of a large number of working men. . . . There will always be a certain amount of sympathy with [malingerers] because from a psychological point of view they are not altogether to be blamed for being the possessors of a weak mental stamina, often the fault of heredity."[123]

Not surprisingly, there were also a few physicians who felt that women, because of their nervous temperament, were more prone to exaggerating the symptoms of back pain. For example, Dr. Martin Delaney, in his article "Significance of Pain in the Back," remarked, "Women often exaggerate more to impress and get the necessary relief than from any other cause."[124]

The picture painted by Collie and these other writers is one of outright class warfare: a battle of wits wherein the worker devises cunning ways of simulating illness and the physician, using the intelligence and instruments at his disposal, protects the virtue of the state by debunking the patient's allegations. Claims for nonspecific back pain became the foremost battleground.

This battle cry was echoed by others on both sides of the Atlantic, including King (1915), Dercum (1916), Mock (1919), and Huddleson (1932) in the United States, Fraser (1930) in Canada, and McKendrick (1927) in Great Britain. They all suggested that the physician's primary weapon was a thorough physical examination, and each doctor provided elaborate technical advice on various tests, postures, and clinical procedures that could uncover the subterfuge of the malingerer.

These medical authorities believed that the primary goal of the clinical examination was assessing the legitimacy of back injuries and differentiating them from other nontraumatic congenital or disease conditions. They all believed that one recently developed technique, radiography, was potentially decisive in this endeavor.

The Introduction of X-Ray Technologies

Upon their discovery by Wilhelm Roentgen in 1895, X rays had been immediately put to use in medical applications. The Vienna Press, in its first announcement about X rays, commented on the exciting possibilities for medicine opened up by the discovery. Physicians quickly realized the tremendous potential brought about by the capacity to visualize internal body structure noninvasively. One of the most obvious and successful of these applications was to structural disorders of the musculoskeletal system, because of the excellent resolution of the bones observed in X-ray images. Within the first few years after the discovery, a whole new science—radiology—had gathered momentum. Historians of the period note that progress during this initial period was "staggering," and that there was clear "over-enthusiasm" displayed by the medical community to the possibilities presented by the new technique.[125]

In the 1920s, many cases of back pain were thought to be psychological in origin, devoid of any organic basis. Other cases were considered "real," insofar as it was possible to discover a specific pathological lesion responsible for the symptoms of the back pain. To determine definitively that an individual's complaint was not feigned and not a manifestation of psychoneurosis, physicians believed that it was necessary to discover an underlying anatomic pathology. Many advocated the routine use of X rays in all cases of alleged back injury.[126]

However, many of those advocating the use of X rays in all cases of alleged industrial back strain were not concerned with the objective verification of a patient's claim. On the contrary, some physicians in the 1920s realized that the results of radiographic analysis of the back could rarely confirm the presence of back injury, since the muscle strains of the sort alleged would not be detectable through standard X rays.[127] Rather, the goal of radiography was often to acquire evidence to help debunk the patient's claim for compensation, as an adjunct to other clinical tests aimed at identifying malingerers.[128] X rays were potentially helpful in this respect in two ways.

On the one hand, a "normal" X ray could be used to demonstrate that there was no underlying lesion in those workers complaining of severe back injury. Such findings were often offered as evidence of malingering, especially in patients whose condition had followed a traumatic event. For example, "concussion of the spine" (railway spine), as expounded in Erichsen's original theory, would have led to structural lesions of the spine that should be manifest in back X rays. The absence of such spinal lesions was offered as alleged proof that the patient's complaints were fabricated.

Another way that back X rays could supposedly detect malingering was by demonstrating the presence of various underlying lesions unrelated to industrial injury. This X-ray evidence of spinal pathology could be claimed as an alternative explanation for a patient's back pain, thereby scientifically challenging a worker's assertion that pain resulted from occupational trauma. For example, it was known that X rays could provide firm evidence of arthritis, tuberculosis, scoliosis, congenital abnormalities, and other somatic conditions. The appearance of such congenital and systemic abnormalities was often introduced in workers' compensation hearings to help "prove" that the patient's complaints, though legitimate, were really the result of nonoccupational causes.[129]

Contemporary studies show that neither of these intended uses of back X rays is valid. Considerable empirical evidence suggests that there is a poor association between X-ray findings and the symptoms of back pain.[130] Indeed, the current view is that standard X rays are not sensitive to many legitimate disorders of the back, including prolapse of intervertebral discs.[131] Furthermore, a large proportion of the "normal" asymptomatic population exhibits various spinal "abnormalities" during X-ray examination.[132] For these reasons, most authorities now argue against relying on standard X rays as a means of accurately diagnosing cases of nonspecific back pain.[133]

Nevertheless, during the early twentieth century, the introduction of X-ray evidence in cases of alleged industrial back pain became extremely common. By 1930, sentiment was growing both in the medical community and among the public that malingering was a major problem for the workers' compensation system. X rays were used increasingly to scientifically challenge claims of occupational causation in cases of nonspecific back pain.

The accumulation of this evidence, combined with the growing popularity of Freudian psychoanalytic theory and the documented occurrence of war-induced "traumatic neuroses," strengthened the arguments of those who perceived nonspecific industrial back pain as essentially a psychological disorder, fabricated deliberately or subconsciously. The stage was set for nonspecific industrial back pain to be redefined as a manifestation of modern neurosis, and thereby dismissed as a legitimate medical concern, in much the same way as spinal irritation in the 1870s, railway spine in the 1890s, and, at the same period (1910–1930) was transforming occupational neuroses of the hands and wrists into a psychological phenomenon.

But the growth of back pain in the workers' compensation system did not decline, but rather continued to increase through World War II. During the 1930s, a number of factors firmly established back pain as the leading cause of work-induced disability. One that was to prove extremely important was the continued advancement of X-ray technology and its eventual role in the discovery and acceptance of the concept of the ruptured disc, which became the predominant medical explanation for occupational back pain after 1934.

The Ruptured Disc Model of Mixter and Barr

A major advance in radiography during the early twentieth century was the use of contrast media to enhance the detail observable in X rays. One such viewing method, lipiodol myelography, was developed in 1922 in France by Jean-Athanase Sicard and Jacques Forestier for studying abnormalities in the spinal canal.[134] This technique gained wide acceptance in the late 1920s through the work of W. E. Dandy and William ("Jason") Mixter. Dandy's work, published in 1929, described two cases where X-ray myelography had identified complete blockage of the spinal canal. Surgical exploration in these cases revealed loose cartilage from intervertebral discs that simulated a spinal tumor.[135] In the same year, German physician G. Schmorl reported a post mortem study documenting the protrusion of an intervertebral disc into the spinal canal.[136] Others, including J. E. Goldthwaite (1911), Middleton and Teacher (1911), Elsberg (1928), and Bucy (1930), also speculated about the possible relationship between intervertebral disc abnormalities and various clinical conditions.

But it was principally the work in the early 1930s of Mixter and Joseph S. Barr, two physicians from the Massachusetts General Hospital, that led to the widespread recognition of a causal association between intervertebral disc lesions and cases of industrial back pain.[137] Mixter, a neurosurgeon, and Barr, an orthopedist, were familiar with the work of Dandy and Schmorl. Building upon this earlier work, they formulated the theory that many cases of severe back pain previously thought to be caused by spinal tumors ("enchondromas") were actually the result of spinal nerve compression resulting from the protrusion of intervertebral disc material into the spinal cavity. Along with Dr. A. O. Hampton, they perfected a new type of lipiodol myelography to identify this lesion.[138] A number of surgical and pathological studies provided evidence in support of this hypothesis.

The results of this investigation were first presented by Barr in 1933, and the first paper describing their theory and the supporting evidence was published in the *New England Journal of Medicine* in 1934.[139] A further elaboration of these ideas authored by Mixter and J. B. Ayer appeared in the same journal in 1935. In this paper the authors advocated use of the descriptive term *rupture* or *herniation* of the disc rather than the phrase "prolapse of the nucleus pulposus," which had originally been suggested by Schmorl in 1929.[140]

The development of the herniated disc model was attractive for occupational physicians because it offered, for the first time, a plausible underlying pathology to account for a large portion of the back pain symptoms existing in the working population. The manner in which Dandy, Mixter, Barr, Ayer, and other researchers presented their results reinforced the connection to industrial trauma.

Dandy, who correctly identified the lesion as a dislodged fragment of intervertebral disc in two patients with severe sciatica and cauda equina syndrome, declared, "the lesion is undoubtedly of traumatic origin." Echoing the claims that Erichsen had made sixty years earlier, he emphasized that the lesion can be induced by "the repetition of minor traumas" and that each of the repeated traumas may be "relatively trivial and slight." Apparently he came to this conclusion based on the histories of his two patients, one of whom was not able to remember any precipitating trauma until after his surgeon explained the nature of the disc lesion that had been discovered in his spine. It was only then that the patient recalled first feeling lumbar pain while riding horseback three months earlier. The other patient developed pain shortly after pushing an automobile out of his driveway. To support his view that the lesion is caused traumatically, Dandy further observed, "it is also not without significance that both of these patients are men."[141]

Mixter and Barr also believed that the lesion was due to traumatic origin. They noted that, in their series of nineteen cases, "there is often a history of trauma not immediately related to the present condition."[142] In reality, according to the detailed case summaries provided in their article, only eight of the nineteen patients reported a history of trauma. Of those eight, three episodes occurred many years before the onset of symptoms (fall onto buttocks twenty years before onset, fall of seventy feet five years before onset, and a wartime shell explosion "several years" before onset). Two of the nineteen patients reported "sudden onset while lifting a weight." This sketchy evidence did not preclude Mixter and Ayer from surmising, in 1935: "Trauma, as an immediate cause of rupture, appears to be quite certain in over one-half of our lumbrosacral group, and in this we are in agreement with Dandy, Alpers and others. . . . We are unable to establish any type of individual patient or any occupation in which disc hernias predominate, but the excess of males over females so afflicted is worthy of comment, and in this respect we are in general agreement with other writers."[143]

It was only many years later, in 1961, that Barr, in recounting the history of the ruptured disc discovery, admitted:

> We had some difficulty in deciding what we would call these things, whether they would be called protrusions or ruptures or what. That led to a very long period in which there was a great deal of indecision and lack of knowledge about what the actual causes of these protrusions were. I think our Swedish confreres have pretty well proven that degenerative change is a primary cause. . . . Probably degenerative change which is a weakening process plus some acute strain is the basis for most of our disk lesions. Certainly only 30–40 percent of our cases give an out-and-out clearcut history of antecedent trauma which one can really relate to. In New England almost everybody has been skating as a kid and has had his feet slide out from under him and has sat down hard. I wonder if that might not be the cause of a great many more disk lesions in the New England area.[144]

Despite the relatively sketchy epidemiologic evidence presented at the time, the pronouncements of Dandy, Mixter, Ayer, and other researchers helped convince most authorities that the condition was essentially traumatic in nature.[145]

In light of the extensive historical background, it is remarkable that none of these researchers specifically addressed the relevance of their findings to the traditional controversies that had surrounded spinal irritation, railway spine, and other similar disorders that had attracted so much attention during the nineteenth century. The similarity of the descriptions concerning the potential for significant spinal injury from repeated minor trauma is striking. So is the concept that symptoms can develop at some distance in both time and location from the point of the original trauma.

Although the discovery was not reported in this historical context, Mixter, Barr, and Ayer were aware of the implications of their findings for workers' compensation. Mixter and Ayer (1935) remarked, "We realize that this subject opens up an interesting problem in industrial medicine. Injuries to the spine have long been a fruitful source of industrial accident compensation. It is unfortunate that we must further complicate this subject by adding another to the long line of possible injuries of the spine."[146] The choice of the words "fruitful source" and "unfortunate" may have reflected their realization that their discovery of the ruptured disc lesion held tremendous potential for explaining (and substantiating) a great deal of the severe yet obscure back pain that was so prevalent among industrial workers.

None of these physicians had any special background in occupational medicine or reason to be especially sympathetic to the need for workers to legitimize compensation claims. Their personal backgrounds reflected lives of privileged status and association with conservative social institutions.[147] There is no evidence to suggest that the identification of the ruptured disc lesion as traumatic stemmed from a surreptitious desire on their part to influence the course of industrial compensation. On the contrary, they probably felt that the association of ruptured discs with compensation issues was unfortunate insofar as their discovery would be used by many workers as a basis for claims that back pain was work-related.

At first, Mixter and Barr's ideas met with skepticism from some physicians. But over the next ten years, as the suspected lesion was repeatedly uncovered during surgeries performed around the world, the theory of Mixter and Barr gained widespread and enthusiastic acceptance by the medical profession. J. Grafton Love, of the Mayo Clinic, came to observe Mixter and Barr's work at the Massachusetts General Hospital and then popularized the surgical treatment of the condition by performing more than three hundred operations for removal of prolapsed disc tissue at the Mayo Clinic between 1935 and 1939.[148] In Great Britain, J. E. A. O'Connell reported on seventy-five such surgeries that he performed between 1937 and 1943.[149] In many cases, dramatic postoperative improvement in the clinical condition of patients was observed. In their report on the first hundred disc operations performed at the Mayo Clinic, Love and Walsh (1938) termed the results "excellent and gratifying," and could barely contain their excitement in declaring, "It may safely be said that today, protrusion of intervertebral discs constitutes one of the major causes of sciatic pain. Indeed, it is quite as antiquated to make a diagnosis of 'sciatica' today as it is to make a diagnosis of 'headache.'"[150]

As a number of contemporary critics have noted, these early reports led to an unprecedented rush of surgical enthusiasm for the new "ruptured disc" diagnosis and treatment during the 1940s and 1950s. During this period, the criteria used for diagnosing cases of ruptured intervertebral discs and selecting surgical candidates expanded significantly. For example, a number of physicians began identifying patients for surgery based on the presentation of clinical symptoms alone, without the need for confirmatory lipiodol myelography.[151] The expansion of this concept was so dramatic that by 1945, J. E. Key was able to claim in the *Annals of Surgery*: "Intervertebral disc lesions are the most common cause of back pain with or without sciatica."[152]

Some commentators have gone one step further in suggesting that the development and popularization of the ruptured disc model by Mixter and Barr became the predominant stimulus behind the acceptance and increased reporting of nonspecific back pain within the state workers' compensation systems. One well-known authority, Dr. Nortin Hadler of the University of North Carolina, has presented this view repeatedly in a number of publications; the following passage is typical.

> In 1934, two surgeons, Mixter and Barr, described the syndrome of discal herniation in a series of patients, many of whom had cauda equina syndrome with bowel/bladder dysfunction and several of whom improved following surgical intervention. In this paper they suggested that discal herniation was an explanation even for regional [idiopathic] backache, and they labeled the disease "rupture" of the disc. Their suggestion took hold over the next decade throughout the Western world; regional backache was thought to be a surgically remedial disease particularly if abnormality of discal anatomy was present. Even more dramatic was the implication of the label of "rupture"; everywhere, the judiciary held that, if the clinical result was so violent as to be a "rupture," the details of the causal event should not be determinative. In this fashion, regional backache became back injury, and backache occurring on the job and ascribed to discal herniation became compensable.[153]

Hadler is right in observing that the development of the ruptured disc model furnished, for the first time, a demonstrable pathology to account for a large proportion of industrial back injuries. In addition, it offered the possibility of a new, and potentially effective, therapeutic technique to address the plight of those suffering from chronic back pain and sciatica. Hadler also correctly points out that the terminology in which the "rupture" model was couched provided a ready-made "bridge" for lawyers and plaintiffs to use in "fitting" back pain cases to the "injury" and "accident" requirements of the state workers' compensation systems.[154] As Hadler has observed,

> "Rupture" is a highly emotive term; it describes the condition of being broken or burst! A patient who is told "you ruptured your disk" should envision major anatomic dissolution. This message was heard by the patient and as vividly by society at large. It was also heard by the Workers' Compensation administrators who are faced with a pressing need to define the "injury" that arose "out of and in the course of employment." Rupture is so horrible that even if there is no accidental cause, it must still be an accidental result. To this day, in almost every jurisdiction, if a worker's backache is certified by a physician to result from a ruptured disk, the worker will be compensated. Furthermore, in the operating sociopolitical climate, the performance of a laminectomy is considered a validation of the certification. It is by virtue of such certification that backache is legally declared an injury. By World War II, this exercise in heuristic logic was so pervasive that all backache was regarded as the result of injury. The chief complaint of the sufferer became and remains "I injured my back" rather than "Oh, my aching back!"[155]

Of equal importance as the question of workers' compensation, lipiodol myelography provided physicians with a way of physically documenting the basis of their diagnosis. In the words of Dandy, the use of lipiodol myelography "makes the diagnosis and localization [of spinal lesions] almost foolproof."[156] This gave claimants and physicians the "physical evidence" needed to establish the presence of injury that they were under pressure to produce by the requirements of the compensation system. The ability to portray the "injury" by X-ray image appealed to insurance claims representatives, lawyers, and workers' compensation administrators, who had become accustomed to depending on X rays of fractures, amputations, and other traumatic incidents to establish the nature of injury and the extent of disability. Myelography even allowed a person without special medical training to visualize the underlying "assault" that had occurred to the worker. Even today, state laws dictate that X-ray diagnosis is a necessary condition for granting workers' compensation for some disorders (for example, silicosis).[157]

Thus, the development of X-ray techniques such as myelography during the late 1920s and early 1930s not only was crucial for Mixter and Barr's discovery of a possible pathology underlying low back pain, it also provided the scientific basis for the entire sequence of diagnosis, surgical treatment, and physical documentation that was important for establishing back pain as compensable within state workers' compensation systems.

Hadler's reason for bringing this history to light is to challenge the medical and workers' compensation communities to reconsider the basis upon which back pain has come to be identified as a disorder with a specific cause, treatment, and relation to trauma suffered on the job. Indeed, since 1934 many tenets of Mixter and Barr's paradigm have been seriously discredited. First, it is now known that relatively few cases of occupational back pain are legitimately ascribable to discal herniation.[158] In fact, true discal herniation is difficult to diagnose, and is not necessarily strongly associated with chronic back pain.[159] Second, the process of discal herniation has been commonly found to occur quite gradually, often from nonspecific degenerative factors, rarely being an event that occurs suddenly or during an identifiable time period.[160] For this reason Hadler ridicules Mixter and Barr's terminology, calling the term *rupture* a "malapropism."[161] Last, the common surgical interventions of laminectomy, spinal fusion, and spinal decompression have been found to have a limited effectiveness in relieving pain symptoms in most cases of nonspecific back pain.[162] Even in cases of specific lumbar disc prolapse causing sciatica, the results of conservative and operative therapy have been shown to be nearly identical at six months after initiation of treatment.[163]

Based upon these considerations, Hadler urges a return to a conservative medical policy regarding the diagnosis, treatment, and compensability of back pain, based only upon evidence and techniques that can be confirmed clinically. In the case of most regional back pain, that approach would not provide sufficient data to substantiate unequivocally the decisions that are needed within the workers' compensation system. Therefore, Hadler urges physicians and others involved in that system to be cautious about expressing and accepting judgments on such matters as the source of "injury," the projected course of a patient's disability, and the underlying pathology of most nonspecific back pain.

Although Hadler is justified in emphasizing the influence of the ruptured disc discovery, his view that the movement toward the compensability of back pain was predominantly a result of the Mixter–Barr model is misleading. For one thing, it is important to recognize that a substantial number of back pain cases were occurring in the workers' compensation system prior to 1934.

In addition, Hadler's narrow focus on the Mixter and Barr discovery in

1934 fails to recognize the associated importance of other social forces that influenced the growth of compensable back pain during the late 1930s and 1940s. Of primary importance in this regard were (1) an emerging crisis in occupational diseases, particularly silicosis, which resulted in more liberal criteria for the inclusion of these claims under state workers' compensation statutes, (2) a growing public acceptance of social welfare legislation to deal with the serious occupational hardships brought on by the Depression, and (3) the growth of orthopedics specialization and orthopedic surgery in the years between World War I and World War II. The significant effect of these social factors on the expansion of criteria for compensable nonspecific back pain will be explored in the remainder of this chapter.

The Liberalization of Occupational Disease Compensation

Mixter and Barr's development of the ruptured disc concept occurred precisely at a time when the state workers' compensation systems were under substantial pressure due to new demands imposed by the rise of occupational diseases, especially silicosis. Anthony Bale uses the phrase "compensation crisis" to describe the turmoil over occupational disease that occurred between the years 1932 and 1936.[164] Historians Gerald Markowitz and David Rosner call this the "silicosis crisis of the 1930s."[165]

Silicosis was not a newly discovered disease. Agricola had written about it in the sixteenth century, as had Ramazzini in the eighteenth century. The relationship of silicosis to dust produced in mining and quarrying had been well documented by the end of the nineteenth century.[166] Frederick L. Hoffman had found elevated levels of silica-induced mortality among granite cutters in community studies conducted in 1921–1922 in Barre, Vermont.[167]

During the late 1920s and early 1930s sporadic reports of occupational silicosis began to appear more frequently, usually associated with deteriorating economic conditions, labor unrest, and public health investigations in specific industries. For example, labor unrest and union concern about workers' health in the zinc-mining region near Joplin, Missouri, led to investigations by the U.S. Public Health Service in 1927–1928 that found a 21.3 percent prevalence of the disease in miners.[168] A 1929 study of rock drilling for the New York City subway by the Columbia University School of Public Health revealed a high rate of silicosis illness and death. The reaction of New York organized labor to that study prompted the *New York Times* to run a story entitled "Silicosis Denounced as 'Murder' of Labor."[169] Beginning in that same year, a severe economic decline in the foundry industry, along with active involvement by the Moulders Union, led to the filing of numerous claims and law suits for silicosis-related death and disability.[170]

Silicosis came to national attention with the tragedy involving the construction of the Hawk's Nest Tunnel near Gauley Bridge, West Virginia, between 1930 and 1933. The history of this incident has been chronicled by Martin Cherniack in *The Hawk's Nest Incident* and will not be repeated here. At least 476 of the 5,000 workers who built that tunnel are thought to have died of silicosis, and 1,500 more became seriously ill. Initially, media coverage of the silicosis outbreak at Gauley Bridge was confined to West Virginia. However, in January 1935 the story broke nationally, prompting widespread attention over the next two years by newspapers, magazines, and even motion pictures portraying the ravages of silicosis and other dust diseases. By January 1936, public concern and anger resulted in widely publicized Congressional hearings on the problem of occupational silicosis.[171]

One aspect of the silicosis crisis that drew particular notice was the question of how workers and their dependents could obtain financial compensation for disability or death resulting from the disease. In West Virginia, surviving workers and widows of those killed at Gauley Bridge were unable to collect remuneration under workers' compensation law because West Virginia's code did not have a provision for recognizing and compensating occupational disease. As a result, they brought actions for redress in liability suits under existing common-law doctrines of negligence. Beginning in the summer of 1932, more than five hundred liability actions were filed by West Virginia workers claiming personal damage from silicosis. Many of these cases were eventually settled out of court, with total payments made to claimants of about $200,000. In response to this incident, the West Virginia House of Delegates enacted a new provision of the state workmen's compensation law in 1935 that established specific conditions for compensating workers with silicosis.[172]

Between 1932 and 1934, similar liability actions for occupational silicosis began to migrate from the mining and tunneling industries into the general manufacturing environment. This trend was most notable in Rochester, New York, where several dozen common-law suits relating to workers' silicosis-related ailments were brought against a number of Rochester companies including General Electric, Merchants Dispatch Transportation Company, Eastman Kodak Company, and American Laundry Machinery Company.[173] Most of the suits were brought by one attorney, William L. Clay. Dr. W. S. McCann, a professor of medicine at the University of Rochester who was sympathetic to industry, claimed that Clay "had been industriously searching the lists of employees and ex-employees of a number of companies for those who had died of tuberculosis or other pulmonary diseases, or for those who were in tuberculosis sanatoria, and later for those who might be expected to have silicosis."[174]

Industry and their insurance carriers panicked. They saw the potential in these suits for an unbridled wave of similar actions throughout New York and the rest of the country, and feared that the economic losses would be substantial. Juries and the public had understandable sympathy for unemployed and disabled workers due to the general hardships brought about by the Depression. Because these were tort actions brought at common law, industry and insurers lost all protection afforded under the schedules and other restrictions incorporated into the workers' compensation system.

One result of this concern was the quick out-of-court settlement of most of the Rochester silicosis cases for sums ranging from $2,000 to $6,000.[175] Another result was a strong call by representatives of insurance companies and industry for the integration of silicosis into the existing state workers' compensation system.[176] Industry felt that subsuming these cases under the system provided an opportunity to exercise greater control over the grounds for compensation.

As of 1930, only eleven states had specific occupational disease provisions within their workers' compensation code. In five states (New York, Ohio, Illinois, Minnesota, and New Jersey), a schedule of recognized occupational diseases limited compensation exclusively to diseases that were on the list. As of 1930, none of those states had recognized silicosis as a compensable occupational disease. In six other states (Wisconsin, North Dakota, California, Connecticut, Massachusetts, and Missouri) a "blanket" occupational disease provision allowed for the compensation of any disease found to be caused by work.

The occupational disease crisis created by the influx of silicosis claims in the early 1930s precipitated an intense reexamination of the goals and assumptions of the workers' compensation system. As Markowitz and Rosner point out, significant questions were raised during this period that challenged traditional notions about the scope and purpose of workers' compensation and the conception of work-related disease. Key new issues concerned the medical basis for distinguishing health problems related to work from those that are not, the role of the workers' compensation system in addressing chronic conditions whose symptoms could appear years after exposure, and whether compensation should be awarded based solely upon the diagnosis of an underlying pathologic condition.[177]

The resolution of these questions during the mid-1930s led to a reformulation of the workers' compensation system. In New York, a new compensation law containing blanket coverage for occupational diseases was enacted in September 1935 with the broad support of industry, labor, and insurance carriers. That support soon dissipated due to increased insurance costs, insurer demands that employees be screened for pre-existing disease, and labor fears about the potential for job losses. As a result, nine months later an amended workers' compensation act tightened eligibility criteria, making it virtually impossible to obtain compensation for any but the most serious and disabling cases of silicosis. This law eliminated civil liability actions for work-related silicosis (since workers' compensation was the exclusive legal remedy for a scheduled occupational disease) and effectively suppressed large-scale payments for the disorder (due to the restrictive criteria and low benefits allowed). Similar laws were soon enacted in a number of other states.[178]

Though silicosis itself was defined in a restrictive fashion by these new laws, the result of the debate inspired by the silicosis crisis was an overall liberalization of the compensation system and a greater recognition of disorders with indistinct etiology and variable latency. For example, in the three years after passage of the amended workers' compensation law, the number of compensated occupational diseases in New York rose steadily from 984 cases in 1936 to 1,522 in 1939 (an increase of 54.7 percent), at the same time that all workers' compensation claims rose only 2.5 percent.[179]

This liberalization of the compensation system laid the groundwork for the increasing acceptance during the latter 1930s of other nontraumatic disorders, of conditions that did not have a clear causal mechanism linking exposure, pathology and symptoms, and of chronic ailments that were not specific to a particular occupation. For example, during the same three-year period (1936–1939), compensable claims in New York for strains from handling (predominantly back strains) rose by 14.6 percent (from 9,386 cases in 1936 to 10,759 in 1939), about six times as great as the growth in all claims.[180]

The liberalization of state compensation systems that occurred in response to silicosis and other occupational diseases helped pave the way for the expanded acceptance of back pain cases that became more common after the mid-1930s. The broader definition of compensable work-related ailments resulting from the debates of the early 1930s had implications that were equally applicable to cases of back pain, for which there was often correspondingly strong (or stronger) diagnostic criteria, X-ray documentation, a plausible underlying pathology, and evidence for a causal linkage with work conditions.

Moreover, medical discussions about back pain cases in the workers' compensation system during the late 1930s began to be cast in terms of some of the same practical and theoretical considerations that had framed the occupational disease debate several years earlier. For example, a major consideration for both was the existence of appropriate X-ray evidence and the ability of physicians to interpret those X rays properly.

As in the case of silicosis, the integration of back pain into the workers' compensation system afforded industry and insurance companies with protection against the unpredictable and often arbitrary awards that could result if actions for compensation were brought through common-law suits. Insurance, business, and governmental representatives had been scared sufficiently by the silicosis crisis of the early 1930s and by the effects of the Depression that when the influx of new back pain and "ruptured disc" cases expanded after 1934, there was little resistance to considering these cases as legitimate work-related disorders and incorporating them into the established workers' compensation process.

Social Legislation and the Depression

The overriding social determinant of the 1930s was the Great Depression. Developments in social legislation, including the workers' compensation system, must be seen within the context of responses to the hardships that the Depression created. By 1931, the nation's economy had essentially collapsed. Between thirteen and fifteen million workers had lost their jobs. Economic misery among the aged, sick, disabled, and other members of the traditional lower classes now extended to a vast number of ordinary middle-class citizens and workers, as well.

By 1933, in response to the economic chaos and Herbert Hoover's failure to take effective responsive action, there was growing public recognition of the need to enact new social legislation at both the state and federal levels to assist the needy. There was also a greater public sympathy during the mid-1930s for expansion of the workers' compensation systems to cover an increasing array of diseases. With despair and misery rampant, it would have seemed merciless to deny "disabled" workers the relief that was available under workers' compensation provisions.

The New Deal legislation, introduced by Franklin Roosevelt upon becoming president, was in keeping with this spirit. According to Walter Trattner, Roosevelt "placed unemployment in the same category as old age, widowhood, and industrial accidents—hazards over which the individual had no control."[181] As governor of New York, Roosevelt had introduced the State Unemployment Relief Act (the Wickes Act) in 1931, the first state legislation to provide unemployment relief. His state labor secretary at that time was Frances Perkins, who later became the U.S. Secretary of Labor. While in New York, Perkins was heavily involved in the state's workers' compensation movement and was an outspoken advocate for extending the occupational disease benefits in the workers' compensation act.[182]

In this vein, the expansion and liberalization of the workers' compensation system during the mid-1930s in New York and elsewhere can be seen as a response to the need for increased social welfare legislation in keeping with the New Deal programs of Roosevelt, Perkins, and other reformers. The state workers' compensation systems were viewed by many progressive thinkers as an important component in the nation's emerging social welfare system.

There was a widespread understanding that the diagnosis of a work-induced disablement provided one means for attaining a rudimentary level of financial security. This function of workers' compensation was noted by such social reformers as Bailey Burritt, general director of the New York Association for Improving the Condition of the Poor, who wrote, "Workmen's compensation is recognized as a family welfare provision." He further noted: "The protection of the economic and social unit of the family through suitable [workers'] compensation awards, instead of proving to be paternalistic and undermining family initiative and morale, is proving itself to be a wise extension of the power of the state to protect its families from economic disaster and make them again, at an early date, independent productive family units."[183]

Anthony Bale has pointed to the very high percentage of unemployed workers who were submitting claims for occupational silicosis in the early 1930s as an indication that compensation for occupational disease was being used as a method for unemployment relief during the Depression. Bale argues that "unemployed workers were filing workers' compensation claims for their disabilities, hoping to receive some income for earning capacity lost in a depression labor market where their previous employment made it even harder to get a job."[184] Rosner and Markowitz make essentially the same point: "Employed workers, fearful of losing their jobs during the Depression, hesitated to report their symptoms to industrial physicians. It was only the unemployed, with nothing to lose, who agitated for recognition of silicosis as a compensable disease."[185]

This recognition that compensation for work-related disease served as one mechanism for obtaining economic relief during the Depression extended to physicians treating back disorders. For example, in a 1937 article entitled "The Compensation Aspects of Low-Back Conditions," Howard Prince, a New York orthopedic surgeon, offered the following perspective: "The compensation case [of back pain] is often influenced by . . . economic conditions. Think of the strain on an injured man's ethics during the past seven years when to get well meant to give up compensation and become jobless! We all saw how hard it was to get the better placed individual off a paying accident policy."[186]

Conservatives were aware of these trends and reacted against them. Markowitz and Rosner provide the following example: "F. Robertson Jones, General Manager of the Association of Casualty and Surety Executives, summarized the fear and the political goals of the insurance industry which worried that workers' compensation would become a tool of reformers seeking to shift the costs of social welfare benefits for unemployment from the public to the private sector: 'The chief trouble today is that we have confused compensation with relief. If we can keep these two ideas separate and can restrict the tendency to turn the compensation system into a universal pension system having no particular relation to employment, we shall have accomplished something.'"[187]

Henry D. Sayer, the former New York Industrial Commissioner, criticized the proposed expansion of New York's occupational disease statute in January 1934:

> Why should we set up a separate, specific class of persons to whom industry shall pay pensions or death benefits, merely because these persons happened to have been working, and after some event has happened, or some illness contracted, a clever doctor and a clever lawyer assume to bring the facts within the scope of your all-inclusive occupational disease provision? That is what we face. We face health insurance; not health insurance by direction, and not health insurance by specific enactment, but by indirection; and we are going to try to take the compensation dollar and divide it up and say, "This much of it shall go for health insurance." That is what it comes down to in the last analysis.[188]

Despite these objections, the workers' compensation systems did undergo further expansion and liberalization at the same time that additional New Deal social legislation was being introduced nationally. This development coincided with the increased reporting of ruptured discs and other occupational back injuries. The gradual expansion of government assistance programs throughout the late 1930s provided a receptive atmosphere for considering these cases to be work-related. Back pain had long been recognized as a common and debilitating disorder, particularly prevalent among manual workers. Within the prevailing framework of expanded social legislation and the growth of government-sponsored economic assistance programs for workers, the disabled, and the unemployed, it was natural for physicians and workers' compensation administrators during the late 1930s and 1940s to react sympathetically to reports of occupational back pain, even if the etiology of the pain was nonspecific or the medical diagnosis uncertain.

The Growth of Orthopedics As a Specialization
The story of the emergence of back pain as a major occupational health problem during the twentieth century is inexorably linked to the correspond-

ing expansion that took place in orthopedic surgery as a field of professional specialization. The ascent of orthopedic surgery in the early part of this century was fostered by the growth of industrial back pain, and vice versa. After 1934, orthopedic surgeons became vocal champions of the ruptured disc model. The discovery by Mixter and Barr was perceived as vindicating many long-held orthopedic doctrines concerning the role of trauma in producing musculoskeletal pain and the primacy of surgical intervention and immobilization as effective modes of therapy. The evolution of the orthopedic specialty in America was particularly rapid in the years between World War I and World War II. The timing of Mixter and Barr's discovery occurred at exactly the right moment to play a decisive role in its growth.

The term *orthopedics* was first coined by the French physician, Nicholas Andry in 1741. It is derived from two Greek words, *orthos* (straight) and *paidios* (child), indicating a focus on the treatment of the congenital deformities of children, the subject of Andry's 1741 book entitled *To Prevent and Correct Deformities of the Body in Children: All By Means Available to Fathers and Mothers and to Everyone Concerned in the Upbringing of Children.*[189]

For the next hundred and fifty years, the practice of orthopedics continued to be limited primarily to the treatment of congenital skeletal deformities of childhood and a few other disabilities of the locomotor system such as tuberculosis of the hip or spine. Two developments at the end of the nineteenth century enlarged this focus. One was Roentgen's discovery of X rays in 1895 which, for the first time, allowed for the noninvasive visualization of the skeletal structure. The other was the refinement of the techniques of general surgery, which grew out of the discoveries of ether anesthesia (W. T. G. Morton, 1846), postoperative antisepsis (J. Lister, 1865), and plaster bandages for immobilization (A. Mathijsen, 1852). By the turn of the century, surgery for correction of musculoskeletal abnormalities became a practical therapeutic alternative. With it came a drive by orthopedists to apply surgical techniques to such common deformities as congenital dislocation of the hip, congenital clubfoot, spastic paralyses, tendon transplants, and the internal fixation of fractures that may occur through trauma.[190]

The other major event that stimulated the modern growth of orthopedics was the unparalleled number of traumatic injuries during World War I. The proliferation of serious wounds, fractures, and amputations required the recruitment and training of many surgeons specializing in musculoskeletal trauma. Following the war, orthopedists like Robert Osgood of Harvard Medical School, who had been a lieutenant colonel in the Marines, saw industrial back pain as fertile ground for applying surgical techniques developed during the conflict. In an address to the 1919 convention of the American Association of Industrial Physicians and Surgeons, Osgood likened back strain to the combat injuries he had treated as a military surgeon several years earlier:

> The specialty I represent appreciates deeply the opportunity of participating in your scientific sessions. Orthopedic surgeons serving with the A.E.F. [American Expeditionary Forces] were trusted with the working out of certain problems. These problems, roughly speaking, were the lesions of the extremities and spinal column, both pre-combat and post combat. Greatly helped by this experience, the specialty is eager to be of more service in peace, convinced that there is no essential difference between certain static and traumatic conditions of civil life and the lesions of the extremities and spinal column which result from pre-combat and combat army life. Perhaps the majority of these lesions in civil life are the results of industrial conditions and industrial accidents. No symptoms are more common, none are less intelligently treated, than those grouped under the term of "Back Strain."[191]

A similar sentiment was expressed in 1919 by Dr. Charles Parker of Chicago to the editor of the *American Journal of Orthopaedic Surgery*: "This is truly the era of orthopedic surgery and the enormous impetus given it by war practice is certain to be reflected in civil practice with results of inestimable value to the multitude of potential cripples constantly repleted from the vast army of citizens engaged in the peaceful pursuits of our normal industrial life."[192] Sixteen years later, John D. Ellis, an orthopedic surgeon from Memphis, Tennessee, was able to claim that Parker's prediction had come true—orthopedic techniques originally developed during World War I had been successfully transferred to the treatment of work-related disabilities: "The surgical experiences of the war and the experiences under [workers'] compensation administration have so overlapped, because the war occurred in the same decade during which compensation legislation was enacted in America, that the improvements in the surgery of injury resulting from the former cannot always be distinguished from those of the latter."[193]

In the years following World War I, orthopedists strove to expand their influence and control over the treatment of fractures and other traumatic injuries.[194] As pointed out by Allan and Waddell, the campaign by orthopedists to broaden the scope of their professional authority stemmed in part from a decline in the incidence of tuberculosis and congenital deformities, which had previously constituted the bulk of the orthopedists' practice.[195] According to British orthopedist Sir Harry Platt, the campaign to expand orthopedists' control over traumatic injuries was waged with intensity: "In the years between the wars the field of orthopaedics was to those of us then young an expanding universe, and we fought the battle for control of fractures with gusto. . . . Our opponents [usually the general surgeons] often accused us of adopting the attitude of the German philosopher Nietzsche— 'that a good fight sanctifies a cause.'"[196]

Similar confrontations arose in the United States. In an account of the modern history of their specialty (written in 1957), several orthopedic surgeons from Massachusetts General Hospital observed, "The broad concept of the scope of orthopedics has not evolved without causing the specialty to experience its share of growing pains. Its followers have been involved in struggles with general surgeons, neurologic surgeons, internists and physiatrists over such questions as who should treat fractures, operate on intervertebral-disk lesions, perform amputations, treat patients convalescing from poliomyelitis and repair severed tendons in the hand. These struggles have at times been bitterly waged."[197] To help enhance their stature and professional identity, several new professional societies were established during that period, including the British Orthopaedic Association in 1918, the American Academy of Orthopedic Surgeons in 1933, and the American Board of Orthopedic Surgery in 1934.

One of the primary issues defining this professional quarrel involved the appropriate means of treating musculoskeletal ailments. A fundamental tenet of the orthopedists was the primacy of rest and immobilization as therapeutic approaches in the management of joint disease. This view stemmed from the pioneering theoretical work of Hugh Owen Thomas in the 1870s and his student (and nephew), Sir Robert Jones, in the early twentieth century. According to this "classic" orthopedic theory, many musculoskeletal disorders were understood as manifestations of bodily reaction to trauma, both acute trauma as occurs in war, as well as the cumulative effect of minor traumas that may occur in civilian life. The principle of enforced rest was based on a perceived need to allow the body time to heal from such traumatic insult. The orthopedists' therapeutic approach was set in opposition to that of the bone-setters—traditional folk healers who, from the mid-1600s to about 1850, treated musculoskeletal disorders with manipulation and exercise.

Consequently, it was in the professional and economic interest of orthopedists for various musculoskeletal disorders to be identified as manifestations of trauma that required treatment in line with the "classic" orthopedic remedy of surgery to correct "deformities," followed by enforced rest. The identification in 1934 of the "ruptured" intervertebral disc by Mixter and Barr and the allegedly successful amelioration of that condition by corrective surgery thus provided to many physicians a crowning vindication of the orthopedic approach. Members of that profession quickly struck a claim of authority over the diagnosis and treatment of the newly discovered syndrome.

Beginning in the late 1930s and continuing through the 1940s, surgery for the removal of ruptured discs flourished. Between 1935 and 1960 more than a million disc excisions were performed, many by leading orthopedists such as Barr, DePalma, and Young.[198] By 1938, one hundred operations for treatment of ruptured intervertebral discs had been performed at the Mayo clinic. By 1950, the number had grown to more than two thousand.[199] Historians have labeled the period between 1938 and the mid-1950s the "dynasty of the disc."[200] A number of writers have commented on the "overenthusiasm" and "over-surgery" during these years.[201]

Evidence began to accumulate between 1950 and 1960 that dampened some of the excitement for surgical intervention. Controlled studies showed there to be a high rate of misdiagnosis and failed surgeries.[202] Despite the potential dangers and ineffectiveness, operations for ruptured discs are still one of the most frequently performed surgical procedures in the United States. Recent estimates are that approximately 3 percent of the American adult population has had low back surgery, with over 250,000 lumbar spine operations performed each year.[203]

The incidence of occupational back pain is still on the rise. Between 1971 and 1981 in the United States, the number of persons disabled due to back pain increased four times faster than the growth rate of the general population.[204] For all the attention it has received during the past hundred years, occupational back pain remains a medical enigma, without a precise cause or cure. The concepts that dominated the debates about railway spine—trauma, injury, pathology, and malingering—still dominate contemporary discussions of this topic, as do the "hidden" underlying themes of corporate culpability and responsibility for disabled workers.

Summary

Various social, economic, and political factors in the history of occupational back pain contributed to its emergence and eventual growth as a work-related disorder. They are summarized below.

1. It is significant that back pain arose first as a major health issue in connection with claims for damages against railroad companies. This thrust the issue of back pain into a broader social debate about the ramifications of the new industrial economy and perceived domination over everyday life by the powerful new capitalist elite. The subject of whether pain ought to be compensated thus became part of a larger question concerning the limits of corporate control and the methods at the disposal of the common person to seek retribution for grievances against alleged wrongdoing by the industrialists.

The legacy of railway spine continued to exert its influence in the early twentieth century when the matter of back pain re-emerged after the introduction of institutionalized government-sponsored insurance programs for the compensation of workers. In both cases, physicians, management, and workers were apt to cast their judgments about the occurrence and legitimacy of back pain in the context of a dialogue characterized by mistrust, accusations, and class conflict. In this respect, the "disease" of back pain became a primary metaphor for a larger social need to assign culpability for human suffering in modern industrial society.

2. The history of railway spine provides an example of how occupational hazards often first receive attention after being perceived as environmental risks potentially affecting the entire community. In this case, new ideas about back injuries arose in the course of medical investigation into the dangers of rail travel, sparked by intense concern from the traveling public. New disease concepts were formulated (for example, railway spine) embodying the notion that back pain can result from spinal injury following repeated minor trauma as well as from severe impacts. Medical discussion about back pain began to be couched in the context of legal debates about the appropriate extent of corporate liability and financial compensation for victims of industrial accidents.

As indicated earlier, there were a number of reasons why heightened public awareness about railway spine during the nineteenth century did not translate immediately into a significant reporting of back injuries by railway workers. However, after enactment of workers' compensation legislation, many of these same issues and medical concepts surfaced in claims for occupational back pain. Public reaction to what was perceived originally as a risk to the community thus laid the foundation for the subsequent recognition of similar traumatic disorders arising in the workplace.

In this respect, the history of back pain is somewhat similar to that of other modern occupational disorders that first gained widespread notice through public reaction to environmental hazards. One recent example, chronicled by Paul Brodeur in *Expendable Americans,* involved asbestos contamination of the public water supply in Duluth, Minnesota, in 1973. In that episode, community alarm was a key factor in bringing to national attention the health hazards of asbestos, which prompted subsequent government intervention to protect workers in asbestos-processing facilities.[205]

3. The history of back pain also exemplifies some of the modern notions of the importance of variations in risk perception. For example, according to the contemporary findings of researchers including Paul Slovic and William Lowrance, individuals are apt to be more concerned with hazards that are perceived to be beyond their control and whose consequences are perceived

to be potentially catastrophic in scale.[206] These findings help to explain why, in the mid-nineteenth century, the public began to attach a degree of importance to a disorder (back pain) that had formerly been considered a relatively minor rheumatic ailment generally analogous to the common cold. When back pain began to be associated with railway disasters, the public began to perceive it as a potential threat arising from the use of technologies that were not within their personal control and that could cause sudden calamities with massive casualties. According to modern theories of risk perception, it is thus not surprising that back pain emerged abruptly as a major health concern during the mid-1800s.

4. With respect to labor activism, the ASRS and other railway unions attempted to arouse public concern over rail safety as a means of achieving specific goals involving wages and working hours. In that limited sense, labor activism could be said to have had an indirect influence in stimulating the emergence of occupational back pain. However, the issue of employee back injuries per se was notably absent from the labor actions of the nineteenth century. This lack of attention was a function of the weak position of labor relative to management, fears of reprisal, preoccupation with more serious injuries, and the campaign for shorter hours and increased job security.

Railway workers in the United States and Britain were chief proponents of the elimination of the traditional common-law employer defenses (fellow servant, assumption of risk, contributory negligence) and so helped spark the enactment of early employer liability and workers' compensation statutes. And thus, to the extent that the passage of workers' compensation laws influenced the growth of occupationally related back pain, labor activism contributed to the emergence of that disorder. But here again, the influence of the labor movement on the growth of occupational back pain would appear to have been at most indirect and limited in importance.

5. In reaction to a variety of political and economic factors, workers' compensation programs were put into place throughout Europe and the United States between 1884 and 1915. These laws were highly influential in stimulating the expanded reporting and diagnosis of occupational back pain, in part by broadening and liberalizing the criteria for reporting of work disability. The establishment of compulsory reporting for occupation-induced disability also led to the accumulation of better statistical data portraying the types and causes of injuries suffered by workers. The manner in which these reports were compiled and categorized helped bring certain important trends to the attention of safety experts and physicians, including the suspected relationship between the performance of materials handling activities at work and the onset of back pain.

The passage of workers' compensation laws in the early twentieth century also proved to be very important in stimulating a medical redefinition of common back pain away from the traditional idea of rheumatism to a new concentration on back injuries, back strains, and other conditions that were deemed to be the result of trauma. This redefinition was related in part to the statutory requirement for compensable work-related disorders to be "injuries," attributable to a discrete traumatic event happening at a specified time and place.

In addition, the outbreak of World War I shortly after passage of the world's major workers' compensation laws, also helped focus medical attention on the issue of trauma, increasing awareness of both major and minor trauma as a root cause of many disorders whose origin had been previously considered obscure.

It is interesting to note a difference in the importance of workers' compensation laws for the emergence of the modern notion of occupationally induced back pain compared to other musculoskeletal disorders. For example, while occupational back pain never emerged as a major issue before the adoption of workers' compensation statutes, the same cannot be said for cumulative trauma disorders of the hands and wrists. A large incidence of writers' cramp and telegraphists' cramp arose well before any institutionalized scheme for the compensation of workers. In the case of cumulative trauma disorders, it does not appear that the compensability of the condition was essential for its medical recognition. However, the history of the growth of occupationally related back pain *does* seem to have been closely connected to issues surrounding its compensation, possibly because of its initial emergence in the context of social debate and public concern about the impact of railway travel.

6. The relative degree of the influence of compensation on the occurrence of back pain has been hotly debated since the mid-1800s. Especially in the late 1800s and early twentieth century, many claimed that a sizable proportion of reported back pain cases were actually "compensation disorders," that is, ailments that were either deliberately or subconsciously concocted in order to derive financial benefit. In response to these suspicions, the role of the physician often became one of a detective, charged with exposing the ruses of the malingerer.

I suggest that the issue of malingering is symptomatic of a deep-seated mistrust between classes and differing perspectives on how and where to fix blame for industrial mishaps. The campaign to interpret industrial back pain as a form of psychoneurotic behavior reflects these underlying social dynamics. By the late 1920s, this campaign threatened to redefine nonspecific back pain as a psychological (rather than a medical) abnormality and thus to disparage it as a subject for legitimate scientific inquiry, in the same manner as it had railway spine, irritable spine, and occupational neuroses of the hands and wrists.

But the history of industrial back pain did not evolve in this way. The turning point came in 1934 with the development of the ruptured disc model by Mixter and Barr, along with the subsequent empirical support that was provided for that model. Mixter and Barr identified a specific demonstrable anatomic lesion and claimed that the lesion was responsible for a large amount of severe back pain previously considered to be idiopathic. Whether these hypotheses were true or not, back pain could no longer be flippantly dismissed as a hysterical neurosis—science had found a way of "proving" that the pain was not all in the heads of deceitful workers.

7. The proponents of the ruptured disc theory went even further in asserting that the lesion was traumatic in origin, and they used the phrases "rupture" and "herniation" to drive home that point. As we have seen, this conclusion was not necessarily based on sound epidemiologic or biomechanical evidence, but rather stemmed from certain a priori assumptions and social perspectives, including the belief that the preponderance of male surgical patients was indicative of traumatic etiology. Despite this shaky foundation, the conception of the traumatic nature of disc lesions took hold and, as emphasized by Hadler, proved to be instrumental in subsequent medico-legal debates about the compensability of back pain within the state workers' compensation programs.

But, in contrast to Hadler's views, the ruptured disc model was not the only factor that promoted increased recognition of back pain as an occupational disorder during the twentieth century. Other social and economic influences included the demand for social welfare assistance to relieve hardships caused by the Great Depression, the liberalization of criteria for work-related compensability of occupational diseases based on public reaction to the silicosis crisis, and the expansion of orthopedics as a surgical specialty.

8. One of the perceived social and political priorities in the 1930s was the need to broaden public assistance given to workers who were unemployed or displaced because of the economic hardships of the Great Depression. This manifested itself in the establishment of new welfare schemes for the compensation of workers and an increased sympathy for workers who were disabled due to disorders that were allegedly work-related. The reformers of the time saw workers' compensation as one of several available methods to provide assistance to needy workers. And this led to an increased acceptance and recognition of many allegedly job-induced disorders whose cause had previously been considered indistinct or vague.

Back pain became a primary example. Just as public sentiment directed against early claimants seeking compensation for railway spine influenced the chances for recovery under the Campbell Act, so the expression of public sympathy for the economic plight of the disabled worker contributed to the growth and acceptance of occupational back pain in the 1930s.

9. During that same period, the country was shocked by the sensational tragedy of silicosis poisoning that had occurred to workers building the Hawk's Nest tunnel in West Virginia. Media attention heightened public reaction to this disaster, and helped expose the underlying social prejudices that prompted this blatant disregard for workers' health. Along with those from the Hawk's Nest calamity, thousands of similar silicosis claims emerged (many in foundries and other industrial settings), frequently submitted by workers who had been laid off because of the depressed economy.

Because diseases like silicosis were not automatically included in the schedules of most state workers' compensation plans, a large number of the silicosis claims were filed as liability actions under common law. The success of many of these suits alarmed employers and insurance companies, who saw in these judgments potentially huge financial losses as similar suits were filed nationwide. Their reaction was to lobby vigorously for the assumption of these diseases under the state workers' compensation systems, as a method for controlling costs and making judgments more predictable.

Ultimately, the compensation system became more liberalized, with expanded acceptance of disorders that did not easily fit into the previous definition of "injuries" by "accident." These changes in the state workers' compensation laws, occurring at about the same time as Mixter and Barr's development of the ruptured disc theory, resulted in a more receptive legal environment for the inclusion of claims for disorders of the back. This also contributed to the growth of back pain as a recognized occupational disorder in the years following 1934.

10. Finally, there was a deliberate campaign between the wars to expand the domain of the orthopedic specialty. It was in the interests of orthopedists for back pain and other musculoskeletal disorders to be interpreted as manifestations of trauma, particularly the type of repeated minor trauma that is common in the working environment. That specialty thus stood to benefit from the frequent diagnosis and surgical treatment of work-induced traumatic back pain. The reported incidence of work-related back pain grew as the orthopedic specialty successfully attained prominence in American medicine.

In addition, the orthopedic principle of immobilization and rest as a preferred therapeutic approach helped bring work "disability" to medical prominence, and as argued by Allan and Waddell, Hadler, and other contemporary scholars, elevated back pain "disability" to the status of a specific medical "disorder" or "syndrome." The modern concept of occupational back pain is thus closely tied to the orthopedic viewpoint. It is still the case that work-induced back pain as a specific diagnostic entity derives much of its legitimacy from the authority of the orthopedic perspective in modern medical practice.

There is now a widespread recognition that prolonged exposure to noise can permanently damage one's hearing ability. In fact, some contemporary authorities have suggested that noise-induced hearing loss (NIHL) is the most common of all occupational disorders. According to otologists Robert and Joseph Sataloff (1993), "Hearing loss due to occupational noise exposure is our most prevalent industrial malady." They estimated in 1987 that there were about eight million people with occupational hearing loss in American industry.[1] Dr. P. W. Alberti, professor of occupational medicine at the University of Toronto, agrees: "Noise is the most ubiquitous of industrial pollutants; there are others more dangerous but none so widespread. Occupational noise is the most common single cause of hearing loss in the developed nations of the world."[2]

If this is true, then the scope of occupational NIHL is potentially enormous, since hearing loss (from all sources) is among the most prevalent medical disorders. Dr. Howard House estimates that "Hearing impairment affects one of ten people in the United States, making it more common than cancer, heart disease, nephritis, diabetes, and stroke put together." The Sataloffs claim that, as of 1993, more than forty million Americans suffer from this condition.[3] The same sentiment has been echoed in the popular press and various technical journals. *Science News* calls noise "the most widespread hazard facing American workers." Headlines in *National Safety and Health News* label NIHL the "major issue facing today's industry."[4]

Reports by U.S. Government agencies lend support to these views. The National Institute for Occupational Safety and Health (NIOSH) has estimated that more than 14 percent of production workers in manufacturing are exposed to levels of industrial noise in excess of the OSHA-permissible exposure limit of 90 decibels (dB) as an eight-hour time weighted average.[5] The final regulatory analysis for OSHA's Hearing Conservation Amendment estimated that "at least one million workers in manufacturing have sustained job-related hearing impairment."[6] Using data collected in the National Health Interview Surveys, the U.S. Centers for Disease Control (CDC) found that 3.2 percent of workers report some degree of hearing loss. Moreover, the CDC discovered a clear dose-response relationship, with a considerably higher level of hearing loss reported by workers having "heavy occupational exposure" to noise.[7] According to the U.S. Environmental Protection Agency (EPA), NIHL accounts for about 28 percent of all reported occupational diseases.[8] Based on reports such as these, NIOSH has officially classified NIHL as one of the nation's ten leading work-related diseases and injuries.[9]

As the awareness of the dangers of job-related noise exposure has grown, workers' compensation claims for noise-induced hearing loss have also emerged as a significant potential problem for American business. All state workers' compensation codes now recognize NIHL as a potentially compensable condition. In 1979, the EPA projected that the cost of workers' compensation claims for NIHL would total more than $800 million for the period 1978–1987.[10] Claims data for 1987–1990 indicate that the average cost of a NIHL claim is $5,330.[11] Alleyne et al. (1989), using Canadian data, found that the average cost per NIHL claim was $14,106 in 1983.[12] There have been some isolated workers' compensation claims for NIHL that exceeded $300,000.[13]

Although compensation for NIHL is now common, there were very few workers' compensation claims for NIHL prior to World War II. In fact, general awareness about the compensability of this condition seems to have developed only after several well-publicized court decisions in the late 1940s and early 1950s. Prior to that time, workers' compensation was awarded only in instances of work-related hearing loss attributable to a single, specifiable traumatic incident such as an explosion or fall. There was little recognition in the workers' compensation system of hearing loss that developed gradually over years of exposure to noises that were loud, but not necessarily painful or traumatic.

In this chapter, I shall explore the history of noise-induced hearing loss to show how this disorder originally emerged as a major occupational health problem.[14] The attempt to define noise-induced hearing loss has been a dynamic, evolving process that has brought about fundamental changes in the way the health profession views the concepts of disability, impairment, and the meaning of occupational disease. The emergence of compensation claims for NIHL after World War II challenged the original intent of the workers' compensation system, stimulating the development of a new conception of NIHL that focused on impairment of sensory function rather than social or work disability. Driving these developments were the actions of organized labor, community concern about environmental noise exposure, business attempts to profit from the growth of NIHL, and employers' legal efforts to limit the economic consequences of this occupational disorder.

Historical Background

Early History

Noise is now so much a part of daily experience that it is difficult to conceive of the time long before the Industrial Revolution when sources of loud noise were uncommon, limited primarily to specific occupational and military activities. Of course, even before the development of any modern technology, people were aware of the sounds emanating from natural sources: the crash of thunder, the rush of wind, the pounding hoofs from a herd of animals. And human sources of noise have always been part of our daily lives: the cry of a baby, a loud shout, and the din from a large crowd. Very early in the human experience, ways of amplifying the human voice were discovered, such as the blowing of a ram's horn as a signal that could be heard for long distances.

But even these natural sounds can have damaging and irritating effects that have been long recognized. Physicians have known for many years that temporary or permanent loss of hearing can result from thunder.[15] In the first century C.E., Pliny the Elder, in his *Natural History,* observed that persons living near one of the larger cataracts of the Nile became hard of hearing.[16] An ancient law in England, in effect until Victorian times, prohibited the beating of wives by their husbands between dusk and dawn, not because of any moral considerations, but rather to keep the noise from disturbing neighbors.[17] The enormous power of sound was also chronicled in many early writings, such as the biblical story of Joshua's trumpet blasts that shattered the walls of Jericho, and the accounts of the great horn of Alexander, which could summon soldiers ten miles away.[18]

One of the earliest and best-known cases of occupationally induced hearing loss was described in *The Hunchback of Notre Dame*. In that novel, set in France of 1482, Victor Hugo recounts the tale of Quasimodo, the church bell-ringer who, at the age of fourteen, was deafened by ringing of the massive bells. Much later, in 1962, A. Bruusgaard investigated and documented "bellringer's deafness," which occurs after ten to fifteen years in those performing as little as twenty-five minutes of bell ringing each week.[19]

Metalworking

To a great extent, the history of occupational noise exposure corresponds to the history of technological advances. As Dan McKensie wrote in 1916, "Civilization is noise."[20] There is evidence that the first major impact of noise on workers occurred with the discovery of the use of metals during the Bronze Age and the Iron Age. Ward (1973) cites the example of the Sybarites, in ancient Greece, who forbade metalwork involving hammering (and also the keeping of roosters) within their city limits.[21] Ecclesiasticus describes the "smith sitting by the anvil, the noise of the hammer and the anvil is ever in his ears—without these cannot a city be inhabited" (6:12). Martial, in the first century C.E., commenting on the noise of ancient Rome, observed that "blacksmiths with their hammer notes, keep up their din the whole day long."[22]

The earliest specific reference to the potentially dangerous effect of metalworking on hearing can be found in the *Regimen Sanitatis Salernitatum,* a medieval treatise in which the physicians of the medical school of Salerno noted:

Our hearing is a choice and dainty sense,
And hard to mend, yet soon it may be marred,
Blows, falls, and noise, all these, as is by sundry proofs appearing,
Breed tingling in the ears, and hurt our hearing.[23]

Ramazzini, the father of occupational medicine, observed in 1713 that coppersmiths became hard of hearing due to the continual din of hammering the metal, and that if they grew old at this work, they become completely deaf.[24] In 1765, Nils Skragge also observed that coppersmiths and blacksmiths usually become hard of hearing after years of hammering.[25]

The first modern scientific study of occupationally induced hearing loss was published in 1831 by John Fosbroke in the British medical journal *Lancet*. Fosbroke was the first to attach a label to this disease entity, referring to the affliction as "blacksmiths' deafness." He describes the disorder as follows: "The blacksmiths' deafness is a consequence of their employment; it creeps on them gradually, in general at about forty or fifty years of age. At first the patient is insensible of weak impressions of sound; the deafness increases with a ringing and noise in the ears, slight vertigo, and pain in the cranial bones, periodical or otherwise, and often violent. No wax is formed. It has been imputed to a paralytic state of the nerve, occasioned by the noise of forging, by certain modern writers, and by the old writers, to permanent over-tension of the membrane, which they compare to fixed dilatation of the pupil."[26] Fosbroke's description is notable for its emphasis on the gradual onset of the disorder, which is a central component in the contemporary scientific understanding of NIHL.

The French investigator Alexandre Layet, in 1875, was one of the earliest to postulate a dose-response relationship, noting that sheet-iron workers, coppersmiths, blacksmiths, and coopers are nearly always hard of hearing and become more so the longer they remain at their trade. Layet was also one of the first to describe correctly many of the now accepted characteristics of NIHL, including the increased effect at high frequencies and the underlying pathology as a lesion to the auditory nerve.[27]

In 1881, J. Gottstein and R. Kayser measured occupational deafness among blacksmiths and metalworkers at a German railway yard, in one of the earliest examples of a cross-sectional study employing modern epidemiologic methodology.[28] In this investigation, Gottstein and Kayser compared the prevalence of hearing decrements in seventy-five smiths and metalworkers to a matched control group of thirty-six bricklayers. They found that 61 percent of the study group had hearing categorized as "bad" or "fairly bad," compared to only 5 percent of the control group. Equally important methodologically, these researchers stratified both groups by age, detecting a clear relationship between age and hearing loss in the exposed workers, but not the bricklayers. This suggested to Gottstein and Kayser that hearing loss increased with cumulative exposure to loud noise and was not merely an effect of increasing age.

By 1883, the Austrian otologist Dr. Adam Politzer felt confident enough about the medical research findings to state: "That occupations which are associated with continuous noise not only act unfavorably upon already existing affections of the ear, but cause ear-disease, is beyond doubt." Agreeing with earlier researchers, Politzer found that special dangers existed in the metal trades: "In the investigation which I undertook in regard to this with different tradesmen, I found that, next to locksmiths, coppersmiths and coopers were most affected by disturbance of hearing. Upon the latter especially, according to their own statement, the so-called hohow stroke when hooping the casks is said to have such a deafening effect, that most of them, if they remain at their trade, become hard of hearing in time."[29]

Military Weaponry and Explosives

In addition to metal hammering and forging, the other major source of occupational noise prior to the Industrial Revolution was gunpowder, which was introduced to Europe about 1300. Unlike metalsmithing, the damaging effects of gunpowder on hearing were usually sudden and traumatic. In 1591 Alberti first mentioned the danger of deafness from cannonading.[30] Admiral Lord Rodney was recorded as being deaf for fourteen days following the discharge of eighty broadsides from his flagship in 1782. During the Battle of Copenhagen in 1801, an officer of Lord Nelson's fleet became permanently deafened by cannon fire.[31] D. J. Glibert (1921), citing De Merrys, reports on the particularly damaging effects to sailors who served in ironclads during the nineteenth century (twenty-four hours after a sea battle many men complained of headache, loss of memory, and deafness).[32]

William Dalby reports an instance of an officer who was discharged for deafness during the Crimean War (1853–1856). He was standing beside a mortar that fired unexpectedly, causing rupture of his tympanic membrane.[33] This may be one of the earliest recorded references of somebody losing his or her job due to occupationally induced hearing loss.

The history of NIHL provides an excellent example of how medical concern about possible occupational hazards is often first stimulated by military conflicts. There are a number of reasons for this. The need to have physically qualified personnel in their ranks has forced the military to establish routine medical testing and surveillance programs to evaluate whether their "workers" are fit for duty. It has also fostered the development and application of new methods and materials for protecting troops from known hazards. Another obvious necessity is the provision of fast and effective medical treatment for all reported casualties and impairments. A third important characteristic of military medicine is the maintenance of comprehensive accident and injury statistical records, along with the military's tradition of investigating the causes of reported incidents. A final influential feature found in the armies of most Western nations is the longstanding tradition of providing pensions for soldiers disabled during military conflicts. The need to determine eligibility for pensions has fostered scientific investigation into the relationship between the conditions encountered in combat and veterans' ensuing health problems. For all these reasons, there has often been a rapid development of medical interest in occupational hazards and a heightening of awareness about work-related disorders during and immediately following military conflicts.

These trends can be seen in the significant increase of attention given to NIHL that resulted from major wars during the past hundred years. For example, Bunch (1930) refers to the influence on medical understanding of NIHL that derived from the large number of studies conducted of hearing loss from the firing of large guns during the Spanish-American War, citing the investigations of Emerson (1898), Kipp (1898), Dench (1898), Simons (1899), Duane (1900), and Lewis (1900). World War I had an even greater effect, in part because of the massive scope of the conflict and the use of more powerful explosives at close range on large numbers of troops. The development of electronic audiometers following the war also provided new options for measuring the influence that the constant exposure to explosions and gunfire had on the ear. In the years during and immediately following World War I, major scientific studies of NIHL were conducted by Love (1916), Got (1916), Bryant (1917), Trible (1917), Jobson (1917), Wilson (1917), Yearsley (1917), and Guild (1918).[34]

Many fundamental concepts now firmly associated with occupationally induced hearing loss came from these investigations. For example, the initial loss of hearing acuity at the higher frequency ranges was verified and measured in the studies conducted by Lieutenant G. B. Ridout of the U.S. Naval Medical Corps.[35] Ingersoll, Yearsley, and Wilson documented the tendency for hearing loss originating from specific acoustic trauma to improve gradually after removal from the exposure.[36] The need to protect soldiers and sailors from the damaging effects of gunfire during World War I also helped stimulate the initial development of acoustic ear plugs and other personal protective devices.

After the war, many researchers began applying the newly invented electronic audiometer to the evaluation of disability incurred by veterans. One military otologist, C. H. Mitchie, advocated audiometric testing for all veterans as a more accurate means of establishing eligibility for disability pensions. Traditional medical examinations of 778 retired army officers had found that about 10 percent had hearing impairment attributable to military experiences.[37] Similar findings were made by S. W. Grimwade, who estimated that about 3 percent of naval personnel had sustained NIHL during the war.[38] Analogous concern for veterans following World War II was a major factor stimulating the initial emergence of NIHL within the workers' compensation system (see below).

Although most of the early medical references are concerned with explosives used in military situations, explosives used in mining and quarrying also posed a considerable hazard of traumatic hearing loss to workers in those trades from the eighteenth century onwards. In 1914, the chief medical inspector of factories in Belgium, D. J. Glibert, advised miners to be as far away as possible when detonating a charge so as not to injure their hearing.[39] F. H. Westmacott (1925) refers to instances of workers rupturing their eardrums from explosions in "mining, blasting and tunneling."[40]

Boilermakers' Deafness

The introduction of powered machinery during the Industrial Revolution marked the beginning of large-scale occupational noise exposure. One group that received particular attention from physicians during the nineteenth century was boilermakers. In this trade, workers often needed to crawl inside the boiler to hold rivets in place while the rivets were hammered onto the exterior. The noise produced by such work has been termed "indescribable."[41] Frequently, this work was performed by youths.[42] Several nineteenth-century writers, including Toynbee (1860), Dalby (1873), Roosa (1874), Holt (1882), Hartmann (1887), Bruhl (1892) and Field (1893), commented on the increased tendency for boilermakers to become hard of hearing.

The early investigations by American physicians D. B. St. John Roosa and E. Eugene Holt are particularly noteworthy. Based upon examinations of workers from boilermaker shops in New York and Portland, Maine, Roosa and Holt observed that, after a period of time, essentially all workers in this industry became deaf. Roosa, in 1874, was apparently the first investigator to use the term "Boiler-maker's Deafness" to describe this condition.[43] Holt employed that label in the title of his 1882 paper "Boiler-maker's Deafness and Hearing in a Noise."[44]

Holt's series included forty boilermakers, and Roosa's, eight. Roosa mentioned that his boilermakers were examined "outside of private practice." Holt explicitly credits the "Boiler-maker's Union" for sending him workers for examination—workers that he describes as "a superior class of intelligent mechanics" who "submitted themselves to the examination with a good deal of interest."[45] It is significant that the Portland, Maine, branch of the Boiler Makers' and Helpers' Protective and Benevolent Union was founded in August 1881, one year before the publication of Holt's study, during a period of national labor strength and union activism.[46] The timing of the union's referral of forty members for hearing tests by Holt indicates that it was probably one of that branch's initial actions. This episode gives an early indication of the concern about the potential damaging effects of noise displayed by boilermakers and their labor organizations, a concern that was to play an important role after World War II in the emergence of NIHL as an issue in the workers' compensation system.

In an early application of occupation-based epidemiology, British physician Thomas Barr, in 1886, compared the hearing acuity of one hundred boilermakers who worked at two shipyards in Glasgow to that of matched groups of one hundred iron-moulders, one hundred letter carriers (who also worked at the shipyards), and one hundred men with apparently "normal" hearing who did not work in this industry. He found that not one of the boiler-makers had normal hearing. In a test of their ability to detect the ticking of a watch at various distances, Barr observed that letter carriers heard the watch at an average of 79 percent of the distance at which it was perceived by the "normal" control group (which was six feet), the iron-moulders at an average of 46 percent of this distance, and the boilermakers at 9 percent of this distance.[47]

Barr, following Roosa and Holt, also adopted the term *boilermakers' deafness* to describe the pervasive hearing loss afflicting these workers. The severity of the exposure and the magnitude of the resulting impairment in this industry was perceived to be so great that until World War II, physicians referred to any case of hearing loss from prolonged exposure to excessive noise as boilermakers' deafness.[48]

The specific site and nature of the underlying anatomic pathology of boil-ermakers' deafness was initially identified by the German investigator I. Habermann (1891), who found degeneration of the organ of Corti and other nerve elements at the base of the cochlea.

Railway Travel

The subsequent history of the growth of NIHL and its recognition as a hazard in various other occupations closely parallels the history of technological advance during and after the Industrial Revolution. It is not surprising that another occupational group to receive attention from the scientific community was railway workers. In 1857 E. A. Duchesne of Paris drew attention to the possible detrimental effect of noise on the brain and nervous system of railway engine drivers.[49] German physician H. Weber expressed a similar concern in 1862.[50] Based on these early warnings, a system for compiling statistics on "diseases of the ear" was established by the German Union of Railroad Directors in 1869. These statistics revealed that about 7–8 percent of engineers and firemen on one Prussian railroad suffered from diseases of the ear between 1851 and 1864.[51] In Great Britain, Thomas Barr conducted a study in 1890 on the injurious effects of railway whistles and recommended design changes to control this source of noise. In this study, Barr cited the "multiplication of underground railways" (the construction of the subway in London) as a factor that "further accentuated this danger [of hearing loss]."[52]

The first systematic studies of NIHL in railway workers were conducted in the 1880s by German researchers responding to growing public concern about the increasing number of serious accidents and collisions on the German railways. As pointed out by Gordon Atherley and William Noble (1985), these German investigations reflected a widespread fear in the late nineteenth century that "occupation-induced deafness might lessen [the] capacity to detect warning signals, and so render the driver or stoker unsafe to drive the train, and thereby unfit for duty."[53] A similar concern had originally surfaced in 1862 in the British investigation of railway safety conducted by the Lancet Commission, which speculated that the continual noise and rattle of railway travel could lead to headache and fatigue, and thus interfere with the safe operation of the train. "The rattle and noise which accompany the progress of the train create an incessant vibration on the tympanum, and thus influence the brain through the nerve of hearing. . . . Amongst the well-known effects are—occasional dizziness, headache, sickness, and mental fatigue."[54]

As suggested earlier in connection with back pain, public anxiety about the adverse health effects of rail travel were deliberately fostered by railway workers and their trade unions as part of their general campaign to achieve higher wages and shorter working hours.

In one of these early German studies, S. Moos of Heidelberg, following the general line of reasoning suggested in the Lancet Commission report, traced the hearing difficulties of engine drivers to the continual vibration and shaking of the train, as well as other factors, including "the repeated hissing of escaping steam, and the thousand repetitions of the scream of the whistle." In 1880 Moos reported on ten cases of hearing loss among railway engineers and firemen, concluding that this form of acquired deafness posed a significant danger to the traveling public. Moos assessed the level of risk to be "more dangerous than color-blindness" insofar as hearing loss can develop gradually and insidiously after an engineer has been on duty for many years. Moos also was one of the first medical researchers to observe that the victim of NIHL is often initially unaware of a hearing defect. In Moos' opinion, this "hidden disorder" created additional special dangers for those traveling by rail.[55] Moos proposed that ear examinations conducted by qualified otologists be provided to all engineers and firemen as a prerequisite for certifying them physically fit for duty: "The ears should be examined very carefully before a certificate of fitness for duty is given; the examination can and should be undertaken by a physician who has made a special study of otology, or, at least, understands how to examine the ear and to test its functions accurately."[56]

The potential ramifications of this recommendation for railway laborers were immediately recognized. If adopted, such a medical criterion could jeopardize the employment of many railwaymen, especially those who were older and more experienced, insofar as the observed diminution of hearing ability was known to increase with age and tenure on the job. In reaction to Moos' suggestion, a heated medical and social debate ensued that was to dominate this field of study for the next several decades. In the following two years (1881–1882), studies by other German researchers challenged the potential usefulness of the proposed medical testing. D. Schwabach and H. Pollnow (1881) measured the hearing ability of thirty-five engineers and firemen using several common clinical tests. In one test, each subject was asked whether he could hear the tick of a watch at gradually increasing distances. Another test assessed the subject's ability to hear a whispered voice at those same distances. Based upon their detailed examinations and measurements, Schwabach and Pollnow concluded that there was indeed a marked reduction of hearing associated with age which most likely reflected the cumulative effect of years of noisiness on the job.[57]

However, Pollnow was not convinced that the results of those particular hearing tests implied any practical incapacity of the railwaymen to perform their jobs safely. To address that question, Pollnow personally traveled on several locomotives and performed additional field tests to evaluate drivers' ability to detect and respond to various auditory signal warnings. In contrast to Moos' stance, Pollnow found that employees were generally able to hear most of the important warning signals, even if they had some measured hearing decrement based on the watch and whisper tests. The most important indicator of the driver's capacity to hear the required acoustic warning signals accurately, concluded Pollnow, was not the standard clinical tests of hearing acuity but rather the employee's demonstrated ability to carry on an ordinary conversation aboard a moving train. Pollnow reasoned as follows:

> These are the results of the test results we have done and we have come to the conclusion that the hearing ability of the engineer and the fireman do not need to be very good, because there is no danger in any way for safety if the hearing ability of the engineer is diminished.
>
> How interesting and worthwhile are the questions raised by Moos and his inquiries about the significance of the hearing ability of the railwaymen, but the practical value for railway administration is not very great, and you can without any difficulty agree with the railway technicians [workers] who say:
>
> Engineers and firemen can hear adequately so long as they can communicate in normal speech to each other.[58]

There is evidence suggesting that Pollnow's motivation for advocating this approach was based as much on economic as it was on medical grounds. Pollnow was acutely aware that the adoption of Moos' examination requirements could result in the layoff of workers and increased operating costs for the railway companies. In a subsequent (1882) rebuttal to Moos, Pollnow wrote:

If there was a real reason why railway workers needed normal hearing for the safety of rail travel, that is, if Moos' views were valid, then the consequence of this position would not only be inconvenient for the railway workers, but would also constitute a threat to the existence of the railway system. My research has shown that after a working period of 15 years, 20.5 percent of the railway workers are hard of hearing, and Moos has argued that they are unfit to work and so must be laid off. Most of them are men between 35 and 45 years old, men with full possession of their strength, the best of the personnel. If it is really necessary to lay-off one-fifth of these men because they no longer have normal hearing, then in the future you wouldn't be able to find enough men for the work of the railway and the payment of pensions would be economically unacceptable.[59]

Pollnow's challenge to Moos' position was thus based on a different approach to the definition of occupationally relevant hearing loss, one based on the identification of practical work disability rather than on decrements in hearing sensitivity as measured by clinical tests. In Pollnow's view, the results of medical employment examinations performed by otologists were not useful as a method for gauging the driver's ability to perform his job safely and thus ensure the welfare of the traveling public.[60]

This challenge to Moos was taken up by several other medical authorities at about the same time. Based on an examination of 146 locomotive engineers, Hedinger (1882) also found substantial evidence of hearing decrements based on the whisper test, with a clear relationship between the prevalence of these hearing decrements and the number of years exposed to noise.[61] But, like Pollnow, Hedinger discovered that railway travel was not at all endangered by a moderate loss of hearing because the acoustic warning signals in common use were loud enough to be heard by all except the very deaf. Additional support for the position of Pollnow and Hedinger came from the studies of Güterbock (1882), Stein (1899), and Zilliacusis (1905).

A number of medical experts sided with Moos. Among them was K. Lichtenberg of Budapest, who concluded in 1891 that "acquired dullness of hearing appears to be more dangerous in regard to signals than does color-blindness" and that a qualifying hearing examination for engineers should be conducted "at least every two years, for the prevention of accidents."[62]

Additional support for Moos' proposal came from Dr. H. Zwaardemaker of Utrecht, who conducted detailed acoustical testing of the major types of warning signals then in use, including ordinary conductor's whistles, signal horns, steam whistles, and explosion signals. Based on his studies, Zwaardemaker agreed with Moos that examination by a trained otologist should be required for employment as a locomotive engineer or fireman, and that minimum hearing requirements should be established: "My experience convinced me that even for the normal ear it is difficult to understand speech when traveling upon a locomotive. . . . Even when the locomotive is at rest, defective hearing gives rise to difficulty and danger through misunderstanding, for we all know how often, under such circumstances, the opposite is done of what has been commanded. Hence, even for older railway employees, I believe the minimum requirement should correspond to that adopted in the military regulations—the whispered speech at one metre."[63]

The debates about the relative merits of clinical hearing tests as an employment screen for railway workers continued into the early twentieth century, with additional contributions made by Stein (1899), Sachs (1905), and Andrews (1907). In time, the debate subsided because periodic medical examinations became a routine practice in the railway industry and also because new optical and electronic warning devices eventually supplanted the use of older acoustical safety signals.[64] But the legacy of the questions first raised in these early studies extended well into the twentieth century. They touch on the fundamental question of how to define an occupational disease and whether physical impairment in the absence of occupational disability ought to be treated as a legitimate medical injury. Now, as then, the answers to those questions have tremendous social and economic implications regarding employment, compensation, and the fixing of blame for industrial mishaps.

Another important concept, first articulated by Pollnow, was the view that the ability to engage in normal spoken conversation ought to be considered the standard for judging the extent of injury resulting from noise-induced hearing loss. The subsequent general acceptance of this suggested criterion by the medical community had a significant impact on the formation of the contemporary understanding of NIHL and the approach to determining whether workers' compensation for NIHL should be awarded.

Telephone Communication
In the late nineteenth century, technological progress in the field of electronics brought amplified sound to the ears of millions of persons for the first time. The invention of the telephone by Alexander Graham Bell and Elisha Gray in 1876 met with immediate commercial success. By 1885 there were more than 140,000 subscribers and 800 telephone exchanges in the United States alone. The public's reaction to this new means of communicating at long distance was one of astonishment and awe. One can only imagine the profound exhilaration that ordinary people must have felt when they first experienced the ability to hear the voice of another conveyed by electricity

over a metal wire. Soon after the telephone was invented, demonstrations of the new technology were presented to enthusiastic audiences at concert halls and expositions throughout the United States.[65]

As with the introduction of many new technologies, there was also a sense of trepidation about possible adverse health effects. Medical concern was articulated in 1879 by the British physician F. M. Pierce, who wrote in the *British Medical Journal*: "The introduction of new inventions amongst the practical requirements of civilized life brings with it its disadvantages. The telephone, when further improved, is no doubt destined to become a most useful agent in daily intercourse; and I do not wish to create unnecessary alarm by pointing out a possible source of inconvenience in its use. The following case which has come under my notice will exhibit a way in which the ear may be more or less injured during the use of the telephone."[66] Pierce described the case of a woman who, in the course of her work as a manager of a manufacturing shop in Manchester, England, was deafened for two weeks by a clap of thunder that had been transmitted through the telephone wire.

In 1878 the American physician Clarence Blake had cautioned the British Society of Telephone Engineers that "habitual use of the telephone would be prejudicial to the hearing in many cases where the hearing was already impaired." In further tests conducted in 1888, Blake found that the need for the ear to absorb energy transmitted by the telephone receiving disc could result in a "decrement of the hearing" and make the ear "peculiarly suscepti-ble to the shock of such metallic sounds as are constantly occurring in the practical use of the telephone."[67] In 1889, much the same finding was made by the French otologist Marie Ernest Gellé, who reported, "The injurious influence of the telephonic sound is analogous to the well-known observa-tions in machinists, in whom changes of the drum-membrane and of the tympanum are found, and also severe attacks of neuralgia, intense tinnitus, extreme hardness of hearing, and vertigo. The conducting and nervous appa-ratuses are equally affected, as well as the general nervous system."[68]

These early medical reports arose against a backdrop of intense public policy debate about the expansion and control of telephone communications, particularly in Europe. For instance, Gellé's report (delivered June 1, 1889) coincided with the French Government's decision (enacted July 13, 1889) to nationalize all telephone service as part of the state telegraph monopoly, as had been done in Germany five years earlier. At about the same time, the British Government was attempting to protect its dominance over inter-urban telegraphic communications by deliberately limiting the allowable size of exchange areas for private telephone companies, a practice it began in 1878 and continued until the mid-1880s.[69]

Historians have noted that the early development of the telephone occurred much more quickly in the United States because of the proliferation of independent telephone exchange companies.[70] In Great Britain and continental Europe, however, the expansion of telephony was impeded due to government concern with maintaining control over the means of communications and protecting existing state-run telegraph monopolies from new competition.

To the best of my knowledge, there is no direct evidence linking the early reports of telephone-induced hearing problems to these political and economic controversies. However, from 1878 to 1888, there was a tremendous amount of public debate and media attention about whether and how aggressively to expand telephone communication, about the appropriate role of the government in its expansion, and about impediments to achieving better telephone service.[71] In this environment, the appearance of public and medical concern about the possible health effects of widespread telephone use makes sense. Indications from physicians about the possible hazards of telephone use would have benefited European governments and others who wished to rein in the development of this technology.

By the early 1900s, public demand for telephone communication forced European governments to relax their restrictions on the commercial development of telephone networks. Large inter-connected telephone systems developed quickly in most Western countries. Along with this development came a corresponding increase in telephone workers. During the first two decades of the twentieth century, a considerable amount of medical research began to be focused on the possible effects of prolonged exposure to telephone transmissions among these workers.

In one of these studies, Braunstein (1904) examined 160 employees of the Munich Telephone Company and found that "the regular use of the telephone does not exert any unfavorable influence on the healthy ear."[72] However, he did find that "severe injuries" to the ear can result from electric discharges through the telephone during thunderstorms. In a study of 450 telephone operators conducted in 1909, N. R. Blegvad found that 26.4 percent of the operators had an abnormal "retraction" of the tympanic membrane in the ear normally in contact with the telephone, yet the other ear was not similarly affected. However, he was not able to detect any reduction in the operators' hearing ability as a result of regular telephone usage.[73]

In Great Britain, physicians worried that infrequent high-voltage discharges producing loud "metallic" or "crackling" noises could damage the hearing of professional telephone operators. The potential danger was identified by a special British medical committee convened in 1911, the same year that the British Post Office acquired the National Telephone Company, thereby nationalizing all of the nation's telephone communications.[74]

Similar concerns were expressed by Bezold and Siebenmann (1907), Koelsch (1907), Capart (1911), Foerster (1911), Koetter (1910), Trétrôp (1914), Kober and Hanson (1916), Cott (1918), and Westmacott (1925). Koetter criticized the telephone companies for advising operators to place the receiver "close to the ear." He argued that conversation could be heard just as well if operators were instructed to hold the receiver lightly to the ear.[75] Westmacott asserted that telephone operators could lose their hearing due to prolonged exposure to noise, in a manner similar to boilermakers. In this regard he wrote: "Barr and others are satisfied that long-continued exposure to noise causes the delicate structures of the perceiving apparatus in the internal ear to lose its power of conveying impressions to the brain. The proof is that air conduction is better than bone conduction. The sensory apparatus, for high-pitched noises especially, becomes absolutely lost. . . . Telephone operators are subject to similar symptoms, induced by constant irritation of the perception apparatus by the instruments or by loud cracking noises due to thunderstorms or intense electrical discharges in the installation."[76] In at least one case, a female telephone operator brought a successful claim for workers' compensation based upon exactly this kind of injury. That 1927 case, from North Dakota, involved a woman who alleged that her deafness was the result of noises produced by her headpiece. At various times she heard intense vibrations, static, loud noises, and ringing bells that caused such severe pain, irritation, and inflammation of her ears that she was forced to leave work after six months.[77]

During the 1920s, articles attempted to explain the supposed hearing problems experienced by telephone operators as manifestations of nervous or hysterical characteristics of the workers. In one of these, Dr. J. A. White concluded (1928), "the probability of harm to the ear from constant use of the telephone among employees of the Telephone Company is only to be considered with those employees who already had some otological trouble or were of a special neurotic tendency."[78] White classifies such workers as "mostly neurasthenics," labels some cases instances of "litigation neurosis," and places them "in the same class as 'railway spine.'" To support his views, he cites the observations of R. Foerster (1911), who, according to White, found that "Most of the cases [hearing loss among telephone operators] were hysterical, neurasthenic or hypochondriac and the effects were not lasting. Also a majority were females and many of them were menstruating at the time of the so-called injury and he considered the nervous instability at that time was enough to precipitate the otological and neurologic symptoms from telephone noises that would not affect them at other times."[79]

The claim that occupational hearing loss is a manifestation of neurosis, especially among menstruating women, is a repeated theme in the medical

Table 4   Employment of Telephone Operators in the United States

Year	Total	Percentage Female
1900	15,327	80.0
1910	88,262	90.2
1920	615,154	93.8
1930	235,259	94.5
1940	197,062	94.6
1941–44	—	99.9

Data: Hooks 1947, p. 80; U.S. Department of Labor 1946, p. 10.

literature of the early twentieth century; it reappears in the relationship of occupational hearing loss to psychoneurosis and the question of malingering.

It is important to note that telephone operators, both in the United States and abroad, were predominantly female. The number of women employed in this industry grew rapidly after World War I (see table 4). A number of reasons accounted for the feminization of this occupation. Employers of the period noted the supposedly greater dexterity, patience, and forbearance of women. Of greater significance was their willingness to work for lower wages than men. The typical telephone operator was an unmarried woman, seventeen to twenty years old, who earned from one-quarter to one-half of what was paid to male laborers.[80]

The interpretation by some physicians that hearing difficulties experienced by telephone operators were psychogenic may have been predicated upon certain social views about the role of women and/or women's innate physical and emotional constitution. Physicians of the period may have been reflecting broader societal perspectives about the suitability of women for permanent employment in industry, particularly in industries where their employment was perceived to be competing with men (see chapter 2). In this case, the hiring of female telephone operators gradually supplanted the employment of telegraph operators, a profession that had been historically male and well-paid.

In addition, the female telephone operators as a group were politically assertive and active in trade unions. Their struggle to create a women's union of telephone operators and the opposition they faced from males within their parent union (the International Brotherhood of Electrical Workers), has been chronicled by labor historians.[81] Highly publicized strikes by militant telephone operators, mostly in New England, took place in 1913, 1919, and 1923. Although the danger of hearing loss apparently was not a significant issue in these strikes, this was the same general period as the medical studies of NIHL from telephone use by the American physicians Kober and Hanson (1916), Cott (1918), Westmacott (1925) and White (1928). The timing of the studies suggests the possibility that the labor struggles undertaken by female telephone operators helped bring attention to the potential health hazards of that occupation.

Textiles and Aviation

In light of its rapid growth during the early stages of the Industrial Revolution, and its extensive use of powered machinery, it is somewhat surprising that virtually no medical reports of occupational hearing loss in the textile industry were made during the nineteenth century. One of the first otologic studies of textile workers was conducted in 1899 by Dr. E. Coosemans, who described temporary deafness among "beetlers" at a linen plant after ten to twelve hours of daily labor.[82] F. Röpke, in 1902, refers to the examination of twenty spinstresses, fourteen of whom were found to be hard of hearing, and fourteen weavers, none of whom heard normally.[83]

In the mid-twentieth century, reports of hearing problems in the textile industry began to increase. The term *cotton-weavers' deafness* was first mentioned in a study by Legge and McKelvie (1927), who found that 24.3 percent of more than one thousand cotton weavers examined had some degree of deafness. In 1930 Canadian physician Frank Pedley wrote: "Dr. Thomas Barr states that . . . 75 per cent of boiler makers either could not hear at all at a public meeting, or could hear only with difficulty. My experience with weavers indicates a somewhat similar condition. The organization of a strike in industries of this class must be very difficult for this reason, for it is hard to conceive of an adequate meeting being held."[84] E. J. Evans of the British National Physical Laboratory, in a 1947 article entitled "Noise in the Factory," made a similar observation. "There are many industries where extremely noisy conditions prevail. In weaving sheds, for example, it is impossible to converse except by shouting."[85]

The subsequent history of NIHL during the twentieth century parallels the dramatic expansion that occurred in the use of powered technology in the workplace. By World War II, the deleterious effects of prolonged exposure to noise had been well-documented in a wide assortment of industries, including woodworking, metalworking, forging, shipbuilding, and mining.

One type of noise exposure that received a considerable amount of attention in the 1920s and 1930s was that incurred by airplane crews in response to the initial expansion of both commercial and military aviation. V. T. Scott, in 1923, was apparently the first to call attention to airplane noise as a factor in hearing loss.[86] Additional studies on aviators' deafness were conducted by Rankin (1925), Bauer (1926), Balla (1929), and Troena (1933). In *Aviation Medicine*, perhaps the most thorough treatment of this subject, Bauer wrote: "The constant roar of a high-powered motor causes diminution of hearing. The pilot who has no protective device in his ears will invariably be markedly deaf. This deafness gradually wears off after a few hours. Constant flying without protection results in permanent impairment of hearing. A large proportion of the flyers in the United States Air Service show diminished hearing. . . . All aviators become deaf and, if the candidate is deaf to start with, he will soon reach the stage where he cannot perform his other military functions. After a flyer is once trained, so long as he has sufficient hearing for his other military duties he may be allowed to fly. For civilian aviators, it is thought that a third of normal hearing is sufficient."[87]

The Measurement of Hearing Ability

By 1940, the contemporary scientific and medical understanding of the nature and pathology of NIHL had essentially been formed. According to the current view, the term *noise-induced hearing loss* is normally used to describe the cumulative loss of hearing that develops gradually over months or years of hazardous noise exposure. It is distinguished from *acoustic trauma*, which refers to hearing loss of a sudden origin. This distinction corresponds to the much-debated dichotomy between acute injury and chronic disease that has been central to the continuing evolution of the workers' compensation system since the 1930s.

According to the contemporary view, NIHL is understood to be sensorineural in nature, involving damage to the auditory nerve and/or sensory organs of the inner ear. NIHL typically begins with a drop in hearing sensitivity at high frequencies (3,000–6,000 Hz), subsequently spreading to lower frequencies with continued exposure. Such impairment in hearing sensitivity is commonly termed a *noise-induced threshold shift*: the difference in the minimum sound intensity that a person can detect, measured before and after exposure to noise. The threshold shift at first is temporary, and hearing sensitivity gradually returns to initial levels after a period of time away from the noise. However, the threshold shift can become permanent, with the decline in hearing acuity eventually spreading to the lower frequencies. In that case, a *permanent threshold shift* has occurred.

Since normal speech frequencies are in the range 500–2,000 Hz, early NIHL is usually not recognized by the affected employee and does not seriously compromise the worker's ability to hear normal conversation and engage in regular work or leisure activities. Further complicating the diagnosis of NIHL is the fact that other common conditions can decrease hearing sensitivity, including advancing age (presbycusis), drugs, toxic chemicals, and various general or infectious diseases. In addition, it is often impossible to distinguish the relative contribution of nonoccupational from occupational sources of noise in persons suffering noise-induced hearing loss. This is especially difficult when there are significant sources of noise in a person's daily life, such as certain hobbies (woodworking, for example) and leisure activities (like listening to amplified music).

As NIHL progresses with continued noise exposure, the employee can begin to have difficulty understanding spoken words in noisy environments, fail to experience high-pitched sounds such as sirens or bells, and hear ringing noises in the ears. Eventually, a debilitating condition can develop, in which the person may not be able to engage in normal conversation or routine job activities. Unfortunately, all sensorineural hearing losses, including NIHL, are irreversible. In addition, the hearing of a worker suffering from NIHL cannot be substantially improved by electronic hearing aids or other medical treatments.

By the beginning of the twentieth century, physicians faced a dilemma of how to detect and measure hearing loss that was due specifically to noise exposure at work. Many authorities believed that relying on worker complaints or manifested difficulty in communicating was unsatisfactory, because these symptoms develop only at later stages of the disorder. Others believed that overt behavioral changes in social discourse should be considered the distinguishing diagnostic criterion, and that any subclinical hearing impairment was essentially inconsequential. Almost all parties realized that the manner in which the "injury" to the worker was to be measured and defined had tremendous potential implication for management-labor relations, the determination of employee fitness for duty, and the economic costs associated with remediation.

"Classical" Hearing Tests

To address this issue, most physicians prior to World War I employed various clinical hearing tests and instruments that had been traditionally used by otologists for measuring hearing sensitivity in the deaf, training musicians and singers, and qualifying soldiers for military duty. These so-called classical tests basically involved the self-reported ability of subjects to hear various types of sounds at increasing distances, including a ticking watch, words whispered and spoken aloud, and tuning forks of differing tones.[88]

A good early example of the use of the "classical" hearing tests in the measurement and diagnosis of occupational deafness is Thomas Barr's 1886 study of boilermakers. Barr measured the ability of his subjects to hear three different kinds of sounds at varying distances: the tick from his pocketwatch, a whispered voice, and a loud spoken voice. In each case, he compared the distance at which the workers heard the sound to a predetermined distance at which a person with "normal hearing" could hear the same sound (he does not explain how the "normal" baseline was established). Barr was aware that there was a potential for large subjective variations in the conduct of the spoken voice test, and he attempted to minimize any discrepancies by selecting certain common utterances for use in his assessment: "A whisper at a yard distance, using such words as 'twenty,' 'brother,' 'America,' 'forty,' 'house,' 'garden.' The use of isolated words is a more reliable method than that of complete sentences, as in the latter, the element of guessing disturbs the result. In normal hearing, a whisper should be heard about 22 yards from the ear. At a yard distance from the ear it was found that fifty-nine men [out of 100] could not hear a whisper with either ear, or heard it very indistinctly."[89]

Along with the traditional clinical tests, Barr also asked the workers to recall whether they had ever experienced difficulty in hearing and understanding a public speaker, as might occur at a church service or a town meeting. Barr believed that it was important to evaluate the workers' hearing problems not only in terms of measured perceptibility, but also with respect to any impairment in their everyday lives: "This particular form of enquiry, namely, as to their power of hearing a public speaker, seemed to me a pretty reliable way of ascertaining the extent to which the deafness of these men interfered practically with their social comfort or usefulness."[90]

As pointed out by Atherley and Noble (1985), Barr's reliance on worker self-appraisal of social handicap represents one early approach to the question of whether occupational hearing loss ought to be defined on the basis of quantified testing of sensory acuity or in terms of the practical social disability created by such impairment. As such, Barr's approach has much in common with the perspective advocated independently by Pollnow in Germany with respect to the otological qualification of railway engineers and firemen. Barr's viewpoint, according to Atherley and Noble, "represents a significant scientific insight" on an important issue that has continued to dominate scientific and political discussion about NIHL up to the present time.[91]

Many authorities realized that the classical hearing tests were inherently subjective and unreliable, in that there was a significant potential for variability in the administration of the test, both because of the possibility for the investigator to produce test sounds of differing intensity, as well as the likelihood that changing environmental conditions might affect the test results.

Audiometric Testing

For these reasons, there was a considerable effort made by physicians and acoustical researchers to develop more consistent and accurate measurement techniques. Beginning in the early nineteenth century, a number of new tests were developed that utilized mechanical instruments to produce standardized sounds. These early devices, which relied on subjective response to various tones and sounds that were generated by the instruments, included Wolke's (1802) and Itard's (1821) construction of mechanical "acuity meters," and the invention by Wheatstone (1827), Weber (1834), and Muller (1838) of instruments that employed tuning forks (invented by the English musician John Shore in 1711) to generate sounds of different frequencies.[92]

In response to technological advances in electronics, most notably the development of the induction coil by E. Du Bois Reymond in 1849 and the telephone by Bell and Gray in 1876, a number of electronic sound-generating devices were built in the late nineteenth century. Otologists and acoustical engineers were particularly influenced by the invention of the telephone, and immediately saw in that device the potential to generate standardized tones and speech for medical testing purposes. Within two years after that breakthrough, sound-generating instruments for the medical testing of hearing perception were built by A. Hartmann (1878), E. Högyes (1878), J. Blyth (1878), and D. E. Hughes (1879).[93]

According to most historians, the initial use of the term *audiometer* to describe these kind of electronic devices is credited to B. W. Richardson, who in 1879 made the following comments about a device that had been developed by Hughes in London: "The world of science in general and the world of medicine in particular is under a deep debt of gratitude to Professor Hughes for his simple and beautiful instrument, which I have christened the audimeter, or less accurately, but more euphoniously, the audiometer."[94] Although similar terms, including acumeter, sonometer, and electric hearing meter, were introduced at about the same time, *audiometer* was soon generally adopted, and *audiometry* came to signify the science of testing human hearing by the use of these electronic devices.[95]

Despite the initial enthusiastic reception by Richardson and other otologists, these early audiometers never met with widespread acceptance or application in a clinical setting.[96] One reason was the high cost of these machines compared to the classical testing methods. Another source of resistance to their use involved technical difficulties, such as the inability to create pure tones at different specific frequencies, which many otologists considered a critical component for hearing tests.[97] W. S. Bryant (1898) summed up many otologists' misgivings about electronic audiometry when he stated, "The objections to the use of electricity in testing are the bulkiness of the apparatus, the amount of care required to keep it in running order and, lastly, the expense."[98] Owing to these problems, there was almost no widespread audiometric testing conducted prior to World War I.[99]

The real breakthrough in the ability to assess human hearing quantitatively occurred with the introduction of the electronic vacuum tube in the early 1920s. Electronic vacuum tubes had first been developed in connection with radiotelephony in the years immediately following World War I. Using this new technology, acoustical scientists could generate electronic tones of any frequency.

Electronic audiometers based on this principle were first presented at the meeting of the Berlin Otological Society of November 21, 1919, by K. L. Schaefer and G. Gruschke, and, independently, at that same meeting, by B. Griessmann and H. Schwartzkopf.[100] Although originally developed by German scientists, the mass production and commercialization of these devices in the United States led to their extensive use in large-scale screening examinations of workers and the general public. Commercialization of this technology was retarded in Germany due to the economic depression there following World War I, while U.S. companies such as the American Telephone and Telegraph Company (AT&T) were aggressively expanding their development and marketing of electronic sound-analysis equipment as a result of their initial tremendous economic success in establishing telephone communications networks.[101]

In 1922, engineers at the Western Electric Company, a subsidiary of AT&T, introduced the first electric audiometer specifically for commercial use, the Western Electric 1A Audiometer.[102] However, the development two years later of a portable model, the Western Electric 2A audiometer, really initiated the era of modern field audiometry. That was soon followed by the introduction of the Western Electric 4A, an audiometer employing phonograph recordings for the testing of speech recognition, which was manufactured between 1924 and 1926. Although the $1,500 price tag of the original 1A audiometer was considered prohibitive by many physicians, the reduced cost of subsequent models ($500–$800 for models 2A and 4A), along with their enhanced acoustical properties, led to the increasing use of these instruments by both researchers and clinicians.[103]

The development of effective, simple, and inexpensive electronic audiometers allowed physicians and acoustical scientists, for the first time, to determine the ranges of hearing possessed by large population groups. To acquire this information, several research organizations initiated extensive public screenings of people's hearing abilities. These testing programs first brought the knowledge of partial hearing loss to the attention of large numbers of individuals and helped transform NIHL from a purely subjective disorder into one that was considered to be definable objectively.

One such well-publicized screening was conducted in 1935–1936 by the

U.S. Public Health Service. In this nationwide survey, audiometric tests were administered to both ears of 9,324 persons. This survey revealed that 50 percent of all men over forty-five years of age had a hearing impairment of 25 dB or more at the high frequencies of 4,096 and 8,192 Hz.[104] According to the study's principal investigator, W. C. Beasley, this survey was conducted as part of the Public Health Service's broader goal of assessing the effects that unemployment and poverty resulting from the Depression were having on the overall health of Americans.[105]

In another screening program that received a great deal of public attention, the hearing of some 550,000 persons attending the 1939 World's Fair in New York was tested using the Western Electric 4A audiometer. This screening program, like that conducted by the Public Health Service, found that more men than women had hearing loss, particularly men who had been exposed to noise on the job. In all, more than 40 percent of males aged ten to fifty-nine exhibited a hearing loss of at least 10 dB for high frequency (7,040 Hz) sounds. However, only about 1.5 percent of the general population had a hearing impairment sufficient to create a significant social handicap, as determined by a hearing loss of at least 40 dB in the lower (880–1,760 Hz) frequency ranges.[106]

Additional mass public testing occurred at the San Diego Fair in 1950 and at the Wisconsin State Fair in 1954 and 1955.[107] One of the main objectives of these screening programs was to determine the hearing capabilities of a normal referent population so that decrements in hearing sensitivity caused by noise or other sources could be expressed both quantitatively and qualitatively (for example, deviation from normal by frequency range).

These screening programs attracted a considerable amount of attention not only from the scientific and medical communities, but also from the popular media, industry and government.[108] One reason for the great amount of attention generated by the early screening programs was the growing public fascination with radios, which had been introduced in large numbers for commercial use beginning in the late 1920s and early 1930s. The inability to hear radio broadcasts clearly was the first signal for many workers and elderly people that there might be some problem with their hearing.

These large-scale public screening programs were stimulated by more than just scientific curiosity; to a great extent, the effort to identify hearing defects in the general population was directly related to the economic interests of some of the sponsors of the tests. Western Electric, for instance, was the sole manufacturer of commercial audiometers throughout most of the 1920s and 1930s.[109] Scientists from Bell Telephone Laboratories, the associated research subsidiary of Western Electric's parent, AT&T, sponsored and conducted the World's Fair screening program of 1939. Initially, Bell Lab's research interest in audiometry had been related to the quality of telephone communication. But AT&T soon discovered that there was a potentially sizable market for the audiometers themselves, especially if the screening programs uncovered large numbers of individuals with measurable hearing defects, who, as a result of this diagnosis, were subsequently referred to their private doctors or industrial clinics for additional audiometric analysis and treatment.[110]

An internal memorandum written in November 1939 by J. C. Steinberg, head of AT&T's audiometry research group, laid out that company's perspective on the potential market opportunities for electronic audiometers, based upon its experience with the World's Fair testing:

> During the past year more than a half a million audiograms have been obtained from people testing their hearing at the Bell System exhibits at the New York and San Francisco fairs.
>
> . . . According to census figures published by the American Medical Association, there are some 169,000 doctors in the United States with some 6,500 specializing in ear, nose, throat disorders. According to a preliminary analysis of our World's Fair hearing test records, about one out of twenty-five persons, or some 5,000,000 people in the United States, have a hearing loss of 25 db or more, for frequencies in the range from 400 to 7000 cycles. As this is a degree of impairment that begins to be noticeable to the individual, there are some 750 people for each specialist that are in need of his services. Since the audiometer is an essential part of his services, a substantial market for such instruments is indicated.
>
> . . . It seems evident that the real market for audiometers has not been reached in the past and is not now being reached.[111]

Recognizing the opportunities presented by the audiometric identification of hearing loss, Western Electric capitalized on the growing need for scientific expertise in noise measurement and control. During the mid-1930s the company started one of the first commercial acoustic consulting services in the United States. According to New York City physician Foster Kennedy (1936), business initiatives such as Western Electric's played a significant role in stimulating the drive for expanded attention to the problem of noise in the workplace: "An acoustic consulting service in sound control, auditorium acoustics and noise abatement has been inaugurated by the Western Electric Company. The National Standards Association representing a number of technical organizations is studying the subject of acoustical measurements.

These movements in industry toward noise prevention are signs of grace, kindness, and enlightened self-interest. The elimination of noise is profitable, so it begins to get some of the attention accorded to other problems such as lighting, heating, and ventilation."[112]

Commercial audiometers and noise consulting services were not the only ways that companies stood to gain from the identification of hearing defects in the general population. Beginning in the 1930s, modern electronics provided a new therapeutic device to improve hearing ability in many persons diagnosed as suffering partial deafness—the electronic hearing aid.

Non-electric hearing aids, including hearing trumpets and hearing tubes, had been used since antiquity to amplify sound for the hard of hearing.[113] The first battery-powered hearing aids were produced in the United States shortly after 1900, based upon the same telephone technology that had been developed by Bell and Gray. However, these early "carbon transmitter" units had limited power of amplification and poor sound quality.[114] Hearing aids utilizing vacuum tubes were first introduced in the early 1920s, but it was not until 1937–1938 that practical, miniaturized electronic hearing aids were commercially available. Acoustically superior and smaller transistor models appeared about 1953.

By 1940, 50,000 people used electronic hearing aids in the United States and Great Britain. The number of users escalated rapidly throughout the 1940s. In 1943, it was estimated that between 125,000 and 150,000 Americans wore hearing aids—by 1947 the number had grown to more than 750,000. One manufacturer alone, the Raytheon Company of Newton, Massachusetts, reported producing four million midget hearing aid tubes between 1939 and 1947 (there were generally two or three midget tubes in each hearing aid).[115]

The major driving force behind the dramatic rise in the use of electronic hearing aids was World War II. Vast numbers of military personnel suffered hearing impairment as a result of that conflict. An estimated 40,000–50,000 American veterans were deafened during World War II. The Veterans Administration reported that 35,000 U.S. veterans were using hearing aids in 1947, and they estimated that they planned to purchase about 11,000 additional devices in 1948 and each year thereafter. In 1948, more than one hundred different hearing aid manufacturers sought Veterans Administration contracts.[116]

Between 1935 and 1948, manufacturers of hearing aids launched a major educational campaign throughout the United States to overcome the prevailing social stigma traditionally associated with the recognition of deafness, and thereby win public acceptance for the wearing of these devices. This

Figure 16 Hearing Aid Advertisement, *Saturday Evening Post,* July 23, 1949, p. 81

campaign was successful, and by 1950 the use of hearing aids had become quite common. Sales rose sharply after the introduction of transistorized models in 1953. Estimated annual sales of hearing aids were as follows: 100,000 in 1943; 150,000 in 1945; 220,000 in 1948; 225,000 in 1953; and 335,000 in 1954.[117]

Although occupational NIHL of the sensorineural variety is not entirely correctable by the wearing of hearing aids, the effort by hearing aid manufacturers to publicize the problem of partial hearing loss nevertheless encouraged many persons to get their hearing audiometrically tested, and it influenced the subsequent move to characterize the problem of occupational hearing loss in terms of subclinical changes in perceptibility rather than on the basis of manifested social handicap.

Immediately following World War II, hearing aids were marketed very aggressively, with dealers often exaggerating and misrepresenting the effectiveness of the devices. For example, existing studies indicating the ineffectiveness of hearing aids in cases of sensorineural deafness did not stop one manufacturer of hearing aids from claiming in 1949 that their model was "powerful enough to serve any hearing loss" (see figure 16). Otologists of the period expressed a great deal of concern about this trend, partly because of the scientific inaccuracies, but also because the treatment of deafness was being taken out of their control and placed into the hands of hearing aid dealers and fitters, who were not medically trained. Watson and Toland noted in 1949 that, "criticism has been directed at the hearing aid dealers and consultants during past years both by hard of hearing individuals, members of the medical profession and others." They attribute this criticism to the presence of those in the hearing aid field "who are poorly trained, who sell inferior equipment, and who render indifferent service."[118] At the meeting of the American Academy of Ophthalmology and Otolaryngology in 1953, otologist Kenneth Day publicly attacked the heavy-handed marketing techniques employed by those profiting from the selling of these new devices: "The manufacturers and distributors of hearing aids are not helping the cause of the hard-of-hearing by their methods of advertising. Do not forget that they are in a competitive business to sell hearing aids and make money. The most effective advertising capitalizes on the psychologic weaknesses of the consumers. Much more stress is put on the size and invisibility of the hearing aids they sell than on the quality and fidelity of response of their instruments. They outdo one another in superlatives and false implications."[119]

As a result of such professional criticism and complaints from consumers, legislation was introduced in several states between 1948 and 1955 to protect the public by regulating the advertising and sale of hearing aids. In 1951, the National Better Business Bureau published recommended standards for hearing aid marketing that prohibited bait advertising, exaggerated claims about the visibility of the hearing aid and its components, inappropriate use of medical terminology, misleading analogies, improper use of superlatives, and disparagement and scare advertising.[120]

This growing use of audiometers to detect hearing impairment in the general public also directly benefited the makers of earplugs and other personal protective devices. These devices had been used widely in the military during World War I, but their application in the industrial environment began to skyrocket only after World War II, as the results of audiometric testing confirmed the large prevalence of partial hearing loss among those exposed to occupational noise. In this sense, the initial mass screening programs provided a means for identifying potential "customers" for ear protection devices and demonstrated to businesses and workers the necessity for taking precautions.

Several commentators have remarked on the influence that the various commercial interests exerted on the contemporary understanding of NIHL. Paul Sabine (1944), for instance, alluded to the importance of the "profit motive" in explaining the contemporary growth of interest in the problem of industrial noise: "One of the sure ways to get remedial action under a capitalist economy is to establish the fact that such action will yield results that can be measured in dollars and cents. About twenty-five years ago [1919], it was found that the noise in business offices could be reduced by the application of sound absorbent treatment to the ceiling and walls of office spaces. . . . While the purely commercial value of quieting for office workers has become a commonplace, yet it has been only within the last few years that any serious attention has been given to the problem of noise in industrial plants."[121]

One consequence of the mass audiometric screening programs conducted between 1939 and 1955 was a vigorous public debate on the question of what constitutes deafness. Many commentators of the period defined deafness in terms of any measured deficiency on audiometric tests, irrespective of the magnitude of the decrement or the sound frequencies affected. Headlines appearing in popular newspapers and magazines often employed the most inclusive criteria in their portrayal of the problem. For example, several magazine articles in the early 1940s declared that the results from the latest mass audiometric screenings meant that "ten million Americans were deafened."[122] Some authorities, including otologists Leland Watson and Thomas Toland (1949), argued that those estimates were misrepresentations, in that they were derived from the number of people showing slight defects (as little as 9 dB) in all tested frequencies, rather than those who were really hard of hearing. Watson and Toland believed that the latter term should be reserved only for those individuals who show "difficulty in hearing speech and definite social handicap" and that a person should not be considered *deafened* unless that person is "unable to hear and understand social conversation." Moreover, they asserted, only decrements of at least 40 dB in the relevant frequencies were sufficient to cause any difficulty in social conversation of the level implied by the use of either diagnostic label.[123]

From an occupational standpoint, routine audiometric tests were introduced by the military during World War II and then expanded into private American industry in 1946–1948. The use of audiometers in the industrial setting was actively promoted by the manufacturers of those devices, who had seen their military market decline after the war and were keenly aware of the potential opportunities for expanded sales to industrial customers. Prior to the outbreak of workers' compensation claims for NIHL, advertising strategy was based on the avoidance of traumatic injuries from accidents related to workers' inability to hear vehicles and other mechanical hazards (see figure 17).

These industrial audiometric screenings prompted a much greater level of awareness among employees about the harmful effects of noise in their workplace. Of great importance, audiometry provided a means for detecting and documenting any previously unrecognized partial loss of hearing that may have insidiously developed over years of employment. Not surprisingly, a large proportion of workers, more than 25 percent in some industries, were found to have some measurable hearing impairment as determined by the audiometric tests.

Figure 17 Audiometer Advertisement, *National Safety News,* March 1948, p. 192

The development of electric audiometers provided workers and physicians with the "physical evidence" needed to demonstrate that bodily harm had been inflicted in the workplace. Various authorities were acutely aware of the potential ramifications that such audiometric evidence could have on legal and workers' compensation treatment of NIHL. In 1929 Canadian physician G. E. Tremble wrote: "Although an instrument such as this is quite mechanical and falls into the field of the specialist, it might also be of interest to others, especially those dealing with compensation cases, now that industrial medicine and medical insurance have come so prominently to the fore. . . . Apart from the audiogram being a permanent record for reporting cases and to note improvement or progression of deafness, it is a common ground for discussion, and in industrial and legal cases a definite loss in percentage of hearing may be determined."[124] Tremble provides a case from his own experience to illustrate this point:

A bricklayer while at work fell from a scaffold, a distance of 15 feet, and suffered a fractured skull. After the injury he complained of deafness in both ears especially the right. During his stay in the hospital of five weeks, the patient's nose, throat and ears were examined. At that time tuning forks were used for the hearing tests. It was finally agreed that the patient had some impairment in both ears, although the drums were normal, but the otologist and the company considered him a malingerer. He was therefore given a certain sum in settlement. Not being satisfied with this amount he consulted a lawyer and the hearing tests were repeated. This time audiogram tracings were taken by three independent observers with very similar results, showing clearly a 50 per cent loss in the right ear and a 27 per cent loss of hearing in the left due to his basal fracture. The patient was subsequently awarded more than three times the original amount.[125]

The introduction of the audiometer and growth of routine audiometric testing of workers set the stage for the emergence, in 1948, of the first claims for compensation of NIHL as an occupational disease under the New York workers' compensation code. Audiometry appealed to insurance claims representatives, lawyers, and workers' compensation administrators, who had become accustomed to depending on quantitative medical evidence to verify the diagnosis of occupational illness and determine the extent of the resulting disability for compensation purposes. In arguing for the merits of an early audiometric testing instrument in 1924, Donald Lyle, a private physician from Cincinnati, Ohio, had observed:

> The chief reason, as I understand it, why most State industrial commissions do not recognize occupational deafness is because there is at present no absolute way of determining whether or not the claimant has become deaf on account of his work.
>
> It is evident that we need two instruments of precision in order to put occupational deafness, due to sound, on an absolute standard. The first is an instrument that covers the whole audible range and produces only fundamental pitch which can be varied in intensity in order to obtain the minimum and maximum audibility. The second is an instrument that receives the sound at the place where the affected man is working and records it so that it may be analyzed into its fundamental pitch or pitches.[126]

By the end of World War II, the development and commercialization of electronic audiometers and portable sound level meters had fulfilled both objectives outlined twenty-five years earlier by Lyle.[127] As he predicted, these instruments provided the quantified data needed to establish the "legitimacy" of occupationally induced hearing loss to state industrial commissions. The door was thus opened to the increased filing of workers' claims for financial compensation of NIHL.

Psychogenic Deafness and Malingering

Some people feared that legitimizing workers' compensation for NIHL would usher in a new wave of malingering and simulated deafness. According to these cynics, compensation for a nonspecific disorder such as NIHL provided an irresistible temptation to workers who might be mentally disturbed or otherwise susceptible to the notion of pretending to be sick. The 1953 warning of Dr. Douglas Wheeler of the American Academy of Ophthalmology and Otolaryngology was representative of this view: "Up to now it has not been of any great importance, but now with the compensation laws being passed in many States, the question of malingering will arise. In other words, these persons will feign a hearing loss or will overlay a psychogenic hearing loss subconsciously in trying to get compensation."[128]

There is a long history of medical skepticism about the legitimacy of deafness, especially of the type that arises in the absence of any overt trauma or disease process. This air of suspicion is related, perhaps, to the ancient association of deafness with insanity—a connection that was drawn by many of the classical medical writers like Celsus and Galen.[129] The legacy of these aspersions resurfaced in the nineteenth century in the guise of a medical discourse on deafness among "nervous" individuals. The noted British physician Sir William B. Dalby (1873) was one of the first modern authorities to attribute deafness to various "nervous" temperaments including excitability, depression, and fatigue. Similarly, American otologist Charles H. Burnett, in 1877, described *hysterical deafness*, which he likened to hallucinations of hearing voices and other sounds by persons with mental illness. Burnett also alluded to the clinical observations of Dr. S. Weir Mitchell, who popularized the "rest treatment" for female neurasthenics during the late nineteenth century. According to Burnett, Mitchell had attended cases of hysterical deafness in young women whose deafness "would apparently come and go during conversation."[130] Dr. P. McBride in 1881 also identified hysteria and violent emotion as causes of nervous deafness.[131] Other physicians provided a cornucopia of scientific terminology and explanations to account for simulated deafness: Dench (1909) attributed it to neurasthenia and mental shock, Bourgeois and Sourdille (1918) to "hystero-pithiatism."

Dalby (1873) was one of the first to link hearing loss specifically with the nervous tendencies and unique biological functions of women: "Among symptoms where impaired hearing is either in part or wholly due to a nervous cause is the experience that the subjects of the affection do not hear so well if they are excited or fatigued, and with women the hearing is commonly very worse during the catamenial periods."[132] In a later work (1893), Dalby expands on his conception of nervous deafness, describing a "typical" patient suffering from this condition as "a young girl of 18 or 20" who suddenly manifests hardness of hearing upon emotional excitement, as might occur from a social event or the birth of a child.[133]

In addition to nervous women and the insane, medical authorities also found that soldiers frequently exhibited hearing disability in the absence of a specific somatic disease. Many physicians interpreted this form of deafness as a deliberate attempt by soldiers to avoid military service. There is an extensive body of literature describing malingering in wartime, especially in those countries having compulsory military service. A number of American writers agreed with the observation of Thomas Barr (1884), who observed that this form of malingering was much less common in the United States, whose military did not depend upon conscripted soldiers. Roosa (1885), for example, offered this opinion: "In countries where liability to military service is universal, there are many malingerers, who claim to be dull of hearing in one or both ears. . . . The only malingerers that I have seen in our country since the close of the civil war, have been among the applicants for the pensions that our Government gives with such liberality to those who were in any way disabled while in the national service."[134]

Thus, a longstanding medical tradition associated deafness with various nonorganic conditions, including psychological and emotional aberrations, nervousness, as well as intentional malingering. In the mid-twentieth century, otologists increasingly came to suggest that hearing loss observed among some industrial workers was also due to malingering and other psychological states. This belief may have been fostered by the influx of women and immigrant groups into the workplace, as well as the well-documented war neuroses suffered by soldiers during World War I.

Malingering was frequently traced to workers' predisposition for seeking undeserved financial compensation. This was the view of the noted American otologist George Shambaugh, who in 1922 said that "it is a very common thing for people to believe that by feigning a defect in the hearing they will be able to get damages for supposed injuries."[135] British otologist Stuart Mawson claimed that most cases of simulated deafness were nefarious attempts to defraud employers: "Cases of malingering are encountered mostly in connection with pensions or compensation claimed as due to deafness resulting from employment. Such allegations are not only the by-product of discontent, but also of social mal-integration. A sense of responsibility is lacking towards any but the subject, and a preoccupation with 'getting,' at a minimal expenditure of effort, is characteristic."[136]

In reaction to the perceived problem of malingering, otologists devised a variety of tests and special instruments for unmasking the ploys of those who attempted to fake hearing impairment. The earliest tests employed various techniques for shifting the source of a sound from one ear to the other, using dual sound tubes, tuning forks, and binaural stethoscopes.[137] Later tests relied on more sophisticated methods utilizing hidden microphones, blindfolds, and electronic lie detectors for measuring galvanic skin response.[138]

By the 1930s, many otologists believed that the electronic audiometer provided a foolproof means to uncover any malingerer's attempt to simulate deafness. G. E. Tremble's excitement about the value of audiometers for industrial medicine was, to a great extent, predicated on this supposed capability of the instrument: "It is sometimes very difficult to distinguish between malingering and true deafness by means of tuning forks, but the audiometer exposes attempts at deception very quickly. If the patient on examination admits hearing any tone in the normal range even very slightly, the reading on the dial should agree with that found for the same tone or tones at subsequent examinations. Any marked variation would at once arouse suspicion."[139] Watson and Toland, in 1949, also displayed considerable enthusiasm about the use of the audiometer in cases of occupational malingering: "In civilian life the problem of detecting malingerers increases daily in proportion to the recognition and publicity attending occupational and traumatic loss of hearing. Every claim or damage suit for loss of hearing which results in a substantial financial settlement is a potential inspiration to would-be malingerers. . . . The modern precision audiometer offers the most reliable proof of whether deafness is real or simulated. If necessary it can actually be brought into a court room for exposing a malingerer to a jury."[140]

The key issue, in the minds of physicians and the courts, was documenting the claimant's hearing ability at various stages of employment. Employers aimed to determine whether new hires had any pre-existing hearing impairment. Workers needed evidence about whether hearing loss had started after assuming a specific work assignment. Physicians and public health advocates desired frequent periodic assessments to spot incipient auditory difficulties at an early stage and in order to provide proper protection and treatment. All parties had a shared goal, to make routine audiometric testing a common practice in industry. It was not long before physicians, safety professionals, lawyers, workers, and management were touting routine audiometric testing as an important technique for controlling the problem of noise-induced hearing loss. This sentiment comes out clearly in essentially all of the scientific and popular literature on this subject since World War II. Manufacturers of audiometers were quick to point out the benefits of their devices in the detection of "fraudulent" law suits (see figure 18).

Most striking is the similarity in perspective on the potential usefulness of audiometric testing shared by the most strident of labor activists and the traditional defenders of business interests. Labor unions petitioned manage-

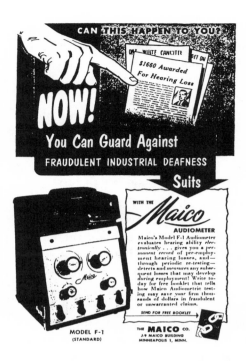

Figure 18 Audiometer Advertisement, *National Safety News,* May, 1952, p. 122

ment to institute periodic audiometric examinations at intervals of every six months.[141] Spokesmen for industry recommended pre-employment audiometric examinations as a way of eliminating compensation payments to workers already deafened by disease, age, war experience, or previous industrial exposure.[142] Not surprisingly, their collective wishes soon came true, and routine audiometric testing emerged as a critical component in the effort to control NIHL in the workplace.

Noise Control Methods

Much can be learned about the initial recognition and emergence of an occupational disorder from examining the history of the corresponding control methodologies. Sometimes the inability to control an occupational hazard is a potential reason why greater attention is not paid to the disorder at an early stage by physicians, management, and workers.

Before the twentieth century, a few attempts were made to prevent NIHL by controlling noise at its source, either through lowering the sound level, isolating it at a distance, or using barriers and other materials to block its transmission. In 1877 the replacement of high frequency railway whistles with those of a deeper tone or by other signals, such as bells, was suggested.[143]

In the early 1900s, new mechanical engineering methods including the use of fiber gears instead of metal and improved machine lubrication, were used to lower noise in production equipment. Physical methods for the reduction of noise in production processes included the redesign or repair of faulty equipment, the use of well-balanced parts to reduce mechanical contact, the incorporation of soundproofing materials into walls, ceilings, and floors, and the use of blankets and curtains as noise-absorptive partitions.[144] The Aetna Life Insurance Company installed sound-absorbing materials in offices occupied by typists, clerical checkers, and punch card operators beginning in 1928.[145] In response to their growing recognition of vibration as a contributing factor to industrial noise, acoustical authorities recommended mounting machinery, when possible, on cork, felt, springs, or other shock-absorbing pads.[146]

The early attempts to control noise at its source through physical means are unusual compared to other occupational diseases, where greater initial reliance was placed on the wearing of personal protective devices by workers. This may have been due to a realization by engineers and industrialists that noisy machinery often is an indication of mechanical inefficiency that ultimately can result in lower productivity and increased cost.

Another early approach to controlling the problem of noise-induced hearing loss was based on identifying and screening out high-risk individuals. D. J. Glibert, in 1921, concluded that the primary "prophylaxis" for NIHL involved the appropriate choice of worker: "Only young people fitted to undergo the normal consequences without damage should be allowed to work in noisy industries." Glibert also recommended that all industrial workers have periodic examinations of their hearing to identify problems at an early stage.[147] In 1967 there were still those who believed that the primary means by which industry should prevent NIHL was the pre-employment audiometric testing and periodic retesting of workers, as exemplified by this passage from a British otology textbook: "The prevention of chronic traumatic deafness [i.e., NIHL] . . . depends on careful audiometric screening of all employees engaged in noise-hazardous operations. Those with preexisting deafness should not be accepted for this occupation, those showing signs of perceptive loss should be otherwise employed."[148]

Wearing personal protective devices in or around the ears to control exposure to industrial noise was a relatively late development in the history of NIHL. With the exception of air crews and other military applications, workers did not wear earplugs, earmuffs, or other personal hearing protection devices in any significant numbers until after the growth of workers' compensation claims in the mid-1950s, and the practice did not become widespread in industry until the enactment of federal noise control standards in 1969.

The earliest reference to the wearing of ear protection as a way of controlling noise exposure appears in Homer's *Odyssey,* thought to be written more than three thousand years ago. Odysseus molded plugs of wax to prevent his sailors from hearing the cries of the Sirens as he sailed past their island. He left his own ears uncovered but ordered his sailors to bind him to the ship's mast. When he heard the Sirens' enchanting songs he begged to be released so that he could jump overboard and swim ashore. However, because of the wax in their ears, his sailors paid no heed and rowed onward until the danger was past.

In modern times, an early reference to personal hearing protection appeared in an anonymous query to the *Lancet* in 1866: "Can anyone of your readers suggest a remedy for preventing hearing loss caused by rifle shooting?" The reply, in a subsequent issue, was "use cotton in the ears."[149] A similar suggestion was made by Roosa (1874), who advised boilermakers to use cotton plugs to protect their hearing: "If care were taken to deaden the sound—that is, to interrupt the vibrations by the use of the cotton plug—I have no doubt that the hearing power of boiler-makers might be materially preserved."[150] Apparently some boilermakers took this advice, as evidenced by Holt's remark in 1882: "The men [boiler-makers] tell me that they have tried stopping the ears with cotton wool, pads, etc." Unfortunately, observed Holt, "they have derived no benefit" from this practice.[151] Thomas Barr, in his 1890 article concerning noise from railway whistles, advised that the use of "a plug of india-rubber" can be helpful for workers like boilermakers and riveters, who are exposed to loud noises in their daily work.

The first widespread use of personal hearing protection against noise was in the military. The use of earplugs in combat extends at least to the late nineteenth century. Barr (1890) mentioned that this form of protection had proved "exceedingly useful" to officers in the army and navy when exposed to the explosion of cannon.[152]

The outbreak of World War I prompted a surge of interest in the development and testing of ear protection for military personnel.[153] In Great Britain, two varieties of mechanical ear protectors were marketed for military purposes. One was the British Tommy, manufactured by George F. Berry of London. The other was the Mallock-Armstrong, which was first constructed by Arnulph Mallock for his personal use at the Armstrong Gun Factory and later offered commercially by the Mallock-Armstrong Defender Company in London.[154] Both of these were distributed in large numbers to British troops on the Western Front. In the United States, ear protectors patented and produced at about the same time included the Baum ear protector, which was constructed of rubber, and a device utilizing a mechanical valve called the Wilson-Michelson hearing defender. Several other devices were also introduced during this period, including the French Verain, Italian gel capsules, and various patented models from other U.S. and British manufacturers including Elliott, Wilson, and Frank.

In 1918, extensive research on these various forms of hearing protection was initiated by C. W. Richardson of the U.S. Army Medical Corps and by G. B. Trible and S. S. Watkins of the U.S. Navy at the Naval Proving Ground in Indianhead, Maryland.[155] These investigations found that most of the available patented hearing protectors were ineffective, as was dry cotton. The only manufactured device that afforded significant protection against noise, according to both studies, was the British Tommy. However, according to Trible and Watkins, the troops were reluctant to use the manufactured earplugs, such as the Mallock-Armstrong, because of "its rigidity and the difficulty of insuring an accurate fit."[156] As a result, soldiers and sailors were actually more apt to use cotton or lamb's wool, both of which were inexpensive and readily available.

Although dry cotton and lamb's wool were determined in the U.S. Navy's analyses to be ineffective, cotton that had been saturated with petroleum jelly or glycerin was discovered to be of value in reducing the effects to the ear of explosive concussion. The final test report delivered by the army to the U.S. Surgeon General in April 1918 recommended that several thousand British Tommy protectors be purchased and issued to the troops and that additional tests be conducted in actual combat to assess their merit compared to saturated cotton.[157]

Following World War I, manufacturers extended their marketing of ear protection devices from the military into new civilian applications. One of the first personal hearing protectors to obtain widespread civilian use in the United States were the Ear Stopples made by the Flents Products Company of Norwalk, Connecticut.[158] These wax-impregnated cotton plugs had been produced in France previously under the trade name of Boules Quies (quiet balls). Stuart Low, Sr., the founder of Flents, first saw these plugs in use in 1927 while on a trip to Paris. They were used not for occupational purposes, but rather by the common citizenry to quiet the annoying turmoil arising from Parisian streets. The disturbing clamor from public sources of noise was a major concern both in Europe and in the United States during that period.

Between 1927 and 1940 at least five other brands of commercial ear protection were introduced in the United States, including the M.S.A. Ear Defenders, Nelson's Ear Stoppers, Nods Noise Mufflers, Olygo Noise Absorbers, and Baum's Mega-Ear-Drum Protectors.[159] These were sold predominantly to the consumer market as personal aids for the reduction of city and domestic noise. The introduction of radios during this period brought electronically amplified sound into private households, contributing to the popularity of these devices. One large retail store in London reported selling 75–100 boxes a week, each box containing twelve ear protectors.[160]

With the start of World War II, ear protection became standard gear for thousands of GIs. During the war, a major new government research initiative was launched to evaluate the effect of prolonged exposure to noise and to evaluate the available varieties of personal hearing protection. This effort was centered first at the University of California, Los Angeles, and later at the Psycho-Acoustic Laboratory of the Harvard School of Public Health under the auspices of the U.S. Office of Scientific Research and Development. This investigation involved the testing of seven types of existing protectors and the engineering development of improved designs for the military. The investigators verified that plain cotton plugs afforded very little effective protection, compared to those made of gum rubber, latex, or plastic. Flexible neoprene devices reduced both continual and blast noises better and were more comfortable.[161] The result of these studies was the development for the military of the V–51R Ear Warden, which was subsequently marketed to the general public and became the most widely accepted brand for personal hearing protection during the two decades following the war.

After the war, the marketing of personal hearing protection devices again shifted to civilian applications, particularly in occupational settings. Despite its success in both the military and consumer markets, ear protection acceptance in the workplace came slowly. The major problem was the initial reluctance of employees to use the devices for a number of reasons, including discomfort, difficulty with communications, fear of ear infections or ear damage, and self-consciousness about appearance.[162] Eventually, most of these objections were overcome and the wearing of earplugs and earmuffs in noisy work environments became a more common practice. The expansion of workers' compensation coverage for NIHL in the mid-1950s and the passage of federal noise control standards in 1969 undoubtedly contributed to the increased use of these devices. In this sense, the growing recognition of NIHL as an occupational hazard encouraged wider acceptance in industry of personal hearing protectors.

But what is less clear is whether the converse is true—whether the aggressive marketing of ear protectors to industry may have helped foster initial awareness about the potential dangers of noise in the workplace. Several articles extolling the benefits of "ear stopples" appeared in *National Safety News* in the late 1940s, and advertising campaigns aimed at convincing industry to use earplugs for factory workers were undertaken by several companies in the early 1950s.[163] In 1952, one brand, "Nelson's Ear Stopples" were already in use at the United States Steel Company, the Western Cartridge Company, and the U.S. Defense Corporation in St. Louis.[164] Mine

Safety Appliances Company began marketing the commercial version of the military V-51R Ear Warden (renamed the MSA Ear Defender) to industry as early as 1955.[165] However, no records have been maintained by manufacturers or trade associations about the number of units distributed during this period, or the success of attempts to spark increased industrial demand.

Community Response to Environmental Noise Exposure

The wearing of personal ear protection by individuals as a means to diminish the annoying effects of noise in homes and streets predates its widespread acceptance in the workplace. This indicates that many persons perceived environmental sources of noise to be a significant problem. As I have suggested previously, the growth of public concern about the adverse effects of an environmental contaminant often spurs increased awareness and recognition of the same hazards existing in the occupational context. When a community becomes sufficiently upset about a harmful or annoying agent occurring in the neighborhood, then the political stage may be set for addressing the corresponding occupational disorders arising in the workplace. There is considerable evidence that exactly this process occurred with respect to noise-induced hearing loss.

Worried citizens voiced consternation about irritating levels of urban noise as far back as 1876, when an editorial entitled "London Noise" appeared in the British journal *The Sanitary Record*. The unnamed author took satisfaction in declaring that "the destructive effects of noise are at last attracting the attention the subject deserves" and went on to identify the major source of London's noise problem as "the effects of the continuous roar and rumble of the leading thoroughfares."[166] In 1882 Eugene Holt reported on a plea made by one London resident to the readers of the *Lancet*:

> In view of the ever increasing noises of the London streets, I venture to ask through your columns, in the interest of those unhappy persons who find it more and more difficult either to sleep well or to work well within the limits of the four-mile radius, why some sort of simple instrument cannot be invented for enabling persons to keep their ears closed (when they wish to do so) in the same way and as effectively as when they apply the tips of their fingers to them? I have tried wool, I have tried the new vulcanite ear-stoppers, but all is useless. Surely it is within the resources of science to solve this difficulty and to confer on nervous and overworked men and women the inestimable boon of "shutting their ears" as easily as they can shut their eyes.[167]

During the twentieth century, commentators have portrayed noise as an inevitable product of the ever-increasing encroachment of mechanization and technological progress onto the lives of ordinary citizens. The social critic Dan McKensie expressed this view in his popular book *The City of Din: A Tirade Against Noise,* published in London in 1916. Many individuals sought relief from this auditory assault by wearing personal hearing protectors like the Boules Quies, which became popular in France by the mid-1920s. The need for such protection can be appreciated from the findings of a study conducted in Paris in 1930, which measured the typical midday sound level on the rue du Faubourg-St-Martin at approximately 90 dB. The main source of this noise was determined to be vehicle traffic, primarily from automobiles and trolleys.[168]

A flurry of activity and concern about the problem of environmental noise in Europe and Great Britain occurred during the 1920s and early 1930s. To some extent, this surge of interest may have been a reaction to the proliferation of combustion engine vehicles. It is also probably not coincidental that vacuum-tube audiometers for the study and measurement of noise were becoming widely available at about this time. Another contributing factor, from a scientific perspective, may have been the increased scholarly interest during that period in the concept of fatigue and the growing realization by researchers that fatigue could be caused by prolonged exposure to loud sounds.

The issue of noise-induced fatigue first came to prominence in the United States through the studies conducted in 1912 by Josephine Goldmark for the National Consumers' League. In her monograph *Fatigue and Efficiency,* Goldmark claimed that fatigue produced by noise from industrial machinery decreases worker efficiency. Noise, she wrote, "not only distracts attention but necessitates a greater exertion or conscious application, thereby hastening the onset of fatigue."[169] Her findings attracted considerable attention from businesspeople and government officials because of the obvious economic consequences implied by the theory that sensory and mental fatigue in workers lowers industrial output. The head of the National Consumers' League at the time of Goldmark's study was Frances Perkins, who later was New York State Industrial Commissioner (1929–1933) and U.S. Secretary of Labor for President Franklin D. Roosevelt (1933–1945).

One of the best-known studies of the relationship between noise and efficiency was undertaken in December 1928 by the Aetna Life Insurance Company. In this experiment, it was discovered that the installation of sound-absorbing materials improved the productivity of office workers by 9.2 percent.[170]

Prompted by the growing scientific and public concern about the potential dangers of noise, several large-scale government-sponsored research initiatives between 1926 and 1930 examined the influence of environmental noise on public health. The International Labor Organization of the League of

Nations conducted one investigation in 1926 that stressed the importance of fatigue caused by occupational exposure to noise. In October 1928, the British Medical Association reported to the Ministry of Health that environmental noise was associated with sleep disturbances, fatigue, nervous conditions, lower work efficiency, and developmental problems in children, as well as with hearing losses.[171]

The Noise Abatement Commission of the New York City Department of Health undertook a similar large research project in October 1929. That commission, comprised of leading medical authorities, physicists, engineers, and lawyers, measured and analyzed noise in more than ten thousand locations throughout New York City. In line with the previous European inquiries, the report (entitled *City Noise*) concluded that exposure to loud urban noises can lead to a wide range of ill health effects, including nervousness, fatigue, and developmental problems. The report expressed particular concern about the potential danger to children, who could be exposed to excessive noise in their homes and schools. Recommendations submitted by the commission eventually culminated in the enactment of city ordinances limiting various sources of disturbing noise, including the sounding of automobile horns.[172]

The activities of the New York Noise Abatement Commission attracted an extraordinary amount of publicity and social comment. A series of eight radio broadcasts by the commission to the people of New York between December 1929 and February 1930 drew large audiences. The commission's final report cites more than 130 newspaper articles throughout the United States and Europe commenting on this project. A preliminary questionnaire from the commission that was printed in major New York newspapers elicited 11,068 complaints about specific sources of annoying community noise. On April 8, 1930, the New York City Board of Health enacted the first noise-control ordinance recommended by the commission, the so-called radio law, which prohibited "loud or excessive noise from radios." When the first conviction for violation of this ordinance was imposed (on June 4, 1930), major stories appeared in the *New York Times,* the *World,* the *New York Telegram,* the *Brooklyn Daily Eagle,* the *Herald Tribune,* and the *Evening World.*[173]

The surge of concern about environmental noise sparked legal actions during the 1930s seeking injunctive relief or damages from industrial operations that were alleged to imperil the health and comfort of nearby residents. In one such New York case, operation of an ice plant was enjoined because noise interfered with the peaceful and normal use of property by residents who lived across the street from the plant.[174] Similar suits during the 1930s originating from New Jersey shut down night operations at a bakery and a laundry, because the sleep of neighbors was being disturbed.[175] In a 1931 decision from New York, an injunction was sought against the construction of an electric substation on the grounds that it would emit a constant hum that would constitute a nuisance to nearby residents.[176] In its ruling, the court in that case remarked: "The art of acoustics has developed rapidly within the personal observation of every one. History may well record this as the decade of audition, for countless minds are to-day intent upon the projection, control, and elimination of sound."[177]

I believe that the flurry of public concern, governmental inquiries, and legal action directed at the issue of community noise during the late 1920s and early 1930s played a significant role in stimulating increased attention to the problem of occupational hearing loss. Evidence for this position can be found in the writings of many key participants in this movement, who expressly credited the heightened awareness of the dangers of urban noise for the increased concern about the plight of affected workers.

For example, in 1930 the Bureau of Women in Industry carried out one of the earliest, largest, and most highly publicized audiometric assessments of noise-induced hearing loss in industry for the New York State Department of Labor. In her cover letter accompanying the final report, the director of the bureau, Frieda S. Miller, described the motivation for undertaking the research project to the New York Industrial Commissioner, Frances Perkins. In September 1930 Miller alluded to the influence of recent studies on environmental noise, presumably including the New York City Noise Abatement Commission's study from earlier that year: "Recent interest in the effect of noise on the general well being of the urban population has become widespread. While the problems involved in industrial noise have not made the same spectacular appeal, it seems certain that they affect those subjected to them at least as vitally as urban noises do the general population."[178]

In 1936 another prominent New York medical authority, Dr. Foster Kennedy, also suggested that public reaction to the problem of community noise helped stimulate increased awareness about the dangers of noise in industry: "Today noise is listed in factory hazards with gases, fumes, dusts, toxic liquids, bacteria, and peculiar chemical and physical radiation. During the last five years there has been much probing of the problem of noise. Probably comment on the activities of the Noise Abatement Commission in New York has pushed the examination of mental and physical effects."[179]

The same association was drawn by F. K. Berrien of Colgate University, who, in 1946, offered his thoughts on some of the reasons behind the growing interest in the problem of noise in the workplace: "Most recently the safety engineers and insurance companies have expressed an interest because of the growing recognition of occupational deafness. One is reminded also of the various noise abatement campaigns which sprang into prominence in the early 1930s."[180] Passages suggesting a possible connection between the emergence of occupational NIHL and concern about the effects of environmental noise can be found in other sources from the period, including Lindahl (1938), Sabine (1944), and Glorig (1961).

The Emergence of Workers' Compensation for NIHL

Considering the extensive number of medical reports from the nineteenth and early twentieth centuries documenting hearing loss among those exposed to industrial noise, it is remarkable that occupational noise-induced hearing loss was not recognized as a compensable disorder by the workers' compensation system of any Western nation until after World War II. A number of potential explanations account for this apparent neglect. For instance, the inability to measure quantitatively the degree of hearing loss prior to the development of modern audiometers made it difficult to "prove" that an injury had occurred. Another possibly more fundamental reason is that, for most occupations, a partial loss of hearing is not critical to the performance of the job. This is particularly true for laborers in heavy industry, such as metalworking, who are most vulnerable to NIHL. Thus, unlike many other occupational diseases with gradual onset, the progression of this ailment does not necessarily presage any decline in task performance or productivity.

A potentially more discerning explanation was offered by Douglas Wheeler in 1953, who interpreted the historical indifference to NIHL as a reflection of the cultural association of loud industrial noise with admired societal traits such as strength, progress, and prosperity. Wheeler reasoned: "Until very recent years industrial noise as a by-product of an industrial process is simply going by default. It's been accepted. It's just simply, as many times as we hear in industry, accepted as evidence that production is going on, and that there is almost in that sense a virtue attached to the noise. If there were no noise apparently the plant would be shut down, which nobody wants."[181]

The Soviet Union was the first nation to recognize gradual-onset NIHL as a disorder qualifying for workers' compensation in 1929.[182] In England, compensation for noise-induced hearing loss was first studied by the Department Committee for Industrial Disease in 1907. At that time, the committee concluded that boilermakers' deafness did not prevent a laborer from continuing in his trade, and therefore was not compensable under British law. It was not until 1965 that NIHL became a prescribed industrial disease in Britain and thus eligible for compensation under the National Insurance Act, but only for acoustic trauma that occurs suddenly. Coverage for NIHL developing gradually was extended only to veterans whose impairment could be clearly related to military service.[183]

From the early days of the workers' compensation system in the United States (1911–1930), all states have had provisions in their workers' compensation statutes covering hearing loss that results from a single traumatic event as might occur in a fall or an explosion. This is in keeping with the system's original intent to compensate workers for "injuries" suffered through "accident"; that is, an incident occurring at a specific place and time in the workplace.

Prior to World War II, no compensation cases were reported for partial hearing loss that developed gradually.[184] There were, however, a few cases involving instances of repeated trauma. One such case, mentioned earlier, involved claims by a telephone operator for hearing loss due to sharp and piercing noises from her headset during a six-month period in 1927. Another early case (*Barker v. Shell Petroleum* 132 Kan. 776) in 1931 involved the repeated loud noise of gun fire on a target range. In a 1932 case (*Vaughn v. Russian Stump* 156 Okla. 25), it was alleged that repeated loud noises of exhaust caused the worker's deafness. The U.S. government had also administered similar claims involving federal workers through the U.S. Bureau of Employees' Compensation. In several states, NIHL had for many years been included in the listing of allowable compensable diseases. In Wisconsin, for example, there had been an inclusive "blanket provision" of the occupational disease code in effect since 1919, which permitted recovery for occupational noise-induced hearing loss.[185]

Nevertheless, it was not until World War II that the first claims began to be filed for compensation of partial hearing loss as a gradually acquired occupational disease. Apparently the earliest such case was that in which a forty-six-year-old welder, Hugh F. Price, who had been employed since 1941 at the California Shipbuilding Company at Terminal Island, California, submitted a claim for compensation for 75 percent loss of hearing in both ears. Because the claim was initially denied by his employer's insurance carriers, Liberty Mutual Insurance Company and Pacific Indemnity Company, an appeal was heard before a referee for the Industrial Accident Commission of the State of California. The referee awarded $3,400 to the claimant, finding that Price had "sustained injury arising out of and occurring in the course of employment to both ears caused by cumulated exposures to excessive noises."[186]

This isolated case did not immediately precipitate similar actions in California. The major turning point in the emergence of large-scale compensation for NIHL came with two landmark decisions a few years later; one in New York in 1948 (*Slawinski v. J. H. Williams & Co.*) and the other in Wisconsin in 1953 (*Wojcik v. Green Bay Drop Forge*).

The first workers' compensation claim for occupational hearing loss in

New York was filed in 1946 by an employee of the Despatch Shops, Incorporated, of East Rochester, New York, a maker of steel freight cars. New York, at that time, had an existing occupational disease provision of its workers' compensation code that included a schedule of allowable payments for each disease depending on the extent of the claimant's disability. In May of 1947, with the assistance of an attorney from the United Steelworkers of America (USW), approximately 300–400 union members at that facility filed similar claims.[187] Apparently, one factor directly precipitating these claims was the introduction of new noisy machinery into one department of the plant.[188] The insurance company representing Despatch Shops, the Liberty Mutual Insurance Company, denied payment for these claims on the grounds that the hearing loss was not a recognized occupational disease according to New York's compensation statute and that no employment "disability" had occurred, as defined under the law. In addition, Liberty Mutual and its attorney, Noel Symons, argued that compensation should be withheld because there was no medical proof that the hearing loss was permanent, insofar as some hearing ability might be recovered after removal from the exposure.[189]

In 1947, several additional claims for hearing loss were made at other facilities in the Buffalo and Rochester areas, including the General Drop Forge Company and J. H. Williams & Company. The New York Compensation Board handed down favorable decisions for the claimants in several preliminary cases, which prompted appeals to the courts by the employers and insurers.[190] The claimant in the *Slawinski* case was Matthew Slawinski, a sixty-year-old machine operator who had worked for several years in the forging area of the J. H. Williams plant where noise levels regularly exceeded 100 dB. At the time of his claim, Slawinski was still employed and had suffered no wage loss.

In July 1948, the New York Court of Appeals determined that Slawinski was suffering from an occupational disease under the legal definition in New York's statute, and that he was entitled to a scheduled award for loss of hearing even though there had been no wage loss. He was granted an award for 45 percent loss of hearing in the left ear and 43.6 percent in the right ear, which entitled him to 66.5 weeks' compensation, amounting to $1,661.[191] The decision established a major new workers' compensation doctrine of a scheduled loss for an occupational disease without loss of earnings. Immediately after the ruling, nearly four hundred similar claims were filed in New York State.[192] By 1952, claims for NIHL had been filed by 730 employees of Despatch Shops, more than 50 percent of the plant workforce.[193]

In December 1951, prompted by the developments in New York, 232 workers at the Hoboken, New Jersey, shipyard of the Bethlehem Steel Company, also represented by the United Steelworkers, filed civil suits seeking some $5 million in damages for deafness due to occupational noise, in part to goad New Jersey into following New York's lead and recognizing NIHL as a compensable disorder under its workers' compensation law.[194]

Wisconsin also had an existing occupational disease provision in its Workers' Compensation Act, with a maximum scheduled award for bilateral hearing loss of $12,333.[195] Despite the fact that the act had been in force since 1919, the first claim for NIHL was not filed until 1947, when an employee of the A. O. Smith Corporation in Milwaukee was awarded $2,000. Apparently, this initial case did not create a great deal of attention, but it did stimulate other companies, such as the Allis Chalmers Company (also located in Milwaukee), to initiate extensive research on the subject and establish a noise abatement program in their plants.[196]

By 1949, awards of up to $5,000 had been made in approximately half a dozen Wisconsin cases. Within the next three years, several hundred similar claims were filed, most of which were against the Ladish Forge Company in the Milwaukee suburb of Cudahy.[197]

As additional cases were filed, employers and their insurance carriers, alarmed over the increasing number of claims, decided to test one case (*Wojcik v. Green Bay Drop Forge*) before the courts. As in New York, the central issue in this seminal Wisconsin case was whether an award for occupational disease could be made in the absence of wage loss. In October 1953, after several contradictory lower court rulings, the Wisconsin Supreme Court upheld an award to the claimant of $1,575.[198] The ruling precipitated the filing in Wisconsin of more than five hundred new claims for NIHL within the next year.[199]

In Wisconsin, organized labor played an active role in pushing for the acceptance of hearing loss claims within the state workers' compensation system and in bringing the problem of NIHL to the attention of the rank and file. Most noteworthy were the efforts of Local 247 of the International Brotherhood of Blacksmiths, Drop Forgers, and Helpers, the union to which all of the claimants in the first several hundred Wisconsin claims belonged. A young union lawyer, Steve Hajduch, filed the initial claims on behalf of the Ladish workers, and represented them throughout the ensuing legal and political challenges.[200] Local 247 led the fight in Wisconsin for recognition of NIHL in the state workers' compensation system and approval for compensation of physical impairment in the absence of wage loss. This platform was first spelled out forcefully in a pamphlet entitled *Occupational Deafness: Real or Imaginary?* which was published by the union in 1953 and distributed widely to Wisconsin workers.

Based on the success of Local 247, the union's International (which in June 1954 had merged with the Boilermakers Union to become the International Brotherhood of Boilermakers, Iron Ship Builders, Blacksmiths, Drop Forgers and Helpers) took up the banner, launching a nationwide educational program on occupational hearing loss in August of 1954, which included the publication of another widely distributed booklet, *Deafness: The Hazard of Occupational Noise*. When the political focus turned to federal regulation in the late 1960s, this union was again in the forefront, leading the drive to enact a national noise control standard through lobbying and educational activities.[201]

An examination of some of the union's publications provides a flavor of how the debates were waged during those years, especially in Wisconsin. For example, Michael Wood, the president of Local 247 and principal author of the 1953 pamphlet, vehemently attacked management's neglect of the problem:

> Today an unheralded abuse of one of the elementary senses granted by nature to man is on the loose. The noise produced by our modern industrial machinery daily causes untold loss of hearing to thousands upon thousands of wage earners. This shocking condition has not only been kept from the general public, but it has also remained an enigma to the very people it victimizes, the workers themselves. Industrial deafness as a result of industrial noise, for the most part is being met with silence by those responsible for creating it. Where silence is not enough to still the protests of forge workers, boilermakers, printing pressmen, machinists, etc., then denial, scientific double talk and legalistic hokum are the device of managerial protest.[202]

Not surprisingly, he attributed management's indifference to its pecuniary motives and maintained that only financial penalties extracted from industry would lead to real progress in addressing any occupational hazard:

> Behind the growing concern of industry, albeit without benefit of fanfare, is the dread speculation of paying the deafened worker for his disability. Compensation in any form (except the absence of it) was never popular with industrial management—and isn't yet. There is little doubt that if the Industrial Commissions of Wisconsin and New York hadn't handed down awards in favor of the claimants whose deafness was well illustrated to be of industrial origin, management and the insurance carriers would hardly show more than curious interest in the problems of industrial deafness. It is well to appreciate the meaning of this fact (i.e., the payment of compensation) for it alone constituted the motivating force required to bring into being the many compensation laws and safety regulations we have today throughout

the United States. Contrary to current myth, not moral or human-itarian considerations are involved herein, but the payment of money adjustments for damages inflicted. The payment of money is a painful step for management to make in matters such as this.[203]

According to the union's historical interpretation of the events in Wisconsin, the publication of *Occupational Deafness: Real or Imaginary?* and the other educational activities of Local 247 had a tremendous impact on swaying the Wisconsin court decisions and achieving compensation for gradual-onset hearing impairment in that state. In this regard, the International wrote, in 1954, that of all the factors involved in the growth of compensation claims in Wisconsin "the publication of the booklet, *Occupational Deafness: Real or Imaginary? . . .* was possibly the one that created the greatest concern, because it was the first attempt on the part of any labor organization to make such a study, and, more important . . . gave many of the views of organized labor on the subject."[204]

Explaining the Sudden Growth of Claims after World War II

Looking back at the initial developments in New York and Wisconsin, one is struck by the extremely abrupt appearance of the initial claims for NIHL, and the startling numbers of claimants who quickly materialized. Equally astonishing was the immediate attention the influx of new claims provoked within the occupational health, safety, business and insurance communities. It is interesting to speculate on why this problem suddenly appeared as it did immediately following the end of World War II, and why the question of industrial hearing loss quickly soared towards the top of the nation's occupational health agenda, emerging as a top priority for workers' compensation and industrial safety. Several factors which together accounted for this extraordinary ascendance have been mentioned in this chapter. The principal catalysts behind the spectacular growth of NIHL claims between 1946 and 1952 appear to be audiometric testing, the return of disabled veterans, commercialization of the noise problem, the environmental noise movement, wartime employment of women, and the strength of organized labor.

Audiometric testing. The development of the modern electronic audiometer provided workers and physicians with a new means for identifying and measuring partial hearing loss. Highly publicized mass screening programs, especially the 1939 New York World's Fair testing, attracted considerable public attention and brought hearing loss to the attention of many individuals who had previously been unaware of the problem. During World War II, large-scale audiometric testing programs for military draftees and active servicemen detected a high prevalence of hearing impairment. Immediately after the war, routine audiometric screening was expanded into the industrial environment, with the active assistance of otologists and audiologists who had gained wartime experience applying these techniques.

Return of disabled veterans. In the aftermath of the war, the nation was confronted with the tremendous social problem of integrating huge numbers of disabled veterans back into productive employment. The United States economy needed to absorb an estimated 1.5 million disabled veterans, approximately 40,000 of which were thought to have war-related hearing loss. The plight of the returning veterans garnered considerable public sympathy, and there was a general recognition that extraordinary measures would have to be taken to accommodate these individuals. Moreover, a large number of veterans had applied for pensions and compensation from the Veterans Administration for injuries acquired in the military. Claims to the VA for NIHL were numerous and were, in general, readily accepted.[205]

In this social environment, it would have been very difficult for workers' compensation administrators between 1946 and 1952 to deny compensation for hearing disorders arising in the workplace, especially those occurring in such war-related industries as steelmaking, shipbuilding, and forging. In general, the prevailing sentiment in America was to respond generously and liberally to claims involving war-related disabilities, among both those who had labored in factories during the war and disabled veterans who may have discovered their hearing loss upon return to industrial employment.

Commercialization of the noise problem. Commercial interests heavily promoted this issue in the late 1940s and early 1950s. The aggressive advertising and marketing campaigns of the hearing aid companies were particularly notorious. Their objective in pushing for the expanded recognition and compensability of partial deafness was to build a larger clientele for their products. The same kind of influence was exerted by businesses like MSA and Western Electric, which stood to profit by the increased use of hearing protectors, industrial noise abatement services, and audiometric test equipment.

Environmental noise movement. The noise abatement campaigns of the late 1920s and early 1930s helped stimulate the original recognition of occupational NIHL. In the years immediately after World War II, there was a resurgence of interest in the problem of environmental noise stemming, at least in part, from the introduction into the community of new sources of noise that had been developed during the war. One of the most visible and provoking of these sources was the sound of commercial and military aircraft, particularly jet planes. Further igniting community response to larger and louder aircraft was the postwar migration to the suburbs, which were often located within earshot of major airports and military bases.

This factor was stressed by Dr. Adam Glorig, who, during the postwar years, was regarded as one of the nation's leading authorities on the effects of noise.

Shortly after World War II, the jet military airplane became quite commonplace and with its husky screaming roar and sonic booms came an avalanche of complaints from the public. The transition from the familiar slow moving piston-engine plane to the unfamiliar fast moving ghostly jet appeared to be the straw that broke the camel's back. Community noise became a serious problem almost overnight. Why? Were the few additional decibels enough to increase the annoyance that much, or was the public unprepared for the sudden intrusion the jet had made into its innermost sanctum—the relative quiet of home?

Suddenly the annoying aspect of noise has changed from a molehill to a mountain. Public reaction is demanding quieter airplanes, rearranged airports, and zoning laws governing airport locations. National and international organizations are demanding noise suppression and noise control ordinances.[206]

Intense concern about environmental noise in New York during the 1930s helps explain why the first workers' compensation claims for NIHL appeared in that state. New York Noise Abatement Commission studies prompted industrial audiometric screenings, which found that significant numbers of workers were being injured by workplace noise. Some of the same individuals who had been instrumental in the Noise Abatement Commission later became major proponents for increased attention to the problem of occupational hearing loss. For example, Dr. Foster Kennedy was one of the first to call specifically for the inclusion of NIHL under the New York state compensation law.[207] In New York, the focus on environmental noise during the early 1930s had created an infrastructure of lawyers, physicians, government officials, and technical experts familiar with the effects of noise on human health. When returning veterans started re-entering the industrial workplace, it is not surprising that the question of compensating victims of noise-induced hearing loss emerged first as a major political priority in New York State.

Women in the workplace. Some commentators have suggested that the increasing numbers of women in the workforce during World War II made employers and physicians more sensitive to the discomforts of working in a loud environment. There is abundant evidence that many felt uncomfortable with the idea of women working in heavy industry, a practice that had become necessary as part of the war effort. The cultural adulation of strength and prowess associated with loud noise was not extended to females—especially by those who felt that "frail" women ought not to be subjected to the rigors of industrial life. Some authorities felt that the accelerating rate of women entering heavy industry during World War II pointed to a need for an intensified effort by medical and safety professionals to detect and control sources of potentially injurious occupational noise. Dr. Paul Sabine suggested this perspective in 1944:

> It has only been within the last few years that any serious attention has been given to the problem of noise in industrial plants. Only with the war demand for increased production and the influx of women workers into heavy industries, has the noise problem received any consideration on the part of industrial management. . . . It is a well established fact that women are more subject to physical strain and have a greater short-sickness rate than men. If women are to retain (which God forbid) any considerable part in heavy industry then, from the standpoint of both public health and efficient management, the greater susceptibility of women to an adverse acoustical environment should be recognized.[208]

Organized labor. Several labor unions initiated aggressive campaigns following the war to educate workers about the dangers of noise and to secure the recognition of compensation for noise-induced hearing impairment. Most noteworthy were the efforts of the International Brotherhood of Blacksmiths, Drop Forgers, and Helpers in Wisconsin and the United Steelworkers in New York. The merger of the former with the International Boilermakers and Ship Builders in 1954 reflected the need of both unions to preserve their membership base in industries that were facing cut-backs as a result of the war's end.[209] It is perhaps not a coincidence that occupational deafness was traditionally considered to be most severe in those particular industries, and that both unions had re-employed a large number of World War II veterans. By focusing their efforts on NIHL in those industries, the unions were tapping into the traditional worker concern about deafness that existed in those trades, and into the apprehension of veterans who feared that the war may have affected their hearing.

The efforts of the USW to promote the filing of claims for NIHL must also be seen as an outgrowth of postwar labor economics in the steel industry. Cut-backs in production immediately after the war and the lifting of wartime price-hike restrictions by the federal government set off a massive wave of nationwide strikes for higher wages by steel, automobile, and coal workers in

Table 5   Historical Trends in the Steel Industry, 1944–1956

	Total Hours	Average Hours per Week	Operating Rate as Percentage of Capacity
1944	1,193,025	46.7	95.5
1945	1,082,529	44.2	83.5
1946	896,679	35.1	72.5
1947	1,057,596	38.6	93.0
1948	1,105,103	39.1	94.1
1949	945,044	34.5	81.1
1950	1,097,781	39.0	96.9
1951	1,189,797	40.2	100.9
1952	1,020,435	35.8	85.8
1953	1,175,370	39.4	94.9
1954	945,637	36.1	71.0
1955	1,118,225	39.2	93.0
1956	1,081,249	38.6	89.9

1946, the same year that initial claims were filed by steelworkers for NIHL. In 1949, when an economic slowdown again affected the steel industry (see table 5), the USW struck again, but this time the issues were fringe benefits and financial security for sickness, disability, and retirement.[210]

In arguing the steelworkers' case before President Harry S. Truman's Steel Industry Board in May 1949, Philip Murray, president of the USW, emphasized the importance of occupational health issues in the contract dispute with the steel producers. He paid special attention to occupational diseases that arise through prolonged exposure which could lead to disability at retirement:

> Particularly in a heavy industry like steel, with its accidents, occupational disease and wearing out processes, workers do not last forever. They become worn out physically and occupationally. Finally, the worker is too old to work and too young to die. He must live in destitution or become a public charge. The costs of his care should be placed squarely on the industry which used his labor and exhausted his sinews.
>
> Illness means a double loss to workers. When a man is unable to work, his pay check stops coming, and it is out of this pay check that he must pay for his medical and hospital bills. At the same time, his regular bills continue, for rent, food, clothing, etc.

So-called industrial health programs (care for on-the-job accidents) and workmen's compensation laws also help out the worker, but only in a partial and inadequate way. They cover only a minor part of his injuries and illnesses. The big burden is still on the individual worker's shoulder to bear as best he can . . . such [medical] bills become especially burdensome when an illness is long. The cost may mean financial ruin to a family . . . Workmen's compensation just covers on-the-job hazards. This is of no help in most of the worker's health problems.[211]

After two government-imposed "truces" and a nationwide forty-five-day strike, the USW finally signed an agreement with the major steel makers in November 1949. It was a mixed victory for the USW; the union won its demands for a fully funded retirement pension, but gained only a 50 percent company contribution toward a scaled-down social insurance plan.[212] After a protracted and bitter strike, the steel workers still had only marginal protection against long-term sickness and medical incapacity at retirement. Murray had made a point of arguing that "the cost of care should be placed squarely on the industry." Based on the agreement, this was only possible in the case of conditions that were deemed to result directly from the occupation. Thus, as the steelworkers entered the 1950s, there was additional incentive for them to push for the recognition of noise-induced hearing loss and other chronic disabling conditions as potentially work-related and thus compensable under state workers' compensation insurance programs.

Reaction to the Rise of Compensation Claims

The special characteristics of noise-induced hearing loss posed fundamental difficulties for workers' compensation administrators. It often takes a long time, commonly ten years or more of exposure, for NIHL to progress to a clearly recognized and debilitating state. This made it difficult to fix a date of injury that was commonly required by most state compensation codes. Also, by the time severe NIHL is recognized, a worker may have reached advanced age. Workers and the medical community found it difficult, if not impossible, to distinguish a claimant's occupational hearing loss from the allegedly natural loss of sensory function (presbycusis) that occurs as people grow older. And unlike many other occupational diseases, such as asbestos or silicosis, significant sources of exposure to this causative agent (that is, noise) are ubiquitous outside the workplace, for example, in daily recreational activities, hobbies, the enjoyment of music, and in other settings throughout one's community. The intent of the workers' compensation system is to provide benefits only for disorders that are demonstrably work-related. Thus, the apparent inability to gauge the precise influence and relative importance of nonoccupational risk factors for noise was considered a major problem.

The supposed potential for NIHL to be reversed also created unique difficulties for the workers' compensation system. Workers suffering a temporary change in hearing sensitivity (a temporary threshold shift) as a result of exposure to noise will generally recover their previous acuity after a period of time away from the exposure. Only after a prolonged period of continued exposure does the threshold shift begin to become permanent. In awarding compensation it is thus critical to determine if permanent or only temporary impairment has occurred, since a worker suffering only a temporary shift will normally regain previous (to exposure) hearing abilities. Even after permanent damage has occurred, some portion of the former hearing sensitivity may return with removal from the noisy environment. There are conflicting medical opinions about how long it takes to regain this portion. So the question arose, at what point in this process to grant compensation? And for what level of impairment? These questions take on added significance given that the vast majority of NIHL cases, even those in which there is permanent threshold shift, do not affect the worker's ability to converse with fellow employees and perform required job duties. In that sense, there is no real "disability" involved with most NIHL cases. Here too, a fundamental dilemma was created for a workers' compensation system originally designed around the concept of employment disability. The basic intent of the system is to provide payment for economic losses that arise because of a worker's inability to perform normal job functions due to workplace injury. In NIHL, there generally is no restriction on function and no corresponding loss of wages. The traditional system had no mechanism for addressing this concern.

Perhaps the most critical difficulty posed by the early workers' compensation claims for NIHL was the sheer number of workers who were potentially affected. Previously, occupational diseases such as lead poisoning and silicosis affected only a limited group of workers in specific industries. By contrast, an estimated twenty million workers (more than 25 percent of the American workforce) were exposed to workplace noise that could damage their hearing. No disease in the history of workers' compensation had come close to NIHL in its potential for creating massive losses for American industry, Floyd Frazier, a spokesman for the insurance industry, observed in 1955. "Unlike the situations which existed when silicosis and lead poisoning became factors in workmen's compensation we are dealing here with an impairment which is not restricted to workers within a few specific industries. Noises of intensity and frequency which may be considered harmful are encountered in practically all industries. The number of workers who might become potential claimants solely on the basis of existing hearing loss unless proper allowances are made for losses not attributable to the job is practically *without limit*" (emphasis added).[213]

The reaction to these developments by employers and their insurance carriers was understandably one of panic. Dire predictions of economic calamity came from many corners. There were estimates that occupational loss of hearing could eventually result in $1–7 billion in claims nationwide and that some employers and insurers might become insolvent as a consequence.[214] C. Richard Walmer, managing director of the Industrial Hygiene Foundation of America, publicly warned that industry was facing a costly tidal wave of claims greater than the "silicosis, radium, and smog cases combined."[215] Magazines and trade journals carried headlines alerting business to the approaching financial disaster, such as "Claims for loss of hearing menace plants financially. Rush is on to lock stable before horse escapes" and "Will industry be deluged with a tidal wave of claims?"[216] Joseph R. Shaw, president of the Associated Industries of New York State, Incorporated, testified to the New York legislature that the influx of new claims for occupational hearing impairment was "the most serious fundamental problem to occur in our workmen's compensation program since its inception in 1914" and predicted that this problem would become "a threatened knockout to industry which is already feeling the effects of substantially higher business costs in New York State."[217] Similar forecasts were made in Wisconsin. Robert Ewens, representing the Wisconsin Manufacturers Association, stated in 1954 that if Wisconsin were to enact new workers' compensation legislation modeled on the Wojcik decision, "the cost would be from $50-$400 million in Wisconsin and that 15 noisy industries were thinking of moving away if some relief can't be given. Michigan, Illinois and other nearby states don't provide similar compensation."[218] He estimated that 50,000 workers in Wisconsin were prepared to submit claims.[219]

In this atmosphere of alarm and apprehension, comparisons were drawn with the silicosis crisis of the 1930s. The collective social memory of that scare exerted a tremendous impact on employers, government and labor, both in eliciting fear of large-scale economic ruination and loss of jobs, and also in furnishing a potential model of how NIHL could be used by labor as a political tactic in the courts and compensation system. An article in *Modern Industry* magazine in 1953 entitled "Noise Is News" articulated this position:

When industry was confronted, in the mid-1930s, with thousands of claims for workmen's compensation for silicosis contracted by employees, many companies faced bankruptcy. Many shut down, and their workers were added to the rolls of the unemployed. The silicosis claims became a high-water mark of seriousness of a new kind of compensation claim for which neither manufacturers nor the insurance industry had prepared.

The situation became so grave that legislatures eventually had to pass new laws dealing with the crisis. Affected companies, given a new lease on life, turned to cutting down hazards, building up insurance reserves, testing employees and working environments, and exclaiming, "Never again!"

The "never" was a little too optimistic. The "again" has come.

This time it is in the form of widespread claims for compensation for loss of hearing due, or allegedly due, to occupational hazards. In New York, New Jersey, Illinois, Maryland, and currently of most interest, in Wisconsin, the threat of a new kind of compensation claim to the financial stability of many companies has become a disturbing reality.[220]

Noel Symons, a prominent business attorney who had represented management at Despatch Shops, also used the legacy of the silicosis crisis of the 1930s to heighten corporate fear and attract support for new restrictive legislation. The initial filing of claims for hearing loss in New York, claimed Symons, "indicates that a trend, analogous to, but far more serious than, the silicosis 'earthquake' of the thirties, is underway." He continued: "This identical problem caused a great deal of trouble in New York when silicosis was first held to be an occupational disease. Thousands of men were thrown out of work because plants with a serious dust exposure could not obtain insurance coverage, and could not operate without it. The crisis did not pass until 1936 when labor itself recognized the need of strong action, and the legislature—at the joint urging of both employee and employer organizations— recognized this problem of accrued liability by barring awards entirely for partial disability and establishing a low schedule of benefits, gradually stepped up over the years, for total disability and death."[221]

In reaction to this prevailing spirit of impending doom, a fascinating alliance of employers, insurance carriers, and legislators quickly emerged to contain what they perceived to be an unbridled threat to the nation's economic interests. A remarkable flurry of activity ensued, and during 1952– 1956 that alliance, together with the medical and scientific communities, molded a new theoretical framework for incorporating the complex features of NIHL into the existing workers' compensation system. Reminiscent of industry's reaction to the influx of silicosis claims in the mid-1930s, the intent of revising the workers' compensation codes was to establish a trade-off of interests by formally recognizing NIHL claims for noneconomic loss of function within the system, in exchange for imposing relatively stringent eligibility criteria and maximum payment limitations on compensation awards. New legislation incorporating these principles was quickly enacted, first in New York and Wisconsin (in 1955), and then in fourteen other states.[222]

A key feature of the new legislation was specific calculational formulae for evaluating and quantifying the extent of hearing impairment, based not only on the threshold shifts that had occurred but also the normally expected effects of presbycusis. Earlier versions of these formulae had been developed in 1929 by H. Fletcher (the so-called Point 8 Rule) and in 1947 by the American Medical Association (AMA) Council on Physical Medicine. The AMA formula was based on pure tone audiometry and used losses at 500, 1,000, 2,000, and 4,000 Hz to determine the percentage of hearing disability.

By contrast, the formulae adopted in the mid-1950s in New York, Wisconsin, and other states were based on the assumption that impairment should be construed as an effect on one's ability to communicate and thus best assessed in terms only of threshold shifts that occur in the lower frequency ranges (500–2,000 Hz).[223] As mentioned earlier, most early noise-induced threshold shifts occur in the higher frequency ranges (3,000–5,000 Hz). The new legislation essentially ignored the early stages of impairment caused by exposure to noise, and compensable NIHL came to be defined primarily in terms of the later-stage manifestations of the disease.

In both New York and Wisconsin, such a formula was included in the legislation at the suggestion of a specially appointed medical advisory panel, which included physicians heavily biased toward industry. For example, in Wisconsin, the principal medical expert proposing this formula was Dr. Meyer Fox, medical director for Ladish Forge Company and a medical consultant to the Liberty Mutual Insurance Company.[224]

Based on the testimony of the medical experts in New York and Wisconsin, the Subcommittee on Noise in Industry of the American Academy of Ophthalmology and Otolaryngology (AAOO) officially adopted the same calculational scheme in 1955, and that version soon came to be the generally accepted model used in most states.[225] In 1963, California took a significant step in liberalizing its approach by adding a consideration of losses occurring at 3,000 Hz. The AAOO (in 1977) and AMA (in 1979) eventually followed suit, inserting the 3,000 Hz measurement as a compromise for those who felt that the determination of impairment must include not only the effect on speech, but also the early-stage hearing decrements that are manifested initially in the higher ranges. The National Institute for Occupational Safety and Health (NIOSH) developed a comparable formula in 1972, which also capped the losses at the level of 3,000 Hz.[226] By 1986, essentially all states had adopted this general practice—only Oklahoma and Oregon specifically included 4,000 Hz losses in their calculation of hearing impairment.[227]

Probably the most influential and controversial aspect of the new legislation was the requirement of a waiting period of six months away from noise exposure before assessment of impairment, and hence compensation, could be granted. From a practical standpoint, the requirement meant that current workers were no longer eligible for awards. This effectively shifted the focus of the workers' compensation program for NIHL away from current workers toward retirees.

Ostensibly, this provision for a "waiting period" was based on available medical evidence that some partial recovery of function may occur in time, even when permanent threshold shifts had taken place. It had been formally adopted on June 30, 1951, as a scientific "statement of policy" by the Committee on Conservation of Hearing of the AAOO: "Hearing loss produced by exposure to loud noise may be considered as permanent six months following complete removal of the individual from the area of loud noise."[228] The same opinion was offered by the Committee of Consultants on Occupational Loss of Hearing, the ad hoc group of experts that had been assembled by the New York Workmen's Compensation Board. In December 1953 it stated: "Until such time as the above discussed research evidence is available on which to base a precise answer, your committee is of the opinion that the present policy of the Board in this matter should be continued, namely, that appraisal of permanency of an occupational hearing loss be made after an interval of not less than six months after the cessation of exposure to the injurious noise."[229]

However, knowledgeable persons knew, even then, that the scientific evidence on this question was inconclusive and marginal at best. The real agenda was to transform the workers' compensation payment system for NIHL into a retirement benefit for which a large percentage of industrial workers would be potentially eligible. Then, as now, legislators and insurers saw something to be gained in shifting cost outflows to future years and making the system more predictable from an actuarial standpoint.

The lack of scientific substantiation for this waiting period concept was cleverly revealed in a heated exchange that took place in 1953 at the annual convention of the International Association of Industrial Accident Boards and Commissions between Adam Glorig, a U.S. Army otologist and prominent medical authority who had helped draft the original AAOO policy statement, and J. Harry Tiernam, Jr., a New York labor official with the United Steelworkers of America:

Mr. Tiernam: I would like to address a question to Dr. Glorig. Doctor, in any case where there is an authenticated loss of hearing due to noise, has there been any one case where it has been established that there is an improvement between the period of twenty-four hours after stopping work and six months after stopping work?

Dr. Glorig: I expected somebody was going to put me on the spot with this question, and I think I'm going to claim my constitutional rights in that if I answer it, I might incriminate myself.

I answered that in my talk, I think, about as good an answer as I can give you at the present time, and we do not talk of individual cases when we talk about a problem as general as this; we talk about probabilities and a majority of cases. I would not be willing to say that I had seen any definite evidence that a large number of cases had come within the confines of this question. We do not know yet. We do not have enough evidence.

Mr. Tiernam: Doctor, to reach a question of probability must you not have one case to show that there's a possibility, and is it not a fact that there has been no such case?

Dr. Glorig: You must have one case to establish a spread, as it is called in statistical jargon; but you don't need one case in order to establish a probability. You need ninety out of a hundred cases or similar figure.

Mr. Tiernam: It isn't the probability I asked about; it was the possibility. Is it even possible that there's such improvement and has there been one case to establish the possibility?

Dr. Glorig: I think that the possibility is always there in anything that concerns humans. We do know that there are people who can work in very loud noises and not develop a hearing loss, but we also know that one man can be exposed to a single pistol shot and suffer almost total hearing loss in one ear. This is the kind of spread that occurs in human susceptibility, so that if you are going to ask if any one case ever improved after twenty-four hours, I suppose it has happened, but I can't say that I've ever seen one that has been measured.

Mr. Tiernam: Thank you, Doctor.[230]

Years later, some of the medical experts who had originally sponsored this position in the early 1950s confessed that it was merely a fabricated device to help save the threatened industries. For instance, Dr. W. Dixon Ward, a leading authority on NIHL after the war, offered this reminiscence in 1969: "In order to keep all the drop-forge industries there from financial ruin as every one of their employees filed suit to collect for their massive hearing losses, the Wisconsin compensation law stipulated that before a worker could file he had to be out of the noise for six months. The *stated* [emphasis in original] reason, of course was that this period was necessary in order to allow complete disappearance of auditory fatigue, but that is so much eyewash. Three months is more than adequate to permit the recovery of whatever sensitivity will be regained; in fact after *one* month of quiet, the additional recovery to be expected is only on the order of a couple of decibels."[231] A similar assessment was made in 1960 by John Zapp of the Du Pont Chemical Company:

> It has been recognized by labor, industry and Government that some rule must be adopted which will permit compensation for hearing loss when deserved, but which at the same time will not create havoc with the economy. The approach adopted in most cases specifies a waiting period of six months after occupational noise exposure ceases before the degree of hearing impairment is calculated. It was at first held that the six months' period was necessary to allow maximum recovery of hearing following cessation of noise exposure. Subsequent studies indicated that maximum recovery would probably occur in a much shorter time, but the six months' waiting period was retained because it postpones the adjudication of many potential claims for hearing loss to some time in the future when the claimant is no longer gainfully employed.[232]

The indications are that this not-so-secret agenda found tacit acceptance among labor leaders, who could inform their constituency both of the victory gained in obtaining formal recognition of nonwage loss awards within the workers' compensation system and, at the same time, in winning a new welfare benefit for workers who are elderly, retired, laid-off, or otherwise incapacitated in their jobs. The fact that approximately one hundred members of the International Brotherhood of Blacksmiths, Drop Forgers, and Helpers were let go at a drop forge plant in Wisconsin in February of 1954 also may have helped convince labor leaders that the alleged economic threat to their industry was real.[233] Both the AFL and the CIO endorsed the 1955 legislative bill in Wisconsin that incorporated the six-month waiting rule. Dr. Stewart Nash, who was retained by the United Steelworkers to provide medical testimony in the Despatch Shops cases in New York, explained (in 1952) the supposed benefits of the compromise in these terms:

1. The industrial plants will be kept in operation.
2. The worker will have continuous employment and will not (in an effort to obtain similar work) be required to remove himself and his family to another locality.
3. Deferring payment of awards until retirement will spread an otherwise ruinous expenditure over a period of years and lighten an almost unbearable financial burden on the employer and carrier.
4. The worker will get his award on retirement when he needs it most.[234]

Richard Ginnold attributes labor's apparently passive acquiescence in Wisconsin to the initial enactment of this legislation primarily to its weak political position in that state. In 1953, when the initial Wisconsin legislation was being crafted, both houses of the legislature had been controlled for more than a decade by Republicans, and Republican Governor Walter Kohler, a large employer himself, was in his second term. The four-member Medical Advisory Committee was headed by Dr. Meyer Fox, a consultant for insurance and business interests. The chairman of the state's three-member Industrial Commission was "Rube" Knutson, a former vice president of Employers Mutual Insurance. According to Ginnold, in this political environment, labor had little choice but to assent to compromise legislation that codified the principle of compensation without wage loss at the price of severely restricting the ultimate economic responsibilities of the employer. Ginnold contends: "Labor was outnumbered from the beginning by the employers and the 'nonvoting' insurance company representatives who had interests identical with employers on most compensation issues and whose 'voice' was as good as a vote in influencing the 'agreed bill.' There was little real bargaining from the time the issue was raised in 1953, since labor had no alternatives beyond the agreed bill."[235]

When workers finally realized that the six-month waiting period effectively cut off any realistic possibility of obtaining compensation for job-related hearing loss, there were efforts in the various state legislatures to relax those restrictions. Industry fought vigorously to save them. The Associated Industries of New York State (AINYS), a lobbying organization for New York business, testified at legislative committee hearings in 1955 that if the six-month waiting period was withdrawn by the Workman's Compensation Board, the resulting avalanche of claims could force many industries out of business.[236] Floyd Frazier of the National Association of Mutual Casualty Companies, and member of the AINYS Committee of Noise in Industry, stated: "If in New York, where the full degree of hearing loss is compensable the 6-months waiting period were to be abrogated, it is entirely possible that many industrial concerns might not be able to assume the financial burden which might result."[237]

The scare tactics of industry accomplished their objective—the six-month waiting period was retained in New York and most other states. Audiometric assessment for compensation purposes in most all states continued to be based on frequency ranges below 4,000 Hz, the level at which noise-induced hearing impairment would normally be expected to begin. As a result of these limitations, the succeeding years saw a continuing, but relatively moderate level of hearing loss claims. Claims which were filed involved primarily the elderly, retirees, and those laid off from work. It was not until 1980 that

New York modified its statute to recognize the wearing of hearing protection by workers as one way of fulfilling the waiting period requirement, thereby expanding the scope of the act to include current workers. However, as of 1981, waiting periods still existed in at least a dozen states.[238]

More important, the sense of urgency that developed during the mid-1950s due to the fear of massive compensation awards helped to stimulate attention from the safety community on the control of noise in the workplace. More than two hundred books and articles were written during the period 1955–1970 on methods for controlling workplace noise. For the first time, management provided workers with hearing protection and encouraged its use. Audiometric testing programs were established, not only for screening purposes, but also to establish baselines of pre-existing hearing loss and to detect incipient cases so that hearing protection or other remedial action could be initiated.

Prompted also by the developments in workers' compensation, a concerted effort began to establish a federal noise standard. The first attempt to regulate noise on the job occurred in December 1960 when the Department of Labor established allowable levels of noise exposure that could be considered administratively to be in compliance with the Walsh-Healy Public Contracts Act. This 1936 act applied to any employers who contracted with the U.S. government in excess of $10,000 per year. The suggested rules covered sound level measurements, hearing conservation criteria, noise control methods, audiometry, personal protective devices, measuring instruments, and recordkeeping. Public debate was marked by considerable dissension, particularly by members of the American Industrial Hygiene Association. It was not until May 1968 that the American Conference of Governmental Industrial Hygienists (ACGIH) adopted a threshold limit value (TLV) for noise and submitted this TLV for inclusion into the proposed Walsh-Healy occupational noise regulation. Finally, on January 17, 1969, the U.S. Department of Labor published its final noise standard (which became effective on May 20, 1969) which included the ACGIH's noise TLV. When the OSHA act came into being on December 29, 1970, the Walsh-Healy Noise Standard was adopted as the OSHA General Industry Noise Standard (29 CFR 1910.95) and the Construction Noise Standard (29 CFR 1926.52) on May 29, 1971. Only agricultural workers were exempted from the occupational noise standard. Because noise is a pervasive occupational health hazard, and sound level meters are relatively easy to use, noise soon became OSHA's most frequent health citation. During OSHA's first ten years, noise citations accounted for nearly 50 percent of all health citations.[239]

Owing to the factors described above, NIHL never reached the epidemic proportions feared by many of the early foreseers of doom during the 1950s.

Despite the reportedly high prevalence of occupationally induced hearing loss in industry, the actual number of workers' compensation claims filed for NIHL has remained relatively modest. A report prepared for the Environmental Protection Agency (EPA) in 1979 found that fourteen states had experienced no claims for NIHL and that in twenty-seven other states, fewer than thirty claims per year were being paid. The EPA report attributed the relatively low number of claims filings to a "variety of factors such as six-month waiting periods before filing, restrictive impairment formulas, severe filing deadlines, lack of worker choice of physician, or deductions for aging."[240]

In Wisconsin, there were only 848 claims awarded for NIHL from 1950 to 1972, an average of thirty-seven cases per year. These claims totaled $1.5 million, less than 0.2 percent of all workers' compensation payments made in Wisconsin during that period.[241] Alleyne et al. (1989), using Canadian data, found that NIHL makes up only 0.3 percent of all workers' compensation claims. Data from the Liberty Mutual Insurance Company for 1987–1990 show that NIHL claims represent only .085 percent of all workers' compensation claims and 3.4 percent of all claims for occupational disease.[242]

Summary

The potentially detrimental effects of noise on hearing have been known for many centuries, and specific scientific studies on the subject have existed since the mid-1800s. Contrary to popular opinion, noise-induced hearing loss did not suddenly emerge after World War II. Medical and political concern about this danger was present in different industries during the past hundred and fifty years, both in Europe and in the United States. There was, however, a surge of heightened interest and awareness about the effects of occupational hearing loss immediately after World War II as a result of the introduction of numerous claims for NIHL into the workers' compensation system in the United States. For many persons, the influx of workers' compensation claims prompted the initial realization that exposure to industrial noise is ubiquitous, and that a great many workers were potentially at risk.

At each stage of its history, certain social, economic, technological, and political forces helped shape the scientific and medical understanding of the relationship between occupational noise and hearing ability. The definition of NIHL itself has been a point of continual debate that reflected profound questions about what constitutes an occupational disease and what society's responsibility ought to be toward affected workers. Underlying this debate are fundamental issues of labor relations, such as whether an employer bears any obligation toward ensuring a laborer's full social or personal functioning outside of employment.

By examining the history of occupational hearing loss, we have been able to identify many of the important social factors that contributed to the scientific and public recognition of this health hazard. Some of the key themes that have emerged from this study are the following.

1. *The introduction of new production technology.* To a great extent the growth of the true prevalence of NIHL is a consequence of modern technological advance. The number of workers exposed to continuous loud noise has gradually increased as machinery and technology developed both before and especially after the Industrial Revolution. The emergence of hearing loss in specific industries parallels the introduction of new power sources into factories and other work settings. For example, the development of powered metalworking machinery (large forging hammers and riveting guns, for example), railway locomotives, military explosives, and modern aircraft have brought a dramatic elevation in the noise levels to which large numbers of workers are exposed, along with a corresponding increase in the reporting of hearing problems.

2. *Risk perception.* Evidence has been presented suggesting that heightened concern about the effects of noise on health followed the introduction of several new technologies, such as jet aircraft, telephones, and radio. At the time, each of these technologies represented a new, unknown danger to the public. According to modern theories of risk perception, individuals are often most concerned about a hazard when it is associated with such alien contrivances. Moreover, contemporary risk perception research has shown that people are generally apt to be more concerned about a hazard that is considered catastrophic. This sentiment may have been at play in Moos' investigations of hearing loss among locomotive engineers in the late nineteenth century. His apprehension about subclinical hearing loss in railway engineers likely reflected the widespread concern about violent rail collisions affecting the traveling public.

3. *Environmental concern.* Public concern about the potential risks of any harmful agent in the general community often arouses sympathy for addressing the corresponding hazard in the workplace. In this case, a growing sense of public frustration and annoyance with urban noise helped bring increased attention to the potential dangers of chronic exposure to occupational noise. Particularly influential were the many government-sponsored studies of environmental noise during the late 1920s and early 1930s. The activities of the New York Noise Abatement Commission appear to have been especially important in stimulating the expanded study of industrial noise in that state. Also prominent were the studies linking noise exposure with fatigue and decreased productivity. These studies placed an economic cost on loud industrial noise, apart from hearing loss, and thereby encouraged business people to identify and measure sources of noise in their workplaces.

4. *Economic interests.* The history of the growth of occupational hearing loss shows how economic interests can accelerate or retard the scientific and medical recognition of an occupational disorder. Commercial enterprises benefited financially from the identification of hearing loss cases, and the marketing of audiometric equipment, hearing protection, sound level meters, hearing aids, and industrial noise abatement services encouraged the increased detection of this disorder among workers. In addition, European governments' desire to retard the expansion of inter-city telephone systems may have promoted the identification of telephone-related hearing loss in those countries. There are also circumstances in which economic influences might exert a negative effect. For instance, the tendency to interpret hearing loss as psychosomatic in female telephone operators may have stemmed, in part, from fears about the loss of traditional male-dominated jobs in the telegraph industry.

5. *Workers' compensation.* Closely allied to economic concerns was the emergence of NIHL in the workers' compensation arena. There is no doubt that the rapid escalation of claims for chronic hearing loss after World War II served to greatly expand medical, business, government, and public concern about the problem of industrial noise. State legislators, workers' compensation administrators, insurance carriers, and employers remembered the similar deluge of claims that occurred in the mid-1930s from silicosis. The strategy that eventually brought the silicosis crisis under control provided business with a model of quickly including NIHL under the occupational disease provisions of the state workers' compensation act in order to placate workers and limit future litigation through the court system. In a political trade-off, the recognition of the disorder as compensable was balanced by the adoption of restrictive eligibility requirements and monetary limitations on maximum allowable payments. Insurers and employers devised mechanisms to shift cost outflows to future years and, at the same time, instill a sense of actuarial predictability to the pricing structure of workers' compensation. Through this process, a new concept of compensation for partial impairment of bodily function in the absence of corresponding disability or loss of earning power emerged.

6. *Audiometry.* The concept of quantitatively measuring hearing loss is closely tied to the medical definition of the disorder. In fact, for most occupational maladies, the two concepts are intimately linked. The development of the electronic audiometer in the 1920s and its use in mass screening programs during the late 1930s and 1940s made possible the modern understanding of NIHL. The aberrant audiogram, which came to be regarded as synonymous with a diagnosis of hearing loss, documented the injury to physicians, judges, and workers' compensation administrators. Most important,

the audiometer brought the effects of potentially harmful industrial noise to the attention of many previously unsuspecting workers who otherwise would have remained oblivious to the dangers. The audiometer gave new meaning to the question originally debated in the 1880s by Barr, Moos, and Pollnow about whether subclinical losses in perceptibility should be used as the primary yardstick for measuring the impact of occupational deafness, or whether it is more important to consider deficiencies in social function.

7. *Military conflicts.* The emergence and recognition of occupational noise-induced hearing loss cannot be understood without considering the role of the military. The development and use of modern military weapons created intense new sources of noise exposure that ultimately resulted in greater deafness among combat troops. The major wars of the twentieth century focused attention on the problem of NIHL and stimulated expanded medical research into the disorder's diagnosis and treatment.

More important, several customary military practices for addressing war-related health hazards brought about expanded recognition of the corresponding occupational hazards during and immediately following the wars. Originally developed to ensure the availability of physically capable fighting personnel, these practices include routine medical testing and surveillance programs, fast and effective medical treatment for casualties and impairment, maintenance of comprehensive accident and injury statistical records, and the provision of pensions for disabled veterans.

In both world wars, these practices led to the establishment of routine audiometric screening programs for new inductees and active service personnel. They also resulted in the development of new forms of personal hearing protection, along with a deeper appreciation for the medical consequences of prolonged exposure to noise. Of equal significance, a large cadre of physicians, audiologists, otologists, and acoustical engineers received their initial professional training and practical experience dealing with NIHL in these military conflicts. After the wars, these individuals applied many of the new techniques to the industrial work environment. The return of thousands of disabled veterans to the workplace brought a greater appreciation for the plight of those deafened by loud noises and encouraged the application of wartime diagnostic and treatment methods, such as routine audiometric testing and the quantified calculation of hearing impairment to the occupational environment.

8. *Labor activism.* Especially following World War II, organized labor played an active role in igniting the drive to have NIHL accepted as a compensable occupational disease within state workers' compensation systems. The eventual success of that campaign, achieved primarily through court decisions, prodded industry to control noise exposures in the workplace and

expedited the passage of noise control standards by the federal government. Particularly noteworthy were the efforts in Wisconsin of the International Brotherhood of Boilermakers, Iron Shipbuilders, Blacksmiths, Forgers, and Helpers, and the United Steelworkers of America in New York. Similar campaigns were waged in the late 1970s by the United Auto Workers in Illinois and New Jersey, and the International Brotherhood of Boilermakers, Iron Shipbuilders, Blacksmiths, Forgers, and Helpers at the Long Beach Naval Shipyard.[243]

Although the involvement of the steelworkers and boilermakers' unions were influential during the postwar years, the question remains as to the ultimate significance of their efforts. The sudden influx of hundreds of claims for hearing loss scared employers in both New York and Wisconsin and was instrumental in bringing greater notice to the issue of occupational noise. To the extent that the unions helped promote these claims, their involvement was central to the contemporary rise of NIHL. But as labor's political power and resources began to decline after the end of the Korean War in 1953, unions were unable to gain a fair and effective resolution of the issue that ensured workers' rights for compensation and guaranteed protection from further injury. For the most part, the legislation for NIHL enacted in most states during the 1950s and 1960s was driven by business and insurance interests, and labor's voice was generally weak.

In summary, organized labor played a significant role in getting business, government, and medical leaders to take notice of the problem of hearing loss in the workplace, but ultimately failed to exert strong influence in determining how to deal with that issue.

In one respect, the history of NIHL can be seen as a successful chapter in the progress of occupational safety and health. The recognition of the problem by physicians, businesses, and unions, accompanied by the development of new noise control technology and audiometric testing instruments, stimulated an aggressive control effort by government, labor, and employers which has generally been effective in limiting further increases in the incidence of NIHL. At the same time, the regulatory development process resulted in a relatively strong and widely enforced OSHA standard. The wearing of hearing protection by workers and hearing conservation programs in industry are now common. In the final analysis, public awareness about the potential danger of noise on the job has been heightened and the hearing of many thousands of workers has been effectively preserved because of these efforts.

Yet the history of NIHL shows how far we still have to go as a society to afford truly effective protection to working men and women. Although the dangers of prolonged exposure to loud industrial noise had been well-documented for centuries, it was only the specter of unbridled compensation losses that spurred business and the government to address the problem. Even then, these interests used legal and legislative maneuvering to redefine the issue so that it became a relatively restricted matter affecting mostly the elderly and retired. Workers were placed in the ironic and untenable position of having to choose between remaining on a job that was known to be injuring their hearing or leaving in order to qualify for the limited compensation that was available. Either way, the compromises reached ignored the most important issue—the maintenance of a healthy workforce.

Conclusion 5

In chapter 1, I suggested that social factors can shape the medical recognition and conception of occupational disease in specific ways. My views were based on a model of occupational disease that gives primacy to two distinct, but interrelated, social contexts. One is the work environment, in which decisions are made that dictate how jobs are performed and what conditions exist in the place of employment. In that setting, economic, political, and other social forces determine how these decisions are reached by management and workers. The other context is the patient-physician relationship, which comes into play when a worker, or former worker, reports to a physician (or other health care provider) for diagnosis or treatment of an ailment. At that point, judgments are often rendered about the disorder's etiology and whether or not it could have been induced by conditions existing in the patient's occupational environment. Because many disorders have a variety of causes, the role of work in bringing about the ailment is frequently uncertain. Nevertheless, in our society, determinations about occupational causality made by physicians are instrumental in establishing the extent of employers' financial obligations, legal responsibility, and other political and economic matters.

Because of medical uncertainty related to indistinct etiology and multifactoral causation, the judgments made in the worker-physician relationship are particularly susceptible to social forces. Moreover, physicians' findings issued in this context appear to be prone to social pressures because of the significant implications of such judgments on broader questions of employers' economic and moral responsibilities toward employees.

Based on previous historical studies of other occupational diseases and considerations of a theoretical nature, twelve hypotheses were formulated of how social factors might determine the way that occupational disorders are initially recognized and conceived (see chapter 1). It was not presumed that each of these factors exert comparable influence in every particular case. Rather, my goal was to determine whether or not these factors are instrumental in the medical recognition of occupational disorders and, if so, to evaluate the extent and nature of their influence.

Of equal importance was the desire to assess the relationships and dependencies among the various factors. My proposed model of occupational disease assumes that the action of these factors is complex, pluralistic, and multi-dimensional. They rarely, if ever, appear in isolation from each other. Some might exert their influence directly on the primary participants (workers, physicians, and so on) while others can act indirectly by affecting the ambient political or social context in which the worker-physician relationship takes place.

Moreover, social factors are, at most, just one of many determinants that enter into a physician's analysis of an occupational disease. They normally occur as a backdrop to other, more overt, considerations, including the physician's knowledge and understanding of scientific, medical, and epidemiological facts and theories, test results, available empirical evidence, and diagnostic modalities. My emphasis on the influence of social forces is not meant to ignore or diminish the significance of scientific and medical knowledge in determining whether a disorder is occupationally related. Rather, in the tradition of Fleck and Kuhn, it is an acknowledgment that scientific observations and theories are always embedded in a social context or "paradigm" that fundamentally shapes the way that scientists understand and apply the available data.

Findings
The historical data presented in the case studies shows that social factors do play a key role in shaping physicians' recognition and conception of occupa-

tional disorders. Appendix I summarizes the major findings from the three case studies separately for each social factor that was presumed to be of prime importance.

Each social factor's apparent impact in shaping the medical conception of the occupational nature of each of the three disorders was assessed on the basis of an interpretation of the entire case history, taking into account such considerations as the timing and magnitude of increases in medical reporting of the disorder subsequent to the social development, the apparent strength of association between the social factor and reports of the disorder, and physicians' own statements and writings concerning their understanding of the relationship between their characterization of the disorder as occupational and the particular social factor. Based upon such considerations, each social factor was ranked according to whether it appeared to have a high, moderate, or low impact for each disorder. In cases where no impact was observed, a summary indication was made to that effect. Appendix II contains a consolidated summary of these rankings.

Whether the impact of a social factor was high, moderate, or low in a particular case represents a professional historical judgment that is not merely the product of a quantified calculation or a precise weighting of the historical events. It provides merely an expedient classification scheme for indicating general patterns and revealing trends.

In some cases, Appendix I indicates the absence of a social factor where an impact might have been expected but was not observed. For example, for the influence of *new technologies,* an increase in reported occupational hand disorders was not observed subsequent to the introduction of typewriters, even though one might have been expected. Such "negative" findings were taken into account when establishing the overall summary ranking for each factor. In other cases, I have indicated that a social factor had a significant impact, but not in the direction that had been originally assumed. For example, some actions by organized labor in the mid-1950s actually served to restrict, rather than to expand, the recognition of occupational NIHL, contrary to the action of labor that was anticipated.

Overall, the historical evidence demonstrates clearly that social factors can affect physicians' recognition of occupational disorders. In fact, nine of the twelve social factors had a high impact on the initial recognition and conception of at least one of the occupational disorders examined. Two of the social factors appeared to have a high impact for at least two of the three disorders studied; those being, the establishment of financial compensation and labor activism. Four factors had at least a moderate impact in all three case studies; those being the introduction of new technologies, the establishment of financial compensation, economic instability, and media attention. No factors failed to exert at least a moderate impact for at least one disorder.

At the same time, there was considerable variability in the effect of these social factors among the three case studies. Few clear patterns or trends emerged, and no factors exhibited a consistently high impact for all the disorders.

These findings indicate a complex social structure that defies simple analysis. Although the evidence is strong that social forces can exert considerable influence in molding physicians' opinions about occupational etiology, the effect of those forces varies significantly by disorder. Each disorder studied has an extremely rich, but unique, social history. This is true even for disorders commonly thought to be closely related, such as back pain and hand and wrist CTDs, which are often grouped together generically in scientific and policy discussions as musculoskeletal ailments.

For example, it is sometimes claimed that the contemporary growth of reported musculoskeletal disorders has been instigated by the actions of organized labor. The data from this study support this conclusion in the case of CTDs, but the historical evidence shows that the actions of organized labor were much less influential in the case of occupational back pain. Likewise, based on the data, cultural and gender stereotyping played a major role in physicians' characterization of occupational neuroses and carpal tunnel syndrome. And yet this sort of stereotyping appears to have played a less important role with respect to back pain and was considerably less evident in physicians' investigations of noise-induced hearing loss.

Some of this variability may be due to differences in the industries in which the disorder first appeared and the type of workers affected. Variability between cases may also reflect the different time periods in which disorders were first reported. For example, one might expect the social dynamics in the early twentieth century—the time of the initial significant reporting of industrial back pain—to be different than in the mid-1800s, when occupational hand disorders first became widely recognized. In addition, the variability and relative influence of the various social determinants may be due, in part, to the ways that they interact. Thus, to understand fully the effect of a particular variable it may be necessary to examine its action relative to others as well as separately. An analysis of the action of each social factor is presented below, along with comments on how the findings from this study compare to those of other social researchers.

New Technologies

This study supports the view that the initial medical reporting of occupational disorders is often associated with the introduction of new production technologies. Many physicians of the time commented on the growth of writ-ers' and telegraphists' cramp following the introduction of steel pens and the Morse telegraph key. During the 1980s, the influx of CTD cases appears to have been stimulated in part by increased high-speed automation in the meatpacking and auto industries. In a similar way, the rise of railway spine was in part a reaction to the nineteenth-century public's initial experience with railway travel. Concern with the effects of noise in the workplace paral-leled the growth of various industrial and military technologies, such as steam boilers, telephones, and military weaponry.

These findings are consistent with those of previous investigators, who have associated the observed increase of concern with coal miners' pneu-moconiosis with advances in mechanized and continuous mining technolo-gies in the 1950s and 1960s.[1] Likewise, the rise in reported silicosis has been related to the introduction of mechanical sandblasting and power tools.[2] Similar findings were reported for other occupational diseases.[3] These find-ings are also consistent with modern research into risk perception, which has shown that people are more concerned with hazards that are new or unfamiliar.[4] As mentioned previously, recent evidence suggests that the per-formance of unaccustomed activity increases the risk of developing cumula-tive trauma disorders.[5]

So there exists relatively strong and consistent evidence that the intro-duction of new technologies helps breed occupational disorders. However, the data from this study also show that the effect of new technology is not always uniform or predictable. For instance, the medical literature contains few, if any, reports of occupational CTDs following the introduction of type-writers or telephone switchboards, both of which seemingly require exten-sive repetitive use of the hands and wrists. Similarly, there was very little medical attention directed to the potential for noise-induced hearing loss among commercial airline crews despite the concern of physicians about NIHL in military pilots. Moreover, there was little reporting of occupational back pain during the nineteenth century due to rail travel or the initial mechanization of industrial processes that necessitated the frequent han-dling of heavy objects.

As suggested by some physicians of the period, these negative findings may be explained on the basis of the magnitude of the exposure—for in-stance, that the use of typewriters and telephone switchboards is less inju-rious from a biomechanical standpoint than is the use of steel pens and Morse telegraph keys. But I suspect that this finding also is the consequence of various social and cultural determinants. For example, telegraphers and professional clerks (scribes, copyists, and so on) in the nineteenth century were predominantly male, whereas workers using typewriters and telephone switchboards were overwhelmingly female.[6] The evidence on cultural stereotyping shows clearly that physicians' social views about women can blind them to occupational disorders occurring among female workers. The strength of that factor, especially in the case of CTDs, can help explain why the introduction of new technologies was not found to have a greater impact.

Likewise, the weakness of British railway labor during the nineteenth century relative to management made it difficult for rail servants to step forward with claims for back pain. This, along with the lack of an effective mechanism for financial compensation of these disorders, accounts for the ostensive failure of the introduction of rail technology to induce the reporting of back ailments in rail workers.

A final point concerning the social effect of new technology involves those directed toward physicians rather than to industrial production. This study provides evidence that such technologies can exert a considerable influence, as exemplified by the role of myelography in the discovery of ruptured discs and of audiometry in identifying cases of NIHL and fundamentally altering the medical conception of that disorder.

Financial Compensation

Considerable evidence has shown that methods for obtaining financial compensation can drive the recognition and reporting of occupational disorders, as in the case of NIHL after the landmark court decisions in New York and Wisconsin authorizing workers' compensation for partial hearing loss, even in the absence of occupational disability. The history of railway spine dramatically illustrates how the availability of financial compensation promoted the recognition of the disorder among passengers, whereas workers, who did not have a comparable means for compensation, were thereby discouraged from reporting the same condition. Additional evidence for the potential influence of workers' compensation can be seen in the surge of reported tenosynovitis after the scheduling of that disease in Ohio's Workers' Compensation Act and the similar increase observed for bursitis and synovitis in New York after the liberalization of its workers' compensation law.

These findings conform with contemporary research showing that, in general, the enactment of new compensation laws and increases in available benefits encourages the expanded reporting and diagnosis of occupational maladies.[7] The evidence is also consistent with other contemporary sociological studies indicating a greater likelihood for patients to seek medical care if they are covered by sickness and disability insurance.[8]

While acknowledging the interdependency of financial compensation and the recognition of occupational disease, some scholars have contended that the attainment of compensability under workers' compensation laws has followed, rather than precipitated, the recognition of a disease's occupational character. For example, it has been argued that the inclusion of silicosis under state occupational disease provisions was a reaction by business and government to the perceived economic threat entailed by the increased incidence of the disorder and its introduction into liability suits brought under common law.[9] Some commentators have observed that in the case of asbestos, workers' compensation was a relatively late-stage development achieved only after labor, political, and media attention had heightened medical awareness of that substance's occupational dangers.[10]

While generally supporting the idea that compensation fosters the medical recognition of occupational disease, this study uncovered instances in which medical awareness of a disorder's work-relatedness developed in the absence of or preceding the availability of financial compensation. For example, there is no indication that any victim of writers' cramp received compensation for the disorder during the nineteenth century. Similarly, telegraphists' cramp was already at epidemic proportions by the time it was scheduled for compensation by the British government in 1908. The early medical attention provided to occupational hearing loss among American boilermakers (for example, Holt 1882, Roosa 1874) and German railwaymen (Moos 1880, Pollnow 1882) provides additional examples of how occupational disorders can be recognized in the absence of effective compensation schemes.

Thus, though financial compensation is potentially quite important in stimulating the initial recognition of occupational disorders, it is not a necessary condition. Contrary to the opinion of some cynics, not all occupational disorders are primarily the result of workers' compensation. In the case of telegraphists' cramp, the laborers' strong political position and active union may have helped generate awareness of the condition despite the unavailability of compensation. In addition, the aggressive reporting of telegraphists' cramp by telegraph workers may have been perceived more as a means for increasing worker control over job conditions and the selection of technology than as a way of attaining recognition or compensation for the disorder. The telegraphers testified before the British Industrial Diseases Committee in 1908 that "Our position is not so much one of compensation. If I may put it so, that is a secondary idea in our minds." The primary idea, according to the telegraphers, was "a reorganization of the work" and "some variation in the work."[11] Much the same sentiment seems to have been why the P–9 strikers at Hormel raised the carpal tunnel syndrome issue in 1985. They pushed for the recognition of the syndrome as an occupational ailment, but their primary objective was better wages and improved job conditions. Injury compensation per se was not the primary driver.

This study also reveals that the effect of financial compensation on fostering a greater awareness of occupational disease may be indirect. For example, one repercussion of the establishment of workers' compensation systems in the early twentieth century was the initiation of compulsory reporting of industrial injuries and the collection and analysis of corresponding statistical accident data. This improved statistical data brought the magnitude of industrial back pain, as well as its relationship to manual materials handling, to the attention of physicians and public health advocates. Likewise, the adoption of "cumulative trauma" legal doctrines in California and Michigan may have had an indirect bearing on the generic terminology that was adopted by scientists and physicians to classify and describe occupational hand disorders in the early 1980s.

An important question unanswered by this historical study is whether payments available under workers' compensation provide a direct monetary incentive (or disincentive) for physicians to regard disorders as work-related. The scant evidence available on that question is generally inconclusive. It is known that during the first decade after passage of the state workers' compensation laws, a considerable number of physicians expressed grave displeasure and bitter opposition to the laws, based primarily on what they saw as the unreasonably low fee schedules that had been adopted by various states.[12] At the same time, however, studies showed that remuneration for physicians' services increased to four to five times what it had been under the old employers' liability insurance system because payments for industrial injuries in tort actions were uncertain, delayed, and sometimes never provided.[13]

In what may be the only empirical study conducted on this question, it was shown in 1976 that 15 percent of dermatologists in California refused to treat workers' compensation patients because of "low fee schedules, excessive paper work, hassles, troublesome patients, and conflicts of interest."[14] Of those treating workers' compensation cases, an equal proportion of the physicians were satisfied (44 percent) and dissatisfied (45 percent) with the available fee schedule. In cases not confined to work injuries, contemporary empirical research has shown marked differences in physicians' diagnostic and therapeutic behavior based on available compensation methods.[15] However, it has not been determined empirically whether a finding of work-relatedness directly benefits physicians making that judgment.

Labor Activism

Labor activism appears to have had a significant impact in the cases of CTDs and NIHL. During the early twentieth century, the strength of the telegraphers' labor organization played a major role in convincing the British Industrial Diseases Committee to recognize telegraphists' cramp as a legitimate occupational ailment. Their influence in that regard has been contrasted to that of the lace makers who, in part because of a weak labor presence, failed to persuade the same committee that twisters' cramp was a disease of occupation. In more recent times, the actions of the UAW, UFCW, and the IAM had an undeniable effect in bringing the problem of work-related CTDs to the attention of physicians, regulators, and the general public.

The same pattern holds for NIHL, in which the early actions of the boiler-makers' union brought that condition to the initial attention of physicians. After World War II, the International Brotherhood of Boilermakers and the United Steelworkers strove to bring awareness of NIHL to their membership, legislators, compensation officials and physicians charged with judging the relationship of partial hearing loss to noise on the job.

And yet this historical study also indicates that the contribution of labor is not always vital to the recognition of occupational disease, nor is it always unidirectional. For example, labor appears to have played a minor role in stimulating the steady growth of the reporting of occupational back pain throughout the twentieth century. The history of that disorder in this century, unlike the history of CTDs and NIHL, is notable for the absence of any major "crises" or significant turning points in which controversies about the condition's work-relatedness became paramount. This suggests that the influence of labor activism might be most pronounced when controversies about a disease's work-relatedness reach crisis proportions, possibly in response to economic instability, changes in production techniques, political issues, or other reasons.

Rather than emanating from crisis, the reporting of occupational back pain seems instead to have grown steadily in association with the gradually increasing level of scientific and medical knowledge linking back pain first to manual materials handling and muscular strain (1915–1930) and later to ruptured discs (1934–1960). In this sense, the history of back pain could be viewed as supporting theories of the gradual accretion of medical knowledge, which hold that the development of a disease concept is the product of ever-deepening scientific knowledge about its etiology and physical nature.

A crisis concerning back pain did develop during the nineteenth century, prompted by public alarm over the dangers of railway travel. This would have been the type of atmosphere in which labor activism could have been most potent in swaying medical judgment about the relationship of the disorder to the working environment. But this did not materialize, owing to the extremely weak position of labor relative to management in that industry at that time.

Even when labor actively sways medical judgment, its influence does not always have the expected effect of expanding recognition of a disorder's occupational nature. This can be seen in the actions of organized labor in the 1950s, which, because of fear of potential job loss, endorsed restrictive conceptions of NIHL, defining it as a transient condition able to be reversed after six months away from the exposure (away from work).

A perplexing finding in this study is the dramatic rise of reporting of writers' cramp in the nineteenth century among scribes, copyists, and clerks, despite their lack of organization and relatively weak political position. The fact that they were almost all male and drawn from the ranks of former tradesmen and farmers may have had some bearing in this respect. The only explanation offered by researchers at the time was that the emergence of writers' cramp was a result of workers' reaction to the introduction of new technologies (such as steel pens) and work methods, as well as a general societal response to the increased pace of work and regimentation of jobs created by the Industrial Revolution. At least one commentator of the period (Poore 1897) also attributed the epidemic to the squalid living conditions of clerks and other low-grade functionaries. Additional research is needed to identify the full range of social and scientific dynamics that were responsible.

Economic Instability

In each case studied, there were indications that the initial recognition of the disorder arose during periods of economic instability and potential job loss. For CTDS, this can be seen most clearly in the case of CTS among meatpackers in the 1980s. Several researchers consider it at least partially responsible for the growth of RSIS in Australia at about the same time. Evidence was also presented that lace makers came forward with reports of occupational Dupuytren's contracture in Nottingham when that industry was in severe decline.

Likewise, NIHL arose among steelmakers in the late 1940s and forgers in the early 1950s when those workers were facing the prospect of layoffs and economic hardship due to recessions in their respective industries. There is also evidence that the reporting of occupational back pain rose during the mid- to late 1930s as disabled and unemployed workers sought relief from the effects of the Great Depression.

These findings conform to those of previous investigators; for example, economic instability in the coal mining industry was an important reason for the rise of concern about black lung disease in the years immediately following a massive (70 percent) drop in coal mining employment.[16] In a similar way, a sizable proportion of the initial reports of occupational silicosis, which started to attract medical attention in the early 1930s, came from workers who had been laid-off or who were facing job insecurity due to deteriorating economic conditions, especially in the foundry industry.[17]

However, overall, the present study indicates that the influence of this social factor is moderate, at best. For every instance where disorders were recognized and/or expanded during periods of economic instability, there seem to be countervailing situations in which they were not. For example, there was no increased awareness or reporting of CTDs or NIHL during the years of the Great Depression. One would think that this would have been a likely time for the resurgence of interest in hand disorders, particularly given their prominence just thirty years earlier. Possibly the stigma of psychoneuroses was still strong, and medical opinion remained colored by the lingering association of nonspecific hand disease with mental abnormality. As shown in Beasley's Public Health survey of 1935–1936, deafness was often a basis for terminating or not hiring individuals during the Great Depression, and so workers with any indication or suspicion of hearing loss might have been loath to seek medical treatment for this condition.[18]

The early history of telegraphists' cramp provides another negative finding with respect to the impact of this social factor. The telegraph industry was strong and growing when the disorder first began to be reported and recognized. Thus, while some disorders initially come to attention during periods of economic instability, the effect of this social factor is not uniform and, apparently, not that decisive in all cases.

Environmental Concerns

Previous historical accounts have shown that public concern about the environmental dangers of asbestos helped bring initial medical attention to the health hazards faced by asbestos workers.[19] Similarly, community fears about exposure to tetraethyl lead in gasoline fostered greater awareness to lead's potential effect in the workplace.[20] However, environmental or community concern has not been identified as a significant consideration by researchers studying the social history of other occupational illnesses, such as black lung disease, byssinosis, radium poisoning, or beryllium poisoning.

The data in this study show that community concerns about environmental exposures of a harmful agent can exert a potentially strong, but variable, influence on the medical recognition of disorders occurring occupationally. Community concern was influential in the case of NIHL, where the noise abatement movement of the late 1920s and early 1930s translated directly into the medical study of workplace exposure. Public apprehension about the dangers of railway travel was instrumental in prompting the medical investigation both of hearing loss among German rail workers and of railway spine among British rail passengers.

But no such effect was observed in the case of CTDs, and public concern about the dangers of rail travel were not sufficient to bring immediate attention to the plight of railway employees.

To some extent, I think that these negative findings can be explained by realizing that harmful contaminants, like asbestos or lead, are perceived by the general population as foreign and unnatural agents—not to be expected in one's community or everyday surroundings, and thus viewed as invasive and threatening. The same was true for powered rail travel during the nineteenth century and for the introduction of loud mechanical noises into residential neighborhoods by industry and jet aircraft during the twentieth century.

By contrast, the handling of materials and the repetitive or forceful use of the hands and wrists is a common and expected part of everyday life for a large majority of individuals. Disorders arising as the result of such daily occurrences, including sore backs and aching hands, may not have been considered to be unusual or worthy of special medical attention. This is especially true for those of lower socioeconomic classes, as shown in the studies conducted in the early 1950s by American sociologist Earl Koos.[21] If environmental hazards are not considered unusual or threatening, then they will probably not elicit much public concern nor stimulate the investigation or recognition of workplace disorders.

Environmental concern also appears to be related synergistically to several other factors. For instance, community concern with the presence of environmental noise, asbestos, and rail travel prompted a considerable amount of *media attention* that elicited greater public concern. The same point could be made with respect to the interdependency of community concern with *labor activism* and *political pressure*.

Gender and Cultural Stereotyping

The effect of gender stereotyping on the history of occupational CTDs is pronounced and dramatic. The contrast between Phalen's and Finkelstein's interpretation and use of patients' work history in determining whether hand disorders are occupationally related provides perhaps the clearest validation of my general thesis that social factors can drive the way that occupational diseases are initially recognized and conceived.

The influence of ethnic, cultural, and gender stereotyping was also evident in the redefinition of occupational neuroses to varieties of psychological abnormalities that occurred around the turn of the century. In addition, the potential contribution of gender stereotyping in explaining the differences in medical recognition afforded telegraphists' and twisters' cramp has been mentioned.

The introduction of gender and ethnic considerations into medical discussions of occupational neuroses in the early twentieth century coincided with the influx of large numbers of women and immigrants into the American workforce. This reflected a general societal reaction to changes in worker demographics and was most threatening to those who were white, male, Christian, and privileged, which generally matched the background of doctors studying these diseases.

The introduction of such considerations may also have been related to the conceptual orientation toward women and Jews taken in the field of neurology. Even before Freud, neurologists had concluded that women had less "nerve energy" than males and thus were more susceptible to nervous exhaustion. Beard formalized and popularized this idea through his development of the concept of neurasthenia. Neurologists, on the whole, also believed that Jews and other ethnic groups possessed distinct nervous characteristics. Thus, the strength of the association between CTDs and cultural stereotyping might, to some extent, have been due to the prominence of neurologists in the study of these disorders and the particular thought paradigms employed in that specialty. In this sense, the effect of cultural stereotyping on influencing the history of CTDs may be related to *medical specialization*.

My discovery of gender-based stereotyping affecting physicians' characterization of CTDs is in accord with contemporary feminist literature that asserts that the medical profession has a longstanding and consistent bias against women. Gena Corea (1977), Phyllis Chesler (1972), Carroll Smith-Rosenberg (1972), Barbara Ehrenreich and Deirdre English (1973), and others have documented the ways that physicians have historically discounted women's health problems, often construing them to be manifestations of the supposed innate temperamental and nervous nature of females.

Smith-Rosenberg and her husband, historian Charles Rosenberg, have examined medical attitudes toward women in nineteenth-century America, concluding that the commonly held view of female patients as nervous, irritable, and prone to hysteria reflected society's growing concern about the movement of women into nontraditional roles outside of the home. These career opportunities had been created, they say, by various social forces during the mid- to late 1800s, such as rapid economic expansion, wider access to higher education, and increased availability of birth control. According to these authors, the medical preoccupation with women's supposed psychological and physiological frailty reinforced the conventional social expectation that women should be passive, domestic, and nurturing, traits suited to their biologically determined function in childbearing.[22] Corea (1977) has argued that this form of gender bias among physicians (usually male and members of a privileged social class), is a way of maintaining social control and preserving status in the prevailing class hierarchy.

These findings are also in agreement with modern sociological research showing differential medical response for different ethnic groups, based on the physician's interpretation of ethnic traits. The classic study in this area, by Irving Zola at Massachusetts General Hospital in the early 1960s, showed that comparable ailments elicited varying medical responses and diagnoses depending on whether the patients were Irish or Italian.[23]

While acknowledging the substantial impact of cultural stereotyping in the history of CTDs, we should note the relatively less influential role it seems to have played in the cases of back pain and NIHL. Dandy, Mixter, and Ayer used the large proportion of males among their patients to argue for the traumatic (and, by implication, potentially industrial) character of the ruptured disc lesion. But overall, the association of back pain with work does not seem to have depended to any great extent on culture- or gender-based considerations. The same can be said for NIHL, for which medical discussions, in general, gravitated toward cultural traits or gender only when dealing with simulated deafness and malingering. For instance, White's attempt to portray hearing problems among telephone operators as psychogenic may have been related to his belief that women were more likely than men to display such behavior. In addition, one otologist (Sabine 1944) suggested that the introduction of women into the industrial workforce during World War II was responsible for bringing increased attention to the dangers of occupational noise—supposedly because women were unaccustomed to loud noise and thus needed special protection.

The comparatively weaker effect of cultural stereotyping in the cases of NIHL and back pain compared to CTDs may be due to the types of industries in which workers reported these ailments. Initial reports of back pain and NIHL came primarily from traditional heavy manufacturing industries—including steelworking, automobile making, shipbuilding, and forging—which would have had a high proportion of male workers. The initial reports of occupational hand disorders during the nineteenth century came generally from such white-collar vocations as clerks and telegraphers. However, by the twentieth century those jobs had evolved into positions (secretaries, telephone operators) that were predominantly female.

Thus, the issue of stereotyping may not have arisen as a significant concern for back pain or NIHL for the same reason that it was not a major issue when writers' cramp and telegraphists' cramp were first noted in the mid-nineteenth century: because the reports of those ailments were from workers representing a traditional, native-born, male-dominated workforce. To clarify this issue further, it would be necessary to acquire information on the gender, ethnic composition, and industrial origin of workers initially reporting back pain and hearing loss during the twentieth century—data that were not obtainable in sources used in this study.

Medical Specialization

Cooter (1987, 1993) and other scholars have noted the intense competition for prestige and turf waged by orthopedists between World War I and World War II. My study shows that this was the period when occupational back pain first became an important medical concern, led by those in the ortho-pedic specialty. Their conception of industrial back pain as an essentially traumatic event helped establish orthopedists' claim to authority over this kind of injury. As the reporting of industrial back pain expanded throughout the century, the domain and influence of the orthopedic practice grew com-mensurably. This history indicates a close interdependency and synergy be-tween the development of the modern medical conception of occupational back pain and the growth of that specialty.

In addition, the new fields of industrial safety engineering and insurance loss prevention, which expanded under the paternalistic corporate welfare programs of the 1920s, were dominated by industrial engineers trained in the tradition of scientific management and Taylorism. Their focus on produc-tion efficiency and engineering methods may have contributed to the recog-nition of the relationship between back pain and production activities involv-ing the lifting and transport of heavy materials.

In the other case studies it was difficult to detect any specialty group that had a preferential "stake" in the recognition or conception of occupational disorders. Identification of a significant incidence of hearing loss in workers benefited not only otologists, but also audiologists and hearing aid dealers. But otologists stood to benefit from the greater application of routine au-diometric testing, irrespective of whether hearing loss was traced to the workplace. Nothing in the historical documents indicates that otologists' conception of occupational NIHL was predicated on self-interest. Audiolo-gists, of course, wanted to promote occupational audiometric testing, as did the manufacturers of audiometers, but those individuals were not physi-cians and did not render medical judgments. Their influence on bringing occupational NIHL to the notice of physicians has thus been considered sepa-rately under the category of marketing efforts.

In the case of CTDs, the historical evidence suggests that writers' cramp and telegraphists' cramp came to prominence in connection with the rise of neurology and neurological theory during the nineteenth century. As aspects of neurology were subsumed by Freudian psychoanalysis and the emergence of professional psychology after 1900, the reporting of hand and wrist oc-cupational neuroses declined. This suggests that the emergence or decline of a medical specialty can determine how occupational maladies are reported and diagnosed.

I have argued that the professional standing of Phalen and Bunnell in the orthopedic community helped convince other physicians that CTS was not job-related. Yet this does not mean that orthopedists had a stake in the characterization of CTS as occupational. If they had been acting strictly out of a sense of self-promotion, then the opposite conclusion would have been expected because more cases of CTS might have been recognized and reported. Despite this, since the early 1980s the number of carpal tunnel release surgeries has increased dramatically, prompting allegations from some critics that hand surgeons have been overly zealous in the diagnosis and surgical treatment of CTS, presumably in hopes of expanding their authority and serving their financial interests.

Perhaps the most significant finding of this study with respect to medical specialization is the apparent lack of involvement by occupational physicians or physicians with special training or familiarity in industrial medicine. Most of the major figures in this study—Phalen, Bunnell, Mixter, Barr, Ayer, and Dandy—apparently had little personal awareness of the special health problems of workers, nor had they spent much time within industrial facilities. With a few exceptions, such as Hayhurst's studies of tenosynovitis and Hamilton's investigation of Raynaud's phenomenon, decisions about the occupational etiology of CTDs, back pain, and NIHL were not made by physicians specializing in workers' diseases.

This finding contrasts with several previous studies in which a decisive factor propelling medical recognition of the relationship between a disorder and work was the role of physicians specially attuned to the problems of workers. For instance, scholars have recognized the major impact of occupational physicians Irving Selikoff, Alice Hamilton, Lorin Kerr, and Harriet Hardy in pushing for recognition of asbestosis, lead poisoning, black lung disease, and beryllium poisoning as occupational ailments. Contemporary historians have pointed to the establishment of workers' own health care facilities as a major influence in transforming the traditional power relationships between doctor and patient, thereby winning recognition for the special medical problems of workers.[24]

The absence of involvement by occupational physicians in the history of CTDs, back pain, and NIHL may reflect the historical evolution of modern occupational medicine from the tradition of public health, which placed considerable emphasis on the control of communicable diseases. As a result, occupational physicians traditionally have focused on chronic systemic diseases induced by chemical or infectious agents. Only during the past few decades has their attention started to shift toward airborne dust-induced diseases, such as asbestosis, silicosis, byssinosis, and coal miners' pneumoconiosis. The present study shows that occupational medicine specialists have, until recently, not paid much attention to disorders caused by nonairborne physical agents.

As a result, physicians who render judgment on occupational etiology, including neurologists, orthopedic surgeons, and otologists, have often been ill-equipped to appreciate and understand fully the nature of work processes and hazards. Acting with limited information about industrial operations, physicians have fallen back on the concepts and premises available to them within their own experience and training. Ultimately, this has introduced additional uncertainty into the medical determination of work-relatedness, thereby increasing the likelihood that social factors will influence physicians' opinion on that subject.

Media Attention

Significant media attention can accompany the outbreak of a new occupational disease. More problematic is the question of whether media publicity actually fosters the initial recognition of such a disease by physicians or whether it is more likely after a disease has been recognized. My study supports both points of view and suggests a relatively complex synergism between the media and the identification of the disease.

For example, in the case of CTDs, it seems evident that intense media coverage in the mid-1980s of labor strikes in the meatpacking industry first helped bring national attention to the issue of CTS, thereby precipitating increased government involvement and medical awareness of the problem. However contemporary media stories about CTD in the United States generally followed rather than preceded the rise in their reporting and diagnosis. By comparing the timing of the rise in reports of CTDs (figure 19) to the timing of news stories appearing in American newspapers and magazines (figure 20), it can be seen that the former started to rise sharply in 1986 and 1987, the latter, not until about one to two years later.[25]

The historical investigations undertaken in this study suggest that media attention might first arise in relation to a "crisis" that develops within a particular industry. The crisis can be precipitated by factors other than occupational health. Examples include the labor strife within the meatpacking industry during the 1980s, rail accidents to British travelers during the nineteenth century, and community noise in New York during the late 1920s and early 1930s. This initial media attention can help increase medical awareness of the occupational hazards and lay the foundation for subsequent reporting of the ailment by workers. However, widespread media attention on the occupational ailment might develop only following a rise in large-scale reporting of the condition by workers and its diagnosis by doctors.

In the case of back pain, a "crisis" involving rail travel elicited consider-

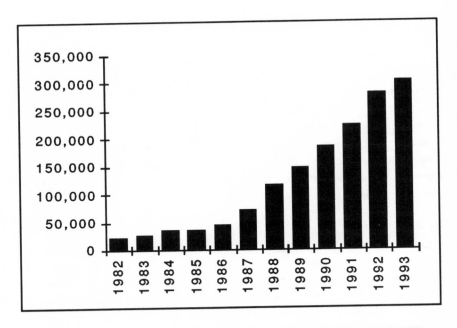

Figure 19 CTD Cases Reported to U.S. Bureau of Labor Statistics (from BLS 1993)

able media attention that helped bring initial medical notice to the problem of railway spine. However, through most of its history, very little media coverage was directed to the specific issue of *occupational* back pain. After the inception of workers' compensation and the rise of reported back injuries subsequent to World War I, stories appeared in the popular media concerning the issue of the "industrial back." However, while bringing attention to the identification of the problem, those stories just as often emphasized its relationship to malingering, making it hard to attribute the subsequent rise in reported back pain between 1930 and 1950 to those articles. Widespread media attention to the problem of occupational back pain seems to have arisen only during the past several decades, as the rising costs and reporting of the condition prompted public concern about its causes, treatment, and economic impact.

For NIHL, early public screening programs (e.g., World's Fair in 1939), as well as the public concern with community noise that peaked in New York in the late 1920s and early 1930s generated significant media attention. Both events seem to have fostered the recognition of the danger of noise in the workplace. However, it was not until the workers' compensation "crisis" of 1948–1954 in Wisconsin and New York that a large number of media stories focused specifically on the issue of occupational NIHL. Here again, while preliminary stories sparked increased medical awareness, the bulk of media

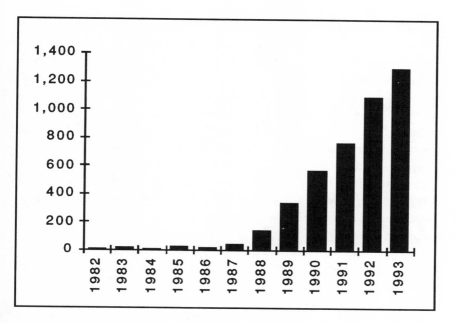

Figure 20 News Stories About CTDs (from Felsenthal 1994)

attention came after large numbers of cases were reported and recognized medically.

Evidence from previous scholarly work into the social history of occupational disease provides some support for this basic view of media action. For example, Alan Derickson (1987, 1991) has shown how national press stories about miners' strikes in 1902 first brought the problem of miners' asthma to the attention of physicians, coal mine operators, and the miners themselves. However, that publicity had a relatively limited effect in prompting the reporting of additional cases of miners' lung ailments. Wide-scale media attention to the problem of miners' lung disease only followed the dramatic rise of silicosis cases that occurred during the early 1930s and the political campaigns of the black lung movement during the late 1960s.[26]

Marketing Efforts

In this study, the impact of marketing efforts by vendors of medical and safety equipment is most evident in the case of NIHL; it is relatively absent in the other two cases of CTDs and back pain. For NIHL, evidence has been presented that manufacturers of audiometers, hearing aids, and personal protective devices all targeted the industrial market for expanded sales. AT&T and its subsidiaries were leaders in both sponsoring efforts to expand the recognition of hearing loss among workers, as well as selling the instrumentation and consulting services needed to identify and fix the problem. Rather than representing a conflict of interests, they perceived this as a public service insofar as it helped direct attention to an important menace to workers' health while offering an effective remedy. In retrospect, this perspective seems to have been generally valid. The motives were evidently less noble in the case of hearing aid manufacturers and dealers, who aggressively marketed their products after World War II even when it was apparent that they were unsuitable for use by those suffering sensorineural hearing loss. Nevertheless, their campaign probably brought increased attention to the occurrence of noise in the workplace. As noted earlier, the data are insufficient to determine whether the marketing of personal hearing protection to industry precipitated or followed the reporting and medical recognition of occupational hearing loss.

Evidence has been presented indicating that typewriters were marketed to telegraphers as a means for preventing telegraphists' cramp. In addition, the apparently excessive amount of hand surgery performed since the early 1980s has indicated to some observers that physicians have wished to profit from the diagnosis of occupational hand disorders (particularly CTS) and thus have overdiagnosed these disorders. The historical analysis in this study was not intended to determine the truth of that allegation. Considering the history of CTDs as a whole, the overall effect of marketing efforts by vendors of medical and protective equipment appears to have had only a limited impact on medical recognition of occupational hand disorders.

I found no evidence that marketing efforts contributed to the recognition or conception of occupational back pain by physicians. Again, as a separate issue, the large number of failed and ineffective back surgeries performed since 1934 has led some commentators to conclude that surgeons overdiagnosed occupational cases of ruptured disks for their own benefit. The effect of that factor has already been considered under the category of medical specialization. It might also be noted that in the 1990s a marketing campaign has been launched by the makers of back belts claiming that those devices prevent industrial back pain, a debatable assertion. However, even if it proves to be correct, this marketing blitz comes too late in the history of occupational back pain to be interpreted as having exerted a significant impact on the recognition of the disorder by the medical community.

It is interesting to speculate on why marketing efforts appear to have been prominent in the case of NIHL but not for back pain or CTDs. It is tempting to attribute the difference to the sophistication of measuring devices needed to assess the degree of injury or the level of exposure. The determination of hearing ability, it could be argued, requires discriminating technology, as does the measurement of noise intensity. The assessment of back pain and

CTDs, by contrast, is straightforward and is based on readily observable weights, forces, postures, and frequency of repetition.

But the determination of whether a person is suffering from back pain or CTS is at least as sophisticated a process as in the case of hearing loss, potentially requiring nerve conduction velocity testing, magnetic resonance imaging, and other diagnostic modalities. Moreover, although the risk factors for back pain and CTD have been measured traditionally by simple observational techniques, there is no reason why more sophisticated approaches like electromyographic measurements of muscle exertion, could not have been used. The fact that generally a quantified approach has been used to assess exposure and outcome for NIHL, but not for back pain or hand pain, cannot be explained solely on the basis of technical requirements.

Moreover, even if NIHL inherently required a more sophisticated and quantified assessment, the same could be said of many other occupational diseases, such as those due to airborne contaminants. For example, air sampling is required to assess the exposure from asbestos and silicosis dust, and spirometry testing and X rays have been used to measure the extent of resulting injury. Yet other historical studies do not indicate that marketing efforts by the vendors of such equipment have contributed to the recognition of asbestosis or silicosis.

To some extent, the significance of this factor in the case of NIHL might be related to the correspondingly high impact noted for the effect of military conflicts. Audiometers and hearing protection first came to widespread use in military applications, and the vendors of those devices might have been looking for ways to replace a market segment that had dissipated after the end of World War II.

Military Conflicts

Military conflicts had a high impact in the case of NIHL and relatively low effect for the other two disorders. In many ways, there seems to be a close association between the history of military medicine and the history of concern about NIHL. Interest in the effects of noise in the military extends back to the 1800s and involves a number of considerations. The paramount reason for the military's emphasis on detecting hearing loss stems from their need to ensure that soldiers are physically fit for duty and can hear and obey commands.

Another traditional motivation for emphasizing detection of hearing loss in the military has been the perceived importance of identifying cases of simulated or psychogenic hearing loss stemming from (1) blatant malingering to avoid military duty, (2) fraudulent attempts to qualify for military pensions, or (3) subconscious post-traumatic effects following combat. This historical preoccupation with the detection of hearing loss in the military led to the institution of diagnostic and preventive approaches that were later applied to industrial settings.

A large proportion of the otologists and other authorities cited in this study of NIHL were directly associated with the military themselves or used military experience to develop and support their views about NIHL in the workplace. In addition, the early development and application of audiometers and hearing protection devices derives in great measure from the military.

Furthermore, many military personnel in both world wars either suffered hearing loss while in the military or learned about it there because of the audiometric and nonaudiometric testing that was performed routinely. It has been suggested that upon the return of those individuals (generally men) into the workforce, accommodation was sought for the resulting disability, if not through veterans' benefits, then through workers' compensation.

The historical ties between otology and the military may help explain why more emphasis was placed on the quantified measurement of hearing loss in industry than on the detection of other ailments caused by physical hazards. In addition, because of the traditional lack of military concern about long-term health effects of airborne contaminants (chemicals, heavy metals, dusts), a commercial market for testing and diagnostic products related to those dangers may not have evolved in the same way that it did for NIHL. This could explain why marketing efforts were not a major factor for back pain, CTDs, or chronic systemic occupational diseases.

In a few limited ways, military medicine influenced physicians' conception of occupational CTDs and back pain. For example, the growth of orthopedics in World War I and its emphasis on traumatic injuries during that conflict colored later descriptions of industrial back pain as a potentially traumatic injury. In addition, Phalen's wartime training in hand surgery might have helped determine his ideas about the kinds of hand disorders that could legitimately be considered "traumatic" and the types of individuals (men, not women) who were susceptible to such injuries.

Political Action

Political considerations had a moderate impact in the cases of CTDs and NIHL and a low impact in the case of back pain. For CTDs, politically inspired reaction against labor during the 1920s helped propel the redefinition of occupational neuroses into forms of psychoneuroses. In the 1980s, the political goals of liberal Democratic leaders Lantos, Jackson, and Babbitt inspired public concern and government investigations of safety conditions in the meatpacking industry, leading to a greater recognition of the CTS problem that existed among meatpacking workers.

Political factors were also evident in the history of NIHL. The conservative political environment in Wisconsin and New York during the mid-1950s encouraged a restrictive conception of NIHL in those states for purposes of workers' compensation. In addition, government action to incorporate NIHL standards in the Walsh-Healy and OSHA acts expanded knowledge about the problem of industrial noise and stimulated the introduction of protective measures for many workers.

In previous historical studies, a more obvious connection has been found between political action and the recognition of occupational disease. In several cases, questions concerning disease recognition became the focus of specific political movements. For black lung disease, the recognition and conception of the disorder became part of a larger political struggle by workers and their sympathizers to recapture political and economic power in the coal mining industry.[27] Angela Nugent (1987) has described another such example in which political organizing by the Consumers' League was critical in prompting medical recognition of workplace radium poisoning as a distinct occupational disease.

In the cases examined in this study, there were no organized political efforts to recognize a disorder's work-relatedness. Unions in specific industries worked hard to secure the recognition of CTDs and NIHL as occupational disorders. But neither disease initially spawned a political movement nor attracted a substantial amount of political support or opposition. This indicates that organized political action is not always necessary for the medical recognition and growth of occupational disorders.

Political discussions about how to define noise-induced hearing loss gradually subsided after 1970 as reporting of the disorder diminished. Contrary to the original prophecies of doom, the incidence of reported NIHL never skyrocketed, nor did it involve excessive costs to industry. In essence, the restrictive conception of NIHL adopted within the state workers' compensation systems, along with industry efforts to control the sources of noise and provide personal protective devices to workers (inspired by the passage of government standards), minimized the impact of occupational NIHL and thereby defused the political sensitivity of that issue.

In the case of back pain and CTDs, the initial absence of political intensity may have been related to the fact that there were no government standards forcing industry to enact protective measures. In the mid-1990s, when a liberal administration in Washington finally issued proposals for enforcement standards, the political debate heated up. In that charged atmosphere, new questions were raised about the medical and legal definition of occupational CTDs and back pain. It will be interesting to see if the medical understanding of these disorders changes as a result of these political pressures.

Economic Costs

Employers' views about the nature of workers' disorders are affected by their perception of the potential economic consequences associated with medical judgments that the disorders are occupational in origin. However, it does not necessarily follow that physicians' perspectives about work-relatedness are affected by the same sorts of considerations. This study found strong evidence that medical opinions are so influenced in the case of NIHL. Less compelling evidence was accumulated for the impact of this factor on physicians' conceptions of CTDs and back pain.

The strength of the economic factor was assessed by examining the statements and expressed views of physicians. Only in the case of NIHL did physicians explicitly indicate the importance of economic costs to business in determining their perspective about the disorder's occupational character. This view was expressed by a number of the physicians involved in debates about the compensability of NIHL in the mid-1950s. The same view was articulated by Pollnow in the case of hearing loss among German rail workers. Early medical warnings about the dangers of telephone use in Europe could have been related to government campaigns to discourage the growth of telephone systems in order to protect the economic base of their telegraph monopolies.

In the other cases, there was only weak circumstantial evidence that physicians' views may have been predicated by an awareness of the business costs associated with the determination of occupational etiology. For example, in the case of back pain the reporting and diagnosis of occupational railway spine was impeded by fears of the economic consequences to the rail industry and rail workers. Mixter and Ayer mentioned that their discovery of a traumatic lesion to the intervertebral disc was "unfortunate," presumably because it could be used to justify the expanded compensation of industrial back pain.

For telegraphists' cramp, a review of the testimony shows that physicians on the Industrial Diseases Committee expressed concern about the economic effect on the British post office if it were found to be due to use of the Morse key. In an episode tinged with irony, Eastman Kodak's initial concern with improved production efficiency (that is, the control of economic costs) prompted the institution of especially thorough accident recordkeeping which ultimately promoted the "discovery" of occupational CTDs at its Windsor, Colorado, facility.

Although only a limited amount of direct evidence is available, a good part of the medical discourse on the subject of malingering and the deliberate feigning of disease seems to be a way for physicians to express tacit concern about what they feel is an unjustified and unethical effort by workers to defraud employers. In that sense, physicians involved with the detection of malingering may be expressing a moral judgment and protecting what they perceive to be the legitimate economic interests of business.

Implications for Policymaking

Considerable evidence has been accumulated in this study to show that social forces often have a dramatic impact on the initial recognition and conception of a disorder's occupational character. But the influence exerted by social factors is neither simple nor uniform. On the contrary, the historical evidence portrays a rich, dynamic, and complex social milieu comprised of a multitude of interrelated forces that impinge upon and mold the perspectives and actions of physicians and others involved in the characterization of occupational disease.

As Marxists have long realized, the unequal power relationship that normally exists between management and workers creates intense, socially predicated reactions to the occurrence of injuries and illnesses, and contrasting perspectives on the role of occupation in causing disease. But the physician charged with diagnosing and treating those disorders has traditionally been considered immune to the effect of such social dynamics. Doctors are supposed to be "neutral" and "objective," applying "scientific" knowledge to determine the root causes of patients' diseases. This study has shown that this view is a myth, at least when workers are the patients.

When workers are involved, the patient-physician relationship takes on a new dimension, infused with the suspense and special significance that comes from the possibility that work might be discovered to have caused harm. In this highly charged context, the potential for social perspectives and interests to exert a strong effect is very great.

To a large extent, the heightened susceptibility for medical judgments about occupational etiology to be swayed by social factors in this context is a result of the physician's role as a "gatekeeper" for determining financial benefits, legal liability, and compensability under workers' compensation laws.[28] This raises the stakes involved in the physician's findings. It also implies that the physician can rarely escape from the necessity of passing some judgment about occupational causation, even when such judgment is not fully supported by the available medical evidence. The difficulty in arriving at this judgment is compounded for disorders that have multiple sufficient causes or otherwise indistinct etiology. The disorders examined in this study are prime examples of those for which it is rarely, if ever, possible to distinguish clearly the relative contribution of occupational and nonoccupational causes for particular patients. Nevertheless, physicians have expended a tremendous amount of time and effort arguing about the occupational character of these ailments. A recognition that disorders potentially stem from a variety of interrelated causes implies that medical judgments about occupational disorders will generally be made in an environment of uncertainty. This uncertainty increases the likelihood that such judgments will be shaped by nonmedical social factors.

The disorders examined in this book are distinctive in that they can arise in almost any industry to workers performing a variety of jobs. The workplace hazards associated with CTDs, back pain, and NIHL are ubiquitous, and it is nearly impossible to imagine a worksite that involves no handling of materials, no need for frequent use of the hands or wrists, and a complete absence of noise. Therefore, if these disorders are judged to be the result of occupation, and if employers are obligated to institute protective measures, then almost every workplace could be affected. The pervasiveness of these particular hazards increases the potential economic consequences issuing from physicians' judgments about work-relatedness and thus heightens the potential for social factors to exert a strong influence on medical assessment of the problem.

In the final analysis, it seems that as long as society places the physician in the position of rendering judgments about whether a disorder should be characterized as work-related, social considerations will have a significant impact on determining the decision that the physician makes. This is especially true when the physician's judgment of occupational etiology confers important financial and legal benefits and obligations.

Physicians' medical opinions depend on social factors because they have been asked to answer social questions. Determining whether a disorder is occupational has become a process for expressing moral judgments, attributing responsibility for harm, assigning blame, and apportioning costs. Society has placed physicians in the position of gatekeepers, expecting them to referee controversies that have significant implications for labor relations and the industrial economy.

The question that needs to be asked is whether we, as a society, really want physicians to perform that role. Do physicians have the appropriate training and skills to fulfill this task effectively? Does the performance of such duties ultimately help them provide better care for patients? In my opinion, the answers are no.

At the same time, we must recognize that workers are entitled to capable and effective health care. In addition, medical knowledge of what causes disease is necessary so that appropriate preventive measures can be taken. Therefore, the issue is not whether physicians have an important role in ensuring a safe and healthy workforce—they do. Rather, the challenge is to identify the specific goals that need to be attained and to establish mechanisms that clarify the role of the physician in achieving those goals, relative to the functions of other individuals and institutions.

The basic goal is health—not only for workers, but for all members of society. The physician's main functions are to promote health and provide care for individuals who are sick or injured. Workers, like other members of society, have basic needs that must be addressed by an effective health care system. They include: access to prompt and effective medical care provided by qualified health professionals; financial insurance covering quality preventive, diagnostic, and therapeutic medical care; income replacement for work incapacity due to illness and injury; and protection against known health hazards, both on and off the job.

In thinking about how to structure a system to achieve these goals, it is important to start with the recognition that many, if not most, disorders have multiple causes. The awareness of multifactoral causation introduces considerable uncertainty into medical determinations of the specific relative contribution of occupational and nonoccupational causes in any particular case of disease. Modern techniques of epidemiological analysis can assess the relative risks posed by these various causes in a population of individuals. However, epidemiological findings concerning the relative strength of various causes are essentially stochastic, applying to the tendencies of populations rather than to individual cases of disease.

Epidemiological approaches can determine if specific workplace hazards pose a risk of disease or injury to a population of workers and thus can be used to identify industrial facilities and processes requiring protective intervention. However, epidemiological analysis cannot specify what caused disease in a particular patient—that determination generally is made by a physician or other qualified health care professional. It is often essential that the physician determines the probable cause of the patient's disease so that appropriate therapeutic modalities can be applied and preventive measures undertaken. The physician may draw upon medical examination and testing, epidemiologic evidence, and the patient's own work history in deciding whether the patient's ailment is "related" to work. Based on this investigation, the physician might explicitly label the ailment as occupational or not. This is often done for purposes of determining eligibility for financial compensation, civil liability, or other social and legal reasons. But, because of the uncertainty created by multifactoral causation, this judgment frequently has little medical significance or credibility.

Challenging the Notion of Occupational Disease

These considerations lead to the question of whether the concept of *occupational disease* is really needed. Can the goals of workers' health described above be achieved without depending on the labeling of disorders as occupational or work-related? What would happen if physicians were free to concentrate on the health of patients without being burdened by the need to render a definitive, yet often unsubstantiated, judgment about occupational causation?

Various social structures could be devised to make this possible. The key components would be an effective means for providing and paying for workers' medical care and lost wages, irrespective of whether the disorder occurred on the job. This kind of system has been adopted in other countries, and similar models are being explored in the United States, including comprehensive national health plans. There have also been attempts to address this need through the mechanisms of collective bargaining, whereby management and workers come to agreement on how health care and wage replacement will be handled, irrespective of specific etiologic determinations. Securing effective health care for patients, without requiring a medical judgment of occupational causation, does not necessarily imply dismantling the state workers' compensation system, as evidenced by reform initiatives under way in various states to enact "twenty-four-hour" coverage programs. There have also been attempts to create methods within workers' compensation for recognizing various disorders presumptively as work-related, based on objective and measurable criteria.

But effective health care is not enough, unless measures also guarantee that employers identify and control workplace hazards known to cause illness or injury. Some persons would say that physicians' judgments about occupational etiology are necessary to spur employers into addressing workplace dangers. Without that incentive, according to this argument, measures to prevent disease among workers would never be adopted.

While acknowledging that strong and effective requirements are needed, I question whether physicians' determinations about occupational etiology in particular patients are necessary to provide that stimulus. Studies have questioned whether the financial incentives and disincentives available to employers in the workers' compensation system actually promote safety.[29] Moreover, the history of occupational safety in the United States shows that, irrespective of workers' compensation, the primary responsibility for ensuring health in the workplace must reside with government safety and health enforcement agencies. Regulations adopted by those agencies ought to be formulated upon the best available population-based epidemiological information about the probability that specific workplace exposure will create a significant risk of disease.

Removing the need for physicians to make individual judgments as to whether particular patients are suffering from "occupational diseases" does not necessarily imply that enforcement of safety and health in the workplace will become any less aggressive. On the contrary, if an insurance and health care system provided quality care and income replacement to patients irrespective of occupational etiology, then it would be more important than ever to ensure that the penalties and enforcement activities of the governmental safety and health agencies are strong and effective.

My proposal varies from today's system in two important ways. First, it presupposes the establishment of clear goals about workers' health and societal commitment to achieve them. Second, it assumes separate and more clearly defined roles for the major participants, notably the removal of the physician from the position of direct gatekeeper for benefits related to workplace disease and disability. In the system I describe each party has a distinct responsibility:

Physicians and other health care professionals provide quality care to patients irrespective of whether their ailment was caused by work.

Epidemiologists, research physicians, and other public health scientists determine whether there are workplace risks of disease for specific populations of workers.

OSHA and other government enforcement agencies adopt strict regulations about the control of workplace hazards and the education of exposed workers, based on the best available epidemiological information.

Government and insurers, with the active involvement of other affected parties, devise a health care plan that provides quality health care for all workers and wage replacement when needed owing to illness or injury.

The historical studies I have presented show that it has taken hundreds of years—and the efforts of many workers, scientists, and physicians—to identify the ways that diseases are caused by work and to gain recognition for the reality of many occupational diseases. I am not proposing that we disregard or reject these efforts. The concept of occupational disease has been of great utility in bringing attention to the fact that certain industries and jobs contain serious health hazards that need to be recognized and ameliorated. This was undoubtedly a primary motivation inspiring many of the great occupational physicians, from the time of Ramazzini and Thackrah to that of Sir

Thomas Legge and Alice Hamilton, to develop the notion of distinct and bounded occupational diseases. We cannot afford to lose the important insights that have been gained through their efforts.

But the traditional notion of occupational illness stemmed from a medical model of disease that linked particular agents in a linear fashion with specific outcomes. With the contemporary recognition of the importance of multifactoral causation, that model has become difficult to apply and interpret. Moreover, the institution of social insurance systems and legal structures predicated on the determination of work-relatedness has forced physicians into the untenable position of having to render critical judgments about occupational etiology with profound social and legal consequences, in the presence of uncertainty and inadequate medical evidence. This has made them quite vulnerable to the influence of various cultural and social forces. Eliminating the burden placed on physicians to serve as our society's moral and financial gatekeepers for occupational disease will allow them to concentrate on the health of the whole individual, both on the job and off.

Appendix 1 Summary of Findings

Key Social Factors (see Chapter 1)	Cumulative Trauma Disorders (CTDS) (Chapter 2)	Back Pain (Chapter 3)	Noise-Induced Hearing Loss (NIHL) (Chapter 4)
1. New Technologies New technologies and the reaction to those technologies by various societal groups can lead to the increased reporting and diagnosis of occupational disorders.	Impact: Moderate • Initial reports of writers' cramp appeared after the introduction of steel pens. • The rise in telegraphers' cramp occurred after the introduction of Morse telegraph keys. • No increase was seen after the introduction of typewriters. • Few reports of CTDS followed the introduction of telephone switchboards. • In Australia, there was some indication that the rise of RSI followed the introduction of computers. • In the U.S., reports of CTDS among users of computers has also increased, but subsequent to the rise of CTDS in meatpacking, automaking, and other heavy industries.	Impact: Moderate • Public fear of railroad travel sparked the initial awareness of railway spine but did not translate into a concern about back pain among workers. • The development of X rays was seen as a way of verifying legitimate back injuries, and disqualifying pseudo-injuries and feigned illness. • The introduction of myelography in 1921 proved to be important in the discovery of the ruptured disc, which was ascribed to trauma, thus supporting claims that back pain is potentially occupational.	Impact: High • Recognition of NIHL among boilermakers and railway workers in the mid-1800s paralleled the growth of steam power and railways during the Industrial Revolution. • Concern with hearing loss in the military followed the development of aircraft and more powerful explosives. • Medical concern about the dangers to hearing immediately followed the invention and commercialization of the telephone. • The development of electronic audiometers was initially seen as a foolproof method for detecting the simulation of hearing loss. • Ironically, audiometers were used to detect unsuspected hearing decrements and thereby expanded the recognition of occupational NIHL.

Key Social Factors (see Chapter 1)	Cumulative Trauma Disorders (CTDS) (Chapter 2)	Back Pain (Chapter 3)	Noise-Induced Hearing Loss (NIHL) (Chapter 4)
1. New Technologies	Impact: Moderate	Impact: Moderate	Impact: High
			• Audiometers provided the "physical evidence" of injury needed to establish claims under workers' compensation.
2. Financial Compensation	Impact: Moderate	Impact: High	Impact: High
Laws and legal decisions establishing financial compensation can bring increased attention to the question of whether or not a disorder is work-related.	• Not present for writers' cramp during the nineteenth century.	• Railway spine arose immediately after passage of the Campbell Act. The lack of effective compensation for workers may have limited occupational reporting of the condition in the nineteenth century.	• Court decisions in New York and Wisconsin after World War II precipitated the increased reporting of occupational NIHL.
	• The rise of telegraphers' cramp preceded compensation.	• Medical reports of occupational back pain began to appear at about the same time as the establishment of workers' compensation laws in Germany (1884), Britain (1897) and the United States (1911–1918).	• Liberal acceptance of hearing loss claims by the VA for returning World War II veterans established similar expectations for industrial workers in the postwar period.
	• The reported incidence of tenosynovitis increased in both Ohio and New York shortly after passage of laws recognizing its compensability.		
	• Through 1980, the overall reporting of Raynaud's phenomenon and de Quervain's disease remained low despite these conditions' acceptance as compensable disorders.		

3. Labor Activism

Union campaigns and labor activism can foster initial concern about the problem of occupational diseases occurring in particular trades.

Impact: High

- Clerks suffering writers' cramp were not unionized.
- Telegraphers had a strong union that pushed for the recognition of telegraphists' cramp.

- The workers' compensation doctrine of "cumulative trauma" affected the selection of generic terminology ("cumulative trauma disorders") to denote occupational hand and wrist disorders.
- The rise of RSI in Australia apparently followed the liberalization of compensation criteria.

Impact: Low

- Rail unions (e.g., ASRS) used public concern about railway spine to win support for shorter working hours and better pay, but they did not push for recognition of the condition as an occupational ailment.

- Workers' compensation requirements for statistical reporting of injuries and their sources fostered the recognition of a relationship between back pain and manual materials handling.
- Initial establishment of workers' compensation systems encouraged the reporting of more minor back ailments.
- The specific *accident* and *injury* requirements of workers' compensation laws helped recast the conception of back pain into the language of injuries, strains, and trauma.
- Liberalization of workers' compensation criteria during the 1930s to include silicosis and other occupational diseases made it easier to pursue claims for nonspecific back pain.

Impact: High

- The International Brotherhood of Boilermakers sent workers to Holt for hearing examinations in 1881.

Key Social Factors (see Chapter I)	Cumulative Trauma Disorders (CTDS) (Chapter 2)	Back Pain (Chapter 3)	Noise-Induced Hearing Loss (NIHL) (Chapter 4)
3. Labor Activism	Impact: High	Impact: Low	Impact: High
	• The lace makers' weak union was unable to get twisters' cramp recognized.	• Rail unions were chief advocates for establishment of workers' compensation laws and thus indirectly fostered the increased reporting of occupational back pain.	• The forgers' union helped press workers' compensation claims in Wisconsin during the 1950s and publicized the problem to its membership.
	• UAW committees helped uncover cases of CTS.		• The United Steelworkers brought attention to NIHL in New York and provided legal assistance to members bringing workers' compensation claims in that state.
	• IAM educated machinists at Pratt & Whitney about CTS, and assisted in the filing of workers' compensation claims for the disorder. This prompted the first widescale epidemiological study of industrial CTS.		
	• Company doctors claimed that activities of the ACTWU helped prompt reporting of CTS at Hanes.		• Labor unions urged institution of periodic audiometric examinations.
	• Local P-9, and later the UFCW, brought increased attention to CTDS among meatpackers as part of a larger labor struggle in that industry.		• Organized labor (e.g., the AFL and CIO) acquiesced to a restrictive legal definition of NIHL that transformed compensability for the disorder into a form of retirement benefit.

- Close ties developed between organized labor and leading CTD researchers at the University of Michigan.
- Activities of the Australian Public Service Association and other trade unions brought early attention to the problem of RSIS.

4. Economic Instability

Occupational disorders are apt to be initially recognized during periods of economic instability and potential job loss.

Impact: Moderate

- CTS in the meatpacking industry appeared at a time of significant lay-offs and wage reductions due to automation, consolidation and the influx of immigrant workers.
- The telegraph industry was strong and growing when telegraphists' cramp began to be reported.
- The Nottingham lace industry was in decline when Dupuytren's contracture became an issue.
- RSI in Australia arose among workers in industries facing job losses due to automation and recession.

Impact: Moderate

- Claims for back pain within the workers' compensation system grew during the mid- to late 1930s as disabled and unemployed workers sought relief from the economic hardships of the Great Depression.

Impact: Moderate

- The U.S. Public Health Service launched an audiometric screening program to assess the effects of the Depression, and found a relationship between unemployment and hearing loss.
- The influx of hearing loss claims among steelmakers in the late 1940s and forgers in the early 1950s arose during precarious times for those workers, with layoffs and recession plaguing both industries.

Key Social Factors (see Chapter 1)	Cumulative Trauma Disorders (CTDS) (Chapter 2)	Back Pain (Chapter 3)	Noise-Induced Hearing Loss (NIHL) (Chapter 4)
5. Environmental Concern	Impact: None Apparent	Impact: Moderate	Impact: High
Medical interest in disorders caused by hazards in the workplace can be aroused by public reaction to similar environmental hazards present in the wider community.		• Public perception of the dangers of rail travel led to concern about railway spine, which laid the foundation for later thinking about the nature of occupational back pain.	• Public concern in Germany about rail accidents during the 1880s prompted studies by Moos and Pollnow on the hearing abilities of rail crews.
			• Reports of hearing damage from loud noises during use of the telephone by the public preceded and may have stimulated studies of NIHL in telephone operators.
			• Public concern with the problem of hearing loss was heightened by the results of mass screening programs (e.g., 1939 World's Fair).
			• Intense public concern with community noise during the 1930s promoted the examination of comparable occupational hazards, particularly in New York State.

Cultural stereotyping based on class, gender, and ethnicity can distort medical opinion about the relationship between occupation and disease.

7. Medical Specialization

The growth of medical specialization and the ensuing competition for professional authority, status, and financial rewards can help shape physicians' perceptions about the connection between disorders and job activities.

- Occupational neuroses were interpreted as psychological disorders, linked to traits of women and Jews and other ethnic groups.

- Occupational Raynaud's phenomenon was identified by studies exclusively in male populations, despite a 3:1 ratio of female to male sufferers in the general population.

- Finkelstein saw de Quervain's disease as an affliction of laborers, even though it occurred mainly among housewives.

- Phalen was convinced that CTS is not occupational, because he did not consider housewives' tasks to be manual work.

Impact: Low

- Occupational neuroses rose with the growth of nineteenth-century neurology and fell with the ascendance of twentieth-century psychology.

- Back pain malingering was interpreted to be a manifestation of differences in class, education, and, to a lesser extent, gender.

- The gender of patients was mentioned by Dandy, Mixter, and Ayer as a reason to think that the ruptured disc lesion was traumatic in origin.

Impact: High

- Interpretation of back pain as a traumatic injury corresponded with the growth and prominence of the orthopedic specialty after World War I.

- Attempts were made to characterize hearing problems among female telephone operators as psychogenic, possibly related to their gender.

- The simulation of hearing loss was attributed to class differences and the "nervous tendencies" of women.

- Some physicians (e.g., Sabine) believed that the increased attention given to industrial noise during World War II stemmed from the need to provide protection for "frail" females who were less accustomed than males to a noisy environment.

Impact: Low

- Otologists, audiologists, and hearing aid dealers all benefited from increased recognition of occupational hearing loss.

Appendix 1 *Continued*

Key Social Factors (see Chapter 1)	Cumulative Trauma Disorders (CTDS) (Chapter 2)	Back Pain (Chapter 3)	Noise-Induced Hearing Loss (NIHL) (Chapter 4)
7. Medical Specialization	Impact: Low	Impact: High	Impact: Low
	• The status of Phalen and Bunnell in the orthopedic community swayed physicians' judgment about the etiology of CTS.	• Industrial and safety engineers focused on the problem of the "industrial back" and its relationship to materials handling during the 1920s.	
8. Media Attention	Impact: Moderate	Impact: Moderate	Impact: Moderate
Attention by the national mass media to a particular workplace disorder can heighten medical awareness of the problem.	• Intense media attention to CTS amidst labor struggle in the meat-packing industry helped promote national awareness of the issue.	• Media attention helped prompt public awareness of railway spine among passengers but did not lead to occupational reporting of the ailment.	• Heavy media coverage of community noise studies in New York in 1930 helped bring attention to noise in the workplace.
	• There was little indication of attention in the mass media to problems of writers' or telegraphists' cramp.	• National media concern about silicosis helped bring about the expansion of workers' compensation eligibility criteria during the 1930s, which indirectly encouraged the filing of claims for back pain.	• Media reports of workers' compensation claims for NIHL in the 1950s helped provoke apprehension among businesses and the public concerning the potential economic consequences of large-scale compensation.
	• Media attention was not apparent in cases of de Quervain's disease or Raynaud's phenomenon.		
	• Recent media attention in the United States has generally followed, rather than precipitated, its rise in various industries.		

Marketing efforts by vendors of diagnostic, protective, and therapeutic equipment can stimulate initial concern about health disorders in workers.

Impact: Low

- Typewriters were marketed to telegraphers to prevent "nervous prostration" (referring to telegraphists' cramp).
- The popularity and profitability of hand surgery for CTS may have helped promote the diagnosis of that disorder.

Impact: High

- Western Electric's efforts to commercialize audiometers and noise control services prompted mass screenings of the public and workers, through which a high prevalence of hearing loss was discovered.
- Aggressive marketing of hearing aids after World War II brought increased attention to the problem of NIHL in workers.
- The marketing of audiometers moved into the industrial setting after World War II to replace military sales, thereby fostering the identification of workers with NIHL.
- Attempts to market personal hearing protection to industry after World War II may have stimulated additional awareness about the dangers of industrial noise.

10. Military Conflicts

Technology, diagnostic procedures, and medical attitudes arising in military conflicts can influence the way that occupational disorders are subsequently studied and understood.

Impact: Low

- Phalen's wartime experience may have influenced his conception of what constitutes a "traumatic" hand disorder.

Impact: Low

- World War I brought heightened medical attention to orthopedics and traumatic injuries, thereby helping to shape the modern conception of back pain as a potentially traumatic condition.

Impact: High

- A large amount of medical study of NIHL derived from military experience in the Spanish-American War, World War I and World War II.
- Widescale audiometric testing was first performed in the military.

Appendix I *Continued*

Key Social Factors (see Chapter 1)	Cumulative Trauma Disorders (CTDS) (Chapter 2)	Back Pain (Chapter 3)	Noise-Induced Hearing Loss (NIHL) (Chapter 4)
10. Military Conflicts	Impact: Low	Impact: Low	Impact: High
			• Modern personal hearing protection for NIHL was developed initially by the military in World War I and World War II.
			• A large number of military personnel in World War II learned of their hearing loss while in the service, or in VA tests conducted after the war. Approaches for accommodating and compensating their hearing disability were sought upon re-entry into the workforce during the postwar period.
11. Political Action	Impact: Moderate	Impact: Low	Impact: Moderate
The actions of particular political parties and candidates can generate public and medical consideration of occupational health problems.	• Conservative reaction against labor after World War I may have encouraged the redefinition of occupational neuroses as psychological ailments.	• Democratic New Deal politics of Roosevelt and Perkins paved the way for liberalization of the workers' compensation system during the 1930s, especially in New York.	• Conservative political environments in Wisconsin and New York in the mid-1950s fostered the adoption of restrictive eligibility requirements for compensable NIHL.

- Political goals of Lantos, Babbitt, and Jackson helped arouse public pressure to address safety concerns in the meatpacking industry.

12. Economic Costs

Resistance to the medical recognition of occupational disease is greatest when there are substantial costs associated with controlling the associated workplace hazards.

Impact: Low

- Kodak's approach to enhancing productivity actually fostered the recognition of CTDs.
- Physicians on the Industrial Diseases Committee expressed concern about the economic effect on the British Post Office that would result from a finding that telegraphists' cramp was due to use of the Morse key.

Impact: Low

- Management resistance to labor demands for changes in work methods and hours may have impeded the reporting of occupational railway spine.
- Mixter and Ayer mentioned that their discovery of a traumatic lesion to the intervertebral disc was "unfortunate," presumably because it could justify the expanded compensation of industrial back pain.

- Development of noise standards under the Walsh-Healy and OSHA acts brought attention to the problem of industrial noise and incited action toward its control.

Impact: High

- Pollnow professed concern about the economic costs to the rail companies if periodic hearing tests were used to identify and disqualify engineers and firemen with hearing difficulties.
- European governments initially retarded the expansion of telephone service, in hopes of protecting their telegraph monopolies. This may have contributed to medical warnings about the dangers of NIHL from telephone use.

- Intense reaction by business and insurers to the allegedly huge economic costs associated with the recognition of hearing loss helped generate a more restrictive legal and medical definition of that disorder.

Appendix II Consolidated Summary of Findings

Key Social Factors	Cumulative Trauma Disorders (Chapter 2)	Back Pain (Chapter 3)	Noise-Induced Hearing Loss (Chapter 4)
New Technologies	Moderate	Moderate	High
Financial Compensation	Moderate	High	High
Labor Activism	High	Low	High
Economic Instability	Moderate	Moderate	Moderate
Environmental Concerns	None Apparent	Moderate	High
Cultural Stereotyping	High	Moderate	Low
Medical Specialization	Low	High	Low
Media Attention	Moderate	Moderate	Moderate
Marketing Efforts	Low	None Apparent	High
Military Conflicts	Low	Low	High
Political Action	Moderate	Low	Moderate
Economic Costs	Low	Low	High

Notes

Chapter One *The Social Context of Occupational Disease*

1. See especially Barth 1980; Boden 1986; Locke 1985; Sagen 1982; and Ashford 1976.
2. Foucault 1973; Rosen 1943, 1947; Rosenberg 1992.
3. A summary of the sociological literature can be found in Cockerham 1986. Especially significant are the studies of Irving Zola (1983). Some of the most notable sources on gender bias in medical care are Ehrenreich and English 1973 and Corea 1977.
4. As described in the original German edition of Fleck's book, the members of a scientific "thought collective" (*Denkkollektiv*) possess a particular "thought style" (*Denkstil*) that predicates and conditions empirical observation. The results and conceptual creations of the thought collective are called "thought structures" (*Denkgebilde*), which are empirically grounded but ultimately derived from and dependent upon the thought style of the collective. Thought collectives are sometimes also referred to by Fleck as "thought communities" (*Denkgemeinschaft*). For additional perspective on Fleck's terminology see the preface to the 1979 English edition by its translator, Thaddeus J. Trenn.
5. Rosner and Markowitz 1987b is a collection of excellent articles on the social analysis of occupational disease. See also Smith 1987; Cherniak 1986; Bale 1986; Barth 1987; Brodeur 1974, 1985; Graebner 1976; Rosner and Markowitz 1991; Bronstein 1984; and Weindling 1985.
6. A good description of social history and its importance for issues of occupational health policy can be found in Weindling 1985. See also Brieger 1980 and MacLeod 1977.

7. Traditionally, the term *disease* has been used quite broadly to denote any abnormal or morbid condition. However, for many physicians the concept of *disease* implies the existence of an underlying organic pathology or lesion (see, for instance, the discussion of this topic in Rosenberg 1992, p. 266). For that reason, there has been a contemporary trend in the medical literature toward the increased use of the word *disorder* as a generic descriptor for any ailment, whether or not there is an identifiable lesion or organic pathology accounting for the malady. Further complicating the medical nomenclature is the distinction between *acute* and *chronic* disorders, as well as that between ailments that are of *traumatic* origin as opposed to those that are not. The concept of *illness* is normally applied to afflictions of nontraumatic origin and is often distinguished from *injuries,* which are deemed to be acute and traumatic in nature. However, these distinctions are becoming increasingly difficult to apply consistently, as evidenced by the uncertainties regarding the status of musculoskeletal ailments such as low back pain and carpal tunnel syndrome. The terms *disorder* and *disease* in the title of this book and in the description of the theoretical model in this section are used in a generic sense that is intended to be neutral with respect to the semantic distinctions and ambiguities mentioned above. One of the intended outcomes of the historical analysis presented in subsequent chapters is a better understanding of the subtle differences in the actual use of these various terms by physicians and other groups, and the ways that medical diagnostic language can be molded by social forces.

8. The model portrayed in figure 4 is applicable to the United States. In other nations, such as those in Scandinavia, employees exercise more control over the selection of work methods. However, in the United States, the employer generally has primary responsibility for that determination. This does not imply necessarily an environment of overt conflict between workers and their bosses. The arrow extending from employers to employees would be as applicable to a traditional paternalistic environment in which employers believed strongly in protecting the welfare of workers and employees accepted and genuinely appreciated the direction given them.

9. I have chosen to use the word *physician* in this model of occupational disease to refer to the individuals diagnosing and treating the disorder and making a determination as to its occupational origin. By using this term I do not intend to ignore or disparage the significant role played by other health care providers, including nurses, chiropractors, osteopaths, and physical therapists, as well as epidemiologists and other researchers who are not medical doctors. To some extent, the choice of the term *physician* represents merely a graphical expediency. On a deeper level, though, it still seems to be true that in our society medical doctors have been invested with the primary authority for rendering judgments about the cause of disease in particular patients. In very recent times, professional epidemiologists have made significant contributions to the identification of occupational risk factors in populations of workers. But historically this role has been the primary domain of the medical doctor. In the historical case studies presented in this book we will see that physicians were at the forefront of the medical recognition and conception of occupational disease, not only from the clinical standpoint but also from the research perspective. In the course of this investigation, I shall cite the contributions of other non-M.D. health professionals and scientists when their contribution seems to be significant to the narrative and the points under discussion.

Chapter Two *Cumulative Trauma Disorders of the Hands and Wrists*

1. For government estimates of CTD incidence see U.S. Department of Labor 1993a, 1993b, 1994. Workers' compensation costs are summarized in Webster and Snook 1994b, pp. 714, 717. Renner 1992 contains information on the cost of surgical cases.

2. Cumulative trauma disorders (CTDs) are generally thought to include a wide variety of conditions affecting the tendons, tendon sheaths, nerves, and muscles and are believed to be caused by repetitive motion. Other commonly used terms used to describe CTDs include repetitive trauma disorders, repetitive strain injuries, occupational cervico-brachial disorders, overuse syndromes, and regional musculoskeletal disorders. Although they can

occur in many different body parts, the tissues of the upper extremities are the most frequently reported sites. Controversy currently exists in the medical and safety communities about whether to consider nontraumatic back pain as a variety of CTD. In this chapter, I shall concentrate specifically on CTDs of the hand and wrist, because of their dramatic growth during the past decade and the ensuing national debate that has resulted regarding their occupational origin. For background information on the current medical understanding of CTDs see Rempel et al. 1992; and Armstrong 1990.

3. An extensive listing of occupation-specific diagnostic terms for CTDs with references is provided in Armstrong 1990, p. 1175. The reference to seamstress's finger is a recent one not mentioned by Armstrong. See Poole 1993.

4. A listing of applicable references is provided in Putz-Anderson 1988, pp. 25–30. See also Armstrong and Silverstein 1987, pp. 335–337.

5. According to the U.S. Department of Labor (1994), repetitive trauma disorders comprised 4.5% of all injuries and illnesses reported in 1993. Using 1989 workers' compensation records from the Liberty Mutual Insurance Company, Webster and Snook (1994b) estimated that upper extremity CTDs account for 0.83% of all workers' compensation claims, and 1.64% of all claims costs. According to Brogmus, Webster, and Sorock 1994, hand and wrist CTDs represented about 2.6% of all workers' compensation claims in 1993.

6. Rempel et al. 1992, p. 838.

7. Armstrong and Silverstein 1987, pp. 339–341.

8. Houston 1989; Dainoff 1992; Verespej 1991.

9. See Ireland 1988; Hadler 1993; and Hadler 1987a. At a conference of the New Jersey Chapter of the Public Risk Insurance Management Association, Dr. Arthur Canario, chief of Orthopedic Surgery at Beth Israel Hospital (Newark, New Jersey) asserted that carpal tunnel syndrome is a "fad injury" that is largely unrelated to occupational causes in the vast majority of cases (reported in Otis 1990).

10. Hadler 1990.

11. Cited in Rosen 1942, p. 1321.

12. Stockman 1920, pp. 4–5; Bach 1948, pp. 13–33.

13. Cited in Thackrah 1832, p. 1.

14. Hippocrates c. 550 B.C.E., *Epidemics*. Book IV, Sec. 50. Discussed in Ramazzini 1713, p. 285.

15. Ramazzini 1713, pp. 229, 421, 423.

16. Thackrah 1832, pp. 73–74, 78. In manual carding, a hand instrument called a card was using for disentangling and ordering cotton or wool fiber preparatory to spinning. The instrument consisted of bent wire teeth set closely in rows. Thackrah's reference to card making refers to the process in which men and children assembled those instruments. In the mid-nineteenth century, manual carding was gradually replaced by the use of mechanical carding machines.

17. For a description of the beat diseases in miners see Rosen 1940; and Rosen 1942.

18. Solly 1864, p. 709. Great Britain Census of 1831, cited in Wade 1833, p. 549. Census estimates for 1900 are derived from data provided in Crozier 1965.

19. Thackrah 1832, p. 175.

20. The disorder was mentioned and described, although not named, by Sir Charles Bell (1830). During the following two decades, over a dozen additional articles appeared on this subject in the medical journals of Germany, France, and England. Some of the earliest references are: Albers 1835; Brück 1835; Cazanave 1836; and Goldschmidt 1839. By 1865, some of the many names that had been used to describe this disorder included writers' cramp, scriveners' palsy, Schreibekrampf, writers' palsy, dysgraphia, crampe des écrivains, and professional cramp.

21. Dana 1894, 468. The American physician Allan McLane Hamilton (1881) observed the same trend: "Writers' cramp is much more rare among those who write and meanwhile compose, than among clerks or copyists who do 'machine work.' Constant use of the pen of this kind is seen to be followed by mischief" (p. 584). Another authority, W. R. Gowers (1896), noted that, "The affection occurs chiefly among those that earn their living by

writing, and clerks furnish the majority of cases. . . . Among clerks who suffer, lawyers' clerks constitute an undue proportion" (pp. 713–714).

22. Solly 1864, pp. 709–710.

23. Gowers estimated that between two-thirds and five-sixths of all sufferers were men (Gowers 1896, p. 711). Of seventy-five cases of writing impairment studied by Poore (1873), all of the confirmed cases of writers' cramp occurred in males. Romberg, in 1853, notes that writers' cramp "has been almost exclusively been met in the male sex" (p. 320).

24. Poore 1897, p. 93.

25. Poore 1873; Dana 1894.

26. Poore 1873, pp. 1–6, 348–349; Poore 1897, pp. 31, 58; Gowers 1896, p. 722; Zuradelli 1857. Poore (1873) explains, "The muscles by which the prehension of the pen is effected need not of necessity obtain any interval of rest for hours together. During all the several acts which constitute writing, these muscles remain in a state of contraction; for the pen, in stroke-making, in horizontal movement, and in ink-dipping, cannot be released from the grasp of the fingers and the thumb. It is acknowledged that by stimulating a muscle for too long a time, too frequently, or too forcibly, we exhaust its irritability, and the muscles of pen-prehension are certainly subjected to too prolonged contraction, and often are made to contract with undue and unnecessary force" (pp. 348–349).

27. Lloyd 1895, p. 458; Poore 1899, p. 655; Dana 1894, p. 468.

28. See Poore 1873, 12; Dana 1894, p. 468; Wood 1893, p. 653; Rosenthal 1879, p. 397; and Lloyd 1895, pp. 463–464. Lloyd remarks, "I have no doubt that the reason why an increase in scriveners' palsy was noted after the introduction of the steel pen was because the latter, when first adopted, had a sharp point in marked contrast with the rather blunt and always soft nib of the old-fashioned quill. There can be no other reason, unless it be in the additional fact that commercial and manufacturing schemes increased vastly about that time, and employed a vastly increased number of hand-writing clerks. The lead pencil, for practically the same reason as that in the case of the stub-pen, is more restful to the hand than a sharp-pointed steel pen." For prophylactic writing devices, see Dana 1894, pp. 475–476; Wood 1893, p. 652; Lloyd 1895, pp. 471–472; Gowers 1896, 726; Poore 1873, pp. 91–92. On stub-pen see Lloyd 1895, p. 463. On typewriter see Wood 1893, p. 653; Gowers 1896, p. 727; Poore 1897, p. 32. Osler (1892) states that "the use of the type-writer has diminished very much the frequency of scrivener's palsy" (p. 965). However, by the early twentieth century a few medical reports began to appear of workers suffering from "typewriters' cramp" (see Kober and Hanson 1916, p. 286).

29. Poore 1873, p. 345. Similar difficulties with the prevailing terminology were expressed by a number of other leading researchers, including Crisanto Zuradelli (1857). James Lloyd (1895) wrote, "It is unfortunate that it [writers' cramp] has been variously named, because not one of its familiar names accurately designates it. Thus Gallard (1877) has said truly that the spasmodic action of the muscles is not a true cramp because it is non-painful. If we call the affection *scrivener's palsy* we are met at once with the objection that true palsy is present in a comparatively small proportion of cases. Such terms as *dysgraphia, graphospasmus,* and *mogigraphia* are pedantic and unfamiliar" (p. 462).

30. Romberg 1853, p. 322.

31. Poore 1873, p. 87.

32. Poore 1897, p. 70.

33. See, for example, Hamilton 1881.

34. Onimus 1875, p. 175. Onimus wrote: "Cette affection ne serait pas très rare parmi les employés au télégraphe, surtout pour ceux qui se servent constamment du télégraphe Morse; ils la designent entre eux par l'expression de mal télégraphique." (This affliction is not that uncommon among telegraphers, especially those who work constantly on the Morse telegraph; among them it is called telegraphers' disease).

35. Robinson 1882; Fulton 1884, p. 369; Dana 1894, p. 474; Cronbach 1903.

36. Robinson 1882, p. 880.

37. Lloyd 1895, p. 473. Thompson and Sinclair 1912, p. 941.

38. Gowers 1896, p. 729. Lloyd 1895, p. 473. Departmental Committee on Telegraphists' Cramp 1911, p. 59. Cronbach 1903, p. 243.

39. Lloyd 1895, p. 476. Fronzblau et al. 1993 and Franco, Castelli, and Gatti 1992 identify the use of a computer mouse as a risk factor for CTDs. Fulton 1884, p. 372. For typist's movements, see Thompson and Sinclair 1912, p. 942. This finding is consistent with contemporary research showing that a good typist may depress the keys seven to eight times per second (25,200–28,800 strokes per hour) and that users of computer keyboards typically make between 8,000 and 27,000 strokes per hour. (Armstrong and Silverstein 1987, p. 334).

40. For example, see Departmental Committee on Telegraphists' Cramp 1911, p. 32.

41. Departmental Committee on Telegraphists' Cramp 1911, pp. 7–9. A written questionnaire was sent to 8,153 telegraphists employed either at the Central Telegraph Office or at the sending side of large provincial offices. Completed questionnaires were received from 7,317 (90%) of the workers. Six percent (437 respondents) reported complaints suggestive of cramp or early stages of cramp. 2,427 others (33.2%) reported miscellaneous difficulties in keying suggestive of muscular fatigue or other problems. The committee chose Division F of the Central Telegraph Office as a representative sample based upon their use of the Morse key approximating the mean of all divisions. Of 182 telegraphists in Division F, 155 answered the questionnaire. All available respondents from Division F (145) were given an objective physical examination by a physician from the investigating committee. Of those examined, 13 (9%) were found to be actually afflicted with cramp (7) or early stages of cramp (6), and 80 (55.2%) to have other varieties of physical discomfort. Thus, the total number of workers experiencing some clinical problems based upon the medical examination was 93 (64.1%). It is interesting to compare these findings with the self-reporting by 155 workers in Division F, where 33 workers described symptoms suggesting cramp (14) or early cramp (19), and 67 described fatigue or other difficulty, for a total of 100 (64.5%) reporting some physical problem.

The percentage of males among United States telegraphists in 1911 was about 87.5% (35,000 males and 5,000 females). Departmental Committee on Telegraphists' Cramp 1911, pp. 60, 9.

42. After 1880, common-law suits were brought under the Employers' Liability Act of 1880, which specified the employers' responsibilities for maintaining a safe workplace, and established guidelines for common-law actions by injured employees.

43. Figlio 1985 discusses the treatment of occupational diseases under the 1906 Act, with particular regard to telegraphists' cramp and twisters' cramp.

44. Departmental Committee on Compensation for Industrial Diseases 1908. Testimony was provided by Dr. J. Sinclair, second medical officer of the General Post Office, that 2.75% of the post office's 19,000 telegraph clerks suffered from telegraphists' cramp (p. 29). Evidence was provided by Sinclair that reported cases of telegraphists' cramp were associated exclusively with the operation of the Morse telegraph instrument. For that reason, members of the committee (principally Drs. Legge and Allbutt) surmised that it was important to restrict the definition of the disease to operation of the Morse instrument. Sinclair and representatives of the Postal Telegraph Clerks Association agreed with this suggestion. Workers representing the Clerks Association testified that by defining the disease in this way, they hoped to induce the Post Office to introduce a greater number of Hughes instruments, which they perceived as easier to operate (see testimony p. 32, §11942–11944 and p. 34, §11985–11986).

The Industrial Diseases Committee struggled with the question of how to differentiate telegraphists' cramp from other similar maladies such as writers' cramp, wrist weakness, tenosynovitis, neurasthenia, neuralgia, neuristis, and muscular paresis (see testimony p. 33, §11925–11939). Sinclair repeatedly testified that the primary differentiating characteristic was the unique and observable coding errors that resulted when affected telegraphers transmitted the Morse signal (e.g., p. 29, §11825; p. 32, §11920).

45. Departmental Committee on Compensation for Industrial Diseases 1913, pp. 8–9, Appendix I, p. xi.

46. Departmental Committee on Compensation for Industrial Diseases 1913, p. 59, §1765.
47. Holcombe 1973, p. 183.
48. Departmental Committee on Compensation for Industrial Diseases 1913, p. 36, §1236.
49. This question was central to discussions of occupational neuroses in the medical literature from 1830 to 1930. Many prominent researchers, including Poore and Lloyd, were convinced that the lesion was located in the peripheral nerves. Others (e.g., Duchenne, Solly, Gowers) asserted that the pathological abnormality could be traced to the brain or higher nerve centers. Anatomical studies that were conducted (typically post mortem) were inconclusive. The prominence of this medical controversy and the lack of a definitive answer was one reason why the eventual discovery of carpal tunnel syndrome and the localization of a specific lesion in the median nerve took on such great medical importance in the mid-twentieth century.
50. Bell 1830, pp. clxii–clxiii.
51. Duchenne 1867, p. 404.
52. Beard 1869a, 1869b, 1881, 1884. Beard 1881, p. 97. Wakefield 1893, p. 302.
53. Two excellent studies are Lutz 1991 and Rabinbach 1990. Other valuable historical studies of neurasthenia include Cayleff 1988, Showalter 1985, Sicherman 1977, and Haller and Haller 1974.
54. For an excellent discussion of the gender bias inherent in the concept of neurasthenia and the differences between the Weir Mitchell Rest Cure for women and Muldoon's Cure for men, see Lutz 1991, pp. 31–37.
55. Lutz 1991, p. 19.
56. Lutz 1991, p. 285.
57. Wood 1893, p. 651. Southard and Solomon 1916, p. 272.
58. Departmental Committee on Telegraphists' Cramp 1911, p. 9.
59. Gowers 1896, p. 725.
60. See, for example, Catton 1919; Collie 1917; Copin 1929; Fisher 1922; Fraser 1930; Jarrett 1917; Jones and Llewellyn 1917; and Osnato 1925. Departmental Committee on Telegraphists' Cramp 1911, p. 6. For follow-up study see Smith, Culpin, and Farmer 1927. This conclusion was based upon psychological tests that found a higher prevalence of severe psychoneurotic tendencies in a study group of telegraphists suffering from cramp (78%) than in four control groups of "noncramp" telegraphists, typists, clerical workers, and learners (17.6–32.5%). Although these results in themselves do not indicate a cause-and-effect relationship, the researchers concluded that psychoneurotic symptoms dispose a person toward cramp, and thus "people who show psycho-neurotic symptoms or poor muscular coordination, and particularly if in combination, should not be advised to take up telegraphy" (p. 35).
61. See Lutz 1991, 31–37. For a historical analysis of female predisposition to neurasthenia see Cayleff 1988, Showalter 1985, and Haller 1971. Rationalizations summarized in Haller1971, pp. 474–481; and Levin 1971, p. 171. Myerson 1920, p. 25. Fulton 1884, p. 374.
62. For historical discussion of this issue see Lutz 1991, pp. 31–37; Haller 1971, pp. 473–482; Haller 1970, pp. 2490–2491; and Smith-Rosenberg and Rosenberg 1981. Hammond 1906, p. 591. Oliver 1916, p. 67. Dwyer cited in Butler 1984, p. 290. Mitchell 1887, p. 10. On the New Woman see Lutz 1991; and Haller 1971.
63. Mock 1919, p. 726.
64. Huddleson 1932, pp. 39, 38. *Jewish Encyclopedia* 1905, p. 225.
65. Church and Peterson 1899, p. 528. Benton 1921, p. 360.
66. Hooks 1947; and U.S. Department of Labor 1950.
67. Wessely 1990, p. 48.
68. On age see Butler 1907, p. 282; Wertheimer 1977, pp. 159, 237; and Davies 1982, p. 76. On duration of employment see Butler 1907, p. 291. On U.S. Women's Bureau Report see Manning 1930; Butler 1907.
69. Drinka 1984, pp. 44–47.
70. A good historical synopsis of Dupuytren's contracture is provided in Elliot 1988 and Elliot 1990. Platar cited in Elliot 1990, p. 1.

71. Cited in Elliot 1990, p. 2.
72. Dupuytren 1862. The full text of the lecture notes from Dupuytren's presentation, translated into English, is provided in Hueston 1963, pp. 1–2.
73. A good summary of contemporary medical knowledge about Dupuytren's contracture can be found in Milford 1988; Welsh and Spencer 1990; and Hueston and Tubiana 1986.
74. Bunnell 1970, p. 226.
75. Raynaud 1862. An English translation of the article is provided in Major 1945. The name *Raynaud's disease* was first mentioned in the medical literature by Thomas Barlow (1883).
76. Raynaud 1862. Cited in Christophers 1972, p. 730.
77. Similar findings had been reported earlier by Loriga (1911) in Italy. Subsequent European studies are described in *Annual Report of the Chief Inspector of Factories and Workshops* 1924, 1930; Teleky 1927; and Seyring 1930.
78. See, for instance, Hunt 1936a; Hunter, McLaughlin, and Perry 1945; Agate, Druett, and Tombleson 1946; Telford, McCann, and MacCormack 1945; Agate 1949; and Dart 1946.
79. Silman et al. 1990; Weinrich et al. 1990; Leppert et al. 1987; and Carpentier et al. 1990.
80. Almost all major studies of occupationally induced Raynaud's phenomenon involve exclusively men: Loriga's 1911 study of miners using pneumatic tools, Alice Hamilton's (1918) study of 123 quarry workers suffering from finger blanching, Maria Seyring's (1930) study among pneumatic tool operators in Germany, the 1924 report of the Chief Inspector of Factories involving stonemasons in Britain, Hunt's (1936) study of riveters, Telford's (1945) study of men working with electrically driven rotating tools, and Agate and Druett's (1947) study of 230 men who were grinding excess metal from small castings. Overall, an estimated 5–6% of the working male population suffers from primary Raynaud's disease, compared with approximately 2–3% in the general male population (see Rom 1992, p. 1167). However, in the general population, Raynaud's disease affects many more females than males, by a ratio of approximately 3:1 (Newmeyer 1988, p. 2421).

    Dupuytren's disease occurs most often among elderly males, especially those of Northern European descent. However, several authorities have speculated that there may be considerable underreporting of the disease among females. For example, Welsh and Spenser (1990) speculate that "the possibility existed, however, that as the disease's main economic import was on manual workers, the incidence in females may have been underestimated." Milford (1988) asserts that "women often accommodate better to the inconvenience of the resulting deformity." The implication here is that women are less likely to receive surgical treatment because they perform less manually strenuous work than men (most of the available epidemiologic data are based on surgical cases).
81. For example, Conn 1931.
82. For a discussion of the factors leading to the growth of the industrial hygiene perspective during the Progressive Era, see Rosner and Markowitz 1991, pp. 30–31.
83. Hayhurst 1923, p. 134. See also Hayhurst 1915, pp. xv–xvii, 1–3.
84. Hayhurst 1923, p. 140.
85. Conn 1931, p. 714. *Ohio Health News* 1934, p. 2.
86. See, for example, Foster 1931; Conn 1931; Hammer 1934; Stein 1927; Schneider 1928; and Finkelstein 1930.
87. The medical terms *tenosynovitis* and *tendovaginitis* are synonymous, referring to the inflammation of a tendon sheath. The etymology of the latter term is the Latin *vagina*, meaning "sheath," and the Greek *-itis*, meaning "inflammation."
88. Finkelstein 1930, p. 509. Schneider also commented on the "relative frequency" of the condition. See Schneider 1928, p. 846.
89. Finkelstein 1930, 511–512, 539.
90. It is unlikely that Finkelstein used the term *houseworker* to refer to women performing contract work at home for the garment industry. A detailed case history for each patient contains background on the disorder's onset, including history of trauma or other unusual manual activities. His case histories of the houseworkers provides no special mention of cutting, sewing, or working with garments, information that is provided on others (e.g., the "cutter") in the series. Moreover, the practice of homework in the garment industry

had been very common in New York prior to 1910, but decreased significantly by 1920 due to legal restrictions on the practice enacted during the Progressive Era.

91. Biographical information on Finkelstein has been obtained from his obituary: "Harry Finkelstein, 91, Orthopedic Surgeon, Dies." *New York Times*, January 25, 1975, p. 30, col. 3, and an interview conducted with Finkelstein's son, Dr. Richard Fenton, on July 14, 1994.

92. New York State Department of Labor 1941. Lapidus and Fenton 1952. Interview with Dr. Richard Fenton, July 14, 1994.

93. New York State Department of Labor 1941, p. 100. *Ohio Health News* 1934, p. 2. For Women's Bureau report, see Mettert 1941. For 1961 Wisconsin data, see Wells 1961.

94. For Public Health survey see Pecora, Udel, and Christman 1960, p. 180. National Institute for Occupational Safety and Health (NIOSH) 1983, p. 5.

95. Lapidus and Fenton 1952, p. 475.

96. Conn 1931, p. 716. For Public Health Service see Pecora, Udel, and Christman 1960, p. 180. Ashe, Cook, and Old 1962, p. 333.

97. On frequency: Data from the Ohio Bureau of Workers' Compensation indicates that, as of 1989, carpal tunnel syndrome accounted for 49.1% of all claims for CTDs of the hands and wrists (Praemer et al. 1992, p. 103). The U.S. Bureau of Labor Statistics reported that "carpal tunnel syndrome is the most common disorder among repetitive motion cases," representing 36% of all disabling repetitive motion cases reported in 1992 (*BLS News*, USDL–94–213, April 26, 1994). The average rate of occurrence of occupational carpal tunnel syndrome is estimated to be about 1.74 cases per 1,000 workers (Franklin et al. 1991, p. 743). But in the automotive and electronics industries, the rate is 25 cases per 1,000 workers. See Madeja 1991, p. 19; and Pfeffer and Gelberman 1987, p. 201.

    On surgical cases see Schenck 1987. Carpal tunnel syndrome release is one of the most frequently performed operations in older adults in the United States and was (in 1988) the tenth most costly surgical procedure performed under Medicare, Part B, according to Louis 1992, p. 146. On media attention: "Carpal Tunnel Syndrome May Be the 'In' Injury, But It Bears Attention," *Chicago Tribune*, October 4, 1989, p. 28; "Carpal Tunnel Syndrome Is a Big Workplace Issue," *Chicago Tribune,* September 27, 1992, Section C, p. 1. Millar 1991. On use as generic descriptor, see, for example, "Carpal Tunnel Lawsuits Are Consolidated," *Wall Street Journal*, June 3, 1992, p. B8; "Hands On Approach to Avoiding Carpal Tunnel Syndrome," *Risk Management*, May 1989, pp. 20–21; "Getting a Grasp on Carpal Tunnel Syndrome," *Risk Management*, March 1990, pp. 40–41.

98. Mosely et al. 1991, p. 375.

99. Putnam 1880, p. 150. The treatment provided by Dr. Putnam to this patient was cannabis. He states that it was too early to access the effectiveness of that therapeutic approach.

100. Phalen 1951; Phalen and Kendrick 1957; Phalen 1966; Phalen 1972.

101. Phalen 1951, pp. 1130–1131. Phalen and Kendrick 1957, pp. 528–529. Phalen 1966, p. 219. Phalen 1972, pp. 33–34.

102. Phalen 1951, p. 1133.

103. Phalen 1966, p. 218.

104. Biographical information on George Phalen is based on archival material supplied by the Cleveland Clinic Foundation, along with telephone interviews with Dr. Phalen on September 29, 1993, and July 18, 1994. Additional information was obtained through conversations with Mrs. Marie Kennedy, a close personal friend of Phalen and his wife. I wish to express my gratitude to Frederick Lautzenheiser, associate archivist of the Cleveland Clinic, for his assistance.

105. Interviews with Phalen, September 29, 1993, and July 18, 1994.

106. Tanzer 1959, p. 627.

107. Tanzer 1959, p. 634.

108. Love 1955, p. 467. Brain, Wright, and Wilkinson 1947, p. 280.

109. See Phalen 1951, p. 1132.

110. Phalen himself suggested this view, for instance, in his 1966 article where he stated, "The fact that the majority of patients with carpal-tunnel syndrome are women at or near the

menopause suggests that the soft tissues about the wrist may be affected in some manner by hormonal changes" (p. 217).

111. For linkages between CTS and occupation, see Birbeck and Beer 1975; Smith, Sonstegard, and Anderson 1977. The state workers' compensation cases are cited and discussed in Hadler 1987a, p. 357. The Missouri case is *Collins v. Neeval Luggage Manufacturing Co. 481 Southwestern Reporter, Second Series (Mo. App. D.K.C. 1972)*, pp. 548–555. The Delaware case is *Warren v. General Motors Corp. 344 Atlantic Reporter, Second Series (Delaware, 1975)* pp. 248–251.

112. MacLeod 1995, p. 111.

113. Wisseman and Badger 1976. Background information on the circumstances leading to this report and the subsequent OSHA citation has been obtained from NIOSH and OSHA records, and from personal interviews conducted with participants in the episode including Tom Majors (July 11, 1994), Don Badger (July 12, 1994), Suzanne Rodgers (July 25, 1994) and several officials from OSHA's Colorado Area and Region offices. At the time of the original investigation in 1976, Colorado maintained its own state OSHA program. However, that program was then in severe jeopardy due to poor financing, inadequate staffing and lax enforcement. As a result of these problems, federal OSHA revoked its authorization of the Colorado state plan in 1977. It was federal OSHA officials from the Denver office who eventually returned to the site in early 1978 to issue citations against Eastman Kodak.

114. Wisseman and Badger 1976, p. 2.

115. OSHA Citation and Notification of Penalty No. C3775–10, issued March 14, 1978.

116. Information obtained through interviews with Tom Majors (July 11, 1994) and Suzanne Rodgers (July 25, 1994), now a private ergonomics consultant in Rochester, New York.

117. Background on Eastman Kodak's involvement in ergonomics can be found in Eastman Kodak Company 1983, pp. 5–6.

118. See Rowe 1983.

119. Cannon, Bernacki, and Walter 1981.

120. Interview with Edward Bernacki, June 23, 1994. Dr. Bernacki is currently an occupational health physician at Johns Hopkins University.

121. See International Association of Machinists 1978. Additional information on worker activities at Pratt & Whitney during 1977–1979 was obtained through interviews with Lou Kiefer and John Harrington of the IAM, and Tim Morris, who was with the New Directions program.

122. Tichauer 1976, 1978; Tichauer and Gage 1977; Chaffin 1975; Greenberg and Chaffin 1977; and Armstrong and Chaffin 1979. Examples of the earlier biomechanical analyses of the hands and wrists performed by Tichauer and Chaffin include Tichauer 1966 and Chaffin 1973.

123. U.S. Department of Labor 1993a, 1993b, 1994.

124. *Wall Street Journal*, January 14, 1983, p. 25. A similar sentiment was expressed by Larry Johnston, director of employee relations for Hanes in an interview with the *New York Times*: "Ailments at Hanes Plant Stir Protest," April 16, 1983, p. 16.

125. U.S. Department of Labor 1987, p. 3.

126. Green 1990.

127. Between 1969 and 1979, one-third of the pork processors in the country closed. Wilson Foods filed for bankruptcy and closed twelve plants in 1983. Dubuque Packing and Rath Packing also shut down major facilities. In all, more than thirty-five plants had closed between 1975 and 1985. See Green 1990, p. 28, and "Misery on the Meatpacking Line," *New York Times*, June 14, 1987, Section 3, pp. 1, 8.

128. "Misery on the Meatpacking Line," *New York Times*, June 14, 1987, Section 3, p. 8. Chain speeds were reported to have increased 84% between 1979 and 1987 (see "Misery," p. 8). According to the UFCW, average hourly wages for meatpackers decreased from $10.69 in 1981 to about $6.79 in 1986 (interview with Deborah Berkowitz of the United Food and Commercial Workers Union, July 28, 1993).

129. Green 1990, pp. 140–260.

130. Green 1990, pp. 22–24.

131. Information concerning UFCW activities with respect to cumulative trauma disorders was obtained through interview with Deborah Berkowitz of the UFCW on July 28, 1993. See also "Unions and Firms Focus on Hand Disorders That Can Be Caused by Repetitive Motions," *Wall Street Journal*, January 14, 1983, pp. 25, 37, which describes the coordinated efforts of eight unions to address this problem and quotes Berkowitz as representative of the AFL-CIO and spokesperson for that effort.

132. "Injury Rate Soaring, Workers at Meatpacking Plant Say," *Los Angeles Times*, March 2, 1987, Section CC/Part IV, p. 1; "Misery on the Meatpacking Line," *New York Times*, June 14, 1987, Section 3, pp. 1, 8; "Plains Slaughterhouse a Union Battleground," *Washington Post*, Aug. 21, 1987, pp. H1–H3.

133. Interview with IBP management officials in "Injury Rate Soaring, Workers at Meatpacking Plant Say," *Los Angeles Times*, March 2, 1987, Section CC/Part IV, p. 1.

134. "OSHA Seeks $2.59 Million Fine For Meatpacker's Injury Reports," *New York Times*, July 22, 1987, p. 1; "Struck Beef Packer Hit With Record Safety Fine." *AFL-CIO News*, July 25, 1987, p. 5; "IBP Confesses Cooking Books on Job Injuries," *AFL-CIO News*, September 26, 1987, p. 2.

135. "IBP Settles Dispute with OSHA," *Business Insurance*, November 28, 1988, p. 37; "Pact Reported on Reducing Meatpacking Injuries," *New York Times*, November 23, 1988, Section I, p. 16; "Major Breakthrough at IBP," *UFCW Action*, January-February, 1989, pp. 8–9.

136. Interview with Deborah Berkowitz, July 28, 1993.

137. Jesse Jackson demonstrated in support of the striking workers in Austin, Minnesota, on April 13, 1986. A similar visit was made by Jackson in support of striking workers at Patrick Cudahy, Inc. in 1987. For an account of these visits, see Green 1990, pp. 224–229, 292. Bruce Babbitt made health and safety hazards in the meatpacking industry a major issue of his brief 1988 presidential campaign, attacking IBP as a "corporate outlaw," and suggesting that the state of Iowa stop giving subsidies to the meatpacking industry. See *New York Times*, January 18, 1988, Section I, p. 13.

138. *New York Times*, November 23, 1988, Section I, p. 16.

139. A good description and analysis of the emergence of the cumulative trauma concept in California can be found in California Workers' Compensation Institute 1978. This report traces the genesis of the cumulative trauma concept to the landmark case of *Beveridge v. IAC, 175 Cal App 2nd 592, 24 CCC 274 (1959)* in which the court decided as follows: "We think the proposition irrefutable that while a succession of slight injuries in the course of employment may not in themselves be disabling, their *cumulative* effect in work effort may become a destructive force. The fact that a single but slight work strain may not be disabling does not destroy its causitive effect, if in combination with other such strains it produces a subsequent disability. The single strand, entwined with others, makes up the rope of causation." The 1978 report of the California Workers' Compensation Institute noted that although this court decision occurred in 1959, very few claims arose under the cumulative trauma (CT) doctrine until the late 1970s. The incidence of CT claims rose threefold between 1974 and 1978, and their costs increased 45% between 1976 and 1978. As of 1978, CT claims primarily involved injuries to the back (34.3%) and heart/vascular system (22.7%). The average age of CT claimants was 52 years old, and nearly 20% of claimants were retired at the time the claim was submitted. It was suggested that the rise in CT cases was due to a deliberate labor effort to encourage retiring workers to file claims routinely under this doctrine at the time of their retirement. See also Cranston 1978.

140. See Silverstein, Fine, and Armstrong 1987; and Silverstein, Fine, and Stetson 1987.

141. *Strains and Sprains* 1982, pp. 7–10.

142. For example, Putz-Anderson 1988.

143. The term *repetition strain injury* was used in Australia as early as 1982 (see National Health and Medical Research Council 1982). The phrase may have originated from the studies conducted in the 1970s by Australian researcher David Ferguson (for example, Ferguson 1971). A historical analysis of the RSI concept in comparison to occupational neuroses of the nineteenth century is provided in Quintner 1991.

144. Task Force Report 1985, p. 120. For example, Hopkins 1990.

145. On labor, see Hopkins 1990, p. 370. On media and unions see Ireland 1992, p. 85. On effects of automation and recession see Acutt 1990; Hall and Morrow 1988, p. 647.
146. Interview with David Michaels, August 19, 1993.
147. Hall and Morrow 1988, p. 647. Ireland 1992, p. 86.
148. See especially Ireland 1992; Hall and Morrow 1988; Gun 1990; Brahams 1992; Bammer and Martin 1988; Lucire 1986; Bloch 1984; and Ferguson 1987.
149. See DeReamer 1980; Haddon, Suchman, and Klein 1964; and Powell et al. 1971.
150. Although there was no labor representation for private-sector clerical workers in Great Britain during the nineteenth century, a few attempts were made in the late 1800s to form clerical unions in the British civil service. However, the first permanent associations were not formed until the 1890s, by which time writers' cramp had become a well-established medical entity. For a history of British civil service clerical unions see Humphreys 1958; Pickard 1955; and Routh 1966.
151. Hadler 1977, p. 1023.

Chapter Three *Back Pain*

1. National Council on Compensation Insurance 1993, p. 3.
2. For basic information about the epidemiology of occupational back pain see Frymoyer and Pope 1987; Andersson 1991; Kelsey and Golden 1987; Bauer 1989; and Snook 1982.
3. Webster and Snook 1994a, p. 1113. According to the National Council on Compensation Insurance (1993), the mean cost of indemnity back injury claims in 1990 was $24,080, considerably greater than the average cost for all workers' compensation indemnity claims of $19,444. Because *indemnity* claims are defined as those for which the injured worker has lost time from work and received payments to compensate for lost wages, they are sometimes referred to as "lost time" claims. A comprehensive analysis of the economic costs of spinal disorders in the United States is contained in Cats-Baril and Frymoyer 1991.
4. Deyo 1987, p. 18 (citing White and Gordon 1982). A study in England of acute back pain treated by general practitioners showed that no specific reason for the back pain could be found in 79% of men and 89% of women. See Dillane, Fry, and Kalton 1966; and Rowe 1969, pp. 7, 34.
5. Andersson 1991, p. 108; Kelsey and Golden 1987, pp. 9–10; Snook 1988, pp. 46–47; NIOSH 1981, pp. 10–12.
6. See Waddell 1990; Burry and Gilkison 1987; Worrall and Appel 1987.
7. For example, Frymoyer and Pope 1987; Kelsey and Golden 1987.
8. See especially Hadler 1991b; Hadler 1989; Hadler 1987b; Hadler 1986; Hadler 1984; and Hadler 1978.
9. A number of excellent studies have been written examining the medical history of back pain. Notable among these are Wiltse 1991; Robinson 1983; and Allan and Waddell 1989. These studies have generally focused on the medical history of back pain, rather than the social forces or occupational factors that are emphasized in this book.
10. See Hippocrates, *Aphorisms,* Sec. IV. pp. 178–179. Ramazzini also refers to Hippocrates' writings on pain in the loins and sciatica, for instance in *On Joints,* LVIII, and *Air, Waters, Places,* xxi.
11. Howarth 1952, pp. 4–5; LeVay 1990, pp. 3–59.
12. Bach 1948, pp. 13–16; LeVay 1990, pp. 2–11.
13. Stockman 1920, pp. 20–23.
14. Brown 1828.
15. The *Index Catalogue of the U.S. Surgeon General's Office* lists references to 161 scholarly articles on spinal irritation appearing in the medical literature between 1828 and 1890. This included articles both in support of and in opposition to Brown's theory.
16. See especially Romberg 1860; Axenfeld 1863; Radcliffe 1868; Rockwell and Beard 1871; and Hammond 1873.
17. Erb 1876. Erb's entire quotation reads as follows: "A good deal of change has taken place in the views entertained respecting the existence, the pathological position and significance

of the group of symptoms which has been so well known by the term 'spinal irritation' since the time of Brown (1828). Sometimes greatly overrated, its importance and frequency exaggerated beyond limit, and used as a common term for many most heterogeneous forms of disease in which pain of the back and sensitiveness of the vertebrae happened to be present, spinal irritation has been considered one of the commonest of diseases; while again, at the time when pathological anatomy was made the sole judge of everything, it was entirely denied recognition, or regarded as at most a frequent and rather meaningless symptom, so that it has almost passed from the memory of the present living generation of physicians" (p. 358).

18. Brandt-Rauf and Brandt-Rauf 1987, p. 69.
19. Curtis 1988, p. 33; Joy 1954.
20. Hippocrates, pp. 178–179.
21. Aurelianus 1950, p. 1019.
22. Ramazzini 1713, p. 285.
23. Ramazzini 1713, pp. 231, 283.
24. Thackrah 1832, pp. 68, 67, 71. For instance, the National Institute for Occupational Safety and Health (NIOSH 1981) has estimated that as many as 60% of all low-back pain episodes may arise as the result of "chronic cumulative trauma" to the musculoskeletal tissues in the lumbar region.
25. Thackrah 1832, pp. 73, 78, 177. Card-setting involves the placement of wire teeth in a hand implement called a card, used for disentangling and ordering cotton or wool fiber preparatory to spinning.
26. For example, no mention is made of possible occupational etiology for lumbago or rheumatism in the following major medical textbooks of the nineteenth century: von Niemeyer 1877; Roberts 1881; Quain 1888, and Bristowe 1890. Articles concerning lumbago and other forms of back pain written by Inman (1860), did not contain any reference to work-induced trauma, manual handling, or other occupational factors.

    In addition to the remarks by Thackrah, another isolated exception to this general trend can be found in a passage from the 1834 book by William and Daniel Griffin entitled *Observations on Functional Affections of the Spinal Cord*. In discussing functional rachialgia (spinal irritation), the Griffins wrote, "The complaints, whatever they may be, are usually relieved by the recumbent posture, always increased by lifting weights, bending, stooping, or twisting the spine, and amongst the poorer classes often consequent on the labour of carrying heavy loads, as in drawing water, carting manure, &c." (Griffin and Griffin 1834, p. 214).

27. The Stockton and Darlington line was opened in 1825, with the Liverpool and Manchester lines following in 1830. For a good history of the British railways see Gourvish 1980.
28. Gourvish 1980, p. 20. In 1862, according to the Lancet Commission, the route mileage existing in Great Britain approximately equaled that existing in the rest of Europe combined (Lancet Commission 1862, p. 16).
29. Gourvish 1980, p. 26, 41. See also Perkin 1970, p. 104.
30. Lancet Commission 1862, p. 82.
31. Schivelbusch 1986, p. 33.
32. Perkin 1970, p. 34.
33. Gourvish 1980, p. 46 citing Wilson 1925.
34. In 1849, 51% of passengers traveled third class. That number increased to 57% in 1860. (Lancet Commission 1862, p. 51). Besides sitting on hard wooden benches in carriages with no vibration-damping springs, there were other reasons why travel in third class was considered more dangerous, such as the open sides on some third-class carriages that permitted passengers to be thrown from the carriage in the case of a collision or sudden stop.
35. Perkin 1970, pp. 289–290; Lancet Commission 1862, p. 17.
36. Perkin 1970, p. 289.
37. Perkin 1970, pp. 290–292.
38. An early version of the Campbell Act (The Fatal Accidents Act) had been originally passed

in 1846. However, it was only in 1864 that the act was extended to cover victims of non-fatal railroad accidents. A similar railroad liability law was passed in Germany in 1871. See Schivelbusch 1986, p. 134.

39. Schivelbusch 1986, pp. 134–135.
40. Hammond 1890, p. 416. According to data in Mitchell 1988, the average conversion rate of U.S. dollars to British pounds in 1865 was 8.54. As of 1995 it was about 1.6.
41. The Lancet Commission Report concluded that most rail accidents occurred because rail crews were overworked. This finding lent support to the efforts of workers and their trade unions, which eventually culminated in the passage of laws in 1893 (the Railway Servants' Hours of Labor Act), 1897, and 1900 establishing maximum working hours for railroad workers.
42. Lancet Commission 1862, p. 83.
43. Erichsen 1867, p. 27.
44. According to Erichsen, this term was used informally even before his first lectures on the subject in 1866. See Erichsen 1867, pp. 22–23.
45. Schivelbusch 1986, p. 139.
46. Page 1883, p. 103, and citing Rigler 1879.
47. Syme 1867, p. 2.
48. See Benedict 1897; Spitzka 1883; Thorburn 1888; Knapp 1888; Rigler 1879; Young 1899; and Sumers 1896.
49. Hodges 1881, p. 363. Hodges did not indicate what his diagnosis was in the remaining 13 cases, an interesting omission given the title of his paper. Hodges 1881, p. 389.
50. See Page 1883, pp. 106, 194.
51. Allen 1900; Alexander 1892. Examples of this sentiment can also be found in Spitzka 1883, Dana 1884; and Bramwell 1886. Spitzka wrote, "There can be very little question, indeed, that speculative actions are frequently based on the erroneous allegation of spinal disease after railroad collisions and similar accidents. And there is little question in my mind that, even when an injury has been done, its results are often magnified or perverted, in order to overbalance the denial of defendants, on the false principle that the best antidote for one lie is another. . . . I should be inclined to believe that over one-half of those in which a verdict has been secured, including several in which very large sums have been obtained, were and are shams."
52. See, for instance, Page 1883; Hammond 1890; Dercum 1889; Grant 1897; and Cullingworth 1886.
53. Oppenheim 1889. See also Clevenger 1889, and Bremer 1889. A contemporary historical analysis of the relationship between railway spine and traumatic neuroses can be found in Fischer-Homberger 1970.
54. Accident statistics from Gourvish 1980, p. 53; and Lancet Commission 1862, p. 16. It has been estimated that in the quarter century between 1875 and 1899, a total of 12,870 British railway workers were killed and 68,575 injured on the job. See Bagwell 1963, p. 95.
55. Outten 1890, p. 21, 29.
56. Lancet Commission 1862, p. 80.
57. Statements made in 1877 by Mr. G. Findlay and in 1900 by Mr. F. Harrison, both general managers of the London and North Western Railway, to British government boards of inquiry. Royal Commission on Railway Accidents. 1877. BPP 1877. Vol. 48, §30817–8; Royal Commission on Railway Accidents. 1900. BPP 1900. Vol. 27, §6044. Their testimony is discussed in Bagwell 1963, pp. 94–95.
58. Wilson 1909, p. 25. A comprehensive summary of this commission's activities is presented in "The Royal Commission of 1874" (chapter 11) in Wilson 1909, pp. 17–33. The commission was appointed on June 8, 1874, and reported in February 1877. The chairman was the Duke of Buckingham and Chandos, and one of its members was Mr. T. Harrison, chief engineer for the Northern division of the North Eastern Railway. The commission heard from 336 witnesses representing management, servants, and government inspectors. The commission presented 43,443 questions to these witnesses.
59. *The Times*, September 16, 1874, p. 1. *The Times* was sympathetic to labor, and supported

ASRS demands for shorter working hours. See Bagwell 1963, p. 94, 100; and Perkin 1970, p. 290.

60. Bagwell 1963, p. 95.

61. Bagwell 1963, pp. 99–100.

62. Threats and intimidation were used by rail management to thwart attempts at worker organization. Written warnings were issued by management to rail servants, such as one written by the directors of three rail companies in 1866 stating that "they will most firmly withstand all dictation by the men; and they give notice that any attempt at combination by the respective employees, will be met by the directors in such a manner as may to them seem fit" (Bagwell 1963, p. 43). A strong statement of this view was expressed at a Labour Commission Inquiry in 1893 by George Findlay, General Manager of the London and North Western Railway, who said "that you might as well have trades unionism in Her Majesty's Army as to have it in the railway service. The thing is totally incompatible." (Perkin 1970, p. 291). It was not until 1872 that railway workers from various trades banded together to form a lasting trade union, the Amalgamated Society of Railway Servants. But even that union was weak, succumbing to pressure from railway management, as well as internal dissension and segmentation, due, in part, to the rigid "grade" system imposed by the companies. (See Kingsford 1970, pp. 77–87). After attracting 17,247 members in 1872, the ASRS had fewer than 6,000 by the end of 1882 (Bagwell 1963, p. 70).

63. Perkin 1970, p. 291.

64. Bagwell 1963, p. 42.

65. In theory, rail servants had at least one other source available to provide financial relief for injury suffered through accidents on the job; the company-subsidized friendly and insurance societies, which were replaced in 1864 by an industry-wide Casualty Fund. However, this means of assistance was generally inadequate, due to incomplete coverage for accidental injuries and lack of participation and financial support by many of the railway companies (see Kingsford 1970, pp. 157–159). The ASRS, while maintaining a protection fund (for strikes) and an orphans' fund, did not provide any direct assistance for injured workers or their families.

Prior to the enactment of workers' compensation laws, workers injured on the job had to sue their employers and prove negligence to recover damages. Employers could use three common-law defenses to resist such lawsuits. Under the "fellow-servant" defense, the employer was not liable if the worker's injury resulted from the negligence of a co-worker. According to the "contributory negligence" defense, employers were not responsible for injuries that were caused in any way by the injured worker's own carelessness. The "assumption of risk" defense freed the employer of liability if the injured worker voluntarily chose to work in an environment known to have specific dangers.

66. Erichsen 1875, pp. 284–285.

67. An excellent exposition of this view is presented in Wolfgang Schivelbusch's book, *The Railway Journey: The Industrialization of Time and Space in the Nineteenth Century* (1986). Schivelbusch quotes a number of nineteenth-century authors who portray the railroad as a representation of the dehumanizing social relations fostered by the new industrial age. As an example, British social commentator John Ruskin observes, "The railroad is in all its relations a matter of earnest business, to be got through as soon as possible. It transmutes a man from a traveler into a living parcel" (Schivelbusch 1986, p. 121).

68. For example: Rubinow 1913, Downey 1924, and Somers and Somers 1954.

69. See Hobbs 1939, p. 70; Somers and Somers 1954, p. 29; Rubinow 1913, pp. 13–15, 106, and Willoughby 1898, pp. 29–35. Willoughby provides a good summary of this perspective: "The reason for the complete conversion of the government to the idea of compulsory insurance, and the occasion for its introduction, however, were due to political conditions. Compulsory insurance was avowedly taken up by Bismarck, for the purpose of checking the rapid growth of the social democratic party. His purpose was to outbid socialism in its own field. There is, however, an important distinction between the socialism of Bismarck and that of the social democratic party—Marxist socialism—was avowedly revolutionary,

and sought for a change in industrial conditions through the complete annihilation of the existing political fabric, and the building anew upon its ruins" (pp. 32–33).

70. Frankel and Dawson 1910, p. 47.

71. Rubinow 1913, p. 55. Given that the railroads employed 1,648,033 persons, the injury rate was approximately one injury for every thirteen employees during the year.

72. New York State Legislative Report 1911, pp. 2–3. This study found that injuries to railway workers accounted for about 30% of all industrial accidents reported in New York during those years.

73. Oppenheimer 1884, pp. 65–66. Strümpell 1893, p. 918. Bailey 1898, p. 246.

74. Gowers (1904) expounds the following view: "We are thus compelled to regard lumbago in particular, and muscular rheumatism in general, as a form of inflammation of the fibrous tissue of the muscles. . . . We may conveniently follow the analogy of 'cellulitis,' and term it [this condition] 'fibrositis.' . . . Another definite form of fibrositis is the traumatic. While any structure may suffer from overstrain, the fibrous attachments of the muscles to the back of the sacrum are especially prone to such traumatic derangement" (pp. 118–119). See also Llewellyn and Jones 1915.

75. Osler 1898, p. 406.

76. Osler 1914, p. 1130.

77. Hoffman 1915, p. 7. I. M. Rubinow voiced a similar opinion in 1913: "Few people in the United States have any conception how enormous is the annual number of accidental injuries to the wage-working population. American information on the subject is yet scant and unsatisfactory. Only within the last few years—when the interest has grown—have a few states undertaken to investigate the problem and demand reports of accidents occurring. In Europe, accident statistics is, and has been for many years, a definite and important branch of statistical and social science. . . . As compared with this comprehensive development [in Europe] accident statistics in the United States is in its infancy. We do not know the number of industrial accidents occurring in this country which might be compared with the European figures. As yet only fragmentary information and more or less arbitrary estimates are available for the United States" (Rubinow 1913, pp. 50, 52).

78. Hoffman 1915, p. 79.

79. Hoffman 1915, p. 81.

80. Hayhurst 1915, pp. 35, 126, 129, 315.

81. State of California 1919, p. 148.

82. Commonwealth of Massachusetts 1919, pp. 106–108.

83. *Annual Report of the Chief Inspector of Factories and Workshops* 1922, p. 35.

84. *Proceedings of the National Safety Council* 1923, p. 881.

85. New York State Department of Labor 1926, pp. 23, 68–70.

86. U.S. Department of Labor 1927, p. 49.

87. Rubinow 1913, pp. 70, 71.

88. Ralston 1922, p. 187.

89. Beyer 1925, p. 6.

90. Beyer and Clair 1929, p. 14.

91. *Annual Report of the Liberty Mutual Insurance Company* 1933, p. 11.

92. Beyer and Clair 1929, p. 68.

93. For example, a summary report of all compensated accidents occurring in the state of New York between July 1914 and June 1922 categorized 13,930 accidents as arising from "Handling Heavy Objects" (18.3% of all workers' compensation cases), and 5,598 of those (40.2%) as a "strain in handling." Of those 5,598 "strains," 5,508 (98.4%) involved "temporary disability." This is a much smaller proportion than all "handling heavy object" cases (85.5% were temporary disabilities) or of all cases (77.1% were temporary). See New York State Department of Labor 1926, Table 2.

94. See Worrall and Appel 1987; and Burry and Gilkison 1987. According to four studies summarized by Worrall and Appel, benefit increases of 10% were followed by increases in claims reporting ranging from 3–10%, which could not be explained by independent changes in production operations, employment levels or other variables.

95. Tunturi and Pätiälä 1980. In the opinion of these researchers, "An increase of this magnitude cannot be attributed to a rise in the incidence of spinal disease; the cause may be supposed to lie in a changed attitude to spinal disease and work as well as in the altered system of social security" (p. 22).
96. See, for example, the British Workmen's Compensation Act of 1897, from which the quoted wording is derived. For a discussion of this topic see Barth 1980, p. 95.
97. King 1915, p. 443.
98. Mock 1919, p. 179.
99. Osgood 1919, pp. 151–152.
100. Hope 1923, p. 697.
101. The term "industrial back" was popularized particularly by Robert Osgood. See Osgood and Morrison 1924. See also Magnuson and Coulter 1921; Kidner 1933; Sever 1923, 1925; Bradford 1921; Brackett 1924; and Bassin 1923. Bassin coined the term "labor back" to describe this condition.
102. Lile 1920, p. 319.
103. Palmer 1926, pp. 9–10.
104. It is a little-known fact that the provision of accident prevention service by insurance carriers was originally imposed as a compulsory feature of some of the early workers' compensation acts. For example, the Massachusetts Compensation Act (1912), entitled "An Act Relative to Payments of Employees for Personal Injuries Received in the Course of their Employment and *to the Prevention of Such Injuries*," required the Board of Directors of the Massachusetts Employees Insurance Association (a mutual insurance company created by the act) to "make and enforce reasonable rules and regulations for the prevention of injuries on the premises of subscribers." See Beyer 1916, p. 4.
105. See, for example, Beyer 1925, pp. 7–8, and Ralston 1922, pp. 185–186.
106. For a review of this literature see Rabinbach 1990; and Frankfurter 1915.
107. *Select Committee* 1890. Cited in Pike 1969, p. 237.
108. *Annual Report* 1909, p. 148.
109. See, for instance, Hewitt and Bedale 1922. See also *Select Committee* 1890 that discusses the potential for misplacements of the womb, miscarriages, and rupture among women using heavy sledgehammers ("olivers") for cutting cold iron. Cited in Pike 1969, p. 238.
110. Sever 1923, pp. 165–166.
111. McKendrick 1916, p. v.
112. Landenberger 1926; Fraser 1930; and Fay 1921.
113. Pollock 1922; Gill 1929; Donohue 1926; and Herndon 1927.
114. See Hurst 1918; Bailey 1918; Benton 1921; Brown 1919; Farrar 1918; and Parsons 1919.
115. Barnett 1909, p. 275.
116. Barnett 1909, p. 278.
117. Conn 1922, p. 1210.
118. King 1915, p. 444.
119. Landenberger 1926, p. 51.
120. Donohue 1926, pp. 56–57.
121. Donohue 1926, p. 58.
122. Collie 1917, pp. 258, 29, 18–19.
123. Dewar 1912, pp. 223–224.
124. Delaney 1920, p. 321.
125. Brecher and Brecher 1969, p. 233.
126. See King 1915, p. 443; McKendrick 1916, pp. 112–123; Osler 1914 (8th edition and later); Sever 1919, p. 139; Crain and Slater 1921, p. 129; and Bradford 1921, p. 332.
127. In his 1923 article, "Diagnosis of Industrial Back Conditions," James Sever admits, "Precision in diagnosis, however, even under the most favorable conditions is not often obtainable, due to the fact that many cases show no demonstrable bone lesions by X-ray examination, and the impossibility of differentiating muscle and ligamentous tears is evident. The best that can be done is usually to be content to differentiate bony from soft-part injuries" (p. 165). But in the same article, in regard to industrial back sprains, Sever says,

"An X-ray examination is always of assistance, if possible to have one, even purely on a negative basis" (p. 166).

128. A lengthy section on the use of various X-ray techniques to expose malingerers can be found in Collie 1917, pp. 234–257.

129. See Landenberger 1926, p. 53.

130. A comprehensive summary of this issue is provided in Deyo 1987. See also Frymoyer et al. 1984; Magora and Schwartz 1976; and Torgeson and Dotler 1976.

131. Deyo, Bigos, and Maravilla 1989. Even in the case of modern myelography, there is a significant rate of false-negative results. As many as 30% of lateral disc herniations may be missed by this imaging technique. See Hlavin and Hardy 1993; McCall 1987; and Macnab and McCullough 1990.

132. The classic study on this issue was conducted by Hult (1954). Jensen et al. 1994 found that a large proportion (64%) of asymptomatic individuals without any history of back pain have an abnormality (bulge, protrusion, or extrusion) in at least one intervertebral disc, as determined through MRI (magnetic resonance imaging) scans. This finding is consistent with other studies (e.g., Bell et al. 1984) showing that 55% of asymptomatic patients have disc abnormalities based on CT scans.

133. McCall 1987; Gibson 1987; LaRocca and Macnab 1969. See also Deyo 1988, pp. 19–20; DeLuca and Rhea 1981; and Liang and Komaroff 1982.

134. Sicard and Forestier 1922. The history of myelography is discussed in Brecher and Brecher 1969, pp. 242–243. For more information on the development of modern radiology see Brecher and Brecher 1969 and Dewing 1962.

135. Dandy 1929.

136. Schmorl 1929. Schmorl correctly identified prolapses of intervertebral disc material into the spinal canal in his post mortem studies. However, he believed these "nodules," as he called them, were asymptomatic in life.

137. More extensive information on the history of Mixter and Barr's discovery of the prolapsed intervertebral disc can be found in Allan and Waddell 1989, pp. 6–8, and Robinson 1983, pp. 235–237. Also, Mixter and Barr provided their own descriptions of the events surrounding this discovery in Mixter 1949 and Barr 1977.

138. Mixter and Ayer 1935, p. 387; Allen and Waddell 1989, p. 7.

139. Mixter and Barr 1934. The presentation is described in Barr 1977, p. 6.

140. Mixter and Ayer 1935. Their explanation for preferring this terminology is a bit enigmatic: "Dr. Charles Kubik, neuropathologist at the Massachusetts General Hospital, has reviewed many of these specimens and feels that both nucleus and annulus are represented in most. At operation one is impressed with the fibrous character of the extruded fragment. We believe, therefore, that the term herniation or rupture of the intervertebral disc is more descriptive than 'prolapse of the nucleus pulposus' as coined by Schmorl" (pp. 385–386). Mixter and Ayer apparently wanted to distinguish their terminology from Schmorl's, whose use of the word *prolapse* implies a displacement of the nucleus pulposus rather than its extrusion through a breach in the surrounding annulus fibrosus. In addition, they evidently wanted to emphasize that the fragments ("nodules") contain both annulus and nucleus tissue, rather than just nucleus pulposus, as conjectured by Schmorl. Barr, in his historical recollection (1977), portrays the adoption of this terminology as a deliberate attempt to reflect the supposed traumatic etiology of the extrusion process. It is likely that all three physicians assumed that trauma was the most likely way for the normal disc structure to have been compromised.

141. Dandy 1929, pp. 669, 660, 672.

142. Mixter and Barr 1934, p. 212.

143. Mixter and Ayer 1935, p. 391.

144. Barr 1977, p. 7.

145. The staunch adherence to the view of traumatic etiology, even in the face of contradictory epidemiological evidence, can be seen vividly in the article by Love and Walsh (1938) in which the following seemingly inconsistent thoughts are presented: "It is the opinion of most authors that abnormal protrusion of an intervertebral disk into the spinal canal is in

the majority of cases the result of trauma. . . . It is probable that repeated trauma may be necessary in many cases to produce sufficient protrusion of the nucleus pulposus to cause clinical symptoms. In only thirty-two (32 per cent) of the 100 cases in this series did the patient feel that his pain or other symptoms began immediately after a certain injury. In thirty-nine cases, however, the patient remembered one or more injuries but could not say whether the symptoms had begun immediately afterward or even within the next few months. In twenty-nine cases there was no history of injury the patient could recall. This would lead one to suspect that in many cases, at least, it is difficult to say that a certain injury had caused protrusion of the disk" (p. 397). Nevertheless, they conclude, "Frequently a recurrence of symptoms [in the 100 cases] followed trauma to the back or heavy lifting. . . . We feel that it is probable that the protruded nucleus pulposus in many cases returns into the intervertebral space, only to be extruded again by additional trauma" (p. 397).

146. Mixter and Ayer 1935, p. 391.
147. William J. ("Jason") Mixter was the product of an old New England family. His father was a doctor, as was his grandfather, his uncle, his son, his nephew, and his brother-in-law. In fact, his father, Samuel J. Mixter, was also a renowned neurosurgeon who practiced at Massachusetts General Hospital (MGH) until his death in 1926. Joseph S. Barr came to MGH after receiving his M.D. degree from Harvard in 1926. He served with distinction as chief of orthopedic surgery at Bethesda Naval Hospital during World War II and in 1952 attained the rank of rear admiral in the Naval Reserves. When Barr became chief of orthopedics at Massachusetts General Hospital in 1946, he instituted several interdisciplinary research projects of low back pain and sciatica in collaboration with the American Mutual Insurance Company and the department of structural engineering at MIT. James B. Ayer was the son, grandson, and great-grandson of doctors. His father, also named James Ayer, had made a fortune producing and selling sarsaparilla. At the time of his work at MGH, Ayer was the James Jackson Putnam Professor of Neurology at Harvard University Medical School and president of the American Neurological Association.

The first industrial clinic in any American hospital was the Occupational Medical Clinic at Massachusetts General, begun in 1913 under the direction of Dr. Wade Wright. It functioned from 1913 to 1917 and again from 1917 to 1928. However, the clinic was not in operation at the time of Mixter and Barr's work and was not reopened until 1949, when, under the guidance of Dr. Harriet Hardy, the clinic was re-established in response to the outbreak of beryllium poisoning among workers in the fluorescent lamp manufacturing industry. Hardy continued her work at the Massachusetts General clinic until 1963.

Dandy, of Johns Hopkins University, was born to immigrant parents in a Missouri railroad town. His father, a railway engineer, was an ardent supporter of the Socialist Labor Party and a Christian fundamentalist. Although Dandy became a member of the Democratic party upon his marriage in 1924, his own personal life remained apolitical and privileged. See Faxon 1959; Castleman, Crocett, and Sutton 1981; Hardy 1983; and Fox 1984. I am also indebted to Richard J. Wolfe, historian at the Countway Library of Harvard Medical School, for providing me with additional archival material on Mixter, Barr, and Ayer.

148. Love and Walsh 1940.
149. O'Connell 1943.
150. Love and Walsh 1938, pp. 396, 400.
151. Allan and Waddell 1989, p. 8. Mixter and Ayer (1935) attempted to warn against the diagnosis of ruptured disc in the absence of myelographic evidence: "We believe that this condition is rare as compared with back strain, fracture, sacro-iliac strain and the like, and that the diagnosis should not be made, even provisionally, without the proper evidence. We have stated that the examination of the spinal fluid and X-ray examination with lipiodol are of the greatest importance" (p. 391). However, this warning did not stop some surgeons of the 1940s from rushing headlong into the diagnosis of ruptured disc. Aitken and Bradford (1947) cite one example in which a surgeon stated, "The presence of back-

ache with sciatica, worse on coughing and sneezing, makes the diagnosis of ruptured disc unmistakable" (p. 365).

152. Key 1945.
153. Hadler 1989, p. 824. This same passage appears in its entirety in Hadler 1991b, p. 80. See also Hadler 1993, pp. 172–186; Hadler 1991b, p. 80; Hadler 1984, pp. 56–57; Hadler 1989, p. 824; Hadler 1978, p. 995; Hadler 1986, p. 6; and Hadler 1987b, pp. 9–10.
154. Hadler 1987b, p. 10; Hadler 1986, p. 6; Hadler 1978, pp. 993–995. For a summary of the American legal cases in which the diagnosis of ruptured disc influenced the determination that compensation should be awarded for a back injury see Schneider 1959, pp. 69–75.
155. Hadler 1987b, p. 10.
156. This statement was made by Dandy (1925) in discussing the use of lipiodol myelography for visualizing spinal tumors. His enthusiasm for this technique directly influenced Mixter and Ayer, who had been disappointed in their first use of lipiodol myelography in 1923. See Brecher and Brecher 1969, pp. 243–246.
157. Barth 1980, p. 87.
158. Waddell 1990, p. 38; Frymoyer 1988; and Quinet and Hadler 1979, p. 265. One Finnish study (Heliövaara, Knekt, and Aromaa 1987) of 8,000 adults found that 13.2% of reported low back pain was attributable to herniated discs.
159. Deyo 1987, p. 31; Hadler 1989, p. 824.
160. Deyo 1987, p. 34; Aufrang et al. 1957, p. 12; Aitken and Bradford 1947, p. 374; and Friberg 1954. Several other contemporary authorities agree that the terms *rupture* and *herniation* are not precise or accurate descriptors of the abnormalities occurring in the intervertebral discs. For example, based on MRI studies of asymptomatic individuals, Jensen et al. (1994) conclude that "the term 'herniation' may be too generic for clinical relevance " (p. 72). Instead, they advise physicians to distinguish between bulges, protrusions, and extrusions.
161. Hadler 1989, p. 824.
162. Deyo 1994, p. 115; Deyo 1987, p. 39; DePalma and Rothman 1970; Hadler 1984, pp. 38–42; Quinet and Hadler 1979, p. 231; and Pheasant and Dyck 1982.
163. Haklius (1970) measured the results of treatment at 6 months and at long-term (mean=7 years) for 583 patients with sciatica and indication of L5–S1 disc protrusion, on the basis of a number of criteria, including recurrence of symptoms, residual sciatica, working capacity, and activity restrictions. He found no substantial difference in outcome for those receiving operative and nonoperative therapy. Other studies have found little or no difference in long-term success between surgical and conservative treatment of herniated disc. See Weber 1983; Spangfort 1972; Saal and Saal 1989; and Alaranta et al. 1990. See also the discussion by Quinet and Hadler (1979, p. 283).
164. Bale 1986.
165. Markowitz and Rosner 1989.
166. Cherniak 1986.
167. Hoffman 1922.
168. Rosner and Markowitz 1991, p. 145. A discussion of silicosis reporting during the 1920s is provided on pp. 38–48, 143–145.
169. *New York Times*, March 7, 1929.
170. Rosner and Markowitz 1991, pp. 49–74.
171. Cherniak 1986, pp. 92–105, 52–73; Bale 1986, p. 678.
172. Cherniak 1986, pp. 69–73.
173. Memorandum dated June 12, 1934, archives of the Liberty Mutual Insurance Company.
174. McCann 1934, p. 1. Clay was a celebrated and flamboyant Rochester lawyer and an active member of the Democratic Party. He had worked in a factory for several years prior to attending Georgetown University Law School, where he supported himself by working as a tally clerk in the Pennsylvania Railroad freight yards. Clay's publicity stunts included showing up in court dressed in pajamas and using his fists to fight his way into a locked room in which one of his clients was being questioned by police. Best known for his representation of silicosis plaintiffs in about 160 legal cases, Clay made front-page headlines

after writing the following letter to jury members who had ruled against his client in one of the silicosis suits: "Dear Sir: When I carried the news of your verdict to the bedside of Lawrence Forte [the plaintiff] last evening he said to me, 'I feel I die right away. What shall become of my poor wife and children?' I am conscious that a great wrong has been done to this man, a wrong which you yourself on your death bed may realize./Very truly yours,/William L. Clay" (*Rochester Democrat-Chronicle*, April 25, 1934, p. 1). After complaints from insurance company attorneys, Clay was suspended from legal practice for six months by an Appellate Court for having written the letter. The state Court of Appeals reversed the suspension. See "W. L. Clay, 77, Lawyer Dies." *Rochester Times Union*, July 6, 1970, p. 1B, 4B; and Clune 1947, pp. 234–240.

175. McCann 1934, p. 2.
176. Markowitz and Rosner 1989, pp. 237–245.
177. Markowitz and Rosner 1989, p. 229.
178. Rosner and Markowitz 1991, pp. 91–96.
179. New York State Department of Labor 1941.
180. New York State Department of Labor 1941.
181. Trattner 1984, p. 262.
182. Two of the major architects of Roosevelt's New Deal legislation had their roots in the workers' compensation system. Frances Perkins had previously served as a member of the state Industrial Board and as that state's industrial commissioner. As Secretary of Labor she showed great interest in reviewing workers' compensation laws, and advocating their liberalization. Likewise, Arthur Altmeyer, a Department of Labor official and one of the primary designers of the Social Security Act in 1935, had been the secretary of the Wisconsin Industrial Commission, where he was primarily involved in administration of the state workers' compensation system. In general, New Deal legislation drew heavily on the state workers' compensation model as a precedent for designing the new Federal social legislation programs (see Berkowitz and Berkowitz 1985, pp. 164–165).
183. Burritt 1928, p. 377.
184. Bale 1986, p. 588.
185. Rosner and Markowitz 1991, pp. 90–91.
186. Prince 1937.
187. Markowitz and Rosner 1989, p. 238.
188. Sayer 1934, pp. 5–6.
189. For general information on the history of orthopedics, including the contributions of Nicolas Andry, see LeVay 1990, Vigliani 1978, Howorth 1952, and Aufrang et al. 1957.
190. See Vigliani 1978.
191. Osgood 1919, p. 150.
192. Cited in LeVay, p. 425.
193. Ellis 1935.
194. Cooter 1993, 1987; Jones 1920.
195. Allan and Waddell 1989, p. 4.
196. Platt 1959, p. 313.
197. Aufrang et al. 1957, p. 934.
198. DePalma and Rothman 1970; Semmes 1964.
199. Love and Walsh 1938; Ghormley 1951.
200. Naylor 1990, p. 4; Allan and Waddell 1989, p. 7; Cauthen 1988, p. 1. This phrase was apparently first coined by Ian Macnab. See Macnab 1971.
201. Naylor 1990, p. 3; Allan and Waddell 1989, p. 8.
202. Naylor 1990, p. 21; Waddell 1990, p. 46; Aitken and Bradford 1947; Aitken 1952, 1953; and Rehfeldt 1966. For a summary of this issue see DePalma and Rothman 1970, pp. 324–353. According to DePalma and Rothman, "No operation in any field of surgery leaves in its wake more human wreckage than surgery on the lumbar discs" (p. 347).
203. Frymoyer 1990, p. 34. See also Andersson et al. 1991, p. 97.
204. Frymoyer and Mooney 1986; Frymoyer 1990, p. 35.

205. Brodeur 1974.
206. Slovic 1987; Lowrence 1976. See also Needleman 1987.

Chapter Four *Noise-Induced Hearing Loss*

1. Sataloff and Sataloff 1993, p. 371; 1987, p. 1.
2. Alberti 1980, p. v.
3. Sataloff and Sataloff 1993, p. 5; House cited on p. v.
4. Ratloff 1982, p. 347; Shipley 1985, p. 35.
5. NIOSH 1972, table VI. The decibel (dB) is a dimensionless unit commonly used to measure sound pressure levels. Most noise regulations, including OSHA's, are based on sound levels in decibels measured on the A-scale (dBA), which is weighted to concentrate on noise at higher frequencies, considered to be most injurious to hearing.
6. U.S. Department of Labor (OSHA) 1981. This report found that about a half million workers have hearing impairment that is considered moderate to severe. OSHA defines *hearing impairment* as greater than a 25-dB average threshold hearing level at 1,000, 2,000, and 3,000 Hz, and *moderate to severe* hearing impairment as greater than or equal to a 40-dB average threshold hearing level at 1,000, 2,000, or 3,000 Hz.
7. U.S. Centers for Disease Control 1988, pp. 158–167.
8. Ginnold 1979. It is interesting to note the involvement of the U.S. EPA in matters of occupational health and workers' compensation. Title IV of the Clean Air Act of 1970 (dealing with noise pollution) authorizes the EPA to establish an Office of Noise Abatement and Control. During the Democratic administration of President Jimmy Carter, that office adopted a broad interpretation of their jurisdiction with respect to protecting the public from the detrimental effects of noise. This led to their sponsorship of several studies on occupational noise including the one cited above, as well as Ashford et al. 1976. When the Reagan administration came to power in 1980, matters pertaining to noise were transferred to local jurisdictions, and the EPA's Office of Noise Abatement and Control was disbanded. It was never revived, and currently the U.S. EPA is not active in the area of noise pollution or control. The fact that the EPA should commission a report into workplace noise provides yet another example of how community (and in this case, government) concern about environmental hazards can lead to increased attention being given to the same exposures occurring occupationally.
9. U.S. Centers for Disease Control 1986.
10. Ginnold 1979, p. 1.
11. Unpublished claims data supplied by Liberty Mutual Insurance Company, the largest writer of workers' compensation insurance in the United States.
12. In this study from Alberta, Canada, "costs" were defined as all costs related to medical treatment, compensation for days lost from work, and pensions paid for disability. The pension payments accounted for 95% of the total claims costs. The relatively liberal pension benefits available in Alberta may account for the higher average cost for claim in this Canadian study compared to that indicated by the Liberty Mutual data.
13. Sataloff 1984, p. 35.
14. Among the best historical studies of noise and industrial deafness are Bunch 1937 (contains extensive literature review) and Atherley and Noble 1985.
15. Macauley 1838, p. 182.
16. Ward 1973, p. 377.
17. House 1957, p. 445.
18. Cox 1958, p. 621; Chadwick 1971, p. 476.
19. Bruusgaard 1962.
20. McKensie 1916.
21. Ward 1973, p. 377.
22. Chadwick 1971, p. 476.
23. Cited in Ward 1969, p. 89; and Chadwick 1971, p. 476.
24. Ramazzini 1713, p. 437.

25. Kylin 1960, p. 8.
26. Fosbroke 1831, p. 648.
27. Layet 1875. See also Glibert 1921, p. 264.
28. Gottstein and Kayser 1881. The relevance of this study for modern epidemiology is explored in the article by Atherley and Noble (1985).
29. Politzer 1883, pp. 190–191. When driving a belly-shaped container shut, wooden truss hoops must be forced down around the open end. Usually this required the efforts of at least two coopers who used heavy short-handled hammers in the process. To accomplish this task, the coopers needed to walk, run, and sometimes jump around the end of the container. The term "hohow stroke" referred to this jumping, frenetic activity, which has been alikened to a wild dance (called by coopers the "hohow dance"). I am grateful to George Monte, the interpreter in the cooperage of the Old Sturbridge Village Museum in Sturbridge, Massachusetts, for supplying this historical information.
30. Cited in Chadwick 1971, p. 476.
31. Fosbroke 1831, p. 648, citing Parry 1825.
32. Glibert 1921, p. 265.
33. Dalby 1875. Cited in Gould and Pyle 1897, p. 537.
34. For a review of these studies see Bunch 1930, pp. 633–635. Further investigations on the effects of gunfire on the development of NIHL in World War I can be found in the work of Colledge and Faulder 1921.
35. Ridout 1930.
36. Ingersoll 1919; Yearsley 1917; and Wilson 1917.
37. Mitchie 1924, p. 61.
38. Grimwade 1925, p. 890.
39. Glibert 1921, p. 264.
40. Westmacott 1925, p. 889.
41. Hunter 1962, p. 872.
42. Glibert 1921, p. 265.
43. Roosa 1874, p 380.
44. Holt 1882. The phrase "hearing in a noise" in the title of Holt's article refers to *paracusis Willisii,* the supposed ability of those with defective hearing to hear better in noisy surroundings. The name of this condition derives from the English physician Thomas Willis, who in 1672 first described a case in which a husband could be heard by his wife only while their servant was beating a drum.
45. Holt 1882, pp. 34–35; Roosa 1874, p. 383.
46. The National Boiler Makers and Helpers Protective and Benevolent Union was organized in October 1880 with eleven branches, including Branch No. 6 in New York. Branch No. 12 was established in August 1881 in Portland, Maine, site of Holt's study. In 1884, the name of the union was changed; see "A Brief History of the International Brotherhood of Boiler Makers and Iron Ship Builders" in that union's *Thirteenth Annual Report,* June 1893, pp. 39–72; and International Brotherhood 1991.

   The period 1878–1884 was an era of labor strength, the growth of unions, and increasing interest in socialist thought and politics. The economic recovery of 1878–1880 (following the Great Depression of 1873–1877) blossomed into a full boom between 1880 and 1884. Major strikes during these years included the great strike of 35,000 iron and steel workers in 1882 and the strike of 4,000 telegraphers in 1883. Numerous smaller-scale walkouts by boilermaker locals, including those in Detroit (1881), St. Paul (1881), and New York (1882), were successful in achieving higher wages.
47. Barr 1886. For a summary of Barr's findings see also Barr 1896, p. 359; and Ballantyne and Martin 1984, p. 210.
48. Shambaugh 1953, p. 118.
49. Duchesne 1857. (Not to be confused with the French neurologist B. A. Duchenne, for whom Duchenne's disease is named.)
50. Weber 1862.
51. Cited in Moos 1880a, p. 321.

52. Barr 1890, p. 675.
53. Atherley and Noble 1985. With respect to the relationship of the early investigations of occupational deafness to rail safety, Atherley and Noble comment, "Rail travel in the late nineteenth century paralleled the place held by air transport now. Spectacular accidents, then as now, heightened the traveling public's concern over safety. Whereas twentieth-century accident analysis seeks equipment deficiencies and systems failures, nineteenth-century analysis sought human errors and worker frailties as chief causes" (p. 103).
54. Lancet Commission 1862, p. 52.
55. Moos 1880a, pp. 326–328.
56. Moos 1880a, p. 329.
57. Schwabach and Pollnow (1881) found that the average distance at which engineers and firemen could hear a ticking watch declined steadily from 56 cm for the youngest workers (under thirty years old) to 2 cm for those over fifty years of age (pp. 213–217). See also Atherley and Noble 1985, p. 105.
58. Schwabach and Pollnow 1881, p. 221. Translated from the German by Brigitt Inderfurth.
59. Pollnow 1882, p. 52. Translated from the German by Brigitt Inderfurth.
60. One could speculate that Pollnow, although professing to have the rail company's economic interests at heart, is acting here on behalf of the welfare of the rail workers. The labor situation in Germany during 1881–1882 was precarious, due to Bismarck's enactment of antisocialist laws banning unionization. Though some labor organizing continued on a clandestine basis, a physician such as Pollnow might have perceived it as dangerous to openly advocate positions that could be construed as protective of the workers. Thus, while it seems in this discussion that Moos is the protector of public health and Pollnow the defender of corporate interests, Pollnow's ardent support of the engineers' rights to retain their positions irrespective of Moos' proposed hearing tests suggests that Pollnow may actually have been representing the more politically liberal position. For additional background on German labor history during this period see Moses 1982.
61. Hedinger (1882) found that at 1–5 years of service, 25% of workers could not hear a whisper a meter away, increasing to 35% at 5–10 years, 50% at 10–15 years, 60% at 15–20 years, and 90% at 20–25 years (pp. 64–65).
62. Lichtenberg 1892, p. 122.
63. Zwaardemaker 1896, p. 392.
64. See Seely 1910; and Swann 1933.
65. For information on the history of the development of telephone communications see Tucker 1978; and Archer 1938.
66. Pierce 1879, p. 162.
67. Blake 1888, pp. 240–241.
68. Gellé 1889, p. 60.
69. Attali and Stourdze 1977; Holcombe 1911; Perry 1977; and Tucker 1978.
70. See Tucker 1978; and Holcombe 1911.
71. In Great Britain, this attention took the form of Parliamentary debates, government inquiries, editorials in the *Spectator* (1884), *Manchester Guardian* (1884), *Times* (1884), *Electrician* (1883), and *Economist* (1888), and petitions by various governmental and business groups, such as the Convention of Royal and Parliamentary Burghs of Scotland (1886, 1887) and the Associated Chambers of Commerce. A similar media barrage occurred during the same years in France and Germany. See Perry 1977 and Holcombe 1911.
72. Braustein 1904, p. 531.
73. Blegvad 1909.
74. *Report of the Committee of Medical Officers* 1911.
75. Koetter 1910, p. 101.
76. Westmacott 1925, pp. 889–890.
77. *Brown vs. North Dakota Workmen's Compensation Bureau*, 214 N.W. 622 (N. Dak. 1927). Cited in Keck 1955, p. 35.
78. White 1928, p. 178. At the time of the writing of this article Dr. Joseph Augustus White (1848–1941) was emeritus professor of laryngology, rhinology, and otology at the Medical

College of Virginia and a distinguished member of Richmond society. White had received medical training in both the U.S. and Germany, and served as an auxiliary surgeon in the Franco-Prussian War of 1870–1871.

79. White 1928, p. 178.
80. Maddox 1977, pp. 262–279; Dempsey 1933, p. 66.
81. See Norwood 1990; Barbash 1952; Foner 1979; and Wertheimer 1977.
82. Cooseman 1899. Beetlers were so called because the textile machine at which they worked resembled a beetle. It was composed of twenty metal hammers, each weighing 100 kilograms and delivering 400 strokes per minute. Cooseman reported that the noise produced by these machines "resembles the continuous rolling of thunder, which shakes the workshop and everything in it." Nevertheless, in his examination of 17 beetle machine operators (ranging from 2 to 39 years of experience working with these machines), Cooseman found that none of the workers was "absolutely deaf," and that those who complained of hearing difficulties at the end of the day reported that most of their hearing returned after two to three hours. This is one of the earliest occupational studies of temporary hearing loss, a phenomenon that was to become prominent in debates about NIHL during the twentieth century.
83. Röpke 1902.
84. Pedley 1930, p. 238; McKelvie 1933.
85. Evans 1947, p. 147.
86. Scott 1923.
87. Bauer 1926, p. 157. Another form of occupational deafness that received a considerable amount of medical attention in the early twentieth century is caisson deafness, caused by rapid changes in air pressure of the type experienced by flyers, professional divers, and caisson workers. A review of this literature can be found in Bunch 1930. However, because this exposure is not related to industrial noise, it will not be considered further in this chapter.
88. Readers interested in a more comprehensive treatment of the history of audiometry should refer to Feldmann 1970, Bunch 1941, Glorig and Downs 1965, Tremble 1930, MacFarlan 1929, and Mester and Stephens 1984. I am indebted to these authors for much of the background material and references presented in this and the next sections. See Feldmann 1970, p. 9, for a discussion of "classical" vs. electronic hearing testing.
89. Barr 1886, p. 228.
90. Barr 1886, pp. 228–229.
91. Atherley and Noble 1985, p. 111.
92. See Feldmann 1970, pp. 19–25; and Bordley and Brookhouser 1979, p. 5.
93. These instruments are discussed in Feldmann 1970, p. 41; Bunch 1940, p. 1101; Mester and Stephens 1984, pp. 209–212.
94. Richardson 1879, p. 66.
95. Feldmann 1970, p. 42; Bunch 1941, p. 1100. According to Bunch, "the word audiometer today among otologists and acoustic engineers is quite generally restricted to instruments in which the stimulus tones are generated electrically."
96. For a discussion of this issue see Mester and Stephens 1984.
97. Bunch 1941, p. 1107; Feldmann 1970, p. 48.
98. Bryant 1893, p. 98.
99. One exception was the audiometric testing of 5,706 Chicago schoolchildren in 1899 using an early audiometer developed by Carl E. Seashore. See Seashore 1899.
100. Schaefer and Gruschke 1921; Griessmann 1921.
101. For additional background on this subject see Feldmann 1970, pp. 48–49; and Bunch 1941, pp. 1111–1112.
102. Fowler and Wegel 1922.
103. For more information on the cost of early audiometers see Mitchie 1924, p. 61; and Glorig and Downs 1965, p. 10.
104. Beasley 1940, pp. 888–889. The concept of "impairment" implies a comparison to a population that is considered to be unimpaired or "normal." The determination of the hearing

ability of a "normal" population continues to perplex audiologists. One of the chief problems is how to find an "unexposed" group of subjects, since virtually everybody is exposed to various loud noises from birth. Another question is how to select the statistical distribution that constitutes the normal or abnormal variation within a study population. In the Public Health Service study, the "normal" sample was selected from those who had been judged as "unimpaired," based on independent self-reporting questionnaires and clinical examinations using classic non-audiometric otological tests. In other mass screening tests, the normal population was selected from younger age groups (e.g., those 20–29 years of age for the 1950 San Diego County Fair; those 18–24 years old for the 1954 and 1955 Wisconsin State Fairs), who were also determined to have no detectable hearing difficulties based on questionnaires and a brief non-audiometric clinical examination. In each of these screening studies, the mean of the sample group's audiometric measurements at each frequency was regarded as the baseline for the group as a whole.

105. The Public Health Survey audiometric screening program was an outgrowth of the National Health Survey of 1935–1936, which was conducted by the U.S. Public Health Service, in cooperation with the Bureau of the Census. In the National Health Survey, health-related information was collected on 2,502,391 persons, or 3.7% of the urban population of the United States. Of those, a representative sample of 9,324 city dwellers was selected for clinical hearing examinations using a Western Electric 2A audiometer. Based on the results of the audiometric tests, the investigators found that the prevalence of hearing loss was correlated with poor socioeconomic conditions, and with unemployment. Beasley (1940) explains these findings in the following way: "The most conspicuous and probably the most significant trend . . . is the excess prevalence of impaired hearing among the unemployed in each occupation class. . . . The significantly higher prevalence of impaired hearing among the unemployed reflects selection by employers in favor of employees who were not hard-of-hearing at the time when large-scale layoffs occurred. Since large numbers of persons were being released from their regular employment due to the industrial and business failures during the period from 1930 to 1935, it is common sense expectation that the less capable (mentally) and the physically handicapped would be discharged before others. The growing unemployed population during this period would naturally accumulate a disproportionately large composition of so-called less fit, incompetent and physically handicapped persons, at least as so viewed by some and possibly most employers" (pp. 881–882). Based on these findings, the Public Health Service concluded: "a. impaired hearing constitutes an unemployment risk, b. the degree of risk increases with stage of deafness; and c. the same stage of deafness varies in risk value for different occupations" (p. 886).

106. Steinberg, Montgomery, and Gardner 1940; Watson and Toland 1949, p. 191.

107. Lichtenstein 1950; Webster, Himes, and Lichtenstein 1950; Glorig 1958.

108. Described in Watson and Toland 1949, pp. 185–200.

109. Bunch 1941, p. 1112.

110. By World War II, the U.S. military alone had acquired over 2,000 audiometers at a cost of about $1.7 million. See Watson and Toland 1949, p. 228. According to Feldmann 1970 (p. 43), another 1,500 audiometers were used in civilian applications as of 1945. The projected market for electronic audiometers in the 1950s was at least 1,000 per year.

111. J. C. Steinberg 1939. Technical memorandum MM–39–328–62, File 53400 (November 2, 1939). Courtesy of the American Telephone & Telegraph Company Archives.

112. Kennedy 1936, p. 1932.

113. For information on the history of non-electric hearing aids see Stephens and Goodwin 1984. Additional information on the history of electric and non-electric aids to hearing can be found in Miller 1972; Berger 1975; and Watson and Toland 1949.

114. Miller 1972, pp. 4–5.

115. Watson and Toland 1949, pp. 424–425; 303–305.

116. The Veterans Administration reported that 42,191 veterans were drawing compensation for hearing disabilities on October 7, 1947, resulting from active service in World War II. The VA also reported an additional total of 16,594 cases drawing compensation for hearing

disabilities connected with World War I. In England, there were 34,000 deafened ex-servicemen on pensions as of 1940. These statistics are reported in Watson and Toland 1949, pp. 224–225, citing Ansberry 1948 and Doctor 1945.

117. Berger 1970, pp. 55, 59. See also Watson and Toland 1949, p. 199.

118. Watson and Toland 1949, p. 421. British audiologists S. D. G. Stephens and J. C. Goodwin (1984) allude to the "expectations of unrealistic effectiveness" that have characterized the selling of modern hearing aids. Many sales approaches, they assert, have catered solely to the vanity of the user with a "concentration on inconspicuous devices which in practice were of little benefit except to a very small minority of individuals. . . . Such approaches are not unknown today" (p. 237).

119. Day 1943, p. 2.

120. For a summary of proposed state legislation and warnings by the National Better Business Bureau see Berger 1970, pp. 130–136.

121. Sabine 1944, pp. 266–267.

122. For examples see Watson and Toland 1949, pp. 183–184.

123. Watson and Toland 1949, pp. 184–185.

124. Tremble 1929, p. 71.

125. Tremble 1929, p. 73.

126. Lyle 1924, pp. 33, 35.

127. The first portable sound level meters for field measurement of sound intensity were introduced by the General Radio Company just prior to World War II. See Hawkins 1976, p. 76. In addition, audiometers themselves could be converted into a sound-level measuring device by the installation of a special microphone (New York State Department of Labor 1930, p. 7, contains a discussion of how the Western Electric 3A audiometer was adapted for this purpose).

128. U.S. Department of Labor 1953, p. 14.

129. Bordley and Brookhouser 1979.

130. Burnett 1877, pp. 594–595.

131. McBride 1881, p. 172.

132. Dalby 1873, p. 176. Dalby used the term *catamenial period* to refer to a woman's menstrual period.

133. Dalby 1893, p. 252.

134. Roosa 1885, p. 58.

135. Shambaugh's comments at the annual meeting of the Section on Laryngology, Otology and Rhinology at the 1922 convention of the American Medical Association, reported in Fletcher 1922, p. 531. Shambaugh said that he had been "stationed at Camp Grant during the most active demobilization period, and I was called to pass on a great many cases in which there was some apparent defect in the hearing, and to determine whether this defect could be the result of war injuries."

136. Mawson 1962, p. 152.

137. Coggin 1879; Politzer 1883, pp. 749–752; Collie 1913, pp. 118–125; Russell 1934.

138. Watson and Toland 1949, pp. 172–182. A good history of malingering tests for defective hearing is contained in Feldmann 1970, pp. 70–73.

139. Tremble 1929, p. 73.

140. Watson and Toland 1949, p. 172.

141. See, for example, the publications of the International Brotherhood of Boilermakers, Iron Ship Builders, Blacksmiths, Drop Forgers, and Helpers, which petitioned management to institute periodic audiometric examinations at intervals of every six months. The union's 1954 brochure entitled *Deafness: The Hazard of Occupational Noise* suggests: "At a very nominal cost, employers can purchase a pure tone audiometer with which the degree of hearing deficiency, if any, of the applicant for employment can be determined prior to his employment, so that the employer would be liable only for the actual amount of additional loss from the date of hiring. Some employers have already adopted this program. By making periodic tests, the employer can also determine the rate of loss and if, because of greater susceptibility, the worker is unduly affected by his noise environment, he can be

moved in the interest of preserving his hearing." See International Brotherhood 1954, p. 12. In a 1969 pamphlet, this union developed a model hearing conservation program that includes a requirement that "audiograms shall be taken at least once every six months for all workers subject to high noise levels." See International Brotherhood 1969, p. 14.

142. This view was advocated repeatedly in the writings of Noel Symons, an attorney representing industry and insurers. In 1951 he wrote: "I hope that those entrusted with the responsibility of enacting and interpreting laws dealing with occupational deafness will not overlook the complication of 'previous employment.' In many cases a man may work in a high noise level for many different companies over a period of years before he files a claim for compensation, and it would seem unfair to place the entire financial burden on the last employer. The difficulty can be eliminated by the adoption of pre-employment audiometric examinations of all new employees" (Symons 1951, p. 50).

143. Glibert 1921, p. 265.

144. Turner 1939, p. 578; McCord 1931.

145. Berrien 1946, p. 149.

146. Knudsen 1939; Turner 1939, p. 578.

147. Glibert 1921, pp. 272–273.

148. Mawson 1967, p. 152.

149. Cited in Glorig 1961, p. 1338.

150. Roosa 1874, p. 381.

151. Holt 1882, p. 41.

152. Barr 1890, p. 675.

153. See especially Guild 1918.

154. Trible and Watkins 1919, p. 53. Information on the development of the Mallock-Armstrong Ear Defender is contained in British patent G.B. 4821 (Feb. 24, 1914).

155. Richardson 1918; Trible and Watkins 1919.

156. Trible and Watkins 1919, p. 51.

157. Richardson 1918, pp. 536–537.

158. Personal communication with Stuart Low, Jr., president of Flents Products.

159. Stevens and Beranek 1943, pp. 2–14.

160. Knudsen 1939, p. 66.

161. Kryter 1946.

162. Coles 1969, Casali 1987, Padilla 1981, Wheeler 1953. See Royster and Holder 1981; Coles 1969; Helmkamp et al. 1984.

163. See, for example, the articles appearing in *National Safety News* in March 1948 (p. 70) and March 1949 (p. 14). Discussion of the marketing to industry of the Lee Sonic Ear Valve is contained in a bulletin (no. 17) issued by Floyd Frazier, director of the industrial division of the National Association of Mutual Casualty Companies, to the Industrial Hygiene Subcommittee of that organization on November 20, 1952. See also the citation on the activities of the J. B. Nelson Company below.

164. Letter written by Dr. J. B. Nelson to Dr. Charles Williams of the Liberty Mutual Insurance Company on May 23, 1952, concerning the acceptance of the Nelson Ear Stopples in several industrial plants.

165. See advertisement of MSA ear protection in *Noise Control*, January 1955, p. 2.

166. "London Noise" 1876, p. 277.

167. Holt 1882, p. 41.

168. McCord 1931.

169. Goldmark 1912, p. 71.

170. Berrien 1946, p. 149. This article contains a good literature review of the studies on noise and fatigue conducted between 1920 and 1940.

171. These are discussed in Kaye 1932, p. 161.

172. New York City Department of Health 1930, pp. 24, 109–110, 214–215. See also Kaye 1932, p. 159.

173. New York City Department of Health 1930, pp. 25–27, 52–53, 77–103, 211–273.

174. *Garber vs. Rubel*, 290 N.Y.S. 633 (N.Y. 1936). See Keck 1955, p. 37.

175. *Friedman vs. Keil*, 166 A. 194 (N.J. 1933); *Abend vs. Royal Laundry Service*, 192 A. 239 (N.J. 1939). See Keck 1955, pp. 36–37.

176. *Miranda vs. Buffalo General Electric Co.*, 251 N.Y.S. 510 (N.Y. 1931). See Keck 1955, p. 37.

177. Cited in Keck 1955, p. 37.

178. New York State Department of Labor 1930, p. 2. In this audiometric study, 23.7% of 1,040 workers tested had sustained some level of permanent hearing impairment. However, a substantial proportion were discovered to have a history of injury or disease unrelated to noise that could have accounted for the hearing loss. Discounting those individuals, 14.9% of the sample had probably been deafened due to noise at work. Among 367 workers considered to have been exposed to the greatest levels of workplace noise, 96 (26.1%) were found to have suffered permanent hearing damage.

179. Kennedy 1936, p. 30.

180. Berrien 1946, p. 141.

181. U.S. Department of Labor 1953, p. 10. A similar view was expressed in 1969 by W. Dixon Ward, who, in his analysis of the rise of hearing loss claims after World War II, wrote: "The trickle of experiments, surveys, and summaries dealing with industrial hearing loss became a flood only a few years ago. Until after World War II, compensation was granted for noise-induced hearing loss only when a Workman's Compensation Board or a civil jury could be convinced that the loss was attributable to a single, specifiable incident—i.e., to 'acoustic trauma.' The gradual loss of hearing that came on insidiously with years of exposure to noises that were loud but not painfully so was either regarded as a necessary evil or indeed displayed proudly as a badge of office, for example signifying long membership in the Ancient Order of He-man Casting Chippers" (Ward 1969, p. 90).

182. Pedley 1930, p. 241; Chadwick 1971, p. 532.

183. Chadwick 1971, p. 531. Coverage under the National Insurance Act for NIHL developing gradually was extended to all workers in 1975, subject to rigorous eligibility criteria. See Action and Grime 1980.

184. Alliance 1981, p. 63; Watson and Toland 1949, p. 208.

185. U.S. Department of Labor 1953, pp. 2–3, 5.

186. Watson and Toland 1949, p. 209.

187. Nash 1952, p. 167; also unpublished records of the Liberty Mutual Insurance Company.

188. Fox 1953, p. 2.

189. Nash 1952, pp. 167–168; also unpublished records of the Liberty Mutual Insurance Company.

190. Symons 1952, pp. 170–175.

191. Frazier 1955, p. 4.

192. Frederickson 1970, p. 1275.

193. Nash 1952, p. 169.

194. "Bethlehem Sued for 5 Million," *New York Journal-American*, December 5, 1951. Employees brought very few other cases of common-law actions for NIHL against their employers. In 1949, a Pennsylvania worker at a factory manufacturing airplane propellers charged that his employer was negligent in creating occupational noise that led to his partial loss of hearing after five years' exposure [*Cool vs. Curtis-Wright*, 66 A.2d 287 (Pa. 1949)]. The worker was forced to sue at tort because his hearing loss did not come under the statutory definition of occupational disease nor result from an "accident" according to Pennsylvania's prevailing workers' compensation act. However, the Pennsylvania Supreme Court ruled that the plaintiff had no cause for action under common law because the employer had no duty to operate other than according to the ordinary practices of the particular industry. (See Stander 1979, p. 2; Keck 1955, p. 36). Pennsylvania law did not change until a state Supreme Court ruling in 1975 [*Hinkle vs. Heinz*, 337 A.2d 907 (Pa. 1975)] that held NIHL to be an "injury by accident," with the accident construed to be repetitive acoustic trauma caused by noise. See Fodor and Oleinick 1986, p. 773.

195. U.S. Department of Labor 1953, p. 5; Sataloff and Michael 1973, p. 163.

196. International Brotherhood 1954, p. 4; Ginnold 1974, p. 683.

197. Ginnold 1974, pp. 683–685; Ginnold 1979, p. 6.
198. Frazier 1955, p. 4.
199. Alliance 1981, p. 65; International Brotherhood 1954, p. 9.
200. Ginnold 1974, pp. 687–690.
201. Beginning in 1963 the International Brotherhood and government officials drafted guidelines for industrial hearing conservation programs. These guidelines eventually were adopted by OSHA into the federal noise control standard. See International Brotherhood 1969, pp. 6–8.
202. Wood 1953, p. 3.
203. Wood 1953, pp. 19–20.
204. International Brotherhood 1954, p. 4.
205. See Watson and Toland, pp. 228–229, 415; also W. T. Donahue and C. Tibbitts, "The Task before the Veteran and Society," *Annals of the American Academy of Political and Social Science* 239 (1945), 1–9. Some major workers' compensation insurance carriers believed that the award of these pensions by the VA exerted a considerable influence on the submission of workers' compensation claims for NIHL by civilians during the late 1940s and early 1950s. A memorandum distributed to field claims representatives of the Liberty Mutual Insurance Company read as follows: "At the end of World War II, the VA handed out disability awards to several hundred thousand returning service personnel for partial hearing impairment caused by service-related noise. It wasn't long before the industrial workers who had manned the forge hammers and refitted the Liberty ships during the war were looking for similar partial impairment awards for hearing loss under the workers' compensation system" (R. W. Hartley, Memorandum on "Special Hearing Loss Provisions," Liberty Mutual Insurance Company, May 22, 1981).
206. Glorig 1961, p. 1342.
207. Kennedy 1936, p. 193. Kennedy wrote: "Undoubtedly, progressive deafness in workers in noisy trades, such as boilermakers, should be included among work hazards to be compensated by insurance, and may come to be recognized as compensable affections."
208. Sabine 1944, p. 267.
209. The International Brotherhood of Blacksmiths, Drop Forgers and Helpers ("the blacksmiths") first decided to seek a merger with the International Brotherhood of Boilermakers, Iron Ship Builders and Helpers of America ("the boilermakers") in April 1950. Negotiations concerning the terms of the merger took place over the succeeding three years, and merger plans were ratified at a consolidated convention of the two groups held in Minneapolis on June 29, 1953. The actual effective date for the merger was June 1, 1954. According to the report of the Blacksmiths' executive board, the reasons for seeking the merger were: "the increasingly complex problems of law, organization, representation and prestige"; "financial considerations," related to "increasing complexities and increasing cost of services and materials"; "the rough-shod actions of other organizations in usurping jurisdiction and the raiding by them of representation units"; the impending merger between the AFL and the CIO "which would undoubtedly affect the jurisdictional position of many of the smaller craft unions"; and "the dire need of insurance to the thousands of members who do not have adequate coverage" (see *Report of the Joint International Executive Council* 1954, p. 7). Underlying this decision was the reality of defense industry cutbacks following World War II: employment in the nation's shipyards plummeted from 213,900 in 1948 to 171,800 in 1949 to 145,200 in 1950, a decrease of 32% in three years (*Report*, p. 47). In 1951 and 1952 there was a temporary resurgence in shipyard employment related to the outbreak of hostilities in Korea, with 266,500 workers in the shipyards by September 1952. However, by 1953–1954, with the end of the Korean War, shipyard employment again dropped precipitously, paving the way both for the final amalgamation of the unions in 1954, and the increased drive for workers' compensation benefits by disabled retirees and unemployed workers in the forging, steelmaking, and shipbuilding industries in 1953–1954.
210. United Steelworkers of America 1961, pp. 12–15.

211. Murray 1949, pp. 19–21.
212. "Bethlehem Signs With Union for Pensions, Welfare Plan; U.S. Steel Seeks New Talks," *New York Times*, Nov. 1, 1949, p. 1.
213. Frazier 1955, p. 12.
214. Nelson 1954, p. 571.
215. Symons 1953, p. 114.
216. "Noise Is News" 1953, p. 48; Symons 1953, p. 114.
217. Frazier 1955, p. 12.
218. Ginnold 1974, p. 685.
219. Ewens is quoted in "Noise Is News" 1953, p. 50.
220. "Noise Is News" 1953, p. 48.
221. Symons 1953, pp. 115, 116.
222. Alliance 1981, p. 77; Ginnold 1979, p. 7.
223. Shipley 1985, p. 37.
224. Ginnold 1979, p. 7, Ginnold 1974, pp. 684–692.
225. American Academy of Ophthalmology and Otolaryngology Committee on Conservation of Hearing 1955.
226. NIOSH 1972, section VI, p. 11.
227. Fodor and Oleinick 1986, pp. 763–777.
228. Frazier 1955, p. 16.
229. Frazier 1955, p. 16.
230. U.S. Department of Labor 1953, p. 19.
231. Ward 1969, p. 95.
232. Zapp 1960, p. 199.
233. International Brotherhood 1954, p. 8.
234. Nash 1952, p. 169. For three years (1947–1950), Nash served simultaneously as medical consultant for the union and the employer's insurance carrier. However, according to Nash, "In litigation proceedings the union representative and I sat beside each other, with a battery of lawyers on the opposite side of the table" (Nash 1952, p. 167). Nash was also a member of the Subcommittee on Noise in Industry of the Committee on Conservation of Hearing of the American Academy of Ophthalmology and Otolaryngology, and the Committee of Consultants on Occupational Loss of Hearing—the special medical advisory panel convened by New York Compensation Board.
235. Ginnold 1974, p. 692.
236. Associated Industries of New York, Inc., Statement of Joseph R. Shaw, President, before the Joint Legislative Committee on Industrial and Labor Conditions in support of the Morgan-Milmoe Bill, Assembly, Int. 754 Print 757, Senate Int. 928, Print 958. Cited by Frazier 1955, p. 12.
237. Frazier 1955, p. 12.
238. Alliance 1981, p. 5. Wisconsin's law by that time required only a two-month absence from noise exposure.
239. Barry 1985, pp. 3–9.
240. Ginnold 1979, p. viii.
241. Ginnold 1974, p. 690. At Ladish Forge Company, about 300 of the original 500 claims were eventually paid, at a cost of about $500,000—an average of approximately $1,000 per case.
242. Unpublished claims data from the Liberty Mutual Insurance Company.
243. Ginnold 1979, pp. 36–37.

Chapter Five *Conclusion*

1. Smith 1981; Smith 1987.
2. Rosner and Markowitz 1991.
3. Graebner 1987; Hardy 1965; Nugent 1987.
4. Slovic 1987; Lowrence 1976; Needleman 1987.
5. Arndt 1990.
6. Since large-scale use of typewriters in business began during the mid-1880s, most typists

in the United States have been women. A historical analysis of the feminization of this occupation is presented in Davies 1982. Kocka 1981 (p. 100) provides employment data showing that the percentage of female typists increased steadily from 63.3% in 1890 to 95.6% in 1930.

7. For a discussion of this topic see the articles in Worrall 1983. See also Walsh and Dumitru 1988; Mendelson 1984; Robertson and Keeve 1983; Leigh 1985; and Hadler 1984.

8. Mockapetris and Craigie 1986.

9. Bale 1986. See also Rosner and Markowitz 1991.

10. Brodeur 1974; Brodeur 1985.

11. Departmental Committee on Compensation for Industrial Diseases 1908, p. 34 §11985–11986.

12. Haller 1988. See also Nehrend 1923; National Industrial Conference Board 1923; Burnham 1915; Crowhart 1915; Rogers 1915; Joughran 1915; Stark 1915; and Codman 1916.

13. Haller 1988, p. 347.

14. Adams 1976.

15. Pauley, Hillman, and Kerstein 1990; Woodward and Warren-Boulten 1984; Hickson, Altemeier, and Perrin 1987; Hillman, Pauly, and Kerstein 1989; Epstein, Begg, and McNeil 1986; Hemenway et al. 1990. Murray et al. 1992; Hillman et al. 1990; and Inglehart 1989, 1990. For a review of this research see Ohsfeldt 1993; and Mitchell and Scott 1992.

16. Smith 1981.

17. Bale 1986; Rosner and Markowitz 1991.

18. Beasley 1940. See chapter 4, note 105.

19. Brodeur 1974; Brodeur 1985.

20. Rosner and Markowitz 1987a.

21. Koos 1954, pp. 30–39. In this examination of illness behavior in a small town in upstate New York, Koos noted that persistent backache is perceived as an expected state of affairs among the majority of lower-class women and thus is not generally considered symptomatic of a disease or pathological state. He found that among women in the lowest socioeconomic class, only 19% recognized persistent backache as needing medical attention.

22. Smith-Rosenberg and Rosenberg 1981, pp. 283, 293–297.

23. Zola 1966.

24. Derickson 1987.

25. U.S. Department of Labor 1993a. Felsenthal derived the data presented in figure 20 using the Mead Data Central Nexis Database. Statistics presented by the BLS and Felsenthal relate to hand/wrist "repetitive stress injuries," which, as used in those reports, are essentially synonymous with cumulative trauma disorders.

26. Smith 1981; Derickson 1991; Kerr 1990; Barth 1987.

27. See Smith 1981.

28. Stone 1979. Stone has observed that the diagnosis of illness by physicians is becoming an increasingly widespread means for certifying eligibility under many government distributive welfare programs, a trend that Stone believes is a political strategy for legitimizing the objectivity of the program, stifling opposition, and restricting the distribution of benefits. See also Stone 1984.

29. See Beckwith 1992; Spieler 1994; Boden 1995; and Dembe 1995.

References

Acton, W. I., and R. P. Grime. 1980. "Noise and Hearing Loss Compensation." *Annals of Occupational Hygiene* 23:205–215.

Acutt, B. 1990. "Repetition Strain Injury (RSI): Legacy of Technology in Changing Times or Human Management Found Wanting?" *Asia Pacific Resources Management* 28:6–13.

Adams, R. M. 1976. "Attitudes of California Dermatologists Toward Worker's Compensation." *Western Journal of Medicine* 125:169–175.

Agate, J. N. 1949. "An Outbreak of Cases of Raynaud's Phenomenon of Occupational Origin." *British Journal of Industrial Medicine* 6:144–163.

Agate, J. N., H. Druett, and J. Tombleson. 1946. "Raynaud's Phenomenon in Grinders of Small Metal Castings." *British Journal of Industrial Medicine* 3:167.

Aitken, A. P. 1952. "Rupture of the Intervertebral Disc in Industry—Further Observations on the End Results." *American Journal of Surgery* 84 (3): 261–267.

———. 1953. "The Industrial Back." In *Proceedings of the Symposium on Industrial Medicine at the Harvard School of Public Health*. April 3–4, 1953, Boston.

Aitken, A. P., and C. H. Bradford. 1947. "End Results of Ruptured Intervertebral Discs in Industry." *American Journal of Surgery* 73:365–380.

Alaranta, H. et al. 1990. "A Prospective Study of Patients with Sciatica: A Comparison

Between Conservatively Treated Patients and Patients Who Have Undergone Operation." *Spine* 15:1345–1349.

Albers, J. F. H. 1835. "Ueber einen eigenthümlichen Krampf der Finger beim Schreiben." *Med. Ztg., Berl.* iv:37.

Alberti, P. W. 1991. "Occupational Hearing Loss." In J. J. Ballenger (ed.), *Diseases of the Nose, Throat, Ear, Head, and Neck.* Philadelphia: Lea & Febiger, pp. 1053–1068.

—— (ed.). 1980. *Personal Hearing Protection in Industry.* New York: Raven Press.

Alexander, H. 1892. "Railway-spine oder Simulation?" *Vrtljschr. f. gerichtl. Med.* (Berlin) 3:109–129.

Allan, D. B., and G. Waddell. 1989. "An Historical Perspective on Low Back Pain and Disability." *Acta Orthopaedica Scandinavica Supplementum* 60 (234): 1–23.

Allen, H. G. 1900. "Simulation After Railway Injuries." *Massachusetts Medical Journal* 20:49–55.

Alleyne, B. C., R. M. Dufresne, N. Kanji, and M. R. Reesal. 1989. "Costs of Workers' Compensation Claims for Hearing Loss." *Journal of Occupational Medicine* 31 (2): 134–138.

Alliance of American Insurers. 1981. *Background for Loss of Hearing Claims.* 2nd ed. Chicago: Alliance of American Insurers.

American Academy of Ophthalmology and Otolaryngology Committee on Conservation of Hearing. 1955. "Guide for the Evaluation of Hearing Impairment." *Transactions of the American Academy of Ophthalmology and Otolaryngology* 63:236–238.

Andersson, G. B. J. 1991. "The Epidemiology of Spinal Disorders." In J. W. Frymoyer (editor-in-chief), *The Adult Spine: Principles and Practice.* New York: Raven Press, pp. 107–146.

Andersson, G. B. J., M. H. Pope, J. W. Frymoyer, and S. H. Snook. 1991. "Epidemiology and Cost." In M. H. Pope, G. B. J. Andersson, J. H. Frymoyer, and D. B. Chaffin (eds.), *Occupational Low Back Pain: Assessment, Treatment and Prevention.* St. Louis: Mosby Year Book, pp. 95–113.

Andrews, A. H. 1909. "The Relation of Impairment of Hearing to Enginemen." *Railway Surgical Journal* 15:58–60.

Annual Report of the Chief Inspector of Factories and Workshops. 1909. His Majesty's Stationery Office, London.

——. 1922. His Majesty's Stationery Office, London.

——. 1924. His Majesty's Stationery Office, London.

——. 1930. His Majesty's Stationery Office, London.

Annual Report of the Liberty Mutual Insurance Company. 1933. Boston.

Ansberry, M. 1948. "The Veterans Administration Program in the Fields of Audiology and Speech Correction." *Journal of Speech and Hearing Disorders* 13:115–118.

Archer, G. L. 1938. *History of Radio.* New York: American Historical Society, pp. 44–51.

Armstrong, J. R. 1952. *Lumbar Disc Lesions.* Edinburgh: E. & S. Livingstone.

Armstrong, T. J. 1990. "Ergonomics and Cumulative Trauma Disorders of the Hand and Wrist." In J. M. Hunter, L. H. Schneider, E. J. Mackin, and A. D. Callahan (eds.), *Rehabilitation of the Hand.* St. Louis: C. V. Mosby, pp. 1175–1191.

Armstrong, T. J., and D. B. Chaffin. 1979. "Some Biomechanical Aspects of the Carpal Tunnel." *Journal of Biomechanics* 12:567–570.

Armstrong, T. J., and B. A. Silverstein. 1987. "Upper-Extremity Pain in the Workplace— The Role of Usage in Causality." In N. M. Hadler (ed.), *Clinical Concepts in Regional Musculoskeletal Illness.* Orlando: Grune & Stratton, pp. 333–354.

Arndt, R. 1990. "Unaccustomed Activity and Cumulative Trauma Disorders." Presentation at symposium, "Occupational Disorders of the Upper Extremity." University of Michigan, Ann Arbor, March 29–30, 1990.

Ashe, W. F., W. T. Cook, and J. W. Old. 1962. "Raynaud's Phenomenon of Occupational Origin." *Archives of Environmental Health* 5:333–343.

Ashford, N. A. 1976. *Crisis in the Workplace: Occupational Disease and Injury*. Cambridge, Mass.: MIT Press.

Ashford, N. A., D. Hattis, E. Zolt, and J. Katz. 1976. *Economic / Social Impact of Occupational Noise Exposure Regulations*. Report No. 550/9–77–352. Washington, D.C.: U.S. Environmental Protection Agency.

Atherley, G., and N. Johnston. 1983. "Audiometry—The Ultimate Test of Success?" *Annals of Occupational Hygiene* 27 (4): 427–447.

Atherley, G., and W. Noble. 1968. "A Review of Studies of Weavers' Deafness." *Applied Acoustics* 1:3–14.

———. 1985. "Occupational Deafness: The Continuing Challenge of Early German and Scottish Research." *American Journal of Industrial Medicine* 8:101–177.

Attali, J., and Y. Stourdze. 1977. "The Birth of the Telephone and Economic Crisis: The Slow Death of Monologue in French Society." In I. de Sola Pool (ed.), 1977. *The Social Impact of the Telephone*. Cambridge, Mass.: MIT Press, pp. 97–111.

Aufrang, O. E., J. S. Barr, T. Brown, and E. E. Record. 1957. "Orthopaedic Surgery." *New England Journal of Medicine* 256:934–940, 991–999, 1040–1050.

Aurelianus, C. 1950. In I. E. Drabkin (ed.), *Acute Diseases and Chronic Diseases*. Chicago: University of Chicago Press, p. 1019.

Axenfeld, A. 1863. *Traité des Névroses*. Paris.

Bach, T. F. 1948. "The History of Arthritis." In T. F. Bach (ed.), *Arthritis and Related Conditions*. Philadelphia: F. A. Davis, pp. 13–33.

Bagwell, P. S. 1963. *The Railwaymen: The History of the National Union of Railwaymen*. London: George Allen & Unwin.

Bailey, P. 1898. *Accident and Injury: Their Relation to Diseases of the Nervous System*. New York: D. Appleton.

———. 1918. "War Neuroses, Shell Shock and Nervousness in Soldiers." *Journal of the American Medical Association* 71:2148–2153.

Bale, A. 1986. "Compensation Crisis: The Value and Meaning of Work-related Injuries and Illnesses in the United States, 1842–1932." Ph.D. diss., Brandeis University.

Balla, A. 1929. "Impaired Hearing of Aviators: Professional Character." *Valsalva* 5:397.

Ballantyne, J., and J. A. M. Martin. 1984. *Deafness*. 4th ed. Edinburgh: Churchill.

Bammer, G., and B. Martin. 1988. "The Arguments About RSI: An Examination." *Community Health Studies* 12 (3): 348–358.

Barbash, J. 1952. *Unions and Telephones: The Story of the Communications Workers of America*. New York: Harper & Brothers.

Barlow, T. 1883. "Three Cases of Raynaud's Disease." *Transactions of the Clinical Society of London* 16:179–188.

Barnett, H. N. 1909. *Accidental Injuries to Workmen with Reference to Workmen's Compensation Act of 1906*. London: Rebman Limited.

Barr, J. S. 1977. "Lumbar Disc Lesions in Retrospect and Prospect." *Clinical Orthopaedics and Related Research* 129:4–8.

Barr, T. 1884. *Manual of Diseases of the Ear*. Glasgow: James Maclehose & Sons.

———. 1886. "Enquiry into the Effects of Loud Sounds Upon the Hearing of Boilermakers and Others Who Work Amid Noisy Surroundings." *Proceedings of the Royal Philosophical Society of Glasgow* 17:223–239.

——. 1890. "Injurious Effects of Loud Sounds Upon the Hearing." *British Medical Journal* 2:675.

——. 1896. *Manual of Diseases of the Ear.* 2nd ed. Glasgow: James Maclehose & Sons.

Barry, J. P. 1985. "Developmental and Enforcement History of the Occupational Noise Standards in the U.S.A.," Paper presented at the conference of the American Industrial Hygiene Association.

Barth, P. S. 1980. *Workers' Compensation and Work-Related Illnesses and Diseases.* Cambridge, Mass.: MIT Press.

——. 1987. *The Tragedy of Black Lung: Federal Compensation for Occupational Disease.* Kalamazoo, Mich.: W. E. Upjohn Institute for Employment Research.

Bassin, J. B. 1923. "Prevention, Rehabilitation, and Medicolegal Aspects of Sprained Backs." *Journal of Industrial Hygiene* 5 (8): 293–298.

Bauer, L. H. 1926. *Aviation Medicine.* Baltimore: Williams and Wilkins.

Bauer, W. I. 1989. "Scope of Industrial Low Back Pain." In W. W. Weisel, H. L. Feffer, D. G. Borenstein, and R. H. Rothman (eds.), *Industrial Low Back Pain: A Comprehensive Approach.* Charlottesville, Va.: Michie.

Beard, G. M. 1869a. "Neurasthenia, or Nervous Exhaustion." *Boston Medical and Surgical Journal* 3:217.

——. 1869b. *A Practical Treatise on Nervous Exhaustion.* New York: E. B. Treat.

——. 1881. *American Nervousness: Its Causes and Consequences.* New York: Putnam's.

——. 1884. *Sexual Neurasthenia: Its Hygiene, Causes, Symptoms and Treatment.* New York: E. B. Treat.

Beasley, W. C. 1940. "The General Problem of Deafness in the Population." *Laryngoscope* 50 (9): 856–905.

Beckwith, G. C. 1992. "The Myth of Injury Prevention Incentives in Workers' Compensation Insurance." *New Solutions* (Winter): 52–73.

Bell, C. 1830. *The Nervous System of the Human Body.* London.

Bell, D. S. 1989. "'Repetition Strain Injury': An Iatrogenic Epidemic of Simulated Injury." *Medical Journal of Australia* 151:280–284.

Bell, G. R., R. H. Rothman, R. Booth, J. M. Cuckler et al. 1984. "A Study of Computer Assisted Tomography: Comparison of Metrizamide Myelography and Computer Tomography in the Diagnosis of Herniated Lumbar Disc and Spinal Stenosis." *Spine* 9:552–556.

Benedict, S. C. 1897. "Railway Spine: A Species of Insanity." *Railway Surgeon* 3:226–231.

Benedikt, M. 1868. *Neurenpathologie und Electrotherapie.* Leipzig: Fues's Verlag.

Benton, G. P. 1921. "'War' Neuroses and Allied Conditions in Ex-Service Men." *Journal of the American Medical Association* 77:360.

Berger, K. W. 1970. *The Hearing Aid: Its Operation and Development.* Lavonia, Mich.: National Hearing Aid Society.

——. 1975. "History and Development of Hearing Aids." In M. C. Pollack (ed.), *Amplification for the Hearing-Impaired.* New York: Grune & Stratton, pp. 1–20.

Berger, O. 1885. "Beschäftigungsneurosen." In *Eulenburg's Real Encyk.* Berlin.

Berkowitz, E. D., and M. Berkowitz. 1985. "Challenges to Workers' Compensation: An Historical Analysis." In J. D. Worrall and D. Appel (eds.), *Workers' Compensation Benefits: Adequacy, Equity, and Efficiency.* Ithaca, N.Y.: ILR Press, Cornell University, pp. 158–179.

Berrien, F. K. 1946. "The Effects of Noise." *Psychological Bulletin* 43 (2): 141–161.

Beyer, D. S. 1916. *Safety Handbook.* Massachusetts Employees Insurance Association. Boston: Houghton Mifflin.

——. 1917. "Accident Prevention in the Textile Industry." Paper presented at the annual meeting of the American Society of Mechanical Engineers (December 4, 1917).

——. 1925. "Safety in Materials Handling." Paper presented at the annual meeting of the American Society of Mechanical Engineers (November 30, 1925).

——. 1928. *Industrial Accident Prevention.* Boston: Houghton Mifflin.

Beyer, D. S., and R. Clair. 1929. "Handling Materials: A Serious Accident Problem for the Food Industry." *National Safety News* 20:13–17.

Bezold, F., and Siebenmann. 1908. *Textbook of Otology.* Translated by J. Holinger. Chicago: E. H. Cosgrove.

Birkbeck, M. Q., and T. C. Beer. 1975. "Occupation in Relation to the Carpal Tunnel Syndrome." *Rheumatology and Rehabilitation* 14:218–221.

Blake, C. J. 1888. "Influence of the Use of the Telephone Upon Hearing Power." *Archives of Otology* 17:240–243.

——. 1916. "Occupational Injuries and Diseases of the Ear." In G. M. Kober and W. C. Hanson (eds.), *Diseases of Occupation and Vocational Hygiene.* Philadelphia: Blakiston, pp. 339–50.

Blegvad, N. R. 1907. "Effets professionels du téléphone sur l'appareil auditif et sur l'organisme." *Annales d'Hygiène publique* 8 (4): 375–377. Abstract in *Journal of Laryngology and Otology* 24:172 (1909).

Bloch, B. 1984. "Repetition Strain Injuries." *Medical Journal of Australia* 140:684–685.

Boden, L. I. 1986. "Problems in Occupational Disease Compensation." In J. Chelius (ed.), *Current Issues in Workers' Compensation.* Kalamazoo, Mich.: W. E. Upjohn Institute For Employment Research.

——. 1995. "Workers' Compensation in the United States: High Costs, Low Benefits." *Annual Review of Public Health* 16: 189–218.

Bordley, J. E., and P. E. Brookhouser. 1979. "The History of Otology." In L. J. Bradford and W. G. Hardy (eds.), *Hearing and Hearing Impairment.* New York: Grune & Stratton, pp. 3–14.

Bourgeois, H., and M. Sourdille. 1918. *War Otitis and War Deafness.* Trans. by J. Dundas Grant. London: University of London Press.

Brackett, E. G. 1924. "Low Back Strain with Particular Reference to Industrial Accidents." *Journal of the American Medical Association* 83 (14): 1068–1075.

Bradford, C. L. 1921. "Diseases and Injuries With Symptoms Referable to the Lumbar Spine." *Proceedings of the National Safety Council,* September 26–30, pp. 329–341.

Brahams, D. 1992. "Keyboard Operators' Repetitive Strain Injury." *Lancet* 339:237–238.

Brain, W. R., A. D. Wright, and M. Wilkinson. 1947. "Spontaneous Compression of Both Median Nerves in Carpal Tunnel: Six Cases Treated Surgically." *Lancet* 1:277–282.

Brandt-Rauf, P. W., and S. I. Brandt-Rauf. 1987. "History of Occupational Medicine: Relevance of Imhotep and the Edwin Smith Papyrus." *British Journal of Industrial Medicine* 44:68–70.

Braustein, H. 1904. "On the Influence of the Use of the Telephone on the Ear." *Archiv für Ohrenheilkunde* 54:240. Abstract in *Archives of Otology* 33:531. (1904)

Brecher, R., and E. Brecher. 1969. *The Rays: A History of Radiology in the United States and Canada.* Baltimore: Williams and Wilkins.

Bremer, L. 1889. "A Contribution to the Study of the Traumatic Neuroses (Railway-Spine)." *Transactions of the Medical Association of Missouri* 32:156–175.

Brieger, G. H. 1980. "History of Medicine." In P. T. Durbin (ed.), *A Guide to the Culture of Science, Technology, and Medicine.* New York: The Free Press, pp. 121–187.

Brill, A. 1922. *Psychoanalysis.* 3rd ed. Philadelphia: W. B. Saunders.

Bristowe, J. S. 1890. *A Treatise on the Theory and Practice of Medicine.* London: Smith, Elder.

Brodeur, P. 1974. *Expendable Americans.* New York: Viking Press.

——. 1985. *Outrageous Misconduct,* New York: Pantheon.

Brogmus, G. E., B. Webster, and G. Sorock. 1994. "Recent Trends in Cumulative Trauma Disorders of the Upper Extremities in the United States." *Proceedings of the Twelfth Triennial Congress of the International Ergonomics Association* 2: 214–216.

Bronstein, J. M. 1984. "Brown Lung in North Carolina: The Social Organization of an Occupational Disease." Ph.D. diss. University of Kentucky.

Brouwer, B. 1920. "The Significance of Phylogenetic and Ontogenetic Studies for the Neuropathologist." *Journal of Nervous and Mental Disease* 51 (2): 113–136.

Brown, C. W. 1888. "Railway Injuries." *New York Medical Journal* 48:683–687.

Brown, T. 1828. "On the Irritation of Spinal Nerves." *Glasgow Medical Journal* 1:131–161.

Brown, W. 1919. "War Neuroses." *Lancet* 1:833.

Brownfield, R. R. 1918. "Detection of Pretended Loss of Hearing." *Journal of the American Medical Association* 70 (9): 597–598.

Brück, A. T. 1835. "Fingerkrampf beim Schreiben. *Wchnschr. f. d. ges. Heilk.*, Berlin, p. 725.

Bruhl, G. 1892. *Atlas and Epitome of Otology.* Philadelphia: W. B. Saunders.

Bruusgaard, A. 1962. "Bell-ringer's Deafness." *T. norske. Laegeforen.* 82:1285.

Bryant, W. S. 1893. In C. H. Burnett (ed.), *A System of Diseases of the Ear, Nose and Throat.* Vol. 1. Philadelphia: J. B. Lippincott, p. 98.

——. 1917. "Prevalence of Ear Injuries and Diseases in the French Army." *Journal of Laryngology and Otology* 32:338.

Bucy, P. C. 1930. "Chondroma of Intervertebral Disk." *Journal of the American Medical Association* 94:1552–1554.

Bunch, C. C. 1929. "Age Variations in Auditory Acuity." *Archives of Otolaryngology* 9:625–636.

——. 1937. "The Diagnosis of Occupational or Traumatic Deafness; A Historical and Audiometric Study." *Laryngoscope* 47 (9): 615–691.

——. 1941. "The Development of the Audiometer." *Laryngoscope* 51 (12): 1100–1118.

Bunnell, S. 1970. *Surgery of the Hand.* 5th ed. Philadelphia: J. B. Lippincott.

Burnett, C. H. 1877. *The Ear: Its Anatomy, Physiology, and Diseases.* Philadelphia: Henry C. Lea.

Burnham, A. C. 1915. "The Role of the Physician in Industrial Medicine Insurance." *Medical Record* 87:854–857.

Burritt, B. B. 1928. "Workmen's Compensation Keeps the Family from Charity." *American Labor Legislation Review* 18:377–384.

Burry, H. C., and M. S. Gilkison. 1987. "The Conceptualization of Low-Back Pain as a Compensable Accident." In N. M. Hadler (ed.), *Clinical Concepts in Regional Musculoskeletal Disease.* Orlando: Grune & Stratton, pp. 317–332.

Butler, E. B. 1984 (rpt. 1907). *Women and the Trades: Pittsburgh, 1907–1908.* Pittsburgh: University of Pittsburgh Press.

Buzzard, T. 1867. "On Cases of Injury from Railway Accidents: Their Influence Upon the Nervous System, and Results." *Lancet* 1:389–391, 453–454, 509–510, 623–625.

California Workers' Compensation Institute. 1978. *A Report to Industry: Cumulative Injury in California—The Continuing Dilemma.* San Francisco.

Cannon, B. W., and J. G. Love. 1946. "Tardy Median Palsy Median Neuritis; Median Thenar Neuritis Amenable to Surgery." *Surgery* 20:210–216.

Cannon, L. J., E. J. Bernacki, and S. D. Walter. 1981. "Personal and Occupational Factors Associated With Carpal Tunnel Syndrome." *Journal of Occupational Medicine* 23: 255–258.

Capart, A. 1911. "Maladies et Accidents Professionnels des Téléphonistes." *Archives Internationales de Laryngologie d'Otologie et de Rhinologie* 31:748–764. Abstract in *Laryngoscope* 22:656 (1912).

Carpentier, P. H., H. R. Maricq, M. Jiguet, O. C. M. Poncot, M. V. Maines, and A. Franco. 1990. "Carpal Tunnel Syndrome Associated with Raynaud Phenomenon: Epidemiologic Evaluation." *Arthritis and Rheumatism* 33:S139 (abstract).

Casali, J. G., S. T. Lam, and B. W. Epps. 1987. "Rating and Ranking Methods for Hearing Protector Wearability." *Sound and Vibration* (December): 10–18.

Castleman, B., D. C. Crocett, and S. B. Sutton. 1983. *History of the Massachusetts General Hospital: 1955–1980*. Boston: Little, Brown.

Cats-Baril, W. L., and J. W. Frymoyer. 1991. "The Economics of Spinal Disorders." In J. W. Frymoyer (editor-in-chief), *The Adult Spine: Principles and Practice*. New York: Raven Press, pp. 85–105.

Catton, J. 1919. "Malingering." *Military Surgeon* 45:706.

Cauthen, J. C. 1988. "Lumbar Pain—An Overview." In J. C. Cauthen (ed.), *Lumbar Spine Surgery: Indications, Techniques, Failures, and Alternatives*. 2nd ed. Baltimore: Williams & Wilkins, pp. 1–4.

Cayleff, S. E. 1988. "'Prisoners of Their Own Feebleness': Women, Nerves and Western Medicine—A Historical Overview." *Social Science and Medicine* 26 (12): 1199–1208.

Cazanave, J. J. 1836. "Perturbations locales de la myotilité empêchant les mouvements de certains doigts de la main droite nécessaires pour écrire. *Gaz. méd. de Paris* 2, s., (iv): 525.

Chadwick, D. 1971. "Noise and the Ear." In J. Ballantyne and J. Groves (eds.), *Diseases of the Ear, Nose and Throat*. 3rd ed. Philadelphia: J. B. Lippincott, pp. 475–539.

Chaffin, D. B. 1973. "Localized Muscle Fatigue." *Journal of Occupational Medicine* 15 (4): 346–354.

——. 1975. "Ergonomics Guide for the Assessment of Human Static Strength." *American Industrial Hygiene Association Journal* (July): 505–511.

Cherniak, M. G. 1986. *The Hawk's Nest Incident: America's Worst Industrial Disaster*. New Haven: Yale University Press.

Chesler, P. 1972. *Women and Madness*. New York: Doubleday.

Christophers, A. J. 1972. "Occupational Aspects of Raynaud's Disease: A Critical Historical Survey." *Medical Journal of Australia* 2:730–733.

Church, A., and F. Peterson. 1899. *Nervous and Mental Diseases*. Philadelphia: W. B. Saunders.

Clevenger, S. V. 1889. *Spinal Concussion: Erichsen's Disease as One Form of Traumatic Neuroses*. Philadelphia: F. A. Davis.

Clune, H. W. 1947. *Main Street Beat*. New York: W. W. Norton.

Cockerham, W. C. 1986. *Medical Sociology*. 3rd ed. Englewood Cliffs, N.J.: Prentice-Hall.

Codman, C. A. E. 1916. "The Workmen's Compensation Law and Its Effect Upon the Medical Profession." *Pennsylvania Medical Journal* 19:739–746.

Coggin, D. 1879. "A New Test for Simulated One-Sided Deafness." *Archives of Otology* 8:177.

Coles, R. A. 1969. "Control of Industrial Noise Through Personal Protection." *ASSE Journal* 14:10–15.

Colledge, L., and T. J. Faulder. 1921. "Injuries to the Ear in Modern Warfare." *Journal of Laryngology and Otology* 36:277–288.

Collie, J. 1917. *Malingering and Feigned Sickness*. 2nd ed. New York: Longmans, Green.

Commonwealth of Massachusetts. 1919. *Annual Report of the Industrial Accident Board*. Boston: Wright & Potter.

Conn, H. R. 1922. "The Acute Painful Back Among Industrial Employees Alleging Compensable Injury." *Journal of the American Medical Association* 79:1210–1212.

——. 1931. "Tenosynovitis." *Ohio State Medical Journal* 27:713–716.

Cooper, A. P. 1822. *A Treatise on Dislocations and Fractures of the Joints*. London: Longman.

Cooseman, E. 1899. "The Hearing Power of Beetlers." *Archives of Otology* 28:413–414.

Cooter, R. 1987. "The Meaning of Fractures: Orthopaedics and the Reform of British Hospitals in the Inter-war Period." *Medical History* 31:306–332.

——. 1993. *Surgery and Society in Peace and War: Orthopaedics and the Reorganization of Modern Medicine, 1880–1948*. London: Macmillan.

Copin, M. 1929. "Nervous Illness in Industry." *Journal of Industrial Hygiene* 11:114.

Copland, J. 1845. *A Dictionary of Practical Medicine*. New York: Harper & Brothers.

Corea, G. 1977. *The Hidden Malpractice: How American Medicine Treats Women as Patients and Professionals*. New York: William Morrow.

Cott, G. 1918. "Telephone Deafness." *Buffalo Medical Journal* 73 (9): 317–320.

Cox, J. E. 1958. "Noise in Industry." *The Laryngoscope* 68 (3): 440–447.

Crain, R. B., and B. J. Slater. 1921. "When Are Disabilities of the Back Arising Out of Pathological Conditions Reportable Accidents." *Journal of Industrial Hygiene* 3 (7): 197–201.

Cranston, J. P. 1978. "An Orthopedic Viewpoint of Cumulative Trauma." Paper presented at a seminar on Cumulative Back Injuries, California Workers' Compensation Institute, San Francisco, October 17, 1978.

Cronbach, E. 1903. "Die Beschäftigungsneurose der Telegraphisten." (Occupation neurosis of telegraphists.) *Archiv für Psychiatrie und Nervenkrankheiten* 37:243–293.

Crowhart, C. H. 1915. "The Relation of the Physician to Compensation." *Wisconsin Medical Journal* 14:268–272.

Crozier, M. 1965. *The World of the Office Worker,* trans. D. Landau. Chicago: University of Chicago Press.

Cullingworth, C. J. 1886. "Fraudulent Damage Claims in Railroad-accident Cases." *Medico-Legal Journal* 3:175–178.

Cumulative Trauma Disorders: History, Description, Cost and Prevention. 1990. Report produced by the Human Resources Committee for the American Apparel Manufacturers Association, Arlington, Va.

Curtis, P. 1988. "Spinal Manipulation: Does It Work?" In R. A. Deyo (ed.), *Back Pain in Workers; Occupational Medicine: State of the Art Reviews*. Philadelphia: Hanley & Belfus. Vol. 3, no. 1, pp. 31–44.

DaCosta, J., and J. Jones. 1923. "Railway Injuries." In *Legal Medicine and Toxicology*. 2nd ed. Philadelphia: W. B. Saunders.

Dainoff, M. J. 1992. "The Illness of the Decade." *Computerworld* April 13, 1992, p. 27.

Dalby, W. B. 1872. "Lectures: Diseases and Injuries of the Ear." *Lancet* 2:873–875.

——. 1873. *Lectures on Diseases and Injuries of the Ear*. London: J. & A. Churchill.

——. 1893. *Lectures on Diseases and Injuries of the Ear*. 4th ed. Philadelphia: Blakiston.

Dana, C. L. 1894. *Textbook of Nervous Diseases*. 3rd ed. New York: William Wood.

Dandy, W. E. 1925. *Annals of Surgery* 81:223–254.

——. 1929. "Loose Cartilage From Intervertebral Disk Simulating Tumor of the Spinal Cord." *Archives of Surgery* 19:660–672.

Dart, E. E. 1946. "Effects of High Speed Vibrating Tools on Operators Engaged in the Airplane Industry." *Occupational Medicine* 1:515–550.

Davies, M. 1982. *Woman's Place Is at the Typewriter: Office Work and Office Workers, 1870–1930.* Philadelphia: Temple University Press.

Delaney, M. 1920. "Significance of Pain in the Back." *International Journal of Surgery* (October): 321.

DeLuca, S. A., and J. T. Rhea. 1981. "Are Routine Oblique Roentgenograms of the Lumbar Spine of Value?" *Journal of Bone and Joint Surgery* 63A:846.

Dembe, A. E. 1995. "Alternative Approaches for Incorporating Safety Into Workers' Compensation Reform Legislation." *Journal of Insurance Regulation* 13 (4): 445–461.

Dempsey, M. 1933. *The Occupational Progress of Women, 1910 to 1930.* U.S. Department of Labor, Women's Bureau, Bulletin No. 104. Washington, D.C.: Government Printing Office.

Dench, E. B. 1909. *Diseases of the Ear.* 4th ed. New York: D. Appleton.

Departmental Committee on Compensation for Industrial Diseases. 1908. *Second Report of the Departmental Committee for Industrial Diseases.* London: His Majesty's Stationery Office.

———. 1913. *Report of the Departmental Committee.* London: His Majesty's Stationery Office.

Dercum, F. X. 1889. "Remarks on Spinal Injuries, More Especially 'Railway Spine,' With Hints on Expert Testimony." *Therapeutic Gazette* 3:304–314.

———. 1916. *Hysteria and Accident Compensation.* Philadelphia: George T. Bisel.

DeReamer, R. 1980. *Modern Safety and Health Technology.* New York: John Wiley & Sons.

Derickson, A. 1987. " 'To Be His Own Benefactor': The Founding of the Coeur d'Alene Miners' Union Hospital, 1891." In D. Rosner and G. Markowitz (eds.), *Dying for Work: Workers' Safety and Health in Twentieth-Century America.* Bloomington: Indiana University Press, pp. 3–18.

———. 1991. "The United Mine Workers of America and the Recognition of Occupational Respiratory Diseases, 1902–1968." *American Journal of Public Health* 81 (6): 782–790.

Dewar, M. 1912. "Medical Training For The Detection of Malingering." *British Medical Journal* 2:223–225.

Dewing, S. B. 1962. *Modern Radiology in Historical Perspective.* Springfield, Ill.: Charles C. Thomas.

Deyo, R. A. 1987. "Reducing Work Absenteeism and Diagnostic Costs for Backache." In N. M. Hadler (ed.), *Clinical Concepts in Regional Musculoskeletal Disease.* Orlando: Grune & Stratton, pp. 25–50.

———. 1988. "The Role of the Primary Care Physician in Reducing Work Absenteeism and Costs Due to Back Pain." In R. A. Deyo (ed.), *Back Pain in Workers; Occupational Medicine: State of the Art Reviews.* Philadelphia: Hanley & Belfus, vol. 3, no. 1, pp. 17–30.

———. 1994. "Magnetic Resonance Imaging of the Lumbar Spine: Terrific Test or Tar Baby?" *New England Journal of Medicine* 331 (2): 115–116.

Deyo, R. A., S. J. Bigos, and K. R. Maravilla. 1989. "Diagnostic Imaging Procedures for the Lumbar Spine." *Annals of Internal Medicine* 111:865–867.

Dillane, J. B., J. Fry, and G. Kalton. 1966. "Acute Back Syndrome—A Study from General Practice." *British Medical Journal* 2:82.

Dixon, F. W. 1935. "A Method to Determine the Percentage of Deafness in Malingerers." *Annals of Otology, Rhinology and Laryngology* 44:483–485.

Doctor, P. V. 1945. "The Rehabilitation of Military Aural Casualties." *American Annals of the Deaf* 90 (2): 99–120.

Donohue, J. D. 1926. "Trauma and its Results from an Administrative Point of View." *Bulletin of the U.S. Bureau of Labor Statistics No. 406.* Washington, D.C.: Government Printing Office.

Downey, E. H. 1924. *Workmen's Compensation.* New York: Macmillan.

Drinka, G. F. 1984. *The Birth of Neurosis: Myth, Malady, and the Victorians.* New York: Simon and Schuster.

Duchenne, G. B. 1855–1872. *Selections from the Clinical Works.* Trans. and ed. G. V. Poore. London (1883).

———. 1867. *Physiology of Motion.* Trans. and ed. E. B. Kaplan. Philadelphia: J. B. Lippincott (1949).

Duchesne, E. A. 1857. *Des Chemins de Fer et de leur Influence sur la Santé des Mécaniciens et Chauffeurs.* Paris.

Dupuis, P. R. 1987. "The Natural History of Degenerative Changes in the Lumbar Spine." In R. G. Watkins and J. S. Collis, Jr. (eds.), *Lumbar Discectomy and Laminectomy.* Rockville, Md.: Aspen.

Eastman Kodak Company. 1983. *Ergonomic Design for People at Work.* Vol. 1. Belmont, Calif.: Lifetime Learning, pp. 5–6.

Ehrenreich, B., and D. English. 1973. *Complaints and Disorders: The Sexual Politics of Sickness.* Old Westbury, N.Y.: Feminist Press.

Eichhoff, E. 1927. "Zur Pathogenese der Tendovaginitis Stenosans." *Bruns' Beiträge z. klin. Chir.* 139:746.

Elliot, D. 1988. "The Early History of Contracture of the Palmar Fascia." *Journal of Hand Surgery* 13B (3): 246–253.

———. 1990. "The Early History of Contracture of the Palmar Fascia." In R. M. McFarlane, D. A. McGrouther, and M. H. Flint (eds.), *Dupuytren's Disease: Biology and Treatment.* Edinburgh: Churchill Livingstone.

Ellis, J. D. 1935. "The Surgeon and the Workmen's Compensation Act." *Memphis Medical Journal* 10 (9): 19–31.

Elsberg, C. A. 1928. "Extradural Spinal Tumours: Primary, Secondary and Metastatic." *Surgical Gynecology and Obstetrics* 46:1–20.

Epstein, A., B. Begg, and B. McNeil. 1986. "The Use of Ambulatory Testing in Prepaid and Fee-for-Service Group Practices." *New England Journal of Medicine* 314:1089–1094.

Erb, W. H. 1876. "Diseases of the Spinal Cord and Medulla Oblongata," in H. W. von Ziemssen (ed.), *Cyclopaedia of the Practice of Medicine.* Vol. 13. New York: William Wood.

Erichsen, J. E. 1867. *On Railway and Other Injuries of the Nervous System.* Philadelphia: Henry C. Lea.

———. 1875. *On Concussion of the Spine, Nervous Shock and Other Obscure Injuries of the Nervous System.* New York: William Wood.

Evans, E. J. 1947. "Noise in the Factory." *Times Review of Industry* (April 5): 14.

Farrar, C. B. 1918. "Neuroses Among Returned Soldiers." *Boston Medical and Surgical Journal* 179:583.

Faulder, T. J. 1921. "Injuries to the Ear in Modern Warfare." *Journal of Laryngology and Otology* 36:277–282.

Faxon, N. W. 1959. *The Massachusetts General Hospital: 1935–1955.* Cambridge, Mass.: Harvard University Press.

Fay, O. J. 1921. "The Lesser Injuries to the Back and Their Industrial Significance." *Transactions of the Western Surgical Association* 31:71–79.

Feldmann H. 1970. "A History of Audiology." *Translations of the Beltone Institute for Hearing Research* 22 (January): 9–107. Trans. of "Die geschichtliche Entwicklung der Hörprüfungsmethoden, kurze Darstellung und Bibliographie von den Anfängen bis zur Gegenwart," in H. Leicher, R. Mittermaier, and G. Theissing (eds.), *zwabglose Abhandlungen aus dem Gebiet der Hals-Nasen-Ohren-Heilkunde*. Stuttgart: Georg Thieme Verlag, 1960.

Felsenthal, E. 1994. "An Epidemic or a Fad? The Debate Heats Up Over Repetitive Stress." *Wall Street Journal*, July 14, 1994, pp. A1, A7.

Ferguson, D. 1971. "An Australian Study of Telegraphist's Cramp." *British Journal of Industrial Medicine*, 28:280–285.

——. 1971. "Repetition Injuries in Process Operators." *Medical Journal of Australia* 2:408–412.

——. 1987. "RSI: Putting the Epidemic to Rest." *Medical Journal of Australia* 147:213.

Field, G. P. 1893. *Diseases of the Ear*. 4th ed. Philadelphia: Lea Brothers.

Figlio, K. 1985. "What is an Accident?" In P. Weindling (ed.), *The Social History of Occupational Health*. London: Croom Helm, pp. 181–206.

Finkelstein, H. 1930. "Stenosing Tendovaginitis at the Radial Styloid Process." *Journal of Bone and Joint Surgery* 12 (3): 509–540.

Fischer-Homberger, E. 1970. "Railway Spine und traumatische Neurose: Seele und Rückenmark." *Gesnerus* 27:96–111.

Fishberg, M. 1911. *The Jews*. New York: Scribner.

Fisher, B. 1922. *Mental Causes of Accidents*. Boston: Houghton Mifflin.

Fleck, L. 1935. *Genesis and Development of a Scientific Fact*. T. J. Trenn and R. K. Merton (ed.), trans. F. Bradley and T. J. Trenn. Chicago: University of Chicago Press (1979).

Fletcher, H. A. 1922. "Determination of Disability as to Loss of Hearing, and the Importance of Vertigo." *Journal of the American Medical Association* 79 (7): 529–532.

Fodor, W. J., and A. Oleinick. 1986. "Workers' Compensation for Occupational Noise-Induced Hearing Loss: A Review of Science and the Law, and Proposed Reforms." *Saint Louis University Law Journal* 30:703–804.

Foner, P. 1979. *Women and the American Labor Movement*. New York: The Free Press.

Fosbroke, J. 1831. "Practical Observations on the Pathology and Treatment of Deafness." *Lancet* 1:533, 645–648.

Foster, G. S. 1931. "Bursitis." *American Medicine* 26:199–203.

Foucault, M. 1973. *The Birth of the Clinic: An Archaeology of Medical Perception*. Trans. by A. M. Sheridan Smith. New York: Pantheon.

Fowler, E. P., and R. L. Wegel. 1922. "Presentation of a New Instrument for Determining the Amount and Character of Auditory Sensation." *Transactions of the American Otological Society* 16:105–123.

Fox, M. S. 1953. "The Hearing Loss Problem." *Occupational Hazards* 15(11).

Fox, W. L. 1984. *Dandy of Johns Hopkins*. Baltimore: Williams & Wilkins.

Franco, G., C. Castelli, and C. Gatti. 1992. "Tenosinovite posturale da uso incongruo di un dispositivo di puntamento (mouse) di un elaboratore." *Medicina del Lavoro* 83 (4): 352–5.

Frankel, L. K., and M. M. Dawson. 1910. *Workingmen's Insurance in Europe*. New York: Russell Sage Foundation.

Frankfurter, Felix. 1915. *The Case for the Shorter Work Day*. Brief delivered to the U.S. Supreme Court in *Bunting v. The State of Oregon*. October 1915. New York: National Consumers' League.

Franklin, G. M., J. Haug, N. Heyer, H. Checkoway, and N. Peck. 1991. "Occupational

Carpal Tunnel Syndrome in Washington State, 1984–1988." *American Journal of Public Health* 81 (6): 741–746.

Franzblau, A., D. Flaschner, J. W. Albers, S. Blitz, R. Werner, and T. Armstrong. 1993. "Medical Screening of Office Workers for Upper Extremity Cumulative Trauma Disorders." *Archives of Environmental Health* 48(3): 164–70.

Fraser, A. J. 1930. *Trauma, Disease, Compensation: A Handbook of Their Medico-Legal Relations*. Philadelphia: F. A. Davis.

Frazier, F. E. 1955. "The Unsolved Factors in Loss of Hearing Claims." Paper presented at the Third Miami Insurance Law Conference, March 29, 1955.

Frederickson, H. M. 1970. "Noise Exposure—The Legal Viewpoint." Paper presented at the 75th Annual Meeting of the American Academy of Ophthalmology and Otolaryngology, Las Vegas, Nev., October 5–9, 1970.

Friberg, S. 1954. "Lumbar Disc Degeneration in Problem of Lumbago Sciatica." *Bulletin of Hospital Joint Disease* 15:1–20.

Fry, H. F. H. 1986. "Overuse Syndrome in Musicians—100 Years Ago." *Medical Journal of Australia* 145:620–625.

Frymoyer, J. W. 1988. "Back Pain and Sciatica." *New England Journal of Medicine* 318:291–300.

——. 1990. "Magnitude of the Problem." In J. N. Weinstein and S. W. Wiesel (eds.), *The Lumbar Spine,* Philadelphia: W. B. Saunders, pp. 32–38.

Frymoyer, J. W., A. Newberg, M. H. Pope, D. G. Wilder, J. Clements, and I. B. MacPherson. 1984. "Spine Radiographs in Patients with Low Back Pain. An Epidemiological Study in Men." *Journal of Bone and Joint Surgery* 66A:1048–1055.

Frymoyer, J. W., and V. Mooney. 1986. "Current Concepts Review: Occupational Orthopaedics." *Journal of Bone and Joint Surgery* 68A:468–473.

Frymoyer, J. W., and M. H. Pope. 1987. "Epidemiologic Insights into the Relationship Between Usage and Back Disorders." In N. M. Hadler (ed.), *Clinical Concepts in Regional Musculoskeletal Disease*. Orlando: Grune & Stratton, pp. 263–279.

Fulton, T. W. 1884. "Telegraphists' Cramp." *Edinburgh Clinical and Pathological Journal* 1 (17): 369–375.

Gellé, M. E. 1889. "Actions du téléphone sur l'organe de l'ouie." *Soc. de Biologie* (June 1). Abstract in *Archives of Otology* 19:58–60 (1890).

Ghormley R. K. 1951. "The Operative Treatment of Painful Conditions of the Lower Part of the Back." *Proceedings of Staff Meetings, Mayo Clinic* 6:112–113.

Gibson, E. S. 1987. "The Value of Preplacement Screening Radiography of the Low Back." In R. A. Deyo (ed.), *Back Pain in Workers; Occupational Medicine: State of the Art Reviews*. Philadelphia: Hanley & Belfus, vol. 3 no. 1, pp. 31–44.

Gill, A. W. 1929. "Hysteria and the Workmen's Compensation Act." *Lancet* 1:811–814.

Ginnold, R. E. 1974. "Workmen's Compensation for Hearing Loss in Wisconsin." *Labor Law Journal* 25 (1): 682–694.

——. 1979. *Occupational Hearing Loss: Workers' Compensation Under State and Federal Programs*. EPA Report 550/9–79–101. Washington, D.C.: U.S. Environmental Protection Agency.

Glibert, D. J. 1921. "Influence of Industrial Noises." *Journal of Industrial Hygiene* 3: 264–275. This paper was originally delivered by Glibert to the Third International Congress on Occupational Diseases in Vienna, August 1914.

Glorig, A. 1958. "A Report of Two Normal Hearing Studies." *Annals of Otology, Rhinology and Laryngology* 67 (1): 93–111.

——. 1961. "The Problem of Noise in Industry." *American Journal of Public Health* 51 (9): 1338–1346.

Glorig, A., and M. Downs. 1965. "Introduction to Audiometry." In A. Glorig (ed.), *Audiometry: Principles and Practice*. Baltimore: Williams and Wilkins, pp. 1–14.

Goldschmidt. 1839. "Die krankhafte Unfähigkeit zu schreiben." *Wchnschr. f. d. ges. Heilk.*, Berl. pp. 29–31.

Goldthwait, J. E. 1911. "The Lumbrosacral Articulation: An Explanation of Many Cases of 'Lumbago,' 'Sciatica,' and Paraplegia." *Boston Medical and Surgical Journal* 164: 365–372.

Gosling, F.G. 1987. *Before Freud: Neurasthenia and the American Medical Community, 1870–1910*. Urbana: University of Illinois Press.

Got, A. 1916. "War Deafness With Lesions of the Internal Ear." *Journal of Laryngology and Otology* 3:374.

Gottstein, J., and R. Kayser. 1881. "Ueber die Gehörsverminderung bei Schlossern und Schmieden." (On hearing defects in locksmiths and blacksmiths.) *Breslauer Aerztliche Z* 18:205–207.

Gould, G. M., and W. L. Pyle. 1897. *Anomalies and Curiosities of Medicine*. Philadelphia: W. B. Saunders.

Gourvish, T. R. 1980. *Railways and the British Economy, 1830–1914*. London: Macmillan.

Gowers, W. R. 1888. *A Manual of Diseases of the Nervous System*. Philadelphia: Blakiston.

——. 1896. *A Manual of Diseases of the Nervous System*. 2nd ed. Philadelphia: Blakiston.

——. 1904. "A Lecture on Lumbago: Its Lessons and Analogues." *British Medical Journal* 1:117–121.

Graebner, W. 1987. "Hegemony Through Science: Information Engineering and Lead Toxicology, 1925–1965." In D. Rosner and G. Markowitz (eds.), *Dying for Work: Workers' Safety and Health in Twentieth-Century America*. Bloomington: Indiana University Press, pp. 140–159.

Grant, W. W. 1897. "Railway Spine and Litigation Symptoms." *Medical Age* 15:649–653.

Gray, L. C. 1895. *A Treatise on Nervous and Mental Diseases*. Philadelphia: Lea Brothers.

Green, H. 1990. *On Strike at Hormel: The Struggle for a Democratic Labor Movement*. Philadelphia: Temple University Press.

Greenberg, L., and D. Chaffin. 1977. *Workers and Their Tools*. Midland, Mich.: Pendall.

Griessmann, B. 1921. "Neue Methoden zur Hörprüfung." *Passow-Schaefers Beitr. Hals-Nas.-Ohrenheilk* 16:47–55.

Griffin, W., and D. Griffin. 1834, *Observations on Functional Affections of the Spinal Cord and Ganglionic System of Nerves, In Which Their Identity with Sympathetic, Nervous, and Imitative Diseases is Illustrated*. London: Burgess & Hill.

Grimwade, S. W. 1925. "Occupational Diseases of the Nose, Throat, and Ear." *British Medical Journal* 2:890–891.

Guild, S. R. 1918. "Tests Upon Devices for the Prevention of War Deafness." *Anatomical Record* 14:36.

Gun, R. T. 1990. "The Incidence and Distribution of RSI in South Australia 1980–81 to 1986–87." *Medical Journal of Australia* 153:376–380.

Güterbock. 1882. *Vierteljahrschr. für öff. Gesundheitspfl.*

Habermann, I. 1891. "Ueber die Schwerhörigkeit der Kesselschmiede." *Archiv für Ohrenheilkunde* 30:1–25. Abstract in *Archives of Otology* 20:171, 177–178. (1891).

Haddon, W., E. Suchman, and D. Klein. 1964. *Accident Research: Methods and Approaches*. New York: Harper & Row, pp. 403–405.

Hadler, N. M. 1977. "Industrial Rheumatology." *Arthritis and Rheumatism* 20 (4): 1023.

——. 1978. "Legal Ramifications of the Medical Definition of Back Disease." *Annals of Internal Medicine* 89 (6): 992–999.

——. 1984. *Medical Management of the Regional Musculoskeletal Diseases.* Orlando: Grune & Stratton.

——. 1986. "Is an Aching Back an Injury." *Occupational Problems in Medical Practice* 1 (3): 6–8.

——. 1987a. "Is Carpal Tunnel Syndrome an Injury That Qualifies For Workers' Compensation Insurance." In N. M. Hadler (ed.), *Clinical Concepts in Regional Musculoskeletal Illness.* Orlando: Grune & Stratton, pp. 355–360.

——. 1987b. "To Be a Patient or a Claimant with a Musculoskeletal Illness." In N. M. Hadler (ed.), *Clinical Concepts in Regional Musculoskeletal Illness.* Orlando: Grune & Stratton, pp. 7–21.

——. 1989. "Disabling Backache in France, Switzerland, and the Netherlands: Contrasting Sociopolitical Constraints on Clinical Judgment." *Journal of Occupational Medicine* 31 (10): 823–831.

——. 1990. "Cumulative Trauma Disorders: An Iatrogenic Concept." *Journal of Occupational Medicine* 32 (1): 38–41.

——. 1991. "Insuring Against Work Incapacity from Spinal Disorders." In J. W. Frymoyer (editor-in-chief), *The Adult Spine: Principles and Practice.* New York: Raven Press, pp. 77–83.

——. 1993. *Occupational Musculoskeletal Disorders.* New York: Raven Press.

Haklius, A. 1970. "Prognosis in Sciatica: A Clinical Follow-Up of Surgical and Non-Surgical Treatment." *Acta Orthopaedica Scandinavia* (Suppl. 129): 1–29.

Hall, W., and L. Morrow. 1988. "'Repetition Strain Injury': An Australian Epidemic of Upper Limb Pain." *Social Science and Medicine* 27 (6): 645–649.

Haller, J. S. 1970. "Neurasthenia: Medical Profession and Urban 'Blahs.'" *New York State Journal of Medicine* 70:2489–2497.

——. 1971. "Neurasthenia: The Medical Profession and The 'New Woman' of Late Nineteenth Century." *New York State Journal of Medicine* 71:473–482.

——. 1988. "Industrial Accidents—Worker Compensation Laws and the Medical Response." *Western Journal of Medicine* 148:341–348.

Haller, J. S., and R. M. Haller. 1974. *The Physician and Sexuality in Victorian America.* Urbana: University of Illinois Press.

Hamilton, A. 1918. "A Study of Spastic Anemia in the Hands of Stonecutters." In *Effects of Use of the Air Hammer on the Hands of Indiana Stonecutters.* Bulletin of the U.S. Bureau of Labor Statistics, Series 19, No. 236, pp. 53–66.

Hamilton, A. M. 1881. *Nervous Diseases—Their Description and Treatment.* 2nd ed. Philadelphia: Henry C. Lea.

Hammer, A. W. 1934. "Tenosynovitis." *Medical Record* (October 3): 353–355.

Hammond, G. M. 1906. "Nerves and the American Woman." *Harper's Bazar* 40:591.

Hammond, W. A. 1890. "Certain Railway Injuries of the Spine in Their Medico-Legal Relations." *Journal of the National Association of Railway Surgeons* 2 (11): 410–424.

Hardy, H. L. 1965. "Lessons in the Control of Man-Made Disease." *New England Journal of Medicine* 273 (22): 1188–1200.

——. 1983. *Challenging Man-Made Diseases: The Memoirs of Harriet L. Hardy.* New York: Praeger Press.

Hartmann, A. 1887. *Diseases of the Ear.* Trans. John Erskine. New York: G. P. Putnam's Sons.

Hawkins, J. E., Jr. 1976. "Experimental Noise Deafness: Recollections and Ruminations." In S. K. Hirsh, D. H. Eldridge, I. J. Hirsh, and S. K. Silverman (eds.), *Hearing and Davis: Essays Honoring Hallowell Davis.* St. Louis: Washington University Press, pp. 73–84.

Hayhurst, E. R. 1915. *A Survey of Industrial Health-Hazards and Occupational Diseases in Ohio*. Ohio State Board of Health. Columbus: F. J. Heer.

——. 1923. "Status of the Occupational Disease Question in Ohio, Based on Official Figures: Retrospect and Prospect." *Ohio's Health* 14:134–140. Reprinted in *Journal of Industrial Hygiene* (1924) 6 (6): 259–65.

Hedinger, A. 1882. "Die Ohrenkrankheiten des Locomotivpersonals." *Deutshe medicinische Wochenschrift* 8:63–65.

Heliövaara, M., P. Knekt, and A. Aromaa. 1987. "Incidence and Risk Factors of Herniated Lumbar Intervertebral Disc or Sciatica Leading to Hospitalization." *Journal of Chronic Disease* 40:251–85.

Helmkamp, J. C., E. O. Talbott, and H. Margolis. 1984. "Occupational Noise Exposure and Hearing Loss Characteristics of a Blue Collar Population." *Journal of Occupational Medicine* 26 (12): 885–891.

Hemenway, D., A. Killen, S. B. Cashman, C. L. Parks, and W. J. Bicknell. 1990. "Physicians' Responses to Financial Incentives: Evidence From a For-Profit Ambulatory Care Center." *New England Journal of Medicine* 322:1059–1063.

Herndon, R. F. 1927. "Back Injuries in Industrial Employees." *Journal of Bone and Joint Surgery* 9:234–269.

Hewitt, E. M., and E. M. Bedale. 1922. "A Study of the Comparative Physiological Costs of Different Methods of Weight Carrying by Women." In *Annual Report of the Chief Inspector of Factories and Workshops*. London: His Majesty's Stationery Office, pp. 106–121.

Hickson, G. B., W. A. Altemeier, and J. M. Perrin. 1987. "Physician Reimbursement by Salary or Fee-For-Service: Effect on Physician Practice Behavior in a Randomized Prospective Study." *Pediatrics* 80 (3): 344–350.

Hillman, A. L., M. V. Pauly, and J. J. Kerstein. 1989. "How Do Financial Incentives Affect Physicians' Clinical Decisions and the Financial Performance of HMOs." *New England Journal of Medicine* 321:86–92.

Hillman, B. J., C. A. Joseph, M. R. Mabry, J. H. Sunshine, S. D. Kennedy, and M. Noether. 1990. "Frequency and Costs of Diagnostic Imaging in Office Practice—A Comparison of Self-Referring and Radiologist Referring Physicians." *New England Journal of Medicine* 323:1604–1608.

Hippocrates. [c. 550 B.C.E.]. In *Works of Hippocrates,* trans. Francis Adams. New York: William Wood. (1908).

Hirt, L. 1893. *The Diseases of the Nervous System*. New York: D. Appleton.

Hlavin, M. L., and R. W. Hardy. 1993. "Clinical Diagnosis of Herniated Lumbar Disc." In R. W. Hardy (ed.), *Lumbar Disc Disease*. 2nd ed. New York: Raven Press.

Hobbs, C. W. 1939. *Workmen's Compensation Insurance*. New York: McGraw-Hill.

Hocking, B. 1987. "Epidemiological Aspects of 'Repetition Strain Injury' in Telecom Australia." *Medical Journal of Australia* 147:218–222.

Hodges, R. M. 1881. "So-Called Concussion of the Spinal Cord." *Boston Medical and Surgical Journal* 104 (16): 361–365; 104 (17): 387–389.

Hoffman, F. L. 1915. *Industrial Accident Statistics*. U.S. Bureau of Labor Statistics Bulletin No. 157. Washington, D.C.: Government Printing Office.

——. 1922. *The Problem of Dust Phthisis in the Granite-Stone Industry*. U.S. Department of Labor. Bureau of Labor Statistics Bulletin No. 293. Washington, D.C.: Government Printing Office. Reprinted in *Monthly Labor Review* 15:178–179.

Holcombe, A. N. 1911. *Public Ownership of Telephones on the Continent of Europe*. Boston: Houghton and Mifflin.

Holcombe, L. 1973. *Victorian Ladies at Work*. London: Archon Books.

Holt, E. E. 1882. "Boiler-maker's Deafness and Hearing in a Noise." *Transactions of the American Ontological Society* 3:34–44.

Hooks, J. M. 1947. *Women's Occupations Through Seven Decades*. U.S. Department of Labor Women's Bureau Bulletin No. 218. Washington, D.C.: Government Printing Office.

Hope, E. W. 1923. *Industrial Hygiene and Medicine*. London: Baillière, Tindall and Cox.

Hopkins, A. 1990. "The Social Recognition of Repetition Strain Injuries: An Australian/American Comparison." *Social Science and Medicine* 30 (3): 365–372.

House, H. P. 1957. "Methods for Conservation of Hearing." *AMA Archives of Industrial Health* 16:445–448.

Houston, P. 1989. "U.S. Officials Call Repetitive Motion Injuries an 'Epidemic.'" *Los Angeles Times*, June 7, 1989, section IV, p. 1.

Howorth, M. B. 1952. *A Textbook of Orthopedics*. Philadelphia: W. B. Saunders.

Huddleson, J. H. 1932. *Accidents, Neuroses and Compensation*. Baltimore: Williams & Wilkins.

Hueston, J. T. 1963. *Dupuytren's Contracture*. Edinburgh: E. & S. Livingstone.

Hueston, J. T., and R. Tubiana (eds.). 1986. *Dupuytren's Disease*. Edinburgh: Churchill Livingstone.

Hughes, A. G. 1928. "Jews and Gentiles." *Eugenics Review* 20:89.

Hult, L. 1954. "The Munkfors Investigation: A Study of the Frequency and Causes of the Stiff-Neck-Brachalgia and Lumbago-Sciatica Syndromes, as well as Observations on Certain Signs and Symptoms from the Dorsal Spine and the Joints of the Extremities in Industrial and Forest Workers." *Acta Orthopaedica Scandinavia* (Suppl. 16): 1–76.

Humphreys, B. V. 1958. *Clerical Unions in the Civil Service*. Oxford: Blackwell & Mott.

Hunt, J. H. 1936a. "Raynaud's Phenomenon in Workmen Using Vibrating Instruments." *Proceedings of the Royal Society of Medicine* 30:171–172.

———. 1936b. "The Raynaud Phenomenon: A Critical Review." *Quarterly Journal of Medicine* 5:399–444.

Hunt, J. R. 1911. "The Thenar and Hypothenar Types of Neural Atrophy of the Hand." *American Journal of the Medical Sciences* 141:224–241.

Hunter, D. 1962. *The Diseases of Occupation*. 3rd ed. Boston: Little, Brown.

Hunter, D., A. McLaughlin, and K. Perry. 1945. "Clinical Effects of the Use of Pneumatic Tools." *British Journal of Industrial Medicine* 2:10–15.

Hurst, A. F. 1918. "Bent Back of Soldiers." *British Medical Journal* 2:621–623.

Hutchinson, J. 1893. "A Typical and Severe Case of Raynaud's Phenomenon—Maternal Grief as Cause—Approach to the Condition of Diffuse Morphea." *Archives of Surgery* 4:177–179.

———. 1901. "Raynaud's Phenomenon." *Medical Press and Circular* 123 (16): 403–405.

Index Catalogue of the Library of the Surgeon General's Office of the U.S. Army. 1892. First Series, Volume 13. Washington, D.C.: Government Printing Office.

Ingersoll, J. M. 1919. "The Otological Work in the U.S.A. General Hospital for Head Surgery." *Transactions of the American Otological Society* 15:68–77.

Inglehart, J. 1989. "Physician Ownership of Health Care Facilities." *New England Journal of Medicine* 321:198–204.

———. 1990. "Congress Moves to Regulate Self-Referral and Physicians' Ownership of Clinical Laboratories." *New England Journal of Medicine* 322:1682–1687.

Inman, T. 1860. *On Myalgia: Its Nature, Causes and Treatment*. London: John Churchill.

International Association of Machinists. 1978. "Bad Medicine." *IAM Shoptalk* (August 1978): 4–7, and (October 1978): 7.

International Brotherhood of Boilermakers, Iron Ship Builders, Blacksmiths, Forgers and Helpers. 1954. *Deafness: The Hazard of Occupational Noise.* Kansas City.

———. 1969. *Industrial Noise Control and Hearing Conservation Program.* Kansas City.

———. 1991. *A Brief Look at Our History: 1880–1991.* Kansas City.

Ireland, D. C. R. 1988. "Psychological and Physical Aspects of Occupational Arm Pain." *Journal of Hand Surgery* 13B (1): 5–10.

———. 1992. "The Australian Experience with Cumulative Trauma Disorders." In L. H. Millender, D. S. Louis, and B. P. Simmons (eds.), *Occupational Disorders of the Upper Extremity.* New York: Churchill Livingstone, pp. 79–88.

Jarrett, M. 1917. "Psychopathic Employee." *Medicine and Surgery* 1:727.

Jensen, M. C., M. N. Brant-Zawadzki, N. Obuchowski, M. T. Modic, D. Malkasian, and J. S. Ross. 1994. "Magnetic Resonance Imaging of the Lumbar Spine in People Without Back Pain." *New England Journal of Medicine* 331 (2): 69–114.

Jepson, P. N. 1933. "Traumatic Backache." *Journal of the American Medical Association* 101 (23): 1778–1782.

Jewish Encyclopedia. 1905. "Nervous Diseases." New York: Funk and Wagnalls, 9:225–227.

Jobson, T. B. 1917. "Normal Gun Deafness." *Lancet* 2:566.

Jones, A., and L. Llewellyn. 1917. *Malingering or the Simulation of Disease.* London: Heinemann.

Jones, R. 1920. "Orthopaedic Surgery in Relation to Hospital Training." *British Medical Journal* 2:773–775.

Joughran, F. W. 1915. "The Theory of Workmen's Compensation." *Medical Record* 87: 501–503.

Joy, R. J. 1954. "The Natural Bonesetters with Special Reference to the Sweet Family of Rhode Island." *Bulletin of the History of Medicine* 28:416–441.

Keck, R. C. 1955. "Legal Aspects of Noise." *Noise Control* (May): 35–60.

Kelsey, J. L., and A. L. Golden. 1987. "Occupational and Workplace Factors." In N. M. Hadler (ed.), *Clinical Concepts in Regional Musculoskeletal Disease.* Orlando: Grune & Stratton, pp. 9–15.

Kennedy, F. 1936. "Fatigue and Noise in Industry." *New York State Journal of Medicine* 36 (24): 1927–1933.

Kerr, L. 1990. "Occupational Health: A Classic Example of Class Conflict." *Journal of Public Health Policy* 11 (1): 39–48.

Key, J. A. 1945. "Intervertebral Disc Lesions are Most Common Cause of Low Back Pain With or Without Sciatica." *Annals of Surgery* 121:534–544.

Kidner, F. C. 1933. "Industrial Backs." *Journal of the Michigan Medical Society* 32:419–428.

King, H. D. 1915. "Injuries of the Back From a Medico-Legal Standpoint." *Texas State Journal of Medicine* 2:442–445.

Kingsford, P. W. 1970. *Victorian Railwaymen: The Emergence and Growth of Railway Labor: 1830–1870.* London: Frank Cass.

Knapp, P. C. 1888. "Nervous Affections Following Injury ('Concussion of the Spine,' 'Railway Spine,' and 'Railway Brain')." *Boston Medical and Surgical Journal* 119:412–449.

Knudsen, V. O. 1939. "Ear Defenders." *National Safety News* (February): 32–68.

———. 1986. "Noise-Induced Hearing Loss." *Medical Times* 114 (1): 27–32.

Kober, G. M., and W. C. Hanson. 1916. *Diseases of Occupation and Vocational Hygiene.* Philadelphia: Blakiston.

Kocka, J. 1981. *White Collar Workers in America: 1890–1940*. London: Sage Publications.

Koetter, A. T. 1910. "Report of a Case of Rupture of the Membrana Tympani While Using a Telephone." *Medical Fortnightly* (St. Louis) 37:99–101.

Koos, E. L. 1954. *The Health of Regionsville*. New York: Columbia University Press.

Kryter, K. D. 1946. "Effects of Ear Protective Devices on the Intelligibility of Speech in Noise." *Journal of the Acoustical Society of America* 18 (2): 413–417.

Kuhn, T. 1970. *The Structure of Scientific Revolutions*. Chicago: University of Chicago Press.

Kylin, B. 1960. "Temporary Threshold Shift and Auditory Trauma Following Exposure to Steady-State Noise." *Acta Oto-Laryngologica Supplementum* 152:1–93.

Lancet Commission. 1862. "The Influence of Railway Traveling on Public Health: Report of the Commission." *Lancet* 1:15–19, 48–53, 79–84.

Landenberger, J. C. 1926. *Chronic Infectious Hypertrophic Arthritis of the Spine and its Relation to Industrial Accidents*. U.S. Department of Labor, Bureau of Labor Statistics Bulletin No. 406. Washington, D.C.: Government Printing Office.

Lapidus, P. W., and R. L. Fenton. 1952. "Stenosing Tendovaginitis at the Wrist and Fingers." *AMA Archives of Medicine* 62:475–487.

LaRocca, H., and I. Macnab. 1969. "Value of Pre-Employment Radiographic Assessment of the Lumbar Spine." *Canadian Medical Association Journal* 101:383–388.

Layet, A. E. 1875, *Encyclopédie d'Hygiène de Rochard*. Paris.

Learmouth, J. R. 1933. "The Principles of Decompression in the Treatment of Certain Diseases of the Peripheral Nerves." *Surgical Clinics of North America* 13:905–913.

Leigh, J. 1985. "Analysis of Workers' Compensation Using Data on Individuals." *Industrial Relations* 24:247–256.

Leppert, J., H. Aberg, I. Ringqvist, and S. Sörensson. 1987. "Raynaud's Phenomenon in a Female Population: Prevalence and Association with Other Conditions." *Angiology* 38:871–877.

LeVay, D. 1990. *The History of Orthopaedics*. Carnforth, England: Parthenon Publishing Group.

Levin, K. 1971. "S. Weir Mitchell: Investigations and Insights into Neurasthenia and Hysteria." *Transactions and Studies of the College of Physicians of Philadelphia* 38: 168–173.

Lewis, R. 1900. "Deafness Due to Concussion from Gun Firing." *Archives of Otology* 29:63.

Lewis, T., and G. W. Pickering. 1934. "Observations Upon Maladies In Which the Blood Supply to the Digits Ceases Intermittently or Permanently, and Upon Bilateral Gangrene of the Digits; Observations Relevant to So-called 'Raynaud's Disease.'" *Clinical Science* 1:327.

Liang, M., and A. L. Komaroff. 1982. "Roentgenograms in Primary Care Patients with Acute Low Back Pain." *Archives of Internal Medicine* 142:1108–1112.

Lichtenberg, K. 1892. "On Disturbances of Hearing in Railway Servants, With Reference to the Traveling Public." Abstract in *Journal of Laryngology and Otology* 6:121–122.

Lichtenstein, M. 1950. "San Diego County Fair Hearing Survey." *Journal of the Acoustical Society of America* 22:473–483.

Lile, S. 1920. "Lumbago as Related to Railroad Injuries," *International Journal of Surgery* 33:319–321.

Lindahl, R. 1938. "Noise in Industry." *Industrial Medicine* 7 (11): 664–669.

Llewellyn, L. L., and A. B. Jones. 1915. *Fibrositis (Gouty, Infective, Traumatic)*. New York: Rebman.

Lloyd, J. H. 1895. *The Diseases of Occupations*. London.

Locke, L. 1985. "Adapting Workers' Compensation to the Special Problems of Occupational Disease." *Harvard Environmental Law Review* 9 (2): 249–282.

"London Noise." *Sanitary Record* (London) 5:277–278.

Loriga, G. 1911. "Il lavro degli scapelli coi martelli pneumatici." *Boll Inspett Lavoro* 2:35–60.

Louis, D. S. 1992. "The Carpal Tunnel Syndrome in the Workplace." In L. H. Millender, D. S. Louis, and B. P. Simmons (eds.), *Occupational Disorders of the Upper Extremity*. New York: Churchill Livingstone, pp. 145–153.

Love, J. G. 1955. "Median Neuritis; Carpal Tunnel Syndrome; Diagnosis and Treatment." *North Carolina Medical Journal* 16:463–469.

Love, J. G., and M. N. Walsh. 1938. "Protruded Intervertebral Disks." *Journal of the American Medical Association* 3:396–400.

——. 1940. "Intra-spinal Protrusions of Intervertebral Discs." *Archives of Surgery* 40: 454–484.

Love, J. K. 1916. "Hearing in the Army." *Journal of the Royal Army Medical Corps* 27:649–651.

Lowrence, W. W. 1976. *Of Acceptable Risk*. Los Altos, Calif.: William Kaufman.

Lucire, Y. 1986. "Neurosis in the Workplace." *Medical Journal of Australia* 145:323–327.

——. 1988. "Social Iatrogenesis of the Australian Disease 'RSI.'" *Community Health Studies* 12:146–150.

Lutz, T. 1991. *American Nervousness*. Ithaca: Cornell University Press.

Lyle, D. J. 1924. "Preliminary Report on a New Method of Determination of Occupational Deafness." *Cincinnati Journal of Medicine* 5 (1): 33–35.

Macaulay, A. 1838. *A Dictionary of Medicine Designed for Popular Use*. 6th ed. Edinburgh: Adam and Charles Black.

MacFarlan, D. 1929. "History of Audiometry." *Archives of Otolaryngology* 29:514–519.

MacLeod, D. 1995. *The Ergonomics Edge: Improving Safety, Quality, and Productivity*. New York: Van Nostrand Reinhold.

MacLeod, R. 1977. "Changing Perspectives in the Social History of Science." In I. Spiegel-Rösing and D. de Solla Price (eds.), *Science, Technology and Society: A Cross-Disciplinary Perspective*. London: Sage Publications, pp. 149–195.

Macnab, I. 1971. "Negative Disc Explorations: An Analysis of Nerve Root Involvement in Sixty-Eight Patients." *Journal of Bone and Joint Surgery* 43A:891–903.

Macnab, I., and J. McCullough. 1990. *Backache*. Baltimore: Williams & Wilkins.

Maddox, B. 1977. "Women and the Switchboard." In I. de Sola Pool (ed.), *The Social Impact of the Telephone*. Cambridge, Mass.: MIT Press, pp. 262–279.

Madeja, P. C. 1991. "Cumulative Trauma Disorders." *Business Insurance* (March 11): 19.

Magnuson, P. B., and J. S. Coulter. 1921. "Workman's Backache." *International Clinics* (series 31) 4:215–253.

Magora, A., and A. Schwartz. 1976. "Relation Between the Low Back Pain Syndrome and X-Ray Findings." *Scandinavian Journal of Rehabilitation Medicine* 8:115–125.

Major, R. H. 1945. *Classic Descriptions of Disease*. 3rd ed. Springfield, Ill.: Charles C. Thomas.

Manning, C. 1930. *The Immigrant Woman and Her Job*. U.S. Department of Labor Women's Bureau Bulletin No. 74. Washington, D.C.: Government Printing Office.

Marie, P., and C. Foix. 1913. "Atrophie Isolée de l'Eminence Thénar D'origine Névritique: Rôle du Ligament Annulaire Antérieur du Carpe Dans la Pathogénie de la Lésion." *Revue Neurologique* 26:647–649.

Markowitz, G., and D. Rosner. 1989. "The Illusion of Medical Certainty: Silicosis and the

Politics of Industrial Disability: 1930–1960." *Milbank Quarterly* 67 (suppl. 2): 228–253.

Mawson, S. 1967. *Diseases of the Ear*. 2nd ed. London: Edward Arnold.

McBride, P. 1881. "Nervous Deafness." *Lancet* 2:172–174.

McCall, I. W. 1987. "Radiological Investigation of the Intervertebral Disc." In M. Jayson (ed.), *The Lumbar Spine and Back Pain*. Edinburgh: Churchill Livingstone.

McCann, W. S. 1934. "Silicosis in Rochester." *Bulletin of the Self Insurers Association* 82:1–3.

McCord, C. P. 1931. *Industrial Hygiene for Engineers and Managers*. New York: Harper and Brothers.

McKelvie, W. B. 1933. "Weavers' Deafness." *Journal of Laryngology and Otology* 48:607–608. Results of this study were first published in T. M. Legge and W. B. McKelvie. 1927. *Annual Report of the Chief Inspector of Factories and Workshops*. London: His Majesty's Stationery Office.

McKendrick, A. 1916. *Back Injuries and Their Significance*. New York: William Wood.

———. 1927. *Medico-Legal Injuries*. London: Edward Arnold.

McKensie, D. 1916. *The City of Din: A Tirade Against Noise*. London: Adlard.

Mendelson, G. 1984. "Compensation, Pain Complaints, and Psychological Disturbance." *Pain* 20:169–177.

Mester, A. F., and S. D. G. Stephens. 1984. "Development of the Audiometer and Audiometry." *Audiology* 23:206–214.

Mettert, M. T. 1941. *The Occurrence and Prevention of Occupational Diseases Among Women*. U.S. Department of Labor. Women's Bureau Report No. 184. Washington, D.C.: Government Printing Office, pp. 18–19.

Middleton, G. S., and J. H. Teacher. 1911. "Injury of the Spinal Cord Due To Rupture of an Intervertebral Disc Due To Muscular Effort." *Glasgow Medical Journal* 76:1–6.

Milford, L. 1988. *The Hand*. 3rd ed. St. Louis: C. V. Mosby.

Millar, J. D. 1991. Presentation at the conference "A National Strategy for Occupational Musculoskeletal Injury Prevention—Implementation Issues and Research Needs." Sponsored by NIOSH and the University of Michigan's Center for Occupational Health and Safety Engineering, Ann Arbor (May 1991).

Miller, M. H. 1972. *Hearing Aids*. Indianapolis: Bobbs-Merrill.

Mitchell, B. R. 1988. *British Historical Statistics*. Cambridge: Cambridge University Press.

Mitchell, J., and E. Scott. 1992. "Physician Self-Referral: Empirical Evidence and Policy Implications." *Advances in Health Economics and Health Services Research* 13:27–42.

Mitchell, S. W. 1887. *Doctor and Patient*. Philadelphia: J. B. Lippincott.

Mitchie, H. C. 1924. "Deafness: A New Method for the Determination of Defective Hearing." *Military Surgeon* 55:49–61.

Mixter, W. J. 1949. "Rupture of the Intervertebral Disk. A Short History of its Evolution as a Syndrome of Importance to the Surgeon." *Journal of the American Medical Association* 140 (3): 278–282.

Mixter, W. J., and J. S. Barr. 1934. "Rupture of the Intervertebral Disc with Involvement of the Spinal Canal." *New England Journal of Medicine* 211 (8): 210–215.

Mixter, W. J., and J. B. Ayer. 1935. "Herniation or Rupture of the Intervertebral Disc into the Spinal Canal." *New England Journal of Medicine* 213 (9): 385–393.

Mock, H. E. 1919. *Industrial Medicine and Surgery*. Philadelphia: W. B. Saunders.

Mockapetris, A. M., and F. C. Craigie. 1986. "Patient Requests in a Family Practice Setting." *Family Practice Research Journal* 5 (4): 216–225.

Moersch, F. P. 1938. "Median Thenar Neuritis." *Proceedings of Staff Meetings, Mayo Clinic* 13 (April 6): 220–222.

Moos, S. 1880. "On the Diseases of the Ear in Locomotive Engineers and Fireman Which May Endanger the Traveling Public." *Archives of Otology* 9:319–329. Originally published in German; "Ueber die Ohrenkrankheiten der Locomotivführer und Heizer, welche sociale Gefahren in sich bergen." *Zeitschrift für Ohrenheilkunde* 9:370–383.

Moos, S., H. Pollnow, and D. Schwabach. 1882. *Die Gehörsstörungen des Locomotivpersonals und deren Einfluss auf die Betriebssicherheit der Eisenbahnen.* (Hearing difficulties of railway personnel and their influence on railway operating safety.) Zweiter Abdruck. Wiesbaden: Verlag von J. F. Bergmann.

Mosely, L. H., R. M. Kalafut, P. L. Levinson, and S. A. Mokris. 1991. "Management of Carpal Tunnel Syndrome." In M. L. Kasdan (ed.), *Occupational Hand & Upper Extremity Injuries and Diseases.* Philadelphia: Hanley & Belfus, pp. 353–402.

Moses, J. A. 1982. *Trade Unionism in Germany from Bismarck to Hitler: 1869–1933.* Totowa, N.J.: Barnes & Noble.

Murray, J. P., S. Greenfield, S. H. Kaplan, and E. M. Yano. 1992. "Ambulatory Testing for Capitation and Fee-for-Service Patients in the Same Practice Setting." *Medical Care* 30:252–261.

Murray, P. 1949. *The Steelworkers' Case for Wages, Pensions and Social Insurance.* Presentation to President Truman's Steel Industry Board. United Steelworkers of America.

Myerson, A. 1920. *The Nervous Housewife.* Boston: Little, Brown.

Nash, C. S. 1952. "Industrial Loss of Hearing: Medical Aspects." In *The Acoustical Spectrum: Sound—Wanted and Unwanted.* Ann Arbor: The University of Michigan Press, pp. 167–169.

National Council on Compensation Insurance. 1993. *Workers' Compensation Back Claim Study.* Boca Raton, Fla.: National Council on Compensation Insurance.

National Health and Medical Research Council. 1982. *Approved Occupational Health Guide. Repetition Strain Injuries.* Canberra, Australia: Commonwealth Department of Health.

National Industrial Conference Board. 1923. *Workman's Compensation Acts in the United States: The Medical Aspect.* Research Report No. 61. New York.

National Institute for Occupational Safety and Health. 1972. *Criteria for a Recommended Standard—Occupational Exposure to Noise.* Report No. HSM 73–110001. Washington, D.C.: U.S. Government Printing Office.

———. 1981. *Work Practices Guide for Manual Lifting.* DHHS Publication 81–122. Cincinnati, Ohio.

———. 1983. *Vibration Syndrome.* Current Intelligence Bulletin No. 38. NIOSH Publication 83–110. Cincinnati, Ohio.

Naylor, A. 1990. "Historical Perspective." In J. N. Weinstein and S. W. Wiesel (eds.), *The Lumbar Spine.* Philadelphia: W. B. Saunders, pp. 1–31.

Needleman, C. 1987. *Science, Technology and Human Values* 12:20–25.

Nehrend, M. 1923. "Status of the Physician in Relation to the Compensation Law." *Pennsylvania Medical Journal* (February): 324–326.

Nelson, H. A. 1954. "Industrial Noise and Occupational Deafness." *Laryngoscope* 64 (7): 568–579.

Newmeyer, W. L. 1988. "Vascular Disorders." In D. P. Green (ed.), *Operative Hand Surgery.* 2nd ed. New York: Churchill Livingstone, p. 2421.

New York State Department of Health. 1930. *Effect of Noise on Hearing of Industrial Workers.* Special Bulletin No. 166. Bureau of Women in Industry. Albany.

New York State Department of Labor. 1926. *Compensated Accidents July, 1914–June, 1922*. Special Bulletin No. 142. Bureau of Statistics and Information. Albany.

———. 1930. *City Noise: The Report of the Commission Appointed by Dr. Shirley W. Wynne, Commissioner of Health, to Study Noise in New York City, and to Develop Means of Abating it*. New York City: Noise Abatement Commission.

———. 1941. *Causes of Compensated Accidents: Four Years, 1936, 1937, 1938, 1939*. Division of Statistics and Information, Special Bulletin No. 210. Albany.

New York State Legislative Report. 1911. *Causes and Prevention of Industrial Accidents*. Albany: J. B. Lyon Company.

"Noise is News." 1953. *Modern Industry* (February 15): 48–52.

Norwood, S. H. 1990. *Labor's Flaming Youth: Telephone Operators and Worker Militancy, 1878–1923*. Urbana: University of Illinois Press.

Notta, A. 1850. "Recherches sur une affection particulière des gaînes tendineuses de la main, caractérisée par le développement d'une nodosité sur le trajet des tendons fléchisseurs des doigts et par l'empêchement de leurs mouvements." *Archives Générales de Médicine* (series 4) 24:142–161.

Nugent, A. 1987. "The Power to Define a New Disease: Epidemiological Politics and Radium Poisoning." In D. Rosner and G. Markowitz (eds.), *Dying for Work: Workers' Safety and Health in Twentieth-Century America*. Bloomington: Indiana University Press, pp. 177–191.

O'Connell, J. E. A. 1943. "Sciatica and the Mechanism of the Production of the Clinical Syndrome in Protrusion of the Lumbar Intervertebral Discs." *British Journal of Surgery* 30:315–327.

Ohio Health News. 1934. Vol 10 (May 1): 2.

Ohsfeldt, R. 1993. "Contractural Arrangements, Financial Incentives, and Physician-Patient Relationships." In J. Clair and R. Allman (eds.), *Sociomedical Perspectives on Patient Care*. Lexington: University Press of Kentucky, pp. 96–113.

Oliver, T. 1916. *Occupations: From the Social, Hygenic and Medical Points of View*. Cambridge: Cambridge University Press.

Onimus, E. 1876. "On Professional Muscular Atrophy." *Lancet* 1:127–128.

Onimus, M. 1875. "Le Mal Télégraphique ou Crampe Télégraphique." *Gazette Médicale de Paris*, p. 175.

Oppenheim, H. 1889. *Die traumatischen Neurosen nach den in der Nervenklinik der Charité in den letzen 5 Jahren, gesammelten Beobachtungen bearbeitet und dargestellt von Dr. Med. Her. Oppenheim, Docent an der Universität*. Berlin: Verlag von Hirschwald.

Oppenheimer, L. S. 1884. "Lumbago: Its Causes and Treatment." *Louisville Medical News* 17 (5): 65–66.

Osgood, R. B. 1919. "Back Strain—An Accident or a Disease." *Journal of Industrial Hygiene* 1:150–157.

Osgood, R. B., and L. B. Morrison. 1924. "The Problem of the Industrial Lame Back." *Boston Medical and Surgical Journal* 191 (9): 381–391.

Osler, W. 1892. *The Principles and Practice of Medicine*. New York: D. Appleton. 3rd ed. (1898), 5th ed. (1902), 6th ed. (1906), 8th ed. (1914).

Osnato, M. 1925. "Industrial Neuroses." *American Journal of Psychiatry* 5:11.

Otis, L. H. 1990. "Carpal Not Occupational, Doctor Says." *National Underwriter* 94 (October 9): 9, 38.

Outten, W. B. 1890. "A Statistical Study of Nine Thousand Three Hundred and Forty-Eight Railway Injuries." *Journal of the National Association of Railway Surgeons* 3:14–36.

Padilla, M. 1981. "Why Some Workers Resent Wearing Earplugs." *Occupational Health and Safety* (January): 6–7.

Page, H. W. 1883. *Injuries of the Spine and Spinal Cord Without Apparent Mechanical Lesion and Nervous Shock in their Surgical and Medico-Legal Aspects.* London: J. & A. Churchill.

Palmer, L. R. 1926. "History of the Safety Movement." *Annals of the American Academy of Political and Social Science* 123:9–19.

Parry, C. H. 1825. *Collections from the Unpublished Medical Writings of the Late C. H. Parry.* Vol 1. London: Underwood.

Parsons, F. 1919. "War Neuroses." *Atlantic Monthly* 123:335.

Pauley, M. V., A. L. Hillman, and J. J. Kerstein. 1990. "Managing Physician Incentives in Managed Care: The Role of For-Profit Ownership." *Medical Care* 28:1013–1024.

Pecora, L. J., M. Udel, and R. P. Christman. 1960. "Survey of Current Status of Raynaud's Phenomenon of Occupational Origin." *American Industrial Hygiene Journal* 21:80–83.

Pedley, F. C. 1930. "The Incidence of Occupational Deafness and Methods for Its Prevention." *Safety Engineering* (October): 237–241.

Perkin, H. 1970. *The Age of the Railway.* London: David & Charles.

Perry, C. R. 1977. "The British Experience 1876–1912: The Impact of the Telephone During the Years of Delay." In I. de Sola Pool (ed.), *The Social Impact of the Telephone.* Cambridge, Mass.: MIT Press, pp. 69–96.

Pfeffer, G. B., and R. H. Gelberman. 1987. "The Carpal Tunnel Syndrome." In N. M. Hadler (ed.), *Clinical Concepts in Regional Musculoskeletal Illness.* Orlando: Grune & Stratton, pp. 201–215.

Phalen, G. S. 1951. "Spontaneous Compression of the Median Nerve at the Wrist." *Journal of the American Medical Association* 145:1128–1132.

———. 1966. "The Carpal Tunnel Syndrome: Seventeen Years' Experience in Diagnosis and Treatment of Six Hundred Fifty-Four Hands." *Journal of Bone and Joint Surgery* 48A (2): 211–228.

———. 1972. "The Carpal Tunnel Syndrome." *Clinical Orthopaedics* 83:29–40.

Phalen, G. S., and J. I. Kendrick. 1957. "Compression Neuropathy of the Median Nerve in the Carpal Tunnel." *Journal of the American Medical Association* 5:524–530.

Pheasant, H. C., and P. Dyck. 1982. "Failed Lumbar Disc Surgery: Cause, Assessment and Treatment." *Clinical Orthopaedics and Related Research* 164:93–109.

Pickard, O. G. 1955. "Clerical Workers and the Trade Unions." *British Management Review* 13 (2): 102–120.

Pierce, F. M. 1879. "The Telephone and Diseases of the Ear." *British Medical Journal* 2:162.

Pike, E. R. 1969. *"Busy Times": Human Documents of the Age of the Forsytes.* New York: Praeger Publishers.

Platt, H. 1959. "British Orthopaedic Association: First Founders' Lecture." *Journal of Bone and Joint Surgery* 41B:231–236.

Politzer, A. 1883. *A Textbook of the Diseases of the Ear.* Philadelphia: Henry C. Lea.

Pollnow, H. 1882. "Noch einmal die Ohrenkrankheiten der Locomotivführer und Heizer." In S. Moos, S. H. Pollnow, and D. Schwabach. 1882. *Die Gehörsstörungen des Locomotivpersonals und deren Einfluss auf die Betriebssicherheit der Eisenbahnen.* Zweiter Abdruck. Wiesbaden: Verlag von J. F. Bergmann.

Pollock, L. J. 1922. "The Neuroses and the Industrial Commission." *Nation's Health* 4:40–42.

Poole, C. J. 1993. "Seamstress's Finger." *British Journal of Industrial Medicine* 50 (7): 668–669.

Poore, G. V. 1872. "On a Case of Writer's Cramp, and Subsequent General Spasm of the Right Arm, Treated by the Joint Use of the Continuous Galvanic Current and the Rhythmical Exercise of the Affected Muscles." *Practitioner* 9:129–137.

———. 1873. "Writer's Cramp: Its Pathology and Treatment." *Practitioner* 40:341–350; 41:1–12, 84–99.

———. 1897. *Nervous Affections of the Hand*. London: Smith, Elder.

———. 1899. "Craft Palsies." In W. Pepper (ed.), *A Textbook of the Theory and Practice of Medicine*." Vol. 1. Philadelphia: W. B. Saunders, pp. 651–654.

Potton, G. 1851. "Researches and Observations on the 'Mal de Vers' or 'Mal de Bassine.'" *Bulletin de l'Académie de Médicale* 17:803.

Powell, P., M. Hale, J. Martin, and M. Simon. 1971. *2000 Accidents: A Shop Floor Study of Their Causes Based on 42 Months' Observation*. London: National Institute of Industrial Psychology, pp. 83–88.

Praemer, A., S. Furner, and D. P. Rice. 1992. *Musculoskeletal Conditions in the United States*. Park Ridge, Ill.: American Academy of Orthopaedic Surgeons.

Prince, H. L. 1937. "The Compensation Aspects of Low Back Pain." *Journal of Bone and Joint Surgery* 19 (3): 805–809.

Proceedings of the National Safety Council. 1923. Twelfth Annual Safety Congress, Chicago, Oct. 1–5, 1923.

Putnam, J. J. 1880. "A Series of Paræsthesia, Mainly of the Hands, of Periodical Recurrence, and Possibly of Vaso-Motor Origin." *Archives of Medicine* 4:147–162.

Putz-Anderson, V. (ed.) 1988. *Cumulative Trauma Disorders: A Manual for Musculoskeletal Diseases of the Upper Limbs*. National Institute for Occupational Safety and Health. Philadelphia: Taylor & Francis.

Quain, R. 1888. *A Dictionary of Medicine*. London: Longmans, Green.

Quinet, R. J., and N. M. Hadler. 1979. "Diagnosis and Treatment of Backache." *Seminars in Arthritis and Rheumatism* 8 (4): 261–287.

Quintner, J. L. 1991. "The RSI Syndrome in Historical Perspective." *International Disability Studies* 13 (3): 99–104.

Rabinbach, A. 1990. *The Human Motor*. Berkeley: University of California Press.

Radcliffe, C. B. 1868. *Reynolds' System of Medicine*, Vol. II. Philadelphia: Lippincott

Ralston, C. E. 1922. "Handling Material." *Proceedings of the National Safety Council*, August 28–September 1, pp. 185–192.

Ramazzini, B. 1713. *De Morbis Artificum (Diseases of Workers)*. Trans. W. C. Wright. Chicago: University of Chicago Press (1940).

Rankin, D. 1925. "Occupational Diseases of the Nose, Throat, and Ear." *British Medical Journal* 2:891–892.

Ratloff, J. 1982. "Occupational Noise—The Subtle Pollutant." *Science News* 121:347–349.

Rayer, P. F. O. 1827. *Traité théoretique et practique des maladies de la peau*. Paris 1826–27. English trans. 1835.

Raynaud, M. 1862. "De l'asphyxie locale et de la gangrène symétrique des extrémités." Paris: Rignoux. Trans. by T. Barlow (1888) *Collected Monographs*. Vol. 121. London: New Sydenham Society.

Rehfeldt, F. C. 1966. "So-Called Ruptured Disc." Paper presented to the Texas Surgical Society, January 1966.

Rempel, D. M., R. J. Harrison, and S. Barnhart. 1992. "Work-Related Cumulative Trauma Disorders of the Upper Extremity." *Journal of the American Medical Association* 267 (6): 838–842.

Renner, M. 1992. "Repetitive Motion Injuries Drive Up Workers Comp Costs." *Journal of Commerce* (July 7): 4.

Report of the Committee of Medical Officers. 1911. "Conditions of Working of Telephonists." London: His Majesty's Stationery Office.

Report of the Departmental Committee on Telegraphists' Cramp. 1911. London: His Majesty's Stationery Office.

Report of the Joint International Executive Council to the Nineteenth Consolidated Convention of the International Brotherhood of Boilermakers, Iron Ship Builders and Helpers of America and International Brotherhood of Blacksmiths, Drop Forgers and Helpers. 1954. Kansas City.

Richardson, B. W. 1879. "Some Researches with Professor Hughes' New Instrument for the Measurement of Hearing: The Audiometer." *Proceedings of the Royal Society of Medicine* 29:65–70.

Richardson, C. W. 1918. "Ear Protectors." *Transactions of the American Otological Society* 14 (Part 1): 525–542.

Ridout, G. B. 1930. "Gunfire Deafness in the Navy." *U.S. Naval Medical Bulletin* 28:736–739.

Rigler, J. 1879. *Ueber die Folgen der Verletzungen auf Eisenbahnen, insbesondere der Verletzungen des Rückenmarks,* Berlin.

Robertson, L., and J. Keeve. 1983. "The Effect of Workers' Compensation and OSHA Inspections." *Health Politics, Policy and Law* 8:581–597.

Robinson, E. 1882. "Cases of Telegraphists' Cramp." *British Medical Journal* 2:880.

Robinson, J. S. 1983. "Sciatica and the Lumbar Disk Syndrome: A Historic Perspective." *Southern Medical Journal* 76 (2): 232–238.

Rockwell, A. D., and G. M. Beard. 1871. *A Practical Treatice on the Medical and Surgical Uses of Electricity.* New York: William Wood.

Rogers, F. T. 1915. "A Study of the Workmen's Compensation Act as it Affects Rhode Island Physicians." *Providence Medical Journal* 16:71–85.

Rom, W. N. (ed.). 1992. *Environmental and Occupational Medicine.* Boston: Little, Brown.

Romberg, M. H. 1853. *A Manual of the Nervous Diseases in Man.* Trans. and ed. E. H. Sieveking. London: Sydenham Society.

———. 1860. *Nervenkrankheiten.* Berlin.

Roosa, D. B. 1874. "A Contribution to the Etiology of Diseases of the Internal Ear." *American Journal of Medical Sciences* 68:377–400.

———. 1885. *Diseases of the Ear.* New York: William Wood.

Röpke, F. 1902. *Die Berufskrankheiten des Ohres und der oberen Luftwege.* Weisbaden: J. F. Bergmann.

Rosen, G. 1940. "The Miner's Elbow." *Bulletin of the History of Medicine* 8 (1): 1249–1251.

———. 1942. "The Worker's Hand." *Ciba Symposia* (July): 1307–1318.

———. 1943. *The History of Miners' Diseases: A Medical and Social Interpretation.* New York: Schuman's.

———. 1947. "What is Social Medicine?" *Bulletin of the History of Medicine* 21:674–733.

Rosenberg, C. 1992. *Explaining Epidemics and Other Studies in the History of Medicine.* Cambridge: Cambridge University Press.

Rosenthal, M. 1879. *A Clinical Treatise on the Diseases of the Nervous System.* New York: William Wood.

Rosner, D., and G. Markowitz. 1987a. "'A Gift of God'?: The Public Health Controversy over Leaded Gasoline During the 1920s." In D. Rosner and G. Markowitz (eds.), *Dying for Work: Workers' Safety and Health in Twentieth-Century America.* Bloomington, Indiana: Indiana University Press, pp. 121–139.

——. 1991. *Deadly Dust: Silicosis and the Politics of Occupational Disease in Twentieth-Century America.* Princeton: Princeton University Press.

Routh, G. 1966. "White-Collar Unions in the United Kingdom." In A. Sturmthal (ed.), *White-Collar Trade Unions.* Urbana: University of Illinois Press, pp. 165–185.

Rowe, M. L. 1969. "Low Back Pain in Industry; A Position Paper." *Journal of Occupational Medicine* 11 (4): 161–169.

——. 1983. *Backache at Work.* Fairport, N.Y.: Perinton Press.

Royster, L. H., and S. R. Holder. 1981. "Personal Hearing Protection: Problems Associated With the Hearing Protection Phase of the Hearing Conservation Program." In P. W. Alberti (ed.), *Personal Hearing Protection in Industry.* New York: Raven Press, pp. 447–470.

Rubinow, I. M. 1913. *Social Insurance.* New York: Henry Holt.

Russell, R. D. 1934. "Detection of Simulated Deafness." *Laryngoscope* 44:201–210.

Saal, J. A., and J. S. Saal. 1989. "Nonoperative Treatment of Herniated Lumbar Intervertebral Disc with Radiculopathy." *Spine* 14:431–437.

Sabine, P. E. 1944. "The Problem of Industrial Noise." *American Journal of Public Health* 34:265–270.

Sachs, R. 1905. "The Hearing Power of Railroad Employees." *Archiv für Ohrenheilkunde* (July). Abstract in *Laryngoscope* 19 (3): 216 (1909).

Sagen, L. A. 1982. "Workers' Compensation for Occupational Illness: A Case Study." In J. S. Lee and W. N. Rom (eds.), *Legal and Ethical Dilemmas in Occupational Health.* Ann Arbor: Ann Arbor Science Press, pp. 277–301.

Sataloff, J. 1984. "WC Hearing Loss Claims Should Be Handled With Care." *Occupational Safety and Health* (March): 35–41.

Sataloff, J., and P. Michael. 1973. *Hearing Conservation.* Springfield, Ill.: Charles C. Thomas.

Sataloff, R. T., and J. Sataloff. 1987. *Occupational Hearing Loss.* New York: Marcel Dekker.

——. 1993. *Hearing Loss.* 3rd ed. New York: Marcel Dekker.

Sayer, H. D. 1934. "Occupational Diseases—What It Means To Employers and the Administrators of the Law." *Bulletin of the Self Insurers Association* 82:4–6.

Schaefer, K. L., and G. Gruschke. 1921. "Über einen neuen elektro-akustischen Apparat zur Hörschärfenmessung mittels einer kontinuierlichen Tonreihe." *Passow-Schaefers Beitr. Hals-Nas.-Ohrenheilk* 16:56–61.

Schenck, R. R. 1987. "Current Treatment of Carpal Tunnel Syndrome: Survey Results." Presented at the Seventeenth Annual Meeting of the American Association for Hand Surgery, San Juan, Puerto Rico, Nov. 4–8, 1987.

Schivelbusch, W. 1986. *The Railway Journey; The Industrialization of Time and Space in the Nineteenth Century.* Berkeley: University of California Press.

Schmorl, G. 1929. "Über Knorpelknötchen an der Hinterfläche der Wirbelbandscheiben." *Fortschr. a. d. Geb. d. Roentgenstralen* 40:629–634.

Schneider, C. C. 1928. "Stenosing Fibrous Tendovaginitis Over Radial Styloid (De Quervain)." *Surgery, Gynecology and Obstetrics* 46:846–850.

Schneider, W. R. 1959. *Schneider's Workmen's Compensation.* Supplemental Text Vol. III. St. Louis: Thomas Law.

Schwab, S. 1911. "Neurasthenia Among Garment Workers." *American Labor Legislation Review* 1:27.

Schwabach, D., and H. Pollnow. 1881. "Die Ohrenkrankheiten der Locomotivführer und Heizer." *Zeitschrift für Ohrenheilkunde* 10:201–221.

Scott, V. T. 1923. "Airplane Deafness and Its Prevention." *Military Surgeon* 52:300–301.

Seashore, C. E. 1899. "An Audiometer." *University of Iowa Studies in Psychology* 2:158–163.

Seely, A. C. 1910. "Importance of Ear, Eye, Nose and Throat Examinations With Railway Service." *California State Journal of Medicine* 8:45–47.

Select Committee of the House of Lords on the Sweating System. 1890. Fifth Report. Vol. 17, pp. xxv–xxxi.

Semmes, R. E. 1964. *Ruptures of the Lumbar Intervertebral Disc, Their Mechanism, Diagnosis, and Treatment*. Springfield, Ill.: Charles C. Thomas.

Sever, J. W. 1919. "The Value of Diagnosis in Back Lesions." *Bulletin of the U.S. Bureau of Labor Statistics No. 248*. Washington, D.C.: Government Printing Office.

———. 1923. "Diagnosis of Industrial Back Conditions." *Bulletin of the U.S. Bureau of Labor Statistics No. 333*. Washington, D.C.: Government Printing Office.

———. 1925. "Backache Due to Industry and Disease." *Boston Medical and Surgical Journal* 192 (14): 647–658.

Seyring, M. 1930. "Erkrankungen durch Arbeit mit Pressluftwerkzeugen." *Arch. Gewerbepath. Gewerbehyg.* 1:359–375.

Shambaugh, G. E., Jr. 1953. "Noise Deafness." *Factory Management and Maintenance* 3 (12): 118–120.

Shipley, L. B. 1985. "Hearing Loss Comp Becoming Today's Major Industry Issue." *National Safety and Health News* (July): 35–38.

Showalter, E. 1985. *The Female Malady: Women, Madness, and English Culture, 1830–1980*. New York: Pantheon Books.

Sicard, J. A., and J. Forestier. 1922. "Méthode Radiographique d'exploration de la Cavité Epidurale par le Lipiodol." *Revue Neurologique* 37:1264–1266.

Sicherman, B. 1977. "The Uses of a Diagnosis: Doctors, Patients, and Neurasthenia." *Journal of the History of Medicine* 32:33–54.

Silman, A., S. Holligan, P. Brennan, and P. Maddison. 1990. "Prevalence of Symptoms of Raynaud's Phenomenon in General Practice." *British Medical Journal* 301:590–592.

Silverstein, B. A., L. J. Fine, and D. Stetson. 1987. "Hand-Wrist Disorders Among Investment Casting Plant Workers." *Journal of Hand Surgery* 12:838–844.

Silverstein, B. A., L. J. Fine, and T. J. Armstrong. 1987. "Occupational Factors and Carpal Tunnel Syndrome." *American Journal of Industrial Medicine* 11:343–358.

Slovic, P. 1987. "Perception of Risk." *Science* 236:280–285.

Smith, B. E. 1981. "Black Lung: The Social Production of Disease." *International Journal of Health Services* 11 (3): 343–359.

———. 1987. *Digging Our Own Graves: Coal Miners and the Struggle Over Black Lung Disease*. Philadelphia: Temple University Press.

Smith, E. W., D. Sonstegard, and W. Anderson. 1977. "Carpal Tunnel Syndrome: Contribution of the Flexor Tendons." *Arch. Phys. Med. Rehabil.* 58:379–385.

Smith, M., M. Culpin, and E. Farmer. 1927. *A Study of Telegraphist's Cramp*. Medical Research Council Industrial Fatigue Research Board Report No. 43. London: His Majesty's Stationery Office, pp. 32–36.

Smith-Rosenberg, C. 1972. "The Hysterical Women: Sex Roles and Role Conflict in 19th-Century America." *Social Research* 39:652–678.

Smith-Rosenberg, C., and C. Rosenberg. 1981. "The Female Animal: Medical and Biological Views of Woman and Her Role in Nineteenth-Century America." In A. L. Caplan,

H. T. Englehardt, Jr., and J. J. McCartney (eds.), *Concepts of Health and Disease: Interdisciplinary Perspectives*. Reading, Mass.: Addison-Wesley, pp. 281–303.

Snook, S. H. 1982. "Low Back Pain in Industry." In A. A. White, 3rd, and S. L. Gordon (eds.), *American Academy of Orthopedic Surgeons Symposium on Idiopathic Low Back Pain*. St. Louis: C. V. Mosby, pp. 23–37.

——. 1988. "Approaches to the Control of Back Pain in Industry: Job Design, Job Placement and Education/Training." In R. A. Deyo (ed.), *Back Pain in Workers; Occupational Medicine: State of the Art Reviews*. Philadelphia: Hanley & Belfus, 3 (1): 45–59.

Solly, S. 1864. "Scriveners' Palsy, or the Paralysis of Writers (Lecture I)." *Lancet* 2:709–711.

——. 1867. "On Scriveners' Palsy." *Lancet* 1:561–562.

Somers, H. M., and A. R. Somers. 1954. *Workmen's Compensation: Prevention, Insurance, and Rehabilitation of Occupational Disability*. New York: John Wiley.

Southard, E. E., and H. C. Solomon. 1916. "Occupation Neuroses." In G. M. Kober and W. C. Hanson (eds.), *Diseases of Occupation and Vocational Hygiene*. Philadelphia: Blakiston.

Spangfort, E. V. 1972. "The Lumbar Disc Herniation—A Computer-Aided Analysis of 2504 Operations." *Acta Orthopaedica Scandinavica* (Suppl. 142): 1–95.

Spieler, E. A. 1994. "Perpetuating Risk? Workers' Compensation and the Persistence of Occupational Injuries." *Houston Law Review* 31:119–264.

Spitzka, A. 1883. "Spinal Injuries as a Basis of Litigation." *American Journal of Neurology and Psychology* 2:540–560.

Stander, I. 1979. "Occupational Hearing Loss." *Pennsylvania Law Journal* (December 10).

Stark, H. S. 1915. "The Physician's Interests in the Workmen's Compensation Law." *Medical Record* 87:567–568.

State of California. 1919. *Report of the Industrial Accident Commission*. San Francisco.

Stein, H. C. 1927. "Stenosing Tendovaginitis." *American Journal of Surgery* 3 (1): 77–78.

Stein, S. 1899. "Functional Investigation of Locomotive Hearing and Signal Hearing." *Northern Medical Archives*. Abstract in *Laryngoscope* 8 (6): 379–380 (1900).

Steinberg, J. C., H. C. Montgomery, and M. B. Gardner. 1940. "Results of the World's Fair Hearing Tests." *Journal of the Acoustical Society of America* 12:291–301.

Stephens, S. D. G., and J. C. Goodwin. 1984. "Non-electric Aids to Hearing: A Short History." *Audiology* 23:215–240.

Stevens, S. S., and L. L. Beranek. 1943. *The Acoustic Performance of Various Ear Plugs*. Harvard University Psycho-Acoustic Laboratory Research Report, August 23, 1943.

Stockman, R. 1920. *Rheumatism and Arthritis*. Edinburgh: W. Green.

Stone, D. A. 1979. "Diagnosis and the Dole: The Function of Illness in American Distributive Politics." *Journal of Health Politics, Policy and Law* 4 (3): 507–521.

——. 1984. *The Disabled State*. Philadelphia: Temple University Press.

Strains and Sprains: A Worker's Guide to Job Design. 1982. Detroit: United Auto Workers.

Strümpell, A. 1893. *A Textbook of Medicine*. New York: D. Appleton.

Sumers, T. O. 1896. "Railway Neurasthenia." *Alabama Medical and Surgical Age* 8:573–580.

Swann, C. C. 1933. "Effects of Noise on Hearing." *International Journal of Medicine and Surgery* 46:314–315.

Syme, J. 1867. "On Compensation for Railway Injuries." *Lancet* 1:2.

Symons, N. S. 1951. "A Lawyer Looks at the Industrial Noise Problem." *Proceedings of the Second Annual Noise Abatement Symposium* (October 5): 42–63.

——. 1952. "Trends in Compensation Attitudes." In *The Acoustical Spectrum: Sound—Wanted and Unwanted*. Ann Arbor: University of Michigan Press, pp. 170–182.

——. 1953. "Industrial Noise: Legal Problems." *Factory Management and Maintenance* 3 (12): 114–117.

Tanzer, R. L. 1959. "The Carpal Tunnel Syndrome; A Clinical and Anatomical Study." *Journal of Bone and Joint Surgery* 41A:626–634.

Task Force Report. 1985. *Repetition Strain Injury in the Australian Public Service*. Canberra: Australian Government Publishing Service.

Teleky, L. 1927. "Pneumatic Tools." In *Occupation and Health Supplement*. Geneva: International Labor Office.

Telford, E. D., M. B. McCann, and D. H. MacCormack. 1945. " 'Dead Hand' in Users of Vibrating Tools." *Lancet* 2:359–362.

Thackrah, C. T. 1832. *The Effects of Arts, Trades, and Professions on Health and Longevity*. Rpt. Canton, Mass.: Science History Publications (1985).

Thompson, H. T., and J. Sinclair. 1912. "Telegraphist's Cramp." *Lancet* 1:888–890, 941–944, 1008–1010.

Thorburn, W. 1888. "On Traumatic Hysteria, Especially in Relation to Railway Accidents." *Medical Chronicle of Manchester* 9:198–265.

Tichauer, E. R. 1966. "Some Aspects of Stress on Forearm and Hand in Industry." *Journal of Occupational Medicine* 2:63–71.

——. 1976. "Biomechanics Sustains Occupational Safety and Health." *Industrial Engineering* 2:46–56.

——. 1978. *The Biomechanical Basis of Ergonomics*. New York: John Wiley.

Tichauer, E. R., and H. Gage. 1977. "Ergonomic Principles Basic to Hand Tool Design." *American Industrial Hygiene Journal* 38:622–632.

Torgeson, W. R., and E. E. Dotler. 1976. "Comparative Roentgenographic Study of the Asymptomatic and Symptomatic Lumbar Spine." *Journal of Bone and Joint Surgery* 58A:850–853.

Toynbee, J. 1860. *Diseases of the Ear*. London: Churchill.

Trattner, W. I. 1984. *From Poor Law to Welfare State: A History of Social Welfare in America*. New York: The Free Press.

Tremble, G. E. 1930. "The Value of the Audiometer in Industrial Medicine." *Canadian Medical Association Journal* 22:71–75.

Trétôp, d'A. 1914. "Troubles auditifs d'origine téléphonique." *Presse otolaryngol. belge.* 13:275.

Trible, G. B. 1917. "Comparative Hearing Requirements in Foreign and American Navies." *Military Surgeon* 40:33–36.

Trible, G. B., and S. S. Watkins. 1919. "Ear Protection." *U.S. Naval Medical Bulletin* 13:48–60.

Troena, F. 1933. "Changes in Hearing in Air Pilots: Statistical Study." *Valsalva* 9:337.

Tucker, D. G. 1978. "Electrical Communication." In T. I. Williams (ed)., 1978. *A History of Technology*. Vol. VII. Oxford: Clarendon Press, pp. 1220–1267.

Tunturi, T., and H. Pätiälä. 1980. "Social Factors Associated with Lumbo-sacral Fusion." *Scandinavian Journal of Rehabilitation Medicine* 12:17–23.

Turner, C. E. 1939. "Industrial Health Education and the Promotion of the Health and Effectiveness of the Worker." In A. J. Lanza and J. A. Goldberg (eds.), *Industrial Hygiene*. New York: Oxford University Press.

U.S. Centers for Disease Control. 1986. "Leading Work-Related Diseases and Injuries—United States." *Morbidity and Mortality Weekly Review* 35:12.

——. 1988. "Self-Reported Hearing Loss Among Workers Potentially Exposed to Industrial Noise—United States." *Morbidity and Mortality Weekly Review* 37 (10): 158–167.

U.S. Department of Labor (OSHA). 1981. *Final Regulatory Analysis of the Hearing Conservation Amendment.* Report No. 723–860/752 1–3. Washington, D.C.: Government Printing Office.

U.S. Department of Labor. 1927. "Record of Industrial Accidents in the United States to 1925." *Bulletin of the U.S. Bureau of Labor Statistics No. 425.* Washington, D.C.: Government Printing Office.

——. 1953. *Panel—Recent Developments in Loss of Hearing Claims,* Presented at the IAIABC Convention in Coronado, Calif., Oct. 4–8, 1953.

——. 1987. *Occupational Injuries and Illnesses in the United States by Industry, 1985.* Bulletin 2278. Washington, D.C.: Government Printing Office.

——. 1993a. *Occupational Injuries and Illnesses in the United States by Industry, 1991.* Bulletin 2424. Washington, D.C.: Government Printing Office.

——. 1946. *The Woman Telephone Operator.* Women's Bureau Bulletin No. 207. Washington, D.C.: Government Printing Office, p. 10.

——. 1950. *Women's Jobs: Advance and Growth.* Women's Bureau Bulletin No. 232. Washington, D.C.: Government Printing Office.

——. 1993b. *Workplace Injuries and Illnesses in 1992.* USDL–93–553 (Dec. 15, 1993). Washington, D.C.: Bureau of Labor Statistics.

——. 1994. *Workplace Injuries and Illnesses in 1993.* USDL–94–600 (Dec. 21, 1994). Washington, D.C.: Bureau of Labor Statistics.

United Steelworkers of America. 1961. *Impact of Technological Change and Automation on the Basic Steel Industry.*

Velpeau A. 1825. *Anatomie des Régions: Traité d'anatomie chirurgicale.* Vol. 1. Paris: Crevot.

Verespej, M. A. 1991. "Ergonomics: Taming the Repetitive Motion Monster." *Industry Week* (October 7): 26–32.

Vigliani, F. 1978. "The Origins of Modern Orthopaedics." *Italian Journal of Orthopaedics and Traumatology* 4 (1): 133–142.

Von Niemeyer, F. 1877. *A Textbook of Practical Medicine.* New York: D. Appleton.

Waddell, G. 1990. "A New Clinical Model for the Treatment of Low Back Pain." In J. N. Weinstein and S. W. Wiesel (eds.), *The Lumbar Spine.* Philadelphia: W. B. Saunders, pp. 38–55.

Wade, J. 1833. *History of the Middle and Working Classes.* London.

Wakefield, E. 1893. "Nervousness: The National Disease of America." *McClure's Magazine* 2:302.

Walsh, N., and D. Dumitru. 1988. "The Influence of Compensation on Recovery From Low Back Pain." *Spine* 3 (1): 109–121.

Ward, W. D. 1969. "The Identification and Treatment of Noise-Induced Hearing Loss." *Otolaryngologic Clinics of North America.* (February): 89–105.

——. 1973. "Noise-Induced Hearing Damage." In M. M. Paparella and D. A. Shumrick (eds.), *Otolaryngology,* Vol. 2. Philadelphia: W. B. Saunders Company, pp. 377–389.

Watson, L. A., and T. Toland. 1949. *Hearing Tests and Hearing Instruments.* Baltimore: Williams and Wilkins.

Weber, H. 1983. "Lumbar Disc Herniation: A Controlled Prospective Study with Ten-Year Observation." *Spine* 8:131–140.

Weber, V. 1862. *Die Gefährdungen des Personals beim Maschinen- und Fahrdienst der Eisenbahnen.* Leipzig.

Webster, B. S., and S. H. Snook. 1994a. "The Cost of 1989 Workers' Compensation Low Back Pain Claims." *Spine* 19 (10): 1111–1116.

——. 1994b. "The Cost of Compensable Upper Extremity Cumulative Trauma Disorders." *Journal of Occupational Medicine* 36 (7): 713–717.

Webster, J. C., H. W. Himes, and M. Lichtenstein. 1950. "San Diego County Fair Hearing Survey." *Journal of the Acoustical Society of America* 22:473–483.

Wechsler, I. 1929. *Neuroses*. Philadelphia: W. B. Saunders.

Weindling, P. (ed.). 1985. *The Social History of Occupational Health*. London: Croom Helm.

Weinrich, M. C., H. R. Maricq, J. E. Keil, A. R. McGregor, and F. Diat. 1990. "Prevalence of Raynaud's Phenomenon in the Adult Population of South Carolina." *Journal of Clinical Epidemiology* 43:1343–1349.

Wells, M. J. 1961. "Industrial Incidence of Soft Tissue Syndromes." *Physical Therapy Review* 41 (7): 512–515.

Welsh, K. I., and J. D. Spencer. 1990. "Immunology and Genetics." In R. M. McFarlane, D. A. McGrouther, and M. H. Flint (eds.), *Dupuytren's Disease: Biology and Treatment*. Edinburgh: Churchill Livingstone.

Wertheimer, B. M. 1977. *We Were There: The Story of Working Women in America*. New York: Pantheon.

Wessely, S. 1990. "Old Wine in New Bottles: Neurasthenia and 'ME'." *Psychological Medicine* 20:35–53.

Westmacott, F. H. 1925. "Occupational Diseases of the Ear, Nose and Throat, and Their Prevention." *British Medical Journal* 2:886–890.

Wheeler, D. E. 1953. "Ear Protection in Industrial Noise Exposure." *American Industrial Hygiene Association Quarterly* 14 (1): 54–58.

White, A. A., and S. L. Gordon. 1982. "Synopsis: Workshop on Idiopathic Low-back Pain." *Spine* 7:141–149.

White, J. A. 1928. "The Telephone and the Ear." *Transactions of the American Otological Society* 18:171–182.

Willan, R. 1798. *Description and Treatment of Cutaneous Diseases*. London.

Willoughby, W. F. 1898. *Workingmen's Insurance*. New York: Thomas Y. Crowell.

Wilson, H. R. 1909. *The Safety of British Railways*. London: P. S. King & Son.

——. 1925. *Railway Accidents, Legislation and Statistics, 1825 to 1924*. London.

Wilson, J. G. 1917. "Injury to the Ear From High Explosives." *Transactions of the American Otological Society* 14:239–255.

Wiltse, L. L. 1991. "The History of Spinal Disorders." In J. W. Frymoyer (editor-in-chief), *The Adult Spine: Principles and Practice*. New York: Raven Press.

Wisseman, C. L., and D. Badger. 1976. *Hazard Evaluation and Technical Assistance Report No. TA-93. Eastman Kodak Company, Windsor, Colorado*. Cincinnati: National Institute for Occupational Safety and Health.

Wood, H. C. 1893. "Functional Nervous Diseases." In W. Pepper (ed.), *A Textbook of the Theory and Practice of Medicine*. Philadelphia: W. B. Saunders, pp. 651–654.

Wood, M. 1953. *Occupational Deafness: Real or Imaginary?* Milwaukee: International Brotherhood of Blacksmiths, Drop Forgers and Helpers, Local 247.

Woodward, R., and F. Warren-Boulten. 1984. "Considering the Effects of Financial Incentives and Professional Ethics on 'Appropriate' Medical Care." *Journal of Health Economics* 3:223–237.

Worrall, J. (ed.). 1983. *Safety and the Workforce: Incentives and Disincentives in Workers' Compensation*. Ithaca, N.Y.: ILR Press.

Worrall, J. D., and D. Appel. 1987. "The Impact of Workers' Compensation Benefits on Low-Back Claims." In N. M. Hadler (ed.), *Clinical Concepts in Regional Musculoskeletal Disease*. Orlando: Grune & Stratton, pp. 281–297.

Yearsley, M. 1917. "An Air Raid Case." *Journal of Laryngology and Otology* 32:273.

Young, J. W. 1899. "Pseudo-railway Spine." *Medical Review* 38:424–426.

Zapp, J. A., Jr. 1960. "Industrial Noise." In A. J. Fleming, C. A. D'Alonzo, and J. A. Zapp, Jr. (eds.), *Modern Occupational Medicine*. 2nd ed. Philadelphia: Lea & Febiger, pp. 191–200.

Zilliacus, W. 1905. "Disturbances of Hearing in Railway Employees." *Finska läkaresällsk. handl.* 47 (2): 345–372. Abstract in *Archives of Otology* 35:502 (1906).

Zola, I. K. 1966. "Culture and Symptoms—An Analysis of Patients' Presenting Complaints." *American Sociological Review* 31:615–630.

——. 1983. *Socio-Medical Inquiries: Recollections, Reflections, and Reconsiderations*. Philadelphia: Temple University Press.

Zuradelli, C. 1857. "Del Crampo degli Scrittori," *Gazz. Med. Ital. Lombardia*, pp. 36–42.

Zwaardemaker, H. 1896. "Acoustic Railway Signals and Acuteness of Hearing." *Archives of Otology* 25:385–392.

Index